THE ETHICS OF LOVE IN THE HUMAN CONTEXT

THE ETHICS OF LOVE IN THE HUMAN CONTEXT

Dr. M. Stephen

Faith Theological Seminary
Manakala–691551
Adoor, Kerala

SERIALS PUBLICATIONS
New Delhi

First Published–2004

ISBN: 81-86771-40-9

Published by

Head Office : **SERIALS PUBLICATIONS**
4, B.S.S. Hall, Khyber Pass Market
Civil Lines, Delhi–110054 (India)
Phone: 23245225
Fax: 91-11-23272135
E-mail: serials@satyam.net.in

Branch Office : 4830/24, Prahlad Street, Ansari Road
Darya Ganj, New Delhi-110002 (India)

Printed at :

PRINTED IN INDIA

Preface

This book *'The Ethics of Love in The Human Context'* is the outcome of my doctoral research. It discusses the need of an evaluative approach in the Indian context which is vey much missing. It is so happened in the ethical decision-making that the normative dimension is asserted to reduce ethics is mere legalism. Joseph Fletcher the proponent of the aposteriori-agapeic approach is mostly dealing with what is evaluative from the Christian perspective, though he considers his approach as normative.

The Indian context is ethically pluralistic and there are several vital issues we find in the society. The religious traditions and the value systems hold diverse perspectives on the issues. In this context, it has been observed how there can be a fitting response to issues related to sexuality and marriage. It is infered that thre is evaluative approach found in the Bible, though there is normative approach. Without legitimizing evil, it is important to show love, mercy and humanness to the victims of the crises. The evaluative approach is found as necessary in the Indian context and for our times, as there is no adequate approach to resolve the life related problems. A methodology is developed to help the persons and communities who undergo the crises. I hope that this book would provide guidelines for resolving the crises in a loving and humane manner. I am greatly thankful to Rev. Dr. Thomas Kalam (Fr. Thomas Kalam) and Rev. Dr. Lukose Kaitharathotty for their valuable guidance and contributions.

Rev. Dr. M. Stephen
Puthenparambil House
Near Railway Station
Kottayam–686 001
Kerala

Introduction

This research deals with the issue of the relevance of Joseph Fletcher's love ethics for the Christian view on sexuality and marriage for our times

Joseph Fletcher is the proponent of situation ethics. He hails from New Jersey in the United States of America. His ethical approach is understood by Paul Ramsey as relativistic, arbitrary and antinomian. Fletcher feels that rules and principles are not helpful to take responsible ethical decision. His approach is an aposteriori-agapeic approach. It is a 'then and there' approach, as it stresses the role of love in particular situations. His approach is against the apriori rules, the conventional wisdom and universally valid rules and principles. Fletcher questions the rigid and fixed rules. For him, they are legalistic. He advocates for the freedom of the individuals to make decisions on different issues. He states that love is the only norm as only it can take responsible shape in diverse situations.

Joseph Fletcher argues that Jesus did not say anything about sexual perversions, sexual manners, birth control and parenthood. He considers with care and concern premarital sex, extramarital sex, homosexuality, and divorce which became the human experience in distinctive situations. He argues that Jesus considers the case of divorce with care, love and mercy as he feels that they best serve the emotional and spiritual welfare of parents and children in a particular family. The Artificial insemination by Donor or Husband (AID/AIH), the surrogate mother and cloning are found by him as the means to overcome the emotional strain and frustration in married life. The reception of third party sperm or ova is not considered by him as adultery.

Fletcher is of the opinion that Apostle Paul drops Jesus' prohibition of divorce. Fletcher will agree that divorce is to be understood as the route to happiness depending on the situation. The apriori rules or norm such as indissolubility of marriage and the sacredness of sex and the understanding of covenant fidelity are not acceptable to Fletcher. So it is important to see the relevance of Fletcher's ethical perspective for the Christian understanding of sexuality and marriage in the light of the New Testament. It is to see whether Joseph Fletcher's situation ethics is a fitting Christian response for our times

The context of India is ethically pluralistic. The context of social change in India, the secularization, the religious traditions, the tribal communities and Indian personal laws contribute to this. The secularization process is contributed by urbanization, westernization and industrialization. There are different religious traditions, tribal communities and other groups with their own norms and practices. They are also having their own ethical dilemma while facing issues like divorce, polygamy, homosexuality, pre-marital and extra-marital sex, prostitution and child molestation. Usually what happens is that the individuals and communities involved in these issues are dealt with contempt in the light of normative principle. There is no adequate approach or attitude developed in order to deal the issue with the principle of Christian charity and generosity. Materialism and individualism have caused the paucity of love in marriage relationship. Marriage is not understood as a permanent association. The normative principle of sanctity of sexuality and sacramental aspect of marriage are being challenged. The concept of sex and marriage are being relativized. The sacredness of sex and indissolubility of marriage are being questioned. Secularization has also positively contributed to challenge the authoritarian structure. It provides freedom of choice and fight against sexual violence, *Sati* and dowry system. Whatever might be the causes, whether secularization, psycho-social or economic, the individuals and communities live with their crises devoid of any help. They are not mercifully dealt with or considered with love and mercy.

The personal laws are also to be dealt with in this connection. We have a common law, but also we have an enactment of personal laws applicable to persons of different religious communities. The Hindu marriage Act, the Muslim personal law, the Christian personal law, the Parsi personal law, and the special marriage Act are the important ones. The Hindu marriage Act applies to Jains, Buddhists and Sikhs also. According to Hindu marriage Act, divorce is possible in the case of adultery, insanity, incurable leprosy or by mutual consent. The Muslim personal law allows four wives. The issue of 'Talaq' is also problematic in the Indian context. This can be exercised as an extra-judicial right by the husbands.

The Parsi personal law does not permit bigamy and consanguine marriages. The grounds for divorce include the insanity, premarital pregnancy, imprisonment of the husband for more than seven years desertion and adultery. The Christian personal law permits monogamy. Adultery is considered as one of the important causes for divorce. The special marriage acts accepts only monogamy. Insanity, impotency, adultery and cruelty can be the grounds for divorce.

The religious traditions have personal laws the tribal communities and other groups have their norms or apriori principles. What is missing is an approach which deals with the issues or moral dilemma in a human manner in the situations. In the light of the complexity of the human situations and ethical dilemma, it is significant to see the relevance of Joseph Fletcher's ethical approach for the Christian view on sexuality and marriage in the context of ethical pluralism of India. The main problem which is to be explored is that, whether Joseph Fletcher's ethical approach (aposteriori-agapeic approach) is a fitting Christian response to the context of ethical pluralism of India.

In the context of the moral dilemma on sexuality and marriage in India which is found in the different religious traditions, the tribal communities, secular groups and personal laws, there is no adequate solution or ethical approach suggested to the problem. So this research is attempting to find out the relevance of Joseph Fletcher's situation ethics for the Christian view on sexuality and marriage in the Indian context. The Christian view is meant here as the New Testament perspective on sexuality and marriage. It should not be confused with the Christian personal law or the views of the Christian churches (denominations). The task is to know how Fletcher's ethical approach is adequate for the New Testament understanding on sexuality and marriage in the context of ethical pluralism of India.

It should be noted that several people and groups including Christians are attracted by Fletcherian views on sexuality and marriage. The secularist values deny the importance of the traditional view of sacredness of sex. There are several issues in the area of sexuality and marriage. The reduction of marriage as a social contract devalues the sacramental element. It contributes to sexual laxity and marital infidelity. The diverse views and understanding regarding the issues on sexuality and marriage held by different communities also bring confusion and flux. So this study has a greater amount of significance and relevance as it investigates the adequacy of Joseph Fletcher's ethical approach as an evaluative principle for the Christian (Biblical) view on sexuality and marriage in the ethically plural context of India.

The role of agape in the situation is important for Fletcher's approach. In the context of ethical pluralism of India, it is important to see how the different communities can co-exist with their apriori norms and the moral dilemma in the situation and what would be the Christian contribution towards it. The focus is what's the role of the ethical approach of Fletcher to help Christians to live together in love, peace, understanding and harmony in the midst of conflicting values.

This thesis deals with the background of situation ethics, the ethical approach of Joseph Fletcher, the New Testament perspective by Sexuality and Marriage and the Indian ethically plural context-view of different religious traditions, personal laws, tribal communities and their practices, and the secularized context. But the focus of this thesis is the issue of sexuality and marriage and it concentrates on the question whether the ethical approach of Joseph Fletcher is a relevant or fitting response for the Christian view of sexuality and marriage in the context of the ethical pluralism of India.

The survey of literature available (Primary and secondary materials) is in the form of books and articles. It involves a critical analysis of the material. This is the method of study that would be applied for this research.

The first chapter deals with the background of situation ethics. The major trends that influenced the emergence of situation ethics of Fletcher would be considered. It will also include the trends that are being influenced by situation ethics.

The second chapter is about the aposteriori-agapeic approach of Joseph Fletcher to the ethical issues such as, the socio-ethical issues, bio-medical issues, the professional ethical issues, and the issues on sexuality and marriage. The concept of sexuality and marriage would be given special attention in this chapter.

The third chapter concentrates on the Biblical understanding of sexuality and marriage. Since the primary source for the Christian understanding is the New Testament, it is used as the source in this chapter to derive the Christian view.

The fourth chapter deals with the understanding of sexuality and marriage in the ethically plural context of India. It includes the study on the sexuality and marriage in the Indian context in general (especially the impact of secularization process); the views of the different religious traditions, the major Christian denominations, the tribal communities and the different personal laws and marriage acts. The ethical issues related to sexuality and marriage such as pre-marital and extra-marital sex, prostitution, divorce and child abuse are also considered in this chapter.

The fifth chapter deal with the relevance of Joseph Fletcher's agapeic approach for our times. It involves the presentation of the moral problem, the values regarding the issue, the attitude of the church to those who are in the crises, the role of sin, guilt and conversion and the significnace of Fletcher's agapeic approach to the issue.

The original title of the thesis is 'the relevance of Joseph Fletcher's agapeic approach for the christian view of sexuality and marriage for our times'. Hope this book entitled 'the ethics of love in the human context' which is a revised form of any doctoral thesis will help the persons and communities to make fitting responses in the issues.

Abbreviations

A.I.D	-	Artificial Insemination by Donor
A.I.H.	-	Artificial Insemination by Huband
A.T.C.	-	Asian Trading Corporation
C.I.S.R.S.	-	The Christian Institute for the Study of Religion and Society
C.L.S	-	Christian Literature Service
C.S.A	-	Centre for Social Action
I.S.I	-	Indian Social Institute
ISPCK	-	The Indian Society for Promoting Christian Knowledge
I.V.P.	-	Inter-varsity Press
L.P.M	-	Lucknow Publishing House
S.C.M.	-	Student Christian Movement
SPCK	-	Society for Promoting Christian Knowledge
T.P.I	-	Theological Publications in India
U.T.C.	-	United Theological College
W.C.C.	-	World Council of Churches

CONTENTS

Chapter 1

The Background of the Situation Ethics

While dealing with the background of situation ethics it is important to discuss the origin and development of situation ethics, the schools of thought that influenced the situation ethics, and the schools of thought that were being influenced by situation ethics. A biographical Sketch of Joseph Eletcher is also given at the beginning.

A. The Biographical Sketch of Joseph Fletcher

According to Millard Erickson, Joseph Fletcher was born in New York, New Jersey, April 10, 1905. He died in the year 1991. He received his B.A.from the University of West Virginia and B.D. from Berkeley Divinity School and also studied at Yale and London. Following pastoral ministry, he served as Paine professor of social ethics, Episcopal theological school, Cambridge, Massachusetts, 1944-1970. He taught Medical ethics at the University of Virginia Medical school. (Millar J. Erickson, "Fletcher, Joseph," *Baker's Dictionary of Christian Ethics,* edited by Carl F.H. Henry, Michigan: Baker Book House, 1973. P. 247).

In the words of Harvey Cox, Joseph Fletcher had worked during his life time as a coal miner, a labourer in a rope industry, a cathedral dean, a social worker and a college chaplain. He was also an admirer of late William

Temple, the Arch Bishop of Canterbury. (Harvey Cox, *The Situation Ethics Debate,* Philadelphia: The Westminster Press, 1967, P.10. Hereafter Harvey Cox, The Situation Ethics Debate). According to John A. Crane of the Unitarian church, California, Joseph Fletcher was reacting against the reigning ethics of American middle class culture which was based on the rigidity and prudery (the aspect of giving extreme importance to the propriety or right or correctness in moral conduct, especially in relation to sexual matters).(Martin J. Heinecken, "Pietism" *A Dictionary of Christian Ethics,* edited by John Macquarrie, London: SCM Ltd., 1967, P. 256).

According to Joseph Fletcher, his father's name was Edward Peres and mother was Annie O' Reilly. (Joseph Fletcher, "Memoir of an Ex-Radical" *Joseph Fletcher: Memoir of an Ex-Radical,* edited by Kenneth Vaux; Louis ville: Westminster John Knox Press, 1993. P.35). His father was a Catholic, and mother a protestant. (*Ibid.,* P. 36). Fletcher, described his father as a lapsed catholic and his mother a nonchurch woman. (*Ibid.,* P. 62). Joseph Fletcher was associated to the episcopal church. He is described by Harvey Cox also as an Episcopalian, ie., a member of the Episcopal church. (*Ibid.,* P. 62).

B. Situation Ethics: Origin and Development

The origin of the term 'situation' ethics, the characteristic of situation characteristics of situation ethics, the salient features of Fletcher's situation ethics are the main concern in this section.

1. Origin of the Term Situation Ethics

'Situation' is a sociological term and the 'situation ethics' is derived from it. W.I. Thomas (1803-1947) has meant the 'situation' as follows: if men define a situation as real, it is real in its consequences. It is explained that if actors define a situation as hostile and threatening, they will act accordingly, for that is their definition of reality. (James Mckee, *Introduction to Sociology,* New York: Holt, Rinehart and Winston inc., 1969, P. 63). James Mackee observes that when he says that action is "situational" he means the conduct of interacting persons, not the stimulated responses of the organisms nor even the attitudinally based behaviour of unique persons (*Ibid.,* P. 63). Every action is taking place or occurs in a situation. According to James Mckee,"One type of situation, such as a social party, permits one kind of interaction, whereas a work situation requires another. Consequently, the interaction of several persons on the job is quite different than when these same persons relax at a friendly bar. The persons are the same, but their interaction is shaped by the situation by which it occurs" (*Ibid.,* P. 64).

Situation is the background or the circumstances in which human action occurs. According to Waldemar Molinski, the term "situation" was introduced into the language of moral theology by T. Steinbuchel.(Waldemar Molinski, "Situation ethics," *Sacramentum Mundi Vol. 6* edited by Karl Rahner, Jan Alfaro et al., Bangalore: Theological publications in India, 1975, P. 94).The influence of existentialism is that the right moral decision in a given moment depends on subjective and objective factors .which are by their very nature unique and they may be summed up as "situation." (*Ibid.*, P. 95). According to Molinski, "Each situation is unique because each man, his social setting (human world) and to some extent his environment (biological world), are in the stream of history. For man can only take ethical action in as much as he is conscious of himself, his social setting and his environment" (*Ibid.,* P. 96). According to Molinski this consciousness is constantly changing, so also the moral agent is developing subjectively. He further states, "He develops in terms of this subjective experiences and decisions, which in turn depends on the constant changes of the environment: he changes, his society changes, his world changes".(*Ibid.,* P. 96).

Situation ethics is grounded on the word situation, and what is the situation is very important for the situationist in the moral decision making. The concrete realities are the main concern rather than the absolute universalized norms.

2. The Characteristics of Situation Ethics

The characteristics of situation ethics in general is dealt with in this sub-section. There are two figures who are quite dominant in the area of new morality. They are John A.T.Robinson and Joseph Fletcher. Robinson's book 'Honest to God' has shaken most Christians as it brings a radical dimension in the ethical decision making. The traditional morality is challenged by Robinson. He stresses the importance of love in each situation. He says, "Love alone, because, as it were, it has a built-in moral compass, enabling it to 'home' intuitively upon the deepest need of the other, can allow itself to be directed completely by the situation". (John A.T. Robinson, *Honest to God,* Philadelphia, The Westminister press, 1963, P. 115). He again talks about love as against prescriptive rules, "It alone can afford to be utterly open to the situation, uniquely and for his own sake, without losing its direction or unconditionality. It is able to embrace an ethic of radical responsiveness, meeting every situation on its own merits, with no prescriptive laws" (*Ibid.,* P.115).

Bishop Robinson talks about three polarities: fixity and freedom, law and love, authority and experience. He explains that "the tension here is between the constant and the variable, the absolute and the relative, the eternal and the changing" (John A. T. Robinson, *Christian Morals Today,* Philadelphia: The Westminster Press, 1964, P. 11). He opines that the old morality estimates the new morality as it betrays the absolutes of right and wrong and selling out to relativism. (*Ibid.,* P. 11). Robinson is for the application of 'agape' in the situation. He states, "Christian ethics, according to this view, is concerned with applying these standards to the changing situation. It starts from the fact that Bible supplies a 'God-given net' or framework of conduct for human affairs. The task of a moral theologian is to keep the net in repair for each generation, and to define its mesh more closely as new occasions teach new duties. (*Ibid.,* P. 12).

He tells that the moral teachings of Jesus and the laws or codes related to are impracticable. He states, "Regarded as a code of conduct, prescribing what one should do in any situation, the Sermon on the Mount is quite impracticable". (*Ibid.,* P. 27,29). For Robinson, ethics is not static, it is variable and all the time changing as the situation is undergoing the rapid changes. (*Ibid.,* P. 27).

In the words of John Milhaven and David Casey, in United States, the trend of situation ethics is variously known as situationism, and new morality, and it is centered around John A.T.Robinson and Joseph Fletcher. (John G. Milhaven and David J. Casey, "Theological Background of the New Morality", *The Theology Digest* vol. xvi, No. 2, (1968), P. 196). According to Louis Dupre, situationist rejects any immanently human standard (subjective or objective) as an absolute criterion of morality. (Louis Dupre, "Situation Ethics and Objective Morality", *TheologicalStudies* vol xxviii., No.2, (1967), P. 246). In his opinion, "A common objection levelled against situation ethics is that it has no absolute principles" (*Ibid.,* P. 246). Absolute rules are questioned by the situationism. Dupre states again that, "For the situationist the human person is an absolute value that cannot be subordinated to anything else." (*Ibid.,* P. 246). According to Louis Dupre the situationist refuses to accept the absolute validity of objective rules of good and evil. He states, The situationist refuses to accept objective rules of good and evil as absolutely valid because the moral intention cannot be determined exclusively by the objective structure of an act (even if this structure is correctly evaluated). Good and evil belong to the interior realm of freedom before belonging to the objective expressions of freedom. Of course, the situationist is well aware that subjectivity is not pure inwardness; the human subject necessarily expresses itself in objective forms for conduct. (*Ibid.,* P. 247).

Dupre also points out that, situation ethics brings out the often neglected element of creativity which would weigh heaviest in any moral theory. (*Ibid.,* P. 248). In the year 1952, Pope Pius XII had made the following remarks about new morality or situation ethics: The situation ethics is 'ethical actualism' or morality of the situation. It is based on particular circumstances. The proponents of this new code affirm that the individual must make his moral judgment entirely on the basis of the actual concrete conditions or circumstances in which he finds himself. The conscience of man making its decision cannot be hampered by ideas, principles and universal laws (Joseph Fuchs, "Situation Ethics and Theology", *Theology Digest,* vol.II, (1954), P. 24). Pope Pius XII was critical of the situation ethics which does not see the significance of the universal laws.

According to Joseph Fuchs, situation ethics can be called as the 'ethics of the moment' (Joseph Fuchs, "Situation ethics and Theology",: *Theology Digest,* vol. II, (1854), P. 25). The situationists, he says, demand that the full, concrete, unique situation be considered when making a moral judgment of human behaviour (*Ibid.*, P. 25). According to Fuchs, "Ethics of the moment fears that a universally valid and absolute law of morality will limit God's absolute freedom and absolute power to decree" (*Ibid.*, P. 25). As a criticism against situationism, he argues that we should not hope to determine the will of God solely from the situation of the moment, without taking into account God's essence and our own. He says further that, "We must rather view each situation in the order of a world freely created and conserved by God; by doing this we can make statements in advance about the morality of a particular situation." (*Ibid.*, P. 26).

As a criticism against new morality John Macquarrie has said, 'Christian love and the concrete personal situation are of the greatest importance, but one can also exaggerate this importance. Because of such exaggeration, the "new morality" has cut itself off from saying anything significant about the really urgent moral issues of our time. (John Macquarrie, *ThreeIssues in Ethics,* London: SCM press Ltd., 1970., P. 30). He says further that, "A situational ethic stresses the uniqueness of each act, but its common characteristics are just as important. In every human life there is need for generalization, and the moral life is no exception" (*Ibid.,* P. 32-33).

He also observes that, "For the situationist, man is simply a "functional" man, he is what he does, in situation after another." (*Ibid.,* P. 33) Macquarrie agrees with Paul Ramsey's comment that no social morality was ever founded or even will be founded, upon a situational ethic. (*Ibid.,* P. 34). He argues that situational ethics is suffering from individualism and subjectivism. (*Ibid.,* P. 34). According to Macquarrie defining the situation is difficult, since every situation has rough edges and merges into the next one. He states,"the truth is that the complex texture of morals includes both a rule element and a situation element. The question is not one of opting for rules or situations, law or love, or however it may be expressed, but of trying to do something far more difficult, namely, to strike a right balance or tension between rules and situations," (*Ibid.,* P. 35). Macquarrie holds the view that the new morality or situation ethics have a valid task of challenging legalism, it is reduced to be subjctivism. He feels that every situation is related with each other and the situation and the rules have a complementary role. According to Joseph Fletcher the situationists are rejecting deontological and teleölogical ethical theories. He argues that, "the deontological and teleological typology of ethical theories in the traditional literature is increasingly unacceptable." (Joseph Fletcher "Situational Ethics" *In Encyclopedia of Bioethics* vol., 1. London: Collier Macmillan Publishers, 1978, P. 422). He summarizes situational ethics as follows: In sum, situation ethics there is a utilitarian or consequentialist ethics, motivated by concern for human well-being, decisionally flexible in method, and guided in its judgments by the greatest good realizable rather than by adhering to prefabricated norms or moral rules. (*Ibid*., P. 423).

According to Gordon H.Clark, situational ethics, though popularly and correctly associated with the name of Joseph Fletcher, it has a background in Nietzsche and Dewey. (Gorden H. Clark, "Situational Ethics", *Baker's Dictionary of Christian Ethics* edited by Carl F. H. Henry, U.S.A: Baker Book House Co., 1973, P. 623). In the words of Erwin W. Lutzer, "situationism does not reject the moral rules of the past, but neither is it bound by them. It seeks to use the rules whenever they are useful, but it discards them if they happen to conflict with "love". Remember, love is regarded as a higher principle than law". (Erwin W. Lutzer, *The Necessity of the Absolutes,* Michigan: Zonderavan publishing House, 1961, P. 29).

Waldemar Molinski analyses the situation ethics as follows: 'Situation ethics denies the generally valid norms of the natural law and the revealed will of God. (Waldemar Molinski, "Situation Ethics" *In Sacramentum Mundi, vol. VI,* edited by Karl Rahner. Juan Alfero *et al.*, Banglore: Theological Publications in India, 1975, P. 94). The situationism is not interested in what is absolute, rigid, fixed and unchanging. It upholds what is variable and relative. It is also very much utilitarian ethics. 'Love' or agape is the commonly accepted norm for situationists or the proponents of new morality, which is applied in each situation. There is no pre-determined idea how it would act in a particular situation ethics. Each case and situation is totally different and unique in their understanding. The prescriptive principles or apriori rules are not regarded much by situation. It is more interested in what is posterior. Situation ethics is an *aposteriori* approach.

3. The Salient Features of Fletcher's Situation Ethics

This analysis is based on the observations and comments by different scholars on Joseph Fletcher's situational approach. Joseph Fletcher is known as the proponent of situation ethics.

Gordon H. Clark observes that Fletcher has a background in Nietzche and Dewey. Nietzsche's evolutionary logic repudiates the Kantian *apriori* forms and it affirms that there are no identical cases in nature. John Dewey stresses the concrete (i.e., individual) situation. (Gorden H. Clark, "Situational Ethics", *Bakers Dictionary of Christian Ethics,* edited by Carl F. H. Henry, U.S.A: Baker Book House Co., 1973, P. 623). Gordon Clark argues that, "Love is what Fletcher wished to substitute for system, commandants, or rules intelligible to all men." (*Ibid.,* P. 623). According to him, Fletcher's method is simply utilitarian calculus applied to love and rejects and misinterprets the Bible. Gordon Clark comments:

Fletcher seriously misinterprets Gal. 5:1 and Matt. 5:27-32; and, of course, discards the ten commandments. How can we appeal to the Bible for the one phrase, "thou shalt love"? A person who believes the Bible can consistently appeal to any verse, as Jesus did in John 10:35; but a person who does not, must give reasons for accepting one verse rather than another. Fletcher gives no reason. To all intents he treats it as if it were a verbally inspired revelation to himself alone. Strange that Fletcher is inherently inspired and the scripture is not. (*Ibid.,* P. 624).

According to Dietritch and Alice Von Hilderbrand, Fletcher makes no distinction between moral laws and positive divine laws, and further confuses the latter with state laws. Fletcher is against the legalistic ethics. He, somehow, develops an allergy to the term 'law' itself. Dietrich and Hilderbrand summarizes the Fletcher's understanding of legalistic morality that, "His presentation of legalistic morality could be summarized as follows:it is a morality subjected to prefabricated laws of conduct that sacrifices the spirit of the letter of the law; it is one which is cold, impersonal and being committed to rules shows little concern for persons." (Dietrich and Alice Von Hilderbrand, *Morality and Situation Ethics, Chicago:* Fransiscan Herald Press, 1966, P. 191). They argue again that "Mr. Fletcher seems to imply that maturity brings about a liberation from all duties and obligations, except the one to love; but he fails to see that the immature person clamors for his rights and forgets his obligations, whereas the mature person recognizes the interdependence of rights and obligations and faces there freely." (*Ibid.*,.P. 182).

According to Erwin Lutzer, traditional Christianity has regarded the precepts of the Bible as having binding authority in all situations (*Ibid.,* P. 182). He states again that Fletcher maintains that legalism must be rejected because it is more concerned with the law than with the people.(Erwin W. Lutzer, *The Necessity of the Ethical Absolutes,* Michigan: Zonder van Publishing House, 1961, P. 28). Erwin Lutzer observes, "For Fletcher the sole arbiter of morality in any situation is love. This is the first premise of situationism we will consider. Fletcher agrees with John A.T.Robinson, who writes, If we have the heart of the matter in us, if our eye is single, then love will find the way, its own particular way, in every individual situation. Therefore, no commandment can infringe on what love demands. Sex relations outside marriage are not intrinsically wrong; the only intrinsic evil becomes the lack of love" (*Ibid.,* P. 36).

According to Erwin Lutzer, situationism affirms that the one absolute love, should be defined in utilitarian terms. This means that actions should be judged by whether or not they contribute to the greatest good to the greatest number. He explains Jeremy Bentham's utilitarian view which affirms that moral actions can be made by calculating the pleasure and the pain that result from any act. A moral action is one that produces more pleasure and less pain than any substitute action. In an immoral action, the pain would outweigh the pleasure. (*Ibid.,* P. 31).He argues that Fletcher along with utilitarians forced to accept the view that the end justifies the means. (*Ibid.,* P. 32). Erwin Lutzer observes that the main criticism against Fletcher's situationism is that love, defined by Fletcher can give no guidance whatever in making moral decisions. Since everyone may have a different opinion of what is loving or unloving in a given situation, and love without ethical content is meaningless. (*Ibid.,* P. 33).

While discussing the ethical thought of Fletcher, Thomas Wassmer has stated, "He is critical of the legalist who enters decision making situations with a barrel of rules and regulations that are applicable *a priori* and who terminates any further ethicizing by appealing to these universal affirmative or negative." (Thomas Wassmer, *Christian Ethics for Today*, Milwarkee: The Bruce Publishing Co., 1969, P. 115). Thomas Wassmer dwells on the six propositions of Fletcher (1) only one thing is intrinsically good, namely love, (2) The ruling norm of Christian decision is love, nothing else, (3) Love and justice are the same, for justice is love distributed, nothing else, (4) love wills the neighbor's good whether we like him or not, (5) Only the end justifies the means, nothing else, (6) Love is decisions are made situationally, nor prescriptively. He comments that, "Fletcher's principal thrust through these six statements is that as soon as we have accepted the Christian ideal of agape, we can in the situation formulate rules or norms of conduct." (*Ibid.,* P. 119).

In his criticism of Fletcher's situationism, Thomas Wassmer observes that "situations are not as discrete and discontinuous as Fletcher seems to think. Each individual situation seems to be unique, unrelated and dissociated from other situations. When this discontinuity of situation is exaggerated there is no question that certain common denominators, explicit or implicit in all situations, are played down. Ethical decisions are always made in the circumstances of the here and now, but some generalizations can be made about values pertaining to human needs and interests." (*Ibid.,* P. 120).

Donald Evans analyses Fletcher's concept of love which is the most dominant theme in Fletcher as follows; (1) Increase of love as the goal of action, (2) The agents love as the test of action, (3) Love as doing good, (4) Love as an ability to discern what to do. (Donald Evans, "Love situations, and Rules" *Norm and Context in Christian Ethics,* edited by Gene H. Outka and Paul Ramsey, New York: Charles Scribner's sons, 1968, PP. 369-374). According to Evans, Fletcher is inconsistent in what he has to say about rules, since he says on the one hand that for situationism there are no rules but on the other hand he seems to accept that rules and principles are to be understood and used in the way appropriate to moral maxims. (*Ibid.,* P. 380).

In his analysis Hanlee Barnett observes that for Fletcher, Christian situation ethics has only one norm-the agape or the commandment love God and neighbor. He found that there is ambiguity in use of the terms situation and love. (Henlee H. Barnett, *The New Theology and Morality,* Philadelphia: The Westminster Press, 1967, PP 39.44). According to him, "Both Robinson and Fletcher are "act utilitarian" (acting in the way that will likely produce the greatest balance of good over evil) when they move from personal to social relations." (*Ibid.,* P. 46).

It is very clear that Fletcher's situation ethics have certain peculiar characteristics compared to the traditional morality. His approach is aposteriori- agapeic. Love is the only norm and it decides then and there. His ethical approach is influenced by pragmatism, personalism, positivism, existentialism and utilitarianism. It rejects the legalism and the rules and the principles. He argues that persons and the Christian principle of agape are important than principles. The denial of loveless rules and laws is found in Fletcher's ethical approach. The characteristics of Flectcher's approach include the role of love or loving concern in each particular situation. His concept of agape makes the ethical approach contextual, agapeic and pragmatic. His ethical approach is an aposteriori-agapeic approach.

Joseph Fletcher emphasizes the significance of agape in each concrete situation. According to Kenneth Vaux "Throughout his career Fletcher struggled against absolutist inclinations in ethics, especially when expressed in inhumane ideologies." (Kenneth Vaux, ed., *Joseph Fletcher; Memoir of an Ex-Radical, Reminiscences and Reappraisal,* Louisville; Westminster, 1993, P. 6). As Fletcher does, it is important to consider the context of each ethical issue. Kenneth Vaux opines again that, "On the issues of women's rights, war and peace, environmental concerns, and the abroad areas of sexuality, baby-making, health care ethics, and consensus of dying, he similarly found himself in contention with church and society that ignore the particular personal and interpersonal pathos of the issues at hand." (*Ibid.,* P. 380).

C. The Schools of thought that Influenced Situation Ethics

There were several theological, philosophical, and cultural factors that influenced the emergence of the situation ethics. The principal elements of influence, especially, in relation to Joseph Fletcher's situation ethics are discussed in this section. Pietism and Puritanism, Natural law tradition, Utilitarianism, Pragmatism, Relativism, Positivism, Personalism and Existentialism are the main influences.

1. Pietism and Puritanism

Fletcher has reacted against the pietism and puritanism since he feels that they are very legalistic. Pietism in Germany had originated as a reaction against the departure from the Reformation emphasis was upon the right proclamation of the gospel as one leading to faith and renewal of life in Christ on the one hand, and on the other, it reacted against the legalistic attempts which were being made to bring order and discipline in the disrupted church life. They advocated for deepening of the inner spiritual life. The chief proponents in Germany were Jacob Spencer (1635-1705) and August Herman Francke (1663-1717).

Pietism insisted on the outward evidence of the inner conversion and the emphasis falls upon the externalities of conduct. It also under- estimated the complexity of the human situation along with the ambiguity of the moral choices, says Martin Heinecken. (*Martin J. Heinecken, "Pietism" A Dictionary of Christian Ethics, edited by John Macquarre, London:* SCM Press, 1967, P. 256) According to him Pietism has forgotten the fact that the will of God is always particular at a time and place, affecting a unique individual within given structures. (*Ibid.,* P. 257). Pietism has upkept a very exclusive life. According to Martin Heinecken, "the danger lies in a self righteous separation from the world instead of a free and joyous living 'in and for the world' in the servant form." (*Ibid.,* P. 257).

There is also a Calvinist Pietism which derives from seventeenth century English Puritanism.[67] (Wenzel Lohff, "Pietism" *Sacramendrum Mundi.* Vol. 6, *Op.Cit.,* P. 24).

According to Wenzel Lohff, "pietism in general must be seen as a part of the great process whereby modern man has been discovering his own autonomous subjectivity." (*Ibid.,* P. 25). But he also stress the fact that, "stressing, however, subjective independence at the expense of tradition, pietism was always in danger of forgetting that the life of faith is an open-ended discussion with history". (*Ibid.*, P. 25). According to Fletcher, though pietism gives support to the secularization of culture and society, it corrupted the religion by separating faith socially, that is reducing the religion to religiosity by making it a personal and internal or mystical affair irrelevant to economic and political matters. (Joseph Fletcher, *Moral Responsibility: Situation Ethics at work,* Philadelphia: The Westminister press, 1967, P. 163; Hereafter *Moral Responsibility)* .Pietism has challenged the traditional rigid nature of the church and advocated for freedom, but it also holds up certain puritanical elements such as the exclusive life from the society.

According to S.J. Knox, Puritanism arose in the sixteenth century as the English expression of Calvinism. When the term 'puritan' is used it is applied by the English Bishops to those clergy who refused to subscribe to the liturgy, ceremonies and disciplines of the established church. A great stress was laid upon man's individual moral responsibility to a righteous God, and aimed at purity of character. (S.J. Knox. "Puritanism", *A Dictionary of Christian Ethics* edited John Macquarrie, Op.Cit..., P. 284). They discouraged those arts and entertainments that were impure or valueless in promoting the good life, according to S.J. Knox. (*Ibid.,* P. 284). The puritans do not approve the moral laxity, especially in the issue of sex.

Richard Baxter (1615-1691) typifies the puritan mind. One of the characteristics of puritan life is sobriety. According to Waldo Beach and Richard Niebuhr, "when the puritan calls on men to be sober, he is simply reminding them that this life is swift and solemn trust, an arena of crucial decision wherein the high values of the religious life are in competition with the cheap and easy values of world's pleasures." (Waldo Beach and H. Richard Neibhur. eds., *Christian Ethics: Sources of Living Tradition,* 2nd edn., New York: Alfred A. Knopf, 1973, P. 302). They continue to say that, "To lead a sober life, one must turn away from the pursuits of the world's enjoyments. Worldiness is the chief enemy of godliness in puritan morality". (*Ibid.*, P. 303).

According to H.G. Wood, the puritans have expressed the importance of submission to God's will which needs the self control. He states "Indeed puritan emphasis on God's sovereignty and man's depravity necessitated a stern and repressive discipline". (H.G. Wood, "Puritanism", *Encyclopaedia of Religion and Ethics vol. 10* edited by James Hastings Edinburg: T. and T. Clark, 1980. P. 513). Mark Rutherford has pointed out two things about puritan morality: (1) an abhorrence of lying, and (2) the conviction that unchastity is a sin and not a venial weakness. (*Ibid.*, P. 513). The puritans have extreme importance to chastity, and they abhorred the lying and sexual immortality and advocated self control. Joseph Fletcher argues that the legalistic puritanism will prevent the loving act (especially in the case of pre-marital sex and the use of contraceptives). (Joseph Fletcher. *Situation Ethics. The New Morality, Philadelphia: The westminster Press, 1966. Hereafter, Situation Ethics*). For Fletcher the puritanism is legalistic and prevent the role of love in the situation.

Joseph Fletcher has no much respect for pietism and puritanism as one is trying to separate religion and society, the other is for the rigid moral rules.

2. Natural Law Tradition

The natural law theory is usually followed by the Roman Catholics. The Protestants have a mixed reaction towards the natural law. The natural law ethic is found so legalistic in olden days, now it is changed as we have even modified natural law theory. The situationism has reacted against the natural law as it is criticized as rigid, legalistic and rule-oriented.

Vernon Bourke expounds the natural law as follows: the view that there are certain precepts or norms of good and right conducts discoverable by all men in the broadest signification of natural law. Sometimes natural law means that part of God's eternal law which governs free actions of men; in another usage, it designates those rules of justice which may be found written in the hearts or conscience of men; or it describes a set of ethical judgments obtained by reflecting on man's ordinary experience, was contrasted with the divine laws that may be supernaturally revealed.(Vernon J. Bourke, "Natural law", *A Dictionary of Christian Ethics,* edited by John Macquarrie, *Op.Cit.,* P. 224).

The early natural law is found in stoic ethics that the good life consists in living in accordance with nature. Aquinas viewed that the natural law is an understanding of God's plan for us, built into the nature by his act of creation. According to Hunter Mabry, Aquinas thought of four laws (1) Eternal law - the ultimate transcendent plan by which all creation is ordered, practically identical with the reason of God, in itself beyond human comprehension due to human finiteness, yet not contrary to human reason, (2) Natural law-eternal law as it is reflected in the created world, discernible by all persons through aided reason (3) Divine law - a gift of God's grace through revelation, particularly as known in the Bible, apprehensible by faith, not contrary to natural law, but not going beyond it, and (4) Human law-rules and regulations enacted by persons and human agencies to guide conduct toward the common good. (Hunter p. Mabry, *Christian Ethics: An Introductory Reader.* Serampore; Indian Theological Library, 1987, PP. 11, 418). For Aquinas law is nothing but the dictate of the practical reason issued by a sovereign who governs a complete community. (*Ibid.,* P. 421).

According to Robin Gill, Thomas Aquinas is convinced that Natural law is ubiquitous in man. Following Aristotle, he believes that man has a natural tendency towards happiness or well-being (eudaimonia), leading ultimately, for the Christian, to the beautific vision of God himself. This is the main spur for morality in all men. Morality is to be discerned through the use of 'practical reason'. There are general principles and secondary principles in it, and general principles cannot be altered, and secondary principles (it comes from the general principles of morality) can be occasionally altered. The error, sin or bad customs may distort the secondary principles. (Robin Gill *A textbook of Christian ethics,* Edinburg: T. and T Clark limited, 1985, PP. 76-77).

According to Jeremiah Newman, the stoics were the first to use the term 'natural law' beginning with Zeno around the year 300 B.C. The prominent among them were Chrysippus, Epictectus, Marcus Aurelius and Cicero. In the opinion of Chrysippus the law is the ruler of all things divine and human, the settled arbiter of good and evil, the guide to justice and injustice, the sovereign lord of all who are by nature political animals. It directs what must be done and forbids the opposite. (Jeremiah Newman, *Conscience Versus Law:Reflections on the Evolution of Natural Law,* Chicago, Fransiscan Herald press, 1971, P. 36). Duncan B. Forester has quoted Cicero to convey the idea of the natural law. In Cicero's opinion, true law is right reason in agreement with nature; it is of universal application, unchanging and it avert from wrong doing by its prohibitions.(Karl H. Peschke. *Christian Ethics vol. I.* Bangalore: TPI., 1967, P. 1334).

The natural law is for the universal valid rules and the absolute norms. This has influenced the Roman

Catholic morality, as they go with the deontological ethics which prohibits lying, abortion, killing, and illicit sex. Felix Podimattam talks about the relativity of the natural law. He states, "Relativity of natural law should sharply be distinguished from relativism of natural law. While relativism admits nothing that is absolute and immutable in natural law, relativity admits some absolutes though they may not be many." (Felix M. Podimattam. *Relativity of Natural Law.,*Bangalore: Asian Trading Corportion, 1976, P. 12, Hereafter, *Relativity of Natural law).*

There are several versions on the understanding of the natural law. Felix Podimattom quotes Bernard Haering's view on natural law. Bernard Haering understands it as the nature of meaning of man in so far as man has the capacity of understanding his nature, meaning and vocation; and consequently of realizing what preserves to the greatest extent the full meaning of his person, what corresponds to his relationship with God, his fellowmen and the created universe. (*Ibid.,* P. 16, quoting Bernad Haering's article entitled "Dynamism and Continuity in a Personalistic Approach to Natural Law", *Norm and context in Christian Ethics,* edited by Gene H. Outke and Paul Ramsey Op.Cit., P. 200). In the view of Bernard Haering, the natural law is not a code of rules and regulations but rather a challenge to act in full accord with our rational principle, says Podimattam. (*Ibid.*, P. 26.)

Bernard Haering explains that the moral law of nature is immutably valid. But its application is variable according to the changeableness of conditions. For example, it is an immutable principle of natural right that every man has the right to his dignity as man to the development of his personal capacities. He has these rights also in regard to his work. From this applied principle we may draw the further conclusion that actual slavery is unlawful at any time. (Bernad Haering. *The Law of Christ, vol. I,* Cork: The Mercier Press, 1961, PP. 245-246). He feels that the natural moral law is immutable at the same time it varies or takes different forms in application in different situations. He is not very rigid in his understanding as he modifies the natural moral law. He looks for the meaningful fulfillment of the law of nature or application of law which transcends the mere letter. (*Ibid.*, P. 247).

Felix Podimatttam tells that, "the moral experience and consciousness of the people of God constitute the principal interpreter of natural law. The fact that natural law is an integral part of supernatural morality, does not deprive the experience and consciousness of the people of God of its competence to interpret natural law because their experience and consciousness too exist in a supernatural state". (Felix M. Podimattam, *Relativity of Natural Law,* P. 55). For him the principles are based on experience as he states that, "experience precedes principles". (*Ibid.*,P. 55). He agrees that though natural law ethic is not strict legalism it has tended to be legalistic. (*Ibid.*, P. 71).

According to James Gustafson the charges against the natural law are three in number: its reliance upon a human natural inclination toward the good does not take sufficiently into account the seriousness of human condition of sin, which is distortion of human reason; its reliance upon reason to formulate principles and norms on which humans can agree is failed; it reflects the medieval periods cultural situation. (James M. Gustafson, *Protestant and Catholic Ethics,*Chicago; The University of Chicago Press, 1978, PP. 62-64).

Joseph Vadackumcherry discusses the issue of situationism and natural law morality. He admits that in the natural law morality God himself is the ultimate norm. He states, "The very moral obligation in order to take universal effect with respect to all men of all times and places, needs to be enjoined upon man through the medium of man's rational power and not by way of supernatural revelation. The natural law becomes palpable and a matter of universal human experience like evident factors of conscious life in the dictates of each one's conscience." (Joseph Vadackumcherry, *Natural-Law-Morality Versus Situationism in Morals.,*Cochin; Louis memorial Press, 1969, P. 31).

The conscience and the rational power also have a very crucial role in moral decision making, along with revelation. Vadackumcherry writes that "Natural law given to man along with his rational nature as law of liberty." (*Ibid.,* P. 31). He points about natural law as follows: "It is the law of his being. It is given as the rational capacity and as norm of free acts discernible through insights into the nature of man and the world by reason alone". (*Ibid.,* PP. 31-32).

Joseph Vadackumcherry comments that situation ethics overlooks the importance of absolute objective norms in discerning one's moral conduct. (*Ibid.,* P. 63). According to him, situation ethics is influenced by positivism and existentialism so it does not realize the permanent value of any principles that is, morality is reduced to merely relative and exclusively focussed on particular and concrete situation of the individual. (*Ibid.,* P.89). It is true that the situation ethics is very much depending on situation and each moment or cases or situation is totally different from the other, but natural law sees that certain principles are universally binding and there can have some generally valid rules as every situation or moment are related and not totally dissociated.

Joseph Fletcher was against the Roman Catholic and Anglican view on natural law morality. For him they are legalistic, based on prefabricated rules. (Joseph Fletcher,. *Moral Responsibility*, P. 73). The situation ethics of Fletcher sees the natural law theory as against the love since he does not approve the importance of the apriori rules. Fletcher was reacting to the natural law tradition and it is reflected in his perspective on law. He sees the law as legalistic and he is allergic to any law. He finds it difficult to recognize the law which does not take into account the value of love in the concrete situations.

3. The Utilitarianism

Jeremy Bentham (1748-1832) and John Stuart Mill are the two important figures in the utilitarianism. In the words of Giesler, "Jeremy Bentham (1748-1832) laid down the principle that one should act so as to produce the greatest good for the greatest number in the long run". (Norman Giesler, *Options in Contemporary Christian Ethics,* Michigan: Book House, 1991. P. 10). The actions that may produce good results for a time will not be best for all persons. So it brings relativism and also situationism. Giesler understands that "utilitarian relativism implies that the end can justify any means." (*Ibid.,* P. 16).

In the opinion of Anthony Quinton, for Bentham and Mill happiness is the sum of pleasure. According to Quinton, utilitarianism is a combination of two principles: "(1) the *consequentialist principle* that the rightness or wrongness of an action is determined by the goodness or badness of the results that flow from it and (2) *the hedonist principle* that the only thing that is good in itself is pleasure and the only thing bad in itself is pain".(Anthony Quinton, *Utilitarian Ethics,* London, Macmillan Press, 1972, P. 1; Hereafter Quinton, *Utilitarian Ethics).*

While discussing the utilitarian thought of Jeremy Bentham, James McGlynn and Jules Toner have said that Bentham talks about two masters namely pain and pleasure which govern the mankind. (James V. McGlynn. Jules J. Toner, *Modern Ethical Theories,* Milwankee, The Bruce Publishing Company, 1961, P. 45). The power and pleasure not only tell us what we ought to do, but they also determine us to do it: right and wrong, cause and effect, are fastened to their throne. (*Ibid.,* P. 46). To Jeremy Bentham, no man acts except to gain pleasure or to avoid pain; and every man is fully determined by desire of pleasure and fear of pain - his own pleasure and his own pain, states James McGlynn and Jules Toner. (*Ibid.,* P. 46). For Bentham, happiness or pleasure and avoidance of pain is the only right and universally desirable end of human action. (*Ibid.,* P. 46). The greatest happiness is the aim of man, and ethics is the art of directing to that goal in Bentham's version. (*Ibid.,*P. 46). To Bentham happiness is pleasure and pleasure is quantitatively measured.

Jeremy Bentham makes in his book, *An Introduction to the Principles of Morals and Legislation*, the following observations: (1) Nature has placed mankind under the governance of two masters, pain and pleasure. (2) By the principle of utility is meant that principle which approves or disapproves of every action whatsoever, according to the tendency which it appears to have to augment or diminish the happiness of the party whose interest is in question: or, what is the same thing in other words, to promote or to oppose that happiness. (3) By utility is meant that property in any object, whereby it tends to produce benefit, advantage, pleasure, good or happiness or to prevent the happening of pain, evil or unhappiness to the party whose interest is considered: if that party be the community in general, then the happiness of the community: if a particular individual, then the happiness of that individual. (Jeremy Benthan, "The Principle of Utility", *Morals and Values,* edited by Marcus G. Singer, New York: Charles Scribner's sons, 1977, PP. 71-72).

John Stuart Mill's moral idea is utility or the greatest happiness principle. According to Anthony Quinton, the idea of Mill is that "To possess utility is to be valuable derivatively, by reason of consequences that are valuable in themselves and the only intrinsic, or non- consequential, value is pleasure and the absence of pain" (Anthony Quinton, *Utilitarian Ethics* P.39). For J.S. Mill, principles or moral should promote happiness. William Lillie has summarized Mill's arguments in the following statements:

(a) Pleasure is the only thing that is desirable.

(b) The only proof that a thing is desirable is the fact that people do actually desire it.

(c) Each person's own pleasure or happiness is a good to that person, so the general happiness is good to everybody.

(d) Man do desire other objects, that they desire them as a means to pleasure.

(e) If one of two pleasures are preferred by those who are competently acquainted with both we are justified in saying that this preferred pleasure is superior in quality to the other. (William Lillie, *An Introduction to Ethics*. New Delhi; Allied Publishers Limited., 1989, P. 167. Hereafter, *Lillie, An Introduction to Ethics*).

According to James McGlynn and Jules Toner, "The utilitarian ethics of Mill gives honour to the man who will sacrifice his own happiness for those whom he sees are concerned, as long as by so doing he is achieving a greater happiness for a greater number. Utilitarianism, he says, does not applaud sacrificing one's own happiness if this sacrifice does not issue in a greater sum of happiness." (James V. McGlynn, Jules Toner, *Modern Ethical Theories, Op.Cit...*, P. 36). It is clear that Mill's view is that greatest happiness is to the greatest number. According to James McGlynn and Jules Toner, "The pleasure spoken of should be qualitatively of the best. And the happiness so conceived is the greatest happiness to the greatest number." (*Ibid.*, P. 56). The action is judged by the end of happiness rather than the moral worth of the person who acts. (*Ibid.*, PP. 56-57).

The following observations are from J.S.Mill's work entitled 'Utilitarianism'. According to J.S.Mill, "the creed which accepts as the foundation of morals, Utility, or the Greatest Happiness principle, holds that actions are right in proportion as they tend to promote happiness, wrong as they tend to produce the reverse of happiness". (John Stuart Mill, "Utilitarianism", *The American State Papers. The Federalist J.S Mill,* Great Books of the Western World series vol.43, edited by Alexander Hamilton, James Madison and John Jay, Chicago: Encyclopaedia Britannica inc., 1982, P. 448). Happiness is understood by him as the absence of pain. Mill states that, according to the greatest happiness principle the ultimate and with reference to and for the sake of which all other things are desirable is an existence exempt as far as possible from pain, and as rich as possible in enjoyments, both in point of quantity and quality; the test of quality, and the rule for measuring it against quantity, being the preference felt by those who in their opportunities of experience, to which must be added their habits of self-consciousness and self-observation, are best furnished with the means of comparison. (*Ibid.*, P. 450).

Henry Sidgwick has pointed out three things about utilitarian morality (1) it may be presented as practical guidance to all who choose "general good" as their ultimate end, whether they do so on religious grounds or through the predominance in their minds or impartial sympathy, or because their conscience acts in harmony with utilitarian principles, or for any combination of these or any other reasons; or (2) it may be offered as a code to be obeyed not absolutely, but only so far as the coincidence of private and general interest may in any case he judged to extend; or again (3) it may be proposed as a standard by which men may reasonably agree to praise and blame the conduct of others, even though they may not always think fit to act on it themselves. (Henry Sidgwick, *Outlines of the History, of Ethics.* Boston; Beacon Press, 1960, P. 248).

According to Frankena, utilitarians hold that what is morally right or wrong is ultimately to be wholly determined by looking to see what promotes the greatest general balance of good over evil. The act-utilitarians hold that in general or at least where it is applicable, one is to tell what is right or obligatory by appealing directly to the principle of utility or, in other words, by trying to see which of the actions open to him is likely to produce the greatest balance of good over evil in the universe. The question one should ask is, what effect will my doing this act in this situation have on the general balance of good over evil?". (William Frankena, *Ethics,* New Delhi: Prentice - Hall India 1988. P-35).

The situationism is fascinated by the utilitarian idea that the pleasure and happiness are important rather than anything else. The consequence of the action in the situation is also an important criteria for utilitarians. Bringing the greatest pleasure is the view of utilitarianism. The situationism is adopting the aspect of good or happiness or pleasure which are the need of utilitarianism (the use or utility in the situation is important for it) which depends on the fact that whether an act will furnish happiness to the individual who acts. Each person's happiness is understood as good to that person in utilitarianism which can even lead to the importance of what is useful and the significance of each case and person in a particular situation. These reflections from utilitarianism must have influenced situationism of Joseph Fletcher.

4. Existentialism

The most important existentialists are Soren Kierkegaard, Jean-Paul Sartre, Martin Heidegger and Friendrich Nietzche. According to Joseph Fletcher, "Sartre refuses to admit any generally valid principles at all, nothing even ordinarily valid, to say nothing of universal laws." (Joseph Fletcher, *Situation Ethics,* P. 25). In the opinion of Carl Michalson, "living by laws, which is a way of knowing what to do, is regarded by existentialist as `bad faith' (Sartre and Simon de Beavoir)." Carl Michalson, "Existentialist Ethics", *A Dictionary of Christian Ethics* edited by John Macquarrie., Op.Cit., P. 124).He continued to say that, "Any abridgement of human freedom is 'bad faith'. A legalistic ethic abridges freedom by taking tensions out of the heads of the responsible selves". (*Ibid.,* P. 124). For existentialist ethics, freedom surpasses all laws. Freedom is understood as a source of man's possibility to act ethically. (*Ibid.,* P. 124).

While Sartre was a rational existentialist, Kierkegaard was a religious existentialist. Kierkegaard talks about the 'teleological suspension of the ethical'. Carl Michalson explains: "Openness to the future has primacy over conformity to the past. To use Sartre's term, one simply 'nihilates' which is to say 'suspends' it, in order to let the demands of the future emerge. The past tells a man what he ought to do. The future is a reliable guide simply because it does not tell a man what to do, but appeal to him to 'invent' or 'create' in the light of the emerging situation". (*Ibid.,* P.124). The existentialism brings a radical subjectivism and personalism in ethics. Sartre believed that there is no place of objective meaning as value to life. (*Ibid.,* P.124).

According to John Macquarrie, the themes such as freedom, decision and responsibility are prominent in all existentialist philosophers. (John Macquarrie. *Existentialism,* New York; Penguin Books,1993, P. 4). He continued to say that, "these matters constitute the core of personal being. It is the exercise of freedom and the ability to shape the future that distinguish man from all the other beings that we know on earth. It is through free and responsible decisions that man becomes authentically himself". (*Ibid.,* P. 4). Existentialism focuses on self as agent and it is concerned with the individual who search for selfhood. (*Ibid.,* P. 4). Macquarrie states that, "Existence is characterized by concreteness and particularity and also by a sheer givenness". (*Ibid.,* P. 41).

Kierkegaard's subjectivism is interested in only one thing, namely, supreme ethical choice. Discussing Kierkegaard's thought Blackham states, "A man can only will absolutely in an original choice, which is also a choice of himself, and which becomes the ground of his subsequent moral decisions". (H. J. Blackham, *Six Existentialist Thinkers.* London: Routledge & Kegan paul, 1985, P. 18). Kierkegaard emphasizes the aspect of living as a particular human being in the same sense as is open to every other human being which is the ethical victory over life. His individualism lays emphasis upon the generically human. (*Ibid.,* P. 21). According to Blackham, Kierkegaard's individualism is concentrated on the individual as the sole source of the universally human, in reflective willing, and authentic choice. The self is so far as it has achieved authentic selfhood in an absolute choice has given itself away absolutely. This absolute subjectivity becomes the absolute objectivity in his total self-displacement before God. (*Ibid.,* PP. 21-22).

According to Beach Waldo and Richard Niebuhr in Kierkegaard's opinion man might seem to be free, for to be what one is by one's own act in freedom. (Waldo Beach and H. Richard Niebuhr, eds. *Christian Ethics, Op.Cit.,* P. 426). God will transfer men, and that he will out of love. In relation to the absolute there is only one sense: the present. For Kierkegard, who is not contemporary with the absolute has no existence. The past is not reality for him, but only the contemporary is reality. Every man can be contemporary only with the age in which he lives. (*Ibid.,* P. 428). For Kierkegaard, says Beach Waldo and Richard Niebuhr,

Existence constitutes the highest interest of the existing individual, and his interest in his existence constitutes his reality. What reality is, cannot be expressed in the language of abstraction. The only reality to which an existing individual may have a relation that is more than cognitive, is his own reality, the fact that he exists; this reality constitute his absolute interest. The ethical demand is that he becomes infinitely interested in existing. (*Ibid.,* PP. 428-429).

Soren Kierkegaard's (1813-1855) understanding of love is explained by Waldo Beach and Richard Niebuhr. According to them, for Soren Kierkegaard, only when it is a duty to love only then is love everlastingly free in blessed independence. Love is not depending on this or that, it is eternally independent. (*Ibid.,* P. 440). The love to God and loving neighbor have a crucial role in human relationship. For Kiekegaard love is independent as it provides freedom to make decisions or to act in the particular situation. Kierkegaard explains the teleological suspension of the ethical that the demand came upon the particular individual in a particular moment, and that individual has to act. (Soren Kierkegaard, *Fear and Trembling The Sickness unto Death,* New york: Doubleday and Co., 1954, P. 72).

The individual exists as the particular in opposition to the universal. If one is justified by his act he is not justified by virtue of anything universal, but by virtue of being the particular individual. (*Ibid.,* P. 72). Kierkegaard on referring to Abraham's sacrifice of Issac which leads to a dilemma of the ethical. Here Kierkegaard feels that every individual has to make his/her own decision in the particular situation.

Martin Heidegger (born 1889) is the next dominant figure in existential thought. For him the 'Dasein' (mode of existence of human being) is important, and the essence of Dasein is in its existence. A man has possibility, he has the power to be. According to Blackham, this existence is in his choice of the possibilities which are open to him, and since this choice is never final, once for all, his existence is indeterminate because not terminated. (H. J. Blackham, *Six Existentialist Thinkers, Op.Cit.,* P. 88). Heidegger was concerned of the immediate world one has and the responsibility towards it. Blackham comments, The mode of existence of the human being has a structure: it is being-in-the world. This being-in-the world which constitutes human being in the being of a self in its inseparable relations with a not-self, the world of things and other persons in which the self always and necessarily finds itself inserted. This manner of existence is not merely accidental, it is a necessity of thought in the sense that the world as I find it in Constitutive of my existence, not merely the place in which I have my existence. There is no separation possible. My pre-occupations in the world, my tasks, concerns, cares, pursuits, exemplify the manner of my existence: I can free myself from this or that task or care but never from pre-occupation of some sort. (*Ibid.*, PP. 88-89).

Every individual is to act in the situation as there is open future and possibilities in Heidegger's thought. Blackham observes, "Dasein, then, being possibility, exists by projecting itself, and these tentative projects (Entwurf) are interpretations, not conceptful but existential. My comprehension conceptful but existential. My comprehension of the world (Verstehen) springs together with my sense of being cast into the world (Befindlichkeit) from a common root in the basic human situation, for I recognize what I exist for in my possibilities and what the things about me exist for in their answering to my possibilities. The meaning of human existence is elaborated in the possibilities of action of Dasein." (*Ibid.*, P. 92).

In Heidegger's view Dasein is seen to be an existence already found in the world in the condition of becoming and therefore face an open fortune with the power to be, and bound up with other beings countered in the world.(*Ibid.*, P. 95).

Heidegger states, "Dasein always understands itself in terms of its existence - in terms of a possibility of itself: to be itself or not itself. Dasein has either chosen these possibilities itself, or got itself into them, or grown up in them already." (Martin Heidegger, *Being and Time, Southampton:* Basial Blackwell, 1983, P. 33).

The mode of our existence is relying on our choice and the decision in particular situation in Heidegger's view. According to John Macquarrie, Heidegger's view on human existence is exhibited as care which constituted of possibility (The entities which are encountered are transformed from being merely 'present-at-hand' to being 'ready-to-hand' to man in their serviceability and out of them man constructs an instrumental world which is articulated on the basis of these concerns, facticity (Man is not pure possibility but factical possibility, that is to say, the possibilities open to him at any time are conditioned and limited by many circumstances which he has never chosen his historical situation), and fallenness (Man flees from the disclosure of anxiety to lose himself in absorption with his instrumental world, or to bury himself in the anonymous impersonal existence of the mass, where no one is responsible. When this happens, man has fallen away from his authentic possibility into an inauthentic existence of irresponsibility and illusory security).[141] (John Macquarrie, Twentieth *Century Religious Thought; The Frontiers of Philosophy and Theology, 1990-1980,* Revised edn. London: SCM Press, 1981, PP. 353-354).

The Heidegger's philosophical thought emphasizes that man has potentialities and there is possibilities, so he has to act in the situation without fail as he is finding an authentic existence.

The existentialist is to be discussed is Jean-Paul Sartre (1905-1980). Freedom is the key idea in Sartre's thought. According to Sartre, it is possible for man to try to conceal from himself the boundless freedom or spontaneity of consciousness and to take refuge in the idea of a stable self which ensures regular patterns of conduct. (Frederick Compleston, *A History of Philosophy,* Vol. VII-IX, New York: Doubleday, 1977, P. 348). He challenges this human attitude and condemn it as the fear. Compleston observes on Sartre's view, "Afraid of boundless freedom, man can attempt to avoid his responsibility by attributing his actions to the determining casuality of the past as precipitated, so as to speak, in the self or ego. He is then in 'bad faith', a theme on which Sartre likes to dwell." (*Ibid.,* P. 348). Using the maximum freedom by the inviduals is promoted by Sartre as he states 'man is condemned to be free'.

Sartre states, For since we ignore the commandments of God and all values prescribes as eternal, nothing remains but what is strictly voluntary. Everyone can do what he likes, and will be incapable, from such a point of view, of condemning either the point of view or the action of anyone else. The individual freedom is affirmed by Sartre. The 'subjectivity' and the first principle of existentialism for Sartre is "Man is nothing but that which he makes himself. (Jean-Paul Sartre, *Existentialism and Humanism,* London: Methuen and Co. Ltd., 1949, P. 24).The existence is prior to essence, so man is responsible for what he is, in Sartre's view. Sartre says,

Thus the first effect of existentialism is that it puts every man in possession of himself as he is, and places the entire responsibility for his existence squarely upon his own shoulders. And when we say that man in responsible for himself, we do not mean that he is responsible only for himself, we do not mean that he is responsible only for his own individuality, but that he is responsible for all men. (*Ibid.*, P. 26).

The subjectivity and freedom are the main theme in Sartre. He states, "Subjectivism means, on the one hand, the freedom of the individual subject and, on the other, that man cannot pass beyond human subjectivity."[146] (*Ibid.*, P. 28). According to him the decisions cannot be prefabricated as he states, "we cannot decide *apriori* what it is that should be done." (*Ibid.*, P. 29).Sartre is not for the deontological ethics, but he advocates for aposteriori decision making which might be situational. The antinominanism is also found in his thinking, as he is arguing for the use of complete freedom by each individual. Sartre questions the laws imposed by social or political authorities which makes one the slave of loveless rules and laws.

The contribution of Friedrich Nietzsche (1844-1900) is the next point to be discussed. He was critical of the values and morals and advocated 'Nihilism'. He said about the importance of nihilism as follows: "Because the values we have had hitherto thus draw their final consequence; because nihilism represents the ultimate logical conclusion of our great values and ideals - because we must experience nihilism before we can find out what value these "values" really had - we require, at some time, new values." (*Ibid.*, P. 49). According to Bertrand Russell, "Nietzsche's ethic is not one of self-indulgence in any ordinary sense; he believes in Spartan discipline and the capacity to endure as well as inflict pain for important ends. He admires strength of will above all things". (Walter Kaufmann, *Existentialism From Dostoevsky to Sartre,* New York: The World Publishing Co., 1967, P. 110). He was against the traditional understanding of good and evil and conventional wisdom. For Nietzsche the higher type of man creates his own values out of the abundance of his life and strength. (Bertrand Russell, *A History of Western Philosophy*. New York: Simon and Schuster, 1945, P. 763).

Nietzsche argues for the 'transvalination of values'. He states that the 'virtue', duty, good, that is the good stamped with the character of impersonality and universal validity are more delusions in which the decline, the ultimate enfeeblement of life express themselves. (Frederick Compleston, *A History of Philosophy* vol. VII, New York: Doubleday, 1974, P. 401). For him the real philosophers are law givers or commanders. (Werkrmeister. *Theories of Ethics,* Lincoln: Johnson Publishing Co., 1961, P. 169). For Nietzsche everything which is characteristic of life can be reduced to one formula: 'will to power'. All motions, appearances and laws are merely symptoms of an inner process. The 'symptoms' is the will to power. (*Ibid.,* P. 169). It is the 'will to power' which evaluates. The value of man lies in its utility, says Nietzsche. (*Ibid.,* P. 189). He says, no one knows what is good or bad. Nietzsche's idea can lead to relativism and anomie. Nietzsche's transvaluation of values' challenges the existing rigid and inhuman rules and regulation and it advocates for freedom.

Karl Jaspers (Born 1883) affirms that science is the measure of all things, for science entertains the personal determination of the free personality. (*Ibid.,* P. 192). The personal choice is understood by him as existential and absolute.(*Ibid.,* P. 211). The liberty is very significant to Karl Jaspers. Blackham observes his thinking as follows no choice without decision, no decision without will, no will without duty, no duty without being. (H.J. Blackham. *Six existentialist Thinkers, Op.Cit...,* P. 47). Another important existentialist is Gabriel Marcel (Born 1889). He repudiated the systems and he stresses the importance of concreteness.(*Ibid.,* P. 49). For him the essence of man is to be in a situation that man is put up in a concrete situation. The existential situation in reliving ourselves in the situation is quite significant in his thinking. He also talks about the autonomy (managing our own affairs) to keep ourselves open as we participate with Transcendence. (*Ibid.,* P. 50).

The existentialism stands for the rejection of traditional values and a kind of desperate nihilism to the general public in the post-war world. (*Ibid.,* P. 67). It is rooted in concrete and everyday human experience and confronts the human situation in its totality, seeking to discover the basic conditions (*Ibid.,* PP. 65-70). of human existence and to find how man can give meaning to his life in terms of there conditions. Existentialism argues that man is nothing and man is free to make something of himself, says James McGlynn and Jules Toner. (James V. McGlynn and Jules J. Toner, *Modern Ethical Theories, Op.Cit...,* P. 93). The existentialism has a closer link with the situationism.

In his discussion on situationism and existentialism, Joseph Vadackumcherry states, "Since the existentialists are so concerned with individual morality, they tend to present it concretely rather than abstractly". (*Ibid.,* P. 94). This is the special feature of existentialist treatment of morality. Since there is a discontinuity of one situation or moment of experience from another, the existentialists are against generalities". (*Ibid.,* P. 94).There is also the element of personalism in existentialism. Fr. Vadackumcherry states, "For Sartre the key to man's moral life is his freedom. In a world without God, human person is an absolute value that can not be subordinated to anything else". (Joseph Vadackumcherry, *Natural-Law-Morality versus Situationism in Morals, Op.Cit..,* P. 68). For Sartre, freedom is the only source of value.

For existentialists freedom is man's existence and all value is, according to Sartre, made by man and for man. There are no God-made laws, but only man made laws, comments Fr. Vadackumcherry. (*Ibid.,* P. 67). According to Fr. Vadackumcherry, "situationism is inspired by the existential philosophy in so far as both the philosophical and theological treatment of ethics tend to undermine the permanent nature (essence) of man. Atheistic existentialism dissolved the permanent essence of man into a series of individual discontinuous acts not linked with any substratum or substance". (*Ibid.*, PP. 68-69).

Joseph Fletcher is definitely influenced by existentialism. He even quotes Paul Tillich and Bultmann who were influenced by existentialism. For both of them the love can only take the varying shape in different situations. Martin Heidegger against the absolutizing of conscience. Fletcher agrees with the existentialist thinking of Heidegger. (*Ibid.*, P. 89). He also quotes Soren Kierkegaard to support him, and he states that Sartre also does not approve any generally valid principles. (*Ibid.*, P. 89). It is clear that the situational approach of Fletcher has a great fascination towards the existentialism.

5. Relativism

The modern cultural, anthropological, sociological and historical analysis argue for relativism. For Harold Kuhn, "Relativism is a theory that the basis for judgements is knowledge, culture, or ethics differs according to persons, events or situations. It connotes a state of mind or a way of thinking in hospitable to absolute claims". (Joseph Fletcher, *Situation Ethics,* P. 53). The present cultural studies argue that the value found in one culture cannot be universalized. The cultural relativism centred in the rejection of universal norms. (*Ibid.,* PP. 111, 23). Kuhn states that, "moral or ethical relativism is a specialized form of cultural relativism in which any universally acceptable criterion for measuring values is rejected. All value systems are viewed as being of equal validity, since they are all culturally conditional and determined". (Harold B. Kuhn, "Ralativism", *Bakers Dictionary of Christian Ethics,* edited by Carl F. Henry, Michigan: Baker Book House, 1981, P. 572).

In the discussion on the pursuit of truth and value of systems, M.G.S. Narayanan comments, "the science-oriented modern man whose mind is liberated from the conventional ideas of God and absolute values will have to confess his limitations, his uncertainty, his unenviable predicament where he tries to experiment with the only tools that are available to him, those of natural science and social science". (M.G.S Narayanan. "A Historian's Approach", *Bangalore Theological Forum* vol. VIII. Nos. 1&2, 1981, P. 25. The modern science-oriented man is advocating relativism).

The cultural relativism is one of the important aspects that contributes to the relativism of values. According to Ruth Benedict, the traits and behaviour and customs can be independent and different in different situations. According to her, "They differ from one another not only because one trait is present here and absent there, and because another trait is found in two regions in two different forms. They differ still more because they are oriented as wholes in different directions". (Ruth Benedict, "Cultural Relativism", *Morals and Values,* edited by Marcus G. Singer, *Op.Cit...,* P. 233). Edwin Lutzer affirms that there are ethical differences among the peoples of the world. (Erwin W. Lutzer, *The Necessity of Ethical Absolutes*, Michgan, Zonderavan Publishing House, 1961, P. 17). Erwin Lutzer comments that, "The clothes we wear, the houses we live in, our sense of justice, and even our understanding of family relationships are shaped in large part by culture. Again we face the question, what makes an action right or wrong? The view we will consider here says that what a given culture accepts determines the answer. Whatever a cultural group approves of becomes right; Whateever a group disapproves of is wrong". (*Ibid.,* P. 17).

According to Erwin Lutzer, the anthropologists agree that culture can make anything right and it also can make anything wrong. What our conscience tells us depends solely upon our tribe or social group. Values are forged by childhood training and by the pressures brought upon us to conform to the ways of the group. (*Ibid.,* P. 18). Lutzer upholds William Graham Sumner of Yale University that every question of conduct receives varying and at times opposing answers from various cultures. (*Ibid.,* P. 18). Lutzer continues to say that,, "Although many tribes believed it was acceptable for a man to have more than one wife, Sumner discovered that in Tibet a woman was encouraged to have several husbands. He also described how some Eskimo tribes allowed deformed babies to die of exposure, and in the Fiji islands, aged parents were killed". (*Ibid.,* P. 19). Lutzer comments that "According to Herskovits, cultures are flexible and so we find that more change over a period of time. Thus the norm for acceptable conduct within a culture may change as the culture shifts its ethical base". (*Ibid.,* P. 19).

Erwin Lutzer observes that the cultural relativism leads to individual relativism. Lutzer states, Cultural relativism also inevitably leads to individual relativism. If there are no transcultural values, where does the group derive the authority to become the source of values? Ultimately, this authority must rest with individuals. The group, the race, or individual becomes the standard. The individual, however, may quite logically reason that he or she need not follow the group, since there is no independent criterion for moral options. (*Ibid.,* P. 24).

Lutzer observes that there is necessity of absolutes, and the reformers come since there is evil in the cultures and its values. (*Ibid.,* P. 25). Auguste Comte also talks about relativism. He was called as the father of Sociology. For him everything is relative and that is the only absolute principle. He has raised relativity to an absolute law. (Jacques Maritain, *Moral Philosophy,* New York; Charles Scribners Sons, 1960, P. 280). Time is the great relativisor. According to Maritain, for Comte "Absolutely speaking, there is nothing good, there is nothing bad; everything is relative, that's the only thing that is absolute". (*Ibid.,*

P. 281).Comtian formula concerns the relativity of "everything", particularly of "good" and "evil" in relation to the dimension of time, all values are relative to time. (*Ibid.,* P. 282). For Auguste Comte the values can be relative as they change as the time goes on.

In the view of historical relativism every human thought is conditioned by history. No moral judgement is universally valid, and that all norms of conduct are essentially relative to time and to the diversity of the moments of history. (*Ibid.,* P. 264).For Ernst Troeltsch, historical contexts are many and they are always changing. What is so in one historical situation may be different in another; what is so today in a given historical context may be different in that same context tomorrow. Historical consciousness seems to imply a radical relativity of all cultures.[187] (Paul F. Knitter, *No Other Name?* Philippines: Claretian publications, 1985, P. 24).

According to Paul Tillich the material cited by sociologists, anthropologists, and psychologists, showing endless difference of ethical ideals is no argument against the unconditional validity of the moral imperative. For him the moral imperative is not a strange law, imposed on us, but it is the law of our being. He states, 'No outside command can be unconditional, whether it comes from a state, or a person, or God if God is thought of an outside power, establishing law for our behaviour". (Paul Tillich, *Theology of Culture,* New York; Oxford University Press, 1964, P. 136). Tillich opined that every situation is different according to the culture, religion and group. He talks about the cultural factor that brings relativism. It is the difference in the spatial dimension, difference of place, group, culture and religions. (Paul Tillich, My Search for Absolutes, *New York; Simon Schuster,* 1967, P. 97).

The moralism, says Paul Tillich, is relative. (Paul Tillich, *Theology of culture, Op.Cit...,* P. 137). He states that no ethnologist should deny the absolute character of the ethical demand. The moral self-affirmations are conditioned by situation, it can be the cultural situation. (*Ibid.*, P.137). According to him, moral systems just because of their intimate connection with a cultural system have the tendency to become oppressive if the general cultural scheme changes. (*Ibid.*, PP.133-134). While discussing relativism Leonard Carmichael has said, "customs related to birth, puberty, marriage, child-rearing, food providing and eating, illness, death, and other standard events of every human life and culture have had many different superficial forms in various ages and societies. This does not suggest that all these patterns of behaviour are equally satisfactory in what may be thought of as on absolute sense".(Leonard Carmichel, "Absolutes, Relativism and the Scientific Psychology of Human Nature", *Relativism and the Study of Man,* edited by Helmut Shock and James W. Wiggins princeton; D. Van Nostrand company, Inc. 1961, P. 8). For him, the aspect of relativism is an undeniable fact.

Eliseo Vivas also affirms the reality of cultural pluralism and cultural relativism. The values of a culture is determined by that culture. According to him the relativists argument is that, "The values determined by a culture are the values that the members of that culture ought to acknowledge". (Eliseo Vivas, "Second thought on cultural Relativism", *Relativism and the Study of Man, Op.Cit...,* P. 47). The cultural relativism is also valid circumstantially for a period of time and at specific places; says Vivas. For him relativism is also retardatarian as the emergence of nationalism and the peoples of the world come together transcending their boundaries even in terms of their moral judgements. (*Ibid.,* PP. 66-67). It is true that because of nationalism and internationalism there are accepted universally valid rules and regulations. Thought few, in the primitive communities also there are some norms which are at least, broadly accepted as absolute universal rules or principles. According to Langmead Casserley, the morality contains several relative elements, but it also acknowledges in its own confused way some absolute elements. (J.V. Langmead Casserly, "Relativism from a Theological Stand Point", *Relativism and the Study of Man, Op.Cit...*, P. 100).

It is evident that the different cultures have their values and there is a divergence. It is difficult to find universal validity of all rules or principles. All norms are also not absolute to all cultures. But it should be accepted that there are some general rules common to all. Embracing good and resist evil is one among them. Do not harm, but love one another in yet another principle. Of course, the perspective and understanding about these norms may be varied, but these can be recognized as the universally accepted principles.

Father Felix Podimattam comments, When we speak of the relativity of the cultural costume of truth, we do not mean, to deny to its validity or some kind of absoluteness. Actually we attribute to it an absoluteness but a temporary one. What we deny is not absoluteness permanent absoluteness. So, a certain formulation of moral truth is absolutely valid for that period of time in which the culture which called for such a formulation endures. (Felix M. Podimattam. *Relativity of Natural Law, Op.Cit...*, P. 34)

The terms relativism and absolute may be redefined. Both are acceptable facts. There is an element of relativism, since there is cultural pluralism, but at the same time, there is a value understanding in local and translocal level.

Joseph Fletcher, the situation ethicist affirms that his ethical approach is a relativistic approach. Fletcher agrees that the tactics of situationism are relativistic. For him the value and the concept of good and the ideas are relativistic. (Joseph Fletcher, *Situation Ethics,* PP. 45-46). In his view the global situation and the cultural contexts are approving the ethical relativism. Fletcher is so much influenced by the relativism as he is allergic to universally valid rules. The cultural diversity and the diverse value systems also ascertain the need for a love oriented and contextual ethical approach.

6. Positivism

Positivism affirms that only what is observed can be believed. According to Fuller, "It involves a rejection of all hypothetical construction of entities regarded as existing apart from and beneath the sensible universe". (B, A.B. Fuller, *A History of Philosophy,* Revised edn. New Delhi; Oxford and IBH Publishing Co., 1976. P. 386).

What is supernatural or the element of revelation is denied by positivism. The laws are not necessarily absolute in the sense of being of necessity universally, for positivism. According to it the establishment of absolute laws, which we could be sure held for everything in all times and places, would require a complete scientific observation of all phenomena whatsoever, past, present, and future throughout the entire universe; and according to Fuller, such completeness is impossible. (*Ibid.*, P. 387). According to him, scientific thinking is relative to the nature of the human organism. Sense data are relative to the kind of sense organs we possess, and the inferences we draw from them are conditional by the nature of human mental processes. (*Ibid.*, P. 387).

Jacques Maritain describes the positivism of Aguste Comte. He states, Despotic norms of conduct prescribed for human life in the name of a universal will inhabiting a supra-temporal world whose existence cannot be proved, and in the name of a supra-temporal law devoid of all content this is the picture which this disaffected Christine ethics that is the ethic of pure practical reason presents to an age for which nothing has any meaning outside of experience, and on which the influence of Darwin will come along to complete that of Auguste Comte. (Jacques Maritain, *Moral Philosophy, Op.Cit.,* P. 263).

For Comte, no moral judgement is universally valid and that all norms of conduct are essentially relative to time and to the diversily of the moments of history. (*Ibid.,* P. 264). Comte has raised relativity to an absolute law. For him everything is relative, that is the only absolute principle. (*Ibid.,* P. 280).

The logical positivism also contributes to the whole concept of positivism. According to Alfred Jules Ayer there are several absolute ethical norms eg. 'good' 'wrong', which are unanalysable because they are pseudoconcepts. (Alfred Jules Ayer, *Language Truth and Logic*, 2nd Edn. New York; Doyer Publications, 1946, P. 107). The ethical judgements are emotive in his view. He states, "It is used to express feeling about certain objects, but not to make any assertion about them". (*Ibid.,* P. 108). He continued to say that, "It is worth mentioning that ethical terms do not serve only to express feeling. They are calculated also to arouse feeling, and so to stimulate action". (*Ibid.,* P. 108). In Gieser's words, for Ayer, "Ethics is not prescriptive; it is simply emotive. Ethical pronouncements are merely ejaculations of our subjective feeling and not divine imperatives about moral duty". (Norman Giesler, *Options in Contemporary Christian Ethics, Op.Cit..,* P. 12). According to A.J. Ayer, a proposition is meaningless unless experience can conclusively establish its truth. (John Passmore, *A Hundered Years of Philosophy,* Middleses; Penguin Books, 1984. P. 386). For him apriori propositions are arbitrary. (*Ibid.,* P. 390).

According to Moritz schlick, "such norms are recognized as the ultimate norms, or highest values, must be desired from human nature and life as facts. Therefore, no result of ethics can stand in contradiction to life, ethics can not declare as evil or false those values which lie at the foundation of life; its norms cannot demand or command anything that is in a real opposition to those final norms recognized by life." (Moritz Schlick. What is the Aim of Ethics?, *Logical Positivism,* edited by A.J. Ayer, Illinois; The Free Press, 1960, P. 258). He again states that the ultimate valuations are facts existing in human consciousness, and even if ethics were a normative science it would not cease because of this to be a science of *facts.* (*Ibid.*, P. 258). Ethics has to do entirely with the *actual.* According to Schlick, ethics should not be so normative that it denies the facts and the circumstances of a person. It should rely on individual's life. According to Joseph Vadackumcherry.

Situationism is bound up with a theological positivism in which faith propositions are posited or affirmed voluntaristically rather than rationalistically. In Fletcher's view it is outside reason, but not against it; thinking supported by faith rather than faith supported by thinking. Thus situationism posits faith in God and reasons out what obedience to his commandment to love requires in any situation. (Joseph Vadackumcherry, *Natural-law-Morality versus Situationnism in Morals, Op.Cit...,* PP. 83-84).

Fletcher agrees that positivism has influenced his ethical approach: "The other approach is theological positivism (or "positive theology"), in which faith propositions are "posited" or affirmed voluntaristically rather than rationalistically". (Joseph Fletcher. *Situation Ethics,* P. 7). The theological positivism does not deny the existence of God and the role of God in the world while the scientific and logical positivism do not affirm the importance of supernatural. He states, 'Christian ethics "posits" faith in God and reasons out what obedience to his commandment to love requires in any situation". (*Ibid.,* P. 47).

7. Pragmatism

The Pragmatism is based on 'what is practical'. Pragmatism is a movement especially, came out as a contribution of America. William James (1842-1910), Charles Sanders Pierce (1839-1914), and John Dewey (1859-1952) are the most important figures in pragmatism. (Robert T. Handy "Pragmatism", *A Dictionary of Christian Ethics,* edited by John Macquarrie. *Op.Cit.,* PP. 267-268). William James' main question is 'what you practically mean' (William James, *Pragmatism and Four Essays from the Meaning of Truth,* New York; A Meradian book, 1974, P. 42). According to him, "The pragmatic method is primarily a method of settling metaphysical disputes that otherwise might be interminable." (*Ibid.,* P. 42). There are mending disputes in the world. In this context William James says.

> The pragmatic method in such case is to try to interpret each notion by tracing its respective practical consequences. What difference would it make to any one if this notion rather than that notion were true? If no practical difference whatever can be traced, then the alternatives mean practically the same thing, and all dispute is idle. Whenever a dispute is serious, we ought to be able to show some practical difference that must follow from one side or the other's being right. (*Ibid.,* PP. 42-43).

Pragmatism comes from the Greek word 'pragma' which means action, from which derives 'practice' and 'practical'. About the pragmatist, William James has stated, "He turns away from abstraction and insufficiency, from verbal solutions, from bad *apriori* reasons, from fixed principles, closed systems, and pretended absolutes and origins. He turns towards concreteness and adequacy, towards facts, towards action and towards power". (*Ibid.,* PP. 42-43).

About the characteristics of pragmatism, William James comments, "pragmatism unstiffens all our theories, limbers them up and sets each one at work. Being nothing essentially new, it harmonizes with many ancient philosophical tendencies. It agrees with nominalism for instance, in always appealing to particulars; with utilitarianism in emphasizing practical aspects; with positivism in its disdain or verbal solutions, useless questions and metaphysical abstractions". (*Ibid.*, P. 45).

The pragmatism is also looking to the facts and consequences says William James: "No particular results then, so far, but only an attitude of orientation, is what the pragmatic method means the attitude of looking away from first things, principles, 'categories', supposed necessities; and of looking towards last things, fruits, consequences, facts." (*Ibid.*, P. 47).

John Dewey is the other important personality behind pragmatism. Pragmatism is also known as 'instrumentalism'. Henry W. Stuart analyses the ethical theory of John Dewey very elaborately. In Stuarts's view, for Dewey, "Methods are justified by their success; results derive none of their worth from the method by which they have been brought to pass". (Henry W. Stuart, "Dewey's Ethical Theory" *In The Philosophy of John Dewey,* 2nd edition New York; Tudor Publishing Co., 1931, P. 293). The experimental inquiry is significant in Dewey. According to him, experimental inquiry or method, is the locus within which, or the supreme principle by which, conceptions of philosophy that are really significant can be understood. It is in this sense; according to professor Dewey, that method - that is to say, the method of experimental inquiry - is supreme", (*Ibid*, P. 295). States Henry Stuart. For Dewey, the situation is precarious, so the direct solution to any problem is not supreme. (*Ibid.,* P. 295).

In the precarious situation, for Dewey, the method is instrumental. He realizes the problem of applying the predetermined rules or principles in that situation. Henry Stuart comments, "A precarious situation is one in which what we already prize and are determined to prize is endangered. In an ethical situation nothing is for us in danger but on success in achieving what shall be better worth our prizing. To identify these two dangers is to empty individual experience and human history of all distinctive meaning." (*Ibid.*, P. 297). Talking about experimentalism Dewey observes that no one lives in a world in which he has found everything at all times perfect. He admonishes the man to learn to be alive to possibilities. Dewey opines, "The potential better will then be regarded as the good - and the only good - of any situation, a statement as applicable to scientific inquiry as to any moral matter. A disposition framed when conditions are overtly not wholly good is capable, like the experimental method itself of exercise when, on the surface, they seem good." (John Dewey, "Experience, Knowledge and Value", *The Philosophy of John Dewey,* edited by Paul Arthur Schilpp, 20 *Op.Cit...,* P. 389).

For Dewey the moral principles are instrumental to make decisions. He states, "No genuine moral principle prescribes a specific course of action; rules, like cooking recipes, may tell just what to do and how to do it. A moral principle, such as that of chastity, of justice, of the Golden Rule, gives the agent a basis for looking at and examining a particular question comes up." (John Dewey, *Theory of the Moral Life*, New Delhi: Wiley Eastern Private Ltd., 1967, P. 1411). He continued to say about the principles that, "It holds before him certain possible aspects of the act; it warns him against talking a short or partial view of the act. It economizes his thinking by supplying him with the main heads by reference to which to consider the bearings of his desires and purposes; it guides him in his thinking by suggesting to him the important considerations for which he should be on the lookout." (*Ibid.*, P. 141).

According to John Dewey, the moral principle is a tool to analyses the situation. He comments, "A moral principle, then, is not a command to act or forbear acting in a given way: It is a tool for analysing a special situation, the right or wrong being determined by the situation in its entirety, and not by the rules as such". (*Ibid.,* P. 141).

According to Charles Pierce the pragmatism is experimental in nature. In his words, "For an experimental phenomenon is the fact asserted by the proposition that action of a certain description will have a certain kind of experimental result; and experimental result are the only result that can affect human conduct." (Charles Sanders Pierce, "The Essentials of Pragmatism" *In philosophical Writings* of Pierce, Dover publications, 1953. P. 262). He continued to say that, "Whenever a man acts purposively, he acts under a belief in some experimental phenomenon, Consequently, the sum of the experimental phenomena that proposition implies makes up its entire bearing upon human conduct". (*Ibid.,* P. 262).The experimental method is a particular application of the rule 'by their fruits you shall know them' states Pierce. (Sanders Pierce, "Pragmatism in Retrospect: A Last formulation" *In Philosophical writings of Pierce, Op.Cit.,* P. 271).

According to Robert Handy, Charles Pierce is concerned of 'how to make our ideas clear'. He affirmed that beliefs are really rules for action which establish habits. Different beliefs are to be distinguished by the different modes of action to which they give rise. To develop a thought meaning, we need only to determine what conduct it is fitted to produce; to attain cleanness in our thought of an object, we need to consider what practical effects the objects may involve. (Robert T. Handy, "Pragmatism", *Distionary of Christian Ethics, Op.Cit..,* P. 267). Pierce was regarding what is practical, and the practical effects as quite important in our life and conduct. Pierce rejected the mechanical conception of natural laws. (John Passmore, *A Hundered Years of Philosophy Op.Cit.,* P. 103).

The pragmatism, instrumentalism or the experimentalism rejects the *apriori* elements. For these what is practical is important, so also feels that the ethics is only instrumental and not concerned of the conclusion. Pragmatism is also experimental. Joseph Fletcher has admitted that he is consciously inspired by American Pragmatism. He quotes the idea of William James that pragmatist turns away from fixed rules, closed systems, and pretended absolutes. (Joseph Fletcher,-*Situation Ethics,* PP. 40-42). One of the main inspiration behind Fletcher's ethical approach is pragmatism. The importance of 'what is practical' played a crucial role in Fletcher's approach.

8. Personalism

According to John H. Lavely, "personalism is a philosophical perspective system which person is the ontological ultimate and for which personality is thus the fundamental explanatory principle". (John H. Lavely, "personalism" *In The Encyclopedia of Philosophy* vol. 6, edited by Paul Edwards New York; The Macmillan Co. and free Press, 1967, P. 107).The personalism is associated to person both in value and being. (*Ibid.,* P. 107).For realist personalism, personality is the fundamental being, and ultimate reality is a spiritual, supernatural being. The idealistic personalism is divided into three: (1) Absolute idealism - reality is one absolute mind, spirit of person, (2) Panpsychistic idealism - Leibeniz' monadology is the paradigm. Reality is a hierarchy of psychic beings (monads) determined by the degree of consciousness possessed by any monad. The supreme monad (God) has created all other monads in pre-established harmony (3) Personal idealism - it is considered as the most typical form. It is idealistic; All reality is personal. Reality is a society of persons. God is the ultimate person and the ground of all being. (*Ibid.*, P. 107).

According to Edgar Brightman (1884-1953), immediate experience in the inescape starting point and the persons are centres of intrinsic value. (*Ibid.*, P. 109). According to R.T. Flewelling the "personalism, in the proper sense of the term asserts a system of themselves related through a supreme personality. It conceives of the supreme person as existing in and through the concrete continuous exercise of his personality, thinking, willing, and sustaining all things". (R. T. Flewelling, "Personalism" *American Philosophy* edited by Ralph B. winn, New Jersey: Littlefiel, Adams and Co. 1965, P. 155). To the personalist, real is that which can act or be acted upon. Personalism is also saved from the vagueness of most forms of idealism by its pragmatic requirements. (*Ibid.*, P. 772).

According to Flewelling, the personalism has passed under various designations such as voluntarism, philosophy of freedom; of effort; of probability ; of contingency; of change. (Ralph T. Flewelling, "Personalism", *American Philosophy,* edited by Ralph B. Winn, New Jersey, Littlefield: Adams & Co., 1965, P. 155). Discussing personalism Flewelling commented, "It is founded upon the doctrine of the sanctity and inviolability of the person, considered as a manifestation of the ultimate energy, which creates the world, and inspires all genius in man as its field of action. Such creative energy, transcendent of time, self- directive and self-conscious, is in the completest sense a person." (*Ibid.*, P. 157). The personalists hold that all reality is in some sense personal; that there are only persons and that which they create; that personality in the possession of self-consciousness and self-directiveness. (*Ibid.*, P. 158).

The personalism is pragmatic, Flewelling observes, "logically, the system is pragmatic, holding that life is more important and convincing than any form of expression, forever bursting the bonds of fixed meanings or verbalisms. Ethically it holds to the way of freedom through which alone moral values are established. Viewing ethical values as creative achievements, it assumes that the risk of error and evil must find justification in the intellectual and potentiality it provides for persons." (*Ibid.,* PP. 158-159). The personalism is pragmatic and it gives freedom for the persons to make their own decisions.

According to Albert Knudson, though there is no fixed definition for the term personalism, it is the philosophy which makes the personality basal and central. (Albert C. Knudson. *The Philosophy of Personalism* second print, New York: the Abingdon Press, 1928, P. 20). Atheistic personalism is represented by J.M.E.McTaggart (1866-1925). He holds that ultimate reality consists of a society of persons. (*Ibid.,* P. 22). For him, "The absolute is not a personal being, it has no independent existence, it exists simply as a system of selves". (*Ibid.,* P. 22). In McTaggart's theory individuals have no real freedom as it is said to be self determined. He rejects freedom and a personal God, so this personalism is found as a departure from the true type. (*Ibid.,* P. 23).

The personalism in Knudson's words' holds six aspects:

(a) Personalism holds that reality is concrete and individual. It thus leans toward pluralism and natural realism. It does so in the interest of the reality and independence of the finite person and also in the interest of a more distinct and cleanly defined conception of the infinite than has prevailed in many philosophies.

(b) It stresses the unity of the world and world around. In this respect it leans towards moralism and absolutism, thus satisfying the religious demand involved in the feeling of absolute dependence and also the intellectual demand for a universe as distinguished from a "multiverse".

(c) It maintains that reality in its essential nature is active. In other words, it interprets substance in terms of causality. It thus falls in line with modern physical theory and also with the modern tendency to conceive of the soul as a mental agent rather than as mere substance.

(d) It takes an important step beyond modern energetics and contends that energy or causality must ultimately be interpreted in terms of volition. Here personalism breaks with the realistic systems of the past and becomes idealistic.

(e) It holds that matter is phenomenal, and that in a more thorough going sense than any realistic theory would admit. This follows necessarily from its interpretation of causality. Not only does personalism deny extra-mental existence to the extended matter of sense-experience but also to its dynamic ground. It conceives of the whole material world as the ceaseless product of the divine energizing. Indeed, in its thorough going form it holds to the complete ideality of space and time.

(f) It contends that personality is the key to ultimate reality. Abstract thought leads to fundamental antimonies such as those between identity and change, the one and the many, freedom and necessity. A solution to these antimonies is possible only in personal experience. Here we have in very fact, however, we may account for it, a union of personal identity with change, of conscious unity with multiplicity of experience, and of freedom or self -control with uniformity or necessity. (*Ibid.,* PP. 178-179).

According to Albert Knudson, "personalism begins its theory with the affirmation that metaphysical existence can be predicated only of that which is individual and concrete. (*Ibid.*, PP. 178-179). Personalism affirms the freedom of personality in the concrete situations. Joseph Fletcher is influenced by personalism. According to him, ethics deals with human relations, and situation ethics puts people at the centre of concern. (Joseph Fletcher, *Situation Ethics* P. 50).The situationists are personalistic, in Fletchers's words. It is the personality which is important rather than principles in Fletcher's perspective. (*Ibid.*, P. 50).

The situation ethics has contributed to an openness in the ethical discussions on one side, and it promoted an evaluative approach on the other. Fletcher's situationism has directly or indirectly influenced the moral thinking in the church and society.

According to Harvey Cox, Joseph Fletcher's book *'Situation Ethics'* has made an important contribution to the democratization of the theological conversation. It has also created a new interest in religions and ethical issues. (Harvey Cox., ed. *The Situation Ethics Debate, Phildelphia; The Westminster Press,* 1968, P. 11, 13). The human experience is taken into account by situation ethics, says Harvey Cox. He states that "Whatever else now happens in theology and ethics, the renewed attention given to the experience of concrete human beings in history can no longer be overlooked". (*Ibid.,* P.18). Harvey Cox writes, "The hundreds of readers who have written to Professor Fletcher or to newspapers, magazines, and journals about his situation ethics, plus editorial treatment and sermons in churches of all traditions, are evidence of some success for his books attempt to interest a wider range of people than just professional thinkers in the growing debate about "How to do ethics", the question of methodology in the formation of conscience". (*Ibid.,* P. 23).

Discussing the strength of situational ethics Hanlee H. Barnette has commented that situation ethics is largely a methodology of ethics that would stimulate for some much needed research in the area of Christian ethics. It enables to make some research in the context of rapid social change which it is the ethical demand today. (*Ibid.*, P. 133). Barnette also feels that situation ethics of Fletcher can contribute to subjectivism. The term love is not described in a systematic fashion that can lead to ambiguity in ethical decision making. (*Ibid.*, P. 135). Charles Curran sees the situation ethics as a corrective to shallow legalism and traditional moral theology which is based on universal prohibitions. (*Ibid.*, P. 191) He argues that Fletcher's approach is more suiting to modern man who places emphasis on the historical the particular, the individual, the changing and the relational. (*Ibid.*, P. 191).

According to Harvey Cox, "The uniqueness of contextualism as an ethical position is to be found in its tendency drastically to minimize the place of principles. Modern situation ethics is allergic to generalized guiding rules and this is where its sickness lies. The epidemic of this disease could have mortal consequences for both church and culture". (*Ibid.*, P. 225). He states again that radical contextualism as we see in Fletcher can eliminate the values of a systematic approach to moral life and it can lead to error and chaos in the area of morality. (*Ibid.*, P. 230). Harvey cox is critical of situation ethics.

It might be true that there are sexual philosophies and theories which have contributed to the emergence of situation ethics. Situationism is understood as relativistic, personalistic, arbitrary, but it takes seriously the issues in the situation in order to deal them with love, generosity and mercy. Situationism can be understood as an evaluative approach which considers the cases (what is termed as posterior) in terms of what is useful, pragmatic loving or agapeic decision in the existential moment.

Chapter 2

Aposteriori-agapeic Approach to Ethical Issues with Special Reference to Sexuality and Marriage

This chapter deals with the ethical approach of Joseph Fletcher. It considers the fundamental aspects of Fletcher's situation ethics and his different perspectives on socio-ethical, bio-ethical and professional ethical issues. The issues like property, abortion, euthanasia etc. are also considered to get an overall picture of his approach. A section would be given to concentrate on the issue of sexuality and marriage. There would also be a comprehensive understanding and evaluation of Fletcher's ethical approach.

A. The Foundational Aspect of Situation Ethics

This section is an analysis of the foundational aspect of the situation ethics. The situation ethics challenges the traditional morality, especially the deontological ethics and the natural law morality. Joseph Fletchen affirms, at the same time, the situation ethics based on love. He questions the loveless rules or principles and dwells on the aposteriori- agapeic approach.

1. The Challenge to Traditional Morality and the Presuppositions of Situationism

According to Joseph Fletcher, the situation ethics or new morality is new either in method or in content, and as a method it is found in the classical tradition of western Christian morals. It is also, he says, "a radical departure from the conventional wisdom". (Joseph Fletcher. *Situation Ethics*, p. 13). He observes that there are three approaches which have played a role in the Western morals. They are legalism, antinomianism (a lawless or unprincipled approach) and situationism. (*Ibid.*, P. 17).

In Fletcher's view, the legalism is rooted in the prefabricated rules and regulations. The codified rules are meant to be directives to be followed. (*Ibid.*, P. 18).Judaism, Catholicism, Protestantism and all major western religious traditions are legalistic in his view.(*Ibid.*, P. 18). He states, "protestantism has rarely constructed such intricate codes and systems of law but what it has gained by its simplicity it has lost through its rigidity, its puritanical insistence on moral rules". (*Ibid.*, P. 19). Legalisms in the Christian tradition has two forms in Fletcher's view - the catholic legalism and the Protestant legalism. About Catholic legalism he says, "In the catholic line it has been a matter of legalistic reason, based on nature or natural law. These moralists have tended to adumbrate their ethical rules by applying human reason to the facts of nature, both human and subhuman, and to the lessons of historical experience. By this procedure they claim to have adduced universally agreed and therefore valid "natural" moral laws" (*Ibid.*, P. 21; Joseph Fletcher, *Moral Responsibility:* 1967, PP. 168-170). The Protestant legalism in his own words as follows:

Protestant moralists have followed the same adductive and deductive tactics. They have taken scripture and done with it what the Catholics do with nature. Their scriptural moral law is, they argue, based on the words and sayings of the Law and prophets, the evangelists and apostles of the Bible. It is a matter of legalistic revelation. One is rationalistic, the other Biblicist; one natural, the other scriptural. But both are legalistic (Joseph Fletcher, *Situation Ethics,* P. 21).

The second approach in the Western morals is the antinomianism, for Fletcher. It literally means lawlessness. It is a form of libertinism which means the laws and rules are no longer applied to Christians. (*Ibid.*, P. 22). About antinomianism Fletcher states, "They follow no forecastable course from one situation to another. They are, exactly, anarchic - ie., without a rule. They are not only "unbound by the chains of law" but actually sheer extemporizers, impromptous and intellectually irresponsible". (*Ibid.*, P. 23). According to Fletcher, antinomianism rejects the demands of love and the Old Testament Torah. (*Ibid.*, P. 23).

Fletcher observes that Sartre refuses to admit to any generally valid principles at all. According to him "Existentialists rightly reject even all principles, all "generally valid" ethical norms or axioms, as well as all rules or laws or precepts that legalistically absolutize (idolize) such general principles" (*Ibid.*, P. 25). Fletcher does not approve the antinomianism, though he is criticized as antinomian.

The third approach is situationism. Situationism is formulated by Fletcher as an alternative, a middle position between legalism and antinomianism. (Joseph Fletcher, *Moral Responsibility,* P. 171). According to Fletcher, "The situationist enters into every decision-making situation fully assumed with the ethical maxims of his community and its heritage, and he treats them with respect as illuminators of his problems. Just the same he is prepared in any situation to compromise them or set them aside in the situation if love seems better served by doing so". (Joseph Fletcher, *Situation Ethics*. P. 26). For him in situation only the love command is categorically good. Fletcher holds that, "Situation ethics goes part of the way with natural law by accepting reason as the instrument of moral judgement, while rejecting the notion that the good is "given" in the nature of things objectively. It goes part of the way with Scriptural law by accepting revelation as the source of the norm while rejecting all "revealed" norms or laws but one command- to love God in the neighbor". (*Ibid.*, P. 26). It is clear that Fletcher's approach is an aposteriori-agapeic approach, and he is against the apriori or normative elements.

Fletcher is found to be against what is normative, but his ethical approach can be accepted as an evaluative one from the Christian understanding as it is very agapeic and merciful in the human dilemma, especially in the cases. It can be also observed as a pastoral approach which is to help people as they are expecting to deal their cases in a loving and merciful manner.

Fletcher argues that the obligation in the situation only is absolute. He explains, "Our obligation is relative to the situation, but obligation in the situation is absolute. We are only "obliged" to tell the truth, for example. "If the situation calls for it; if a murderer asks us his victim's whereabouts on duty might be lie". (*Ibid.*, P. 27). Fletcher's situationism has agape as an absolute norm. Situationism is deciding then and there in Fletcher's view. He reduced aposteriori-agape as his norm.

Love is the highest goal for situation ethics. Fletcher states, 'the situational ethic holds furthermore, that love and only love is intrinsically, inherently good, always and forever, regardless of circumstances. This is the same logically, as saying that only God is absolute and conditional, that all else, all creature and conditions are relative - relative to their total situations and shifting contexts".(Joseph Fletcher, *Moral Responsibility*, P. 171).The values are also relative, according to him, as "what is right in one context could be evil or wrong in another". (*Ibid.*, P. 172).

Speaking about legalism Fletcher states, "Legalism always emphasizes order and conformity and responsibility". (*Ibid.*, P. 177). While talking about situation ethics, Fletcher said, "Precisely, I think that agapism or situation ethics is necessarily consequentialist or teleological. As a teleology, situation ethics is like utilitarianism, and like pragmatism". (William E. May, ed. *Hello Lovers!,* Washington: Corpus books, 1970, P. 6; Hereafter, Mello travers!)

Joseph Fletcher talks about four working principles. They are Pragmatism, Relativism, Positivism and Personalism. (Joseph Fletcher, *Situation Ethics,* PP. 40-56).

1. **Pragmatism:** Joseph Fletcher confesses that his book 'Situation Ethics' is inspired by American pragmatism. He argues that pragmatism is the legitimate tool of ethics. Pragmatism is based on what is practical. (*Ibid.*, P. 41). He says, "Christianly speaking, as we shall see, the norm or measure by which any thought or action is to be judged a success or failure i.e., right or wrong, is love. What "love" is, can wait for later and longer discussion, but here and now let it be clear that the situationist, whether a Christian or not, follows a strategy that is pragmatic". (*Ibid.*, P. 43). He discloses that William James, Charles Pierce and John Dewey have influenced him. He argues that William James turns away from apriori reasons, fixed principles, closed systems, and turns towards concreteness and adequacy, toward facts and actions.(*Ibid.*, P. 43).The basic question of pragmatism is whether the method goes to work. (*Ibid.*, P. 43).Fletcher is very much influenced by the pragmatism which is not insisting on the predetermined rules and conventional wisdom, but insists on what is 'practical' in the situation.

2. **Relativism:** The situation ethics is relativistic. The tactics are relativistic, says Fletcher. He has

the opinion that, "The situationist avoids words like "never", "perfect", "always", and "complete" as he avoids the plague, as he avoids absolutely". (*Ibid.*, P. 44). The aspects of cultural relativity has influenced Fletcher's thinking. He states, "In Christian situationism the ultimate criterion is, as shall be seeing, "agapeic love". It relativizes the absolute, it does not absolutize the relative!" (*Ibid.*, P. 45). Arguing for situationism and the relativity, he says, "Only love is a constant; everything else is a variable. The shift to relativism carries contemporary Christians away from stern iron-bound do's and don'ts, away from prescribed conduct and legalistic morality". (*Ibid.*, P. 45).In order to support the ethical relativism he quotes Paul Tillich's understanding that, "Ethical relativism lies in the moral laws inability to give commandments which are unambiguous both in their general form and in their concrete applications." (*Ibid.*, P. 46). Fletcher points out that the relativity is found in Jesus when he attacked the Pharisees' principle of statutory morality. (*Ibid.*, P. 47).

3. **Positivism:** In theological positivism, Fletcher explains, the faith propositions are "posited" or affirmed voluntaristically rather than rationalistically. (*Ibid.*, P. 47). He says further that Christian ethics affirms or posits faith in God and reasons out what obedience to His commandment to love requires in any situation. (*Ibid.*, P. 47). The moral value judgement, he says, in ethics is not a conclusion but a decision. (*Ibid.*, P. 47). He holds, "Ethical decisions seek justification, whereas cognitive conclusions seek verification. We cannot verify moral choices. They may be vindicated, but not validated". (*Ibid.*, PP. 48-49)

4. **Personalism:** According to Fletcher, "Ethics deals with human relations. Situation ethics puts people at the centre of concern, not things. Obligation is to persons, not to things; to subjects, not objects". (*Ibid.*, P. 50). He clarifies that the legalist is a what asker (what does the law say?) but situationist is a who asker (who is to be helped?), and he says that the situationists are personalistic and it is based on the command to love people, not principles or laws or objects or any other thing. (*Ibid.*, P. 50).He quotes Martin Buber's I - 'Thou' to prove his standpoint telling that to Buber true existence lie in human relationships and not in 'I-it'. (*Ibid.*, P. 50). About values, Fletcher says, "There are no "values" in the sense of the inherent goods - value is what happens to something. When it happens to be useful to love working for the sake of persons". (*Ibid.*, P. 50). There are no intrinsic values for situationists. The situationism is based on extrinsicalism in Fletcher's opinion. (*Ibid.*, PP. 50,51). Fletcher feels that the principles and law do not give much for people to make decisions as it objectifies the persons. The above stated four working principles or the presuppositions are fundamental in Fletcher's situation ethics. The ethical approach of Fletcher is understood to be aposteriori-agapeic, and it does not give importance to the norms or the apriori principles.

Another important aspect that is found in Fletcher is utilitarianism as he himself admits. According to him, "Situation (or contextual) ethics is best classified as act-utilitarianism" (Joseph Fletcher, "Situation Ethics", *Encyclopedia of Bioethics vol.1.,* London: Collier Macmillan publishers, 1978, P. 421). He states further that, "Act-utilitarians determine what is right by electing that course of action which offers the most beneficient consequences or greatest utility in each act, each particular situation". (*Ibid.*, P. 421). He rejects the rule utilitarians who decide what is right by following preconceived rules. (*Ibid.*, P. 421). He affirms that "Love being understood as goodwill or beneficence, the ethics of love is equivalent to utilitarian ethics". (*Ibid.*, P. 422). He quotes John Stuart Mill to justify his view point that, "To do as you would be done by, and to love your neighbour as yourself, constitute the ideal perfection of utilitarian morality". (*Ibid.*, P. 422, Fletcher quotes from Mill's book 'Utilitariantanism') .According to Fletcher "In sum, situation ethics is a utilitarian or consequentialist ethics, motivated by concern for human well-being decisionally flexible in method, and guided in its judgements by the greatest good realizable rather than by adhering to prefabricated norms or moral rules". (*Ibid.*, P. 423).

The ethical approach of Joseph Fletcher is rooted on the elements such as pragmatism, relativism, positivism, personalism and also the utilitarianism. The aspects of existentialism also influenced the thinking of Joseph Fletcher. He challenges the traditionally understanding of ethics based on natural law, pietism and puritanism.

2. The Affirmation of Love and Situation.

The situationism, for Fletcher, is a method of "situational" or "contextual" decision making. (Joseph Fletcher, *Situation Ethics,* P. 11). The role of love in the situation is the most important thing for Fletcher. He states, "The situationist enters into every decision making situation fully armed with the ethical maxims of his community and its heritage, and he treats them with respect as illuminators of his problems. Just as the same he is prepared in any situation to compromise them or set them aside in the situation of love seems better served by doing so". (*Ibid.*, P. 26). The appropriation in the situation is important for situationism. "Situation ethics aims at a contextual appropriateness- not the "good" or the "right" but the fitting".[47] (*Ibid.*, PP. 27-28).

The situational factors are primary for Fletcher, so he says the circumstances alter the rules and principles. (*Ibid.*, P. 29). He gives prominence to love as he quotes Paul: "The written code kills, but the spirit gives life" (II Cor. 3:6) and "You shall love your neighbour as thyself" (Gal s: 14) Which is the whole law fulfilled in one word. (*Ibid.*, P. 30). He says that for the Christian situation ethics what is always good and right is the love or agape regardless of the circumstances. (*Ibid.*, P. 30). Relating Love to the situation and the whole strategy of situation ethics is love. (*Ibid.*, PP. 30-31).Fletcher feels that love is the most important aspect so the absolute norm is love. He argues that, "Love is of people, by people and for people. Things are to be used; people are to be loved. It is "immoral" when the people are used and things are loved. Loving actions are the only conduct permissible". (*Ibid.*, P. 51). He defines love as the Holy spirit working in us: "Love is not the work of the Holy spirit, it is the Holy spirit-working in us." (*Ibid.*, P. 51).

According to Fletcher, "In Christian situationism highest good and only law is love, neighbor-concern, and it decides or chooses its course of action accordingly". (Joseph Fletcher, *Moral Responsibility,* P. 175). He says, "Legalism always emphasizes order and conformity; situationism emphasizes freedom and responsibility. The situationist sees that prescriptive morality falsifies reality situations by oversimplifying them or actually twisting the facts". (*Ibid.*, PP. 177-178). To each question, the moral decision has to be weighed and judged within the situation, in the total context; none of them (the means, for example) can be predetermined to be good or evil" (*Ibid.*, PP. 180-181). The love in the situation is the deciding factor in situation ethics. He classifies that, "Finally in a situational approach, decision must be made not only in the situation but also by the decider in the situation.!". (*Ibid.*, PP. 181). Here also the aversion to Fletcher's perspective towards prescriptive rules in the situation is evident, as his approach is aposteriori-agapeic.

The six prepositions of situation ethics by Fletcher would be considered in the next section. Love is explained as the only norm and only good thing by Fletcher in these propositions. (*Ibid.*, PP. 57-145). The sixth preposition is that love's decisions are made situationally and that love plays a very dominant role in Fletcher's approach. His aposteriori-agapeic approach is formed in this regard also.

According to Joseph Fletcher, there is no universally binding normative principle in Christian ethics than love or loving concern. (Joseph Fletcher. "Situation Ethics in a Changing Situation", *The Christian century* vol. Lxxxviii, No. 49 (December, 1971), P. 1444). He emphasizes that the new morality's only absolute is agapeic or loving neighbour concern, and it seeks the good of the people by decisions tailored to the relativities of each particular situation. (Joseph Fletcher, "Why New?" *Religion in Life* vol xxxv, No. 2 (Spring, 1966), P. 188). Fletcher observes that the relevance of maxims or principles depends on the situation, and he says, "The situationist is prepared in concrete case to suspend, ignore or violate any principle if by doing so he can affect more good than by following it". (Joseph Fletcher, "Love is the only Measure", *Commonweal* vol Lxxx, No. 14, (Jan.14, 1966), P. 428).

The role of love in the situation is the key element in the ethical approach of Joseph Fletcher. He always deal with each particular situation, in each case the love has priority over any maxims, principles, or norms.

Hello Lovers! is a book edited by William May. It deals with a discussion among Thomas Wassmer, William May and Joseph Fletcher on Situation ethics. In this book the aspects of love and situation are explained by Fletcher. According to Joseph Fletcher "essentially there is only one determinant of a moral act, and that is loving concern. A moral agent acts out of loving concern for others according to the realities of the situation and with as much reason and knowledge as possible". (William E. May, ed., *Hello Lovers!, Op.Cit.,* P. 10). According to him only this love as the moral agent can be concerned of others well being. He says that there is only this one moral determinant, loving concern, which can be concerned of the well being the pleasure, the growth and happiness of the others. (*Ibid.,* P. 10). He found agape as the only determinant, but that also in a aposteriori way, by rejecting the validity of the norms which are apriori.

Fletcher argues that his approach is data conscious and fact conscious, informed and reasonable. (*Ibid.,* P. 10). He states, "A genuinely and seriously loving person will recognize that in order to serve love well, he must be rational and well informed". (*Ibid.,* P. 11). The determinants of moral act for Fletcher are, first, the motivation of loving concern and, second, the prospect of consequences appropriate to love. (*Ibid.,* P. 14). He states that agape is intrinsically good and it is the loving concern for the greatest number.(*Ibid.,* P. 49).

Fletcher answers to William May's question, what is a situation? He states, "By situation we mean the objective set of circumstances within which the moral agent makes his decisions, not the subjective belief-system of the agent".(*Ibid.,* P. 60). The situation-love dynamics is the key in Fletcher's approach. He clarifies, "All we are saying is that according to situation ethics, if principles or norms come into conflict with facts, we follow the facts rather than the norms if love is better served thereby". (*Ibid.,* P. 65).It can be observed with Fletcher's approach that he is not interested in the apriori rules as he confronts the people with their crises in the situation. So he is suggesting aposteriori agapeic approach as a solution, to the issues from the context. He is consistently arguing for aposteriori-agapeic approach. Discussing the New Testament and situation ethics Fletcher argues that in Jesus' understanding law is to love and he did not absolutize any ethical norm other than to act lovingly. (*Ibid.*, P. 67). So it is clear that the love and situation play a very crucial role in Fletcher's approach. Fletcher's aposteriori-agapaic perspective can be appreciated as an evaluative approach, but not as a normative principle. His approach emphasizes the role of agape in the situation (the persons and their experiences- cases) and he is not concentrating on the normative or the apriori element in ethics. So his approach is only the evaluative, rather than the normative principle.

B. The Approach to Socio-ethical Issues

The issues such as love and law, and property are considered in the socio-ethical issues. Since the issue of sex and marriage are dealing separately, it is not taken under the socio-ethical issues.

1. The Perspective of Love and Law

The tension between love and law is the over-arching theme in Fletcher's situation ethics. In his view the new morality is not new since the root of it lies in the western Christian moral as a method. (Joseph Fletcher, *Situation Ethics,* P. 13). He also argues that the new morality is a radical departure from the conventional wisdom. He affirms that his approach is neither legalistic nor antinomian, but situational.

As a reaction against the legalists, he said that they cry out for doing the 'right' even if the heaven falls. (*Ibid.*, P. 20). Legalism in Christian tradition he says, has two forms: one is based on reason and natural law (Roman catholic tradition) which argues for universally valid rules, and the other is based on scripture (Protestants) which also advocate for universally valid rules. (*Ibid.*, P. 21). These two groups are making use of two sources, but they are moving towards the direction of legalism according to Fletcher. It has to be noted that legalism is not necessarily anti-love, but it can be reduced to become anti-love when it does not take seriously the responsibility to persons and the changing contexts and realities of life. It is clear from Fletcher‘s words that when the law ethic listens to love, it tries to rise above the legalism. (*Ibid.*, P. 21). In the perspective of Fletcher the principles are not inevitably loveless, but he feels that the stringent rules can become inflexible and will ignore the role of love in the situation.

Joseph Fletcher argues that the greatest virtue is love, but it has to be proved in the situation. (*Ibid* ., p. 15). For Fletcher the love is the foremost norm and not the law. He joins with James pike's argument against the natural law that it is based on universal precepts such as 'avoid the evil, do the good', it defended anything and everything such as feudalism, capitalism, socialism, fascism divine right of things and democracy, the cultural anthropology has made it plain that there is disagreement "on every subject" in morals. The natural law's conclusions are based on faith assertions, and not based on reason at all. (Joseph Fletcher, *Moral Responsibility,* p. 71). Fletcher criticized the legalists (The Protestant legalists rely upon the 'law' of scripture and Roman catholic legalists rely upon the 'law' of nature recording to Fletcher) for their prefabricated principles, precepts and rules. (*Ibid.*, p. 73).His prejudice towards norms which are apriori is seen very clearly in his thinking here.

He criticized the legalists by telling, "They hang on to certain eternally invariable rules of conduct as absolutely valid and universally obliging regardless of the situation". (Joseph Fletcher, "Reflection and Reply", *The Situation Ethics Debate,* edited by Harvey Cox. 1968,

p. 250). The deontological aspect is being challenged by Joseph Fletcher. The ethical absolutes have no place in his thinking except love which is absolutized and relativized by him. He states that situationism is a form of relativism as to both norms themselves as to their use; for Christians it is a Christianly motivated form of ethical relativism. It decides what's good by the facts, not by ideal abstractions. The insistent demand to spell out the content of love marks an insistence on norms as prefabricated decisions. To "fill up" love with rules or laws is to slip back into a new form of legalism. (*Ibid.*, P. 252).

He ascribed legalism to Judaism, Catholicism (all major western religious traditions are legalistic for him), the Pharisees who lived by Torah and oral tradition, and the puritanic Christianity. (Joseph Fletcher, *Situation Ethics,* PP. 18-20). They were criticized for their rigid moral rules by Fletcher. He observes that in the legalistic tradition of Christian morality some of the norms and moral principles of conduct are regarded as intrinsically valid and universally obliging, to be followed obediently under all circumstances, either because they have scriptural authority or because they are alleged to be found in the natural law. (William E. May, ed. *Hello Lovers,*1970, P. 16). He states again, "We are saying that norms cannot be regarded as Prescriptions, that there are no prescriptive principles of loving conduct. We are saying that whether or not we are to follow an ordinarily and usually wise normative principle, derived from the substantiative principle of agape, depends upon the relativities of the concrete situation". (*Ibid* ., P. 16). The ethical approach of Fletcher concentrates on the issues in this situation, so he emphasis what is evaluative in his perspective.

As against the prefabricated rules and principles or the law, Joseph Fletcher places the agape or love as the only norm for making responsible ethical decisions. He has formulated six propositions to illustrate the concept of loving concern:

1. Love only is always good. Whatever suits to love's need and purpose is the foremost one. (Joseph Fletcher, *Stuation Ethics,* P. 57). Good, evil and the values are depending on situation. (*Ibid.*, P. 59). Fletcher argues that the supreme norm is the neighbour love commanded of Christians. He states, "There is only one thing that is always good and right, intrinsically good regardless of the context, and that one thing is love". (*Ibid.*, P. 60).According to him, love alone when well served is always good and right in every situation. For him love is the only universal and it is something we do. (*Ibid.*, P. 61). Love is always good is defined by him as whatever is loving in any particular situation is good. (*Ibid.*, P. 61).Fletcher opines that God's command of love is for the sake of the people. He says, " Love is a way of relating to persons, and of using things". (*Ibid.*, P. 61). The unselfish sacrificial love of Jesus was portrayed by him in the sense that Jesus' going to the cross was His role and vocation in His situation with His obligation as the Son of God. (*Ibid.*, PP. 61-62).For him the situation ethics which is based on love is extrinsic, since it is against the intrinsicalist ethics which is based on "given" or "natural" or "objectively valid" laws and maxims. (*Ibid.*, P. 64). The only universal and objectively valid value is love. Fletcher feels that love only is good in all circumstances of decision-making, Though he speaks about love in the situations, he does not consider the role of love in the form of apriori principles or norms.

2. The second proposition is "The ruling norm of Christian decision is love: nothing else". (*Ibid.*, P. 69; Joseph Fletcher, *Moral Responsibility,* p. 15).Fletcher writes, "Christian situation ethics

> reduces law from a statutory system of rules to the love canon alone". (Joseph Fletcher, *Situation Ethics,* P. 69). In order to justify his view he quotes the instance of Jesus breaking the obligations of Sabbath (M.K. 2: 27-28). He talks about Paul that, "In exactly the same way Paul could eat his food kosher or not, simply depending on whether in any situation it is edifying (upbuilding) for others (1 Cor. 10: 23-26) (*Ibid.*, PP. 61-69). Jesus, of course, was not rejecting the sabbath obligation, but the inhuman element in the sabbath rule. Apostle Paul was also not very liberal at this point. He did not arbitrarily make use of the situation. Jesus was for keeping sabbath as a norm, but he rejects the inhuman regulations attached to sabbath, which is the creation of man.

Fletcher observes that Jesus and Paul replaced the precepts of Torah with the living principle of agape- agape being good will at work in partnership with reason. (*Ibid.*. PP. 61-69).The love, he says, seeks the neighbours best interest with a careful eye to all the factors in the situation. (*Ibid.*, PP. 61-69).For him, the situationist is willing to follow principles and precepts if they serve love. (*Ibid.*, PP. 61-70). The situationist speaks of law of love, says Fletcher. According to Fletcher, "There are no "universal laws" held by all men everywhere at all times, no consensus of all men" (*Ibid.*, PP. 61-71). For Joseph Fletcher love is not one among many other virtues, love has no equals that it supersedes other virtues. (*Ibid.*, P. 76). Agape is, for him, neighbour-regarding (neighbour means everybody) and agape is giving love. (*Ibid.*, P. 79). He condemns the natural law moralists for their denial of love's demands, especially in the case of sterilization. (*Ibid.*, P. 80). By referring Galatians 3: 19-4: 7 and 5:1 he states that the aspect of freedom that is advocated by Paul might be the slogan of Christian situation ethics. He writes, "Situation ethics aims to widen freedom, which is the other face of responsibility. As much as he can, the situationist will prevent law`s procrusteanly squeezing down an iron system of prefabricated decisions upon free people in living situations". (*Ibid.*, PP. 84-85). But it should be noted that no violent means is advocated by law to keep the uniformity. Law is always given to safeguard the interests of the persons and community. But it may be reduced to legalism in certain situations.

The agape is elevated by Fletcher as the only 'norm', as the rigid rules cannot meaningfully relate to the situation. This ethical approach rejects the norms as it is not concerned of what is prior, but it takes seriously what is posterior (the cases or issues in the situation).

3. The Third proposition of Joseph Fletcher is, "Love and Justice are the same, for justice is love distributed, nothing else". (*Ibid.*, P. 87; Joseph Fletcher, *Moral Responsibility,* PP. 17-19).For him"Love is justice, justice is love" (Joseph Fletcher, *Situation Ethics,* P. 89). In his view, since Christians have always more than one neighbour it is difficult to define what is just. He explains, "If to love is to seek the neighbor's welfare, and justice is being fair as neighbors, then how do we put those two things altogether in our acts in the situation? The answer is that in the Christian ethic the twain became one". (*Ibid.*, P. 88). Love is calculating, careful, prudent distributive and doing all that it can. (*Ibid.*, P. 89). "Justice is the many-sidedness of love" says Fletcher. (*Ibid.*, P. 89). He equates love with justice. He states, "We say, however, very positively, that love is justice or that justice loves. They are one and the same. To be loving is to be just, to be just is to be loving."(*Ibid.*, P. 93).

Justice is for him Christian love using its head, calculating its duties, obligations, opportunities and resources. (*Ibid.*, P. 95). In his view love subsumes justice. Both justice and love are neighbour-regarding, but provides all it can and the concern of justice and love are the same, so these two should not be considered separately.

4. The fourth proposition of Fletcher is "Love wills the neighbour's good whether we like him or not" (*Ibid.*, P. 103; Joseph Fletcher, *Moral Responsibility,* PP. 20-21). He defines Christian love as definitely agapeic, not erotic or philic. It is neighbour-concerned, outgoing and not selective or self-centred. (Joseph Fletcher, *Situation Ethics*, P. 103). He argues that, "Agape's desire is to satisfy the neighbor's need, not one's own, but the main thing about it is that agape love precedes all desire, of any kind" (*Ibid.*, P. 104). The loving is most important than the liking for him. The pre-marital sex of engaged couples (by getting pregnant to force a selfish parent to relent his over-bearing resistance to their marriage, is accepted by him if there is loving concern. But he rejects it if there is only mere liking. (*Ibid.*, P. 104). As an evaluative principle, Fletcher's view over here can be accepted but it cannot be understood as a rule to commit pre-marital sex in all cases. The pre-marital or extra-marital sex took place because of certain Psycho- social reasons also. A mistake is committed, so there is also room for love, mercy and forgiveness from the Christian point of view to the victim or to the person who is involved in the mistake. However, the aposteriori agapeic approach of Fletcher is clearly found in this instance. In Fletcher's understanding, love is not emotional or mere liking. (*Ibid.*, PP. 105-106). Agape, he says seeks

the good of anybody and everybody. (*Ibid.*, P. 107).Fletcher has the opinion that, "The radical obligation of the Christian ethic is to love not only stranger-neighbour and the acquaintance-neighbour, just as we love the friend-neighbour. (*Ibid.*, P. 107). He question the selfish love that is loving ourselves for our own sake. He states, "If we love ourselves for God's sake and the neighbour's self-love is right. For to love God and the neighbor is to love one's self in the right way; to love one's neighbor is to respond to God's way in the right way; to love one's self in the right way is to love God and one's neighbors". (*Ibid.*, P. 114).The love is impartial and respecter of persons and it universalizes its concern, says Fletcher. (*Ibid.*, P. 119). Fletcher does not approve the understanding of liking as loving. For him love is more than the aspect of liking.

5. "Only the end justifies the means; nothing else" is the fifth proposition. (*Ibid.*, P. 121; Joseph Fletcher, *Moral Responsibility*, PP. 21-23). He explains that end justifies the means does not mean all old end will justify any old means" (Joseph Fletcher. *Situation Ethics.*, P. 121). He clarifies "we all assume that some end justifies some means; no situationist would make a universal of it." (*Ibid.*, P. 121). The good and evil are only predicates or attribute for him. So he states, "And therefore what is sometimes good may at other times be evil, and what is sometimes wrong may sometimes be right when it serves a good enough end-depending on the situation". (*Ibid.*, P. 123). The situation decides whether any means is a justifiable one or not for Fletcher. He find situations, the experience or the crises of a person only as absolute and he does not see any value of the norm which operate in a context. His aposteriori-agapeic approach evades the question of the significance of the apriori norms. He is always concerned of what is already happened (cases) in the life of persons,

and not about what persons should keep up in one's life. According to him love justifies the means which is justified by the situation. He writes, "The new morality, situation ethics, declares that anything and everything is right or wrong, according to the situation". (*Ibid.*, P. 124). Fletcher challenges the prohibition of certain acts (telling lie or committing suicides are the examples given by Him), regardless of the circumstances. (*Ibid.*, P.125). He argues that "love could justify anything and love has a foremost place in justifying the means" (*Ibid.*, P. 126). There is only one end, one goal, one purpose which is not relative and contingent always an end in itself. Love," says Fletcher (*Ibid.*, P. 129). The highest good is love for Fletcher. In Fletcher's view "Love's method is to judge by particularity not to lay down laws and universals". (*Ibid.*, P. 133).Fletcher observes that love approves divorce if it serves the emotional and spiritual welfare of the parents and children. (*Ibid.*, P. 133). The aposteriori-agapeic approach of Fletcher is not very much concerned of normative principles, but his agapeic approach is concerned of what is posterior- the agape that operates in the life of a person after the violation of rules or norms because of some reasons with one psycho- social or any other.

6. The sixth proposition of Fletcher is "Love's decisions are made situationally, not prescriptively". (*Ibid.*, P. 134; Joseph Fletcher. *Moral Responsibility,* pp. 23-27). For him, love decides then and there. The love's decisions are not based on pre-determined rules, but it is grounded on the situation. The situations he says, cutting himself loose from the dead hand of unyielding law. (Joseph Fletcher. *Situation Ethics,* P. 135). He quotes the story of Arizona lady who terminated the pregnancy as she was fearing that the embryo might be defective since

> she had taken thalidomide. She did it at Sweden as the law prohibits abortion in Arizona. Fletcher said that even if the embryo was not deformed it was a responsible act. He describes, "It was a brave and responsible and right decision, even if the embryo had been all right. It was a Kairos, a fullness of time, a moment of decision". (*Ibid.*, PP. 135-136). It is a good example of Fletcher's aposteriori agapeic approach which only consider the evaluative perspective of agape in the situation.

Fletcher provides two incidents which seem to be different, but he justifies both. The first incident is as follows: In 1841 the ship' William Brown' out of Liverpool to Philadelphia, struck an iceberg and began to sink. The captain, seven seamen and thirty-two passengers were in a boat, which was double of what that boat could carry. The rough sea doomed them. The mate ordered most of the males into the sea. They refused, but Holmes, a seaman, pitched them out. In Philadelphia, Holmes was convicted of murder. Mercy was recommended to him but the court refused it. In Fletcher's words, legalism says Holmes did an evil thing "situation ethics says it was bravely sinful, it was a good thing". (*Ibid.*, P. 136). Fletcher tells another similar story. When captain Scott's expedition to south pole ran into trouble and they were making it back to the coast with no time to spare, one of his men was injured and had to be carried. The stretcher would slow them down dangerously. Scott decided to stick with the man and they all perished. But it was for Fletcher, an authentic Kairos. His argument is that we can't predict the future, so a decision taken in a particular moment of time regardless of past or future is authentic. In Fletcher's view, Scott was not simply legalistic and, he states, "we can't always guess the future, even though we are always being forced to try". (*Ibid.*, P. 136). These two incidents or cases expose the aposteriori agapeic approach of Joseph Fletcher. The normative principles are not taken into account by him, justifies the decisions taken in the context or in a particular case.

In this case the situations are almost similar, but the decisions vary each other and the situational decision in both cases are approved by Fletcher. Paul Ramsey has criticized this as arbitrary subjectivism of situation ethics.(Paul Ramsey, *Deeds and Rules in Christian Ethics* New York: Charles Scribners sons, 1967, pp. 218-219). Hereafter, *Deeds and Rules in Christian Ethics*. Joseph Fletcher advocates for a love ethic that is situational and agapeic- aposteriori agapeic approach. He did not discuss whether the authorities had mistakes or not in both cases, but he looks for the role of agape in the situation.

In Fletcher's perspective, the new morality is a shift away from moral and prescriptive rules. He formulated the essence of it in two proposition: a) We are commanded to love people, not principles, so that the needs of human beings come before adherence to any rule - although adherence to rules is often less opposed to human welfare than sentimental or unreflective persons may be willing to appreciate; and b) we are to love people and use things, "things" including abstractions such as moral principles as well as material objects, so that the immorality lies in loving things and using people - that is, subordinating persons to principles, thus reducing them from subjects to objects. (Joseph Fletcher, "What's in a Rule: A Situationists View", *Norm and Context in Christian Ethics,* edited by Gene H. Outka and Paul Ramsey, London: SCM Press Ltd., 1968, P. 328).

Joseph Fletcher reiterated that no rule can be universalized but the single norm for Christians is agape or neighbour Concern or love for others. (*Ibid.*, P. 321). The law of love is the key for a Christian situationist rather than law of love. (*Ibid.*, P. 337). Love is illustrated by him as the only measure. Nothing is inherently good or evil, except love for a situationist, says Fletcher. (Joseph Fletcher, "Love is the Only Measure", *Commonweal* Vol. Lxxxiii. No. 14 (Jan. 14) 1966. P. 430). Love is understood as the criteria in which every case or situation or action would be measured. The prefabricated rules and principles are unimportant and irrelevant for decision making in the understanding of Fletcher. He argues that agape only is suiting to take responsible decision in all situations.When we examine Fletcher's ethical approach, one can find it as aposteriori-agapeic approach as the normative principles (apriori) are not considered much in his perspective.

2. The Understanding on Property

Joseph Fletcher observes that the modern free-enterprise theory recognizes land, capital and labour as the three important factors of property.[139] (Joseph F. Fletcher, ed., *Christianity and Property,* philadelphia: The West minister press, 1947, P. 176). He warns the tendency to use property as a means to establish power over other, or of exploiting the labour of others as both violate the principle of love and subvert the true order of things. (*Ibid.*, P. 181). This tendency to use property as a means to manipulate makes him to think of distinguishing between property to use and property for power. (*Ibid.*, P. 181).The traditional Christian understanding, for Fletcher, has been that property values are provided in the order of creation, with man's use of enjoyment as their end. (*Ibid.*, P. 181).

In his theological and ethical outlook, he admonishes the share manipulation, holding of land out of use in order to change a higher price for it, and promotion of artificial scarcity. He emphasizes that, "The industrial magnate or firm who promotes artificial scarcity for the sake of higher profits through low supply, as many monopolistic enterprises do, is also sinning". (*Ibid.*, P. 181).In Fletcher's opinion, true ownership is contingent, not absolute; and the criterion or test is use and productivity. (*Ibid.*, P. 182).

In the perspective of Fletcher, the Old Testament view of property is relative and it is a gift from God and man is the steward of this property. In his view, the property rights are only a delegation of God's Lordship of all that he has produced and is still producing through the subordinate agencies of nature and man' (*Ibid.*, P.184). The property rights and possession of property values, whether scarce or plentiful, are stewardly. (*Ibid.*, P. 184). While discussing about wealth, Fletcher expresses the view that "the creationist doctrine is that "the earth is the Lords and the fullness thereof" (I Chron. 29: 14 ; ps. 24: 1), and therefore stewardship is on God's behalf- he is ultimately the only landlord or owner" (Joseph Fletcher, *Moral Responsibility,* P. 190). The equity and the due share of all for the members of the family of God is emphasized by Joseph Fletcher.

Fletcher analyses the story of Ananias and Saphira in the New Testament (Acts of the apostles), and has found more of the sin of selfishness than dishonesty and deceit. (*Ibid.*, P. 185). According to Fletcher's perception the ascetics did not condemn wealth as such, but they forsook the private or individualistic wealth. When dealing with the notion of the property in the Gospels, he has said; perhaps the simplest way to phrase it is to say that the gospel principle is poverty but not destitution-modest possession but not penury or pennilessness". (*Ibid.*, P. 188).

The understanding of Fletcher on stewardship is crucial to the perspective on property. He scorns the sub-Christian twist on sharing as our mercy to the less fortunate. According to Joseph Fletcher, we are not our Stewards but we are God's Stewards to distribute his wealth to his family on earth. (*Ibid.*, P. 191). He finds Stewardship as a vocation closing the gap of the private opulence and public poverty as Stewardship has the crucial task of witnessing to the dangerous imbalances of opulence. (*Ibid.*, P. 197). He has the opinion that a definition of Stewardship must aim at an ethical corrective for consumerism! . (*Ibid.*, P. 208).

He has a very socialistic vision about the concept of Stewardship of the property. He writes about property that, it belongs to God and for the common goal. He describes, "It belongs, therefore, first of all to God and then equally to society and the individual". (*Ibid.*, P. 209). He states again, "social equity and "commonwealth" are elemental features of Christian economic ethics. This is why almsgiving in Christian moral theology has always been treated as justice, not as mercy!. Helping the neighbour in need is only giving him what is his own". (*Ibid.*, P. 210).

The perspective of Fletcher on property and wealth are based on the concept of Stewardship. He opposed any kind of manipulation in production and in the keeping of property in order to exploit the people. The property is understood by him as the gift of God. The essence of Stewardship is to bridge the gap between public property and private opulence. The sharing of resources in a fair manner is found in his thinking. He understood the whole humanity as the family of God and Stewardship means we are to distribute the wealth to our family on earth.

The agapeic approach is found clearly in Fletcher's perspective on the socio-ethical issues. He emphasizes the role of love and the concept of Stewardship. Love is the only norm and it only will help people for responsible decision making for Fletcher. He opposes the pre-determined rules and the principles as rules are loveless ones for him in the situation. Basil Mitchel comments that, "professor Fletcher believes that love, and only love, can determine our moral choices. But he does not make it clear how love does it". (Basil Mitchel, "Ideals Roles and Rules", *Norm and Context in Christian Ethics,* edited by G ene H. Outka and Paul Ramsey, *Op.Cit...* P. 352). Charles Curran thinks that though the situationism is a constant reminder to avoid the pitfalls of legalism, Fletcher is unable to provide the exact meaning and content of agape. (Charles E. Curran, *A New Look at Morality,* London: Sheed and Ward, 1969, PP. 168-169). Fletcher's approach is aposteriori agapeic approach. He dwells on the evaluative elements of agape rather than reflecting on the apriori principles which are normative and agapeic. The approach of Joseph Fletcher highly regards the role of love and mercy in the situation.

In his view on property he upholds equity, justice and the fair distribution of resources. And he criticizes the consumerism and the exploitation. He develops the Biblical concept of stewardship in a proper and meaningful way.

C. The Approach to Bio-ethical Issues

The ethical issues such as abortion, euthanasia, artificial insemination, sterilization and contraception, humanhood; screening, cloning, the question of patient's consent and the organ transplantation are considered under the bio-ethical issues.

1. The Perspective on Abortion

Joseph Fletcher gives a case for abortion in his book Situation Ethics. In 1962 a patient in a mental hospital raped a fellow patient who was an unmarried girl ill with schizophrenic psychosis. Her father requested for abortion of that unwanted embryo. The hospital authorities declined it on the ground of criminal law which allows abortion only for therapeutic reasons when the mother's life is at stake. Fletcher says that the legalists and catholic moral theory will say No, since for them killing is inherently evil. (Joseph Fletcher, *Situation Ethics.,* PP. 38-39). He justifies the abortion stating that there is a rapist who being insane was legally and morally innocent, so also there is an embryo which is innocent. (*Ibid.*, P. 39).

Fletcher also did justify the case of Arizona lady who decided to abort the suspected deformed foetus. (*Ibid.*, P. 136). He stressed that even if the embryo was not deformed, the decision would have been right. Fletcher suggests that mental health and physical health should also be considered when deciding on abortion. In the case of rape and incest, Fletcher holds that "it is even likely they would favour abortion for the sake of the victim's self-respect or reputation or happiness or simply on the ground that no unwanted and unintended baby should ever be born". (*Ibid.*, P. 39). In the two cases Joseph Fletcher was not concerned of the normative principle which reject the abortion or feticide, but applies his aposteriori agape approach.

He considers only of the situation in which two persons who opted for abortion. The Psycho-social reasons are taken into account by Fletcher. It comes clear that he is basing more on aposteriori- agapeic element Paul Ramsey comments that Fletcher does not limit the verdict in the case of schizophrenic girl to this kind of case rather his verdict is a general rule for abortion. (Paul Ramsey, *Deeds and Rules in Christian Ethics.*, P. 160). He stated that,

The assertions that no child should be required to be born or no woman should be forced to accept responsibility for a child, following rape or incest, or that no woman should be required to risk sacrificing her life in giving birth, or to undergo a serious injury to her health, or that (to be yet more forbidding) no unwanted or unintended child should be deemed rightfully born of this required moral suasions upon the mother, are all quite general (correct or mistaken) judgements which Fletcher's situationist reaches, or may reach by love's casuistry. (*Ibid.*, P. 170).

Fletcher agrees for pre-emptive abortion for the defective factors. He prefers the quality of life rather than the traditional understanding of respect of life which accepts the birth of defective babies thinking that abortion is wrong. (Joseph Fletcher "Medicine, Morals and Religion", *Theology Today* vol. xxxi, No. 1 (April, 1974), P. 42). He condemns the traditional concept of sanctity of life and abortion as killing or murder. He advocates for therapeutic abortions. He states, that to the traditional morality sometimes abortion would be right, sometimes wrong. (Joseph Fletcher, "The Ethics of Genetic Control, Some Answers", *On Moral Medicine: Theological Perspectives in Medical Ethics,* Michigan: William B. Eerdmans publishing Co., 1987, P. 345; Hereafter, On *Moral Medicine).* His bias towards the normative (apriori rules) is very explicit over here. He does not want to compromise his aposteriori-agapeic approach for any reason.

He explains that "The basic ethical issue is whether abortion, if it is the "wisest" thing to do, is an evil act which can be excused - or, on the other hand, is a positively good thing to do". (Joseph Fletcher, *The Ethics of Genetic Control.* New York; Anchor press, 1974 P. 31. Hereafter, the Ethics of crenitic control). He continues to say that if any act or policy is the wisest as measured by human need and well being, to them it is positively good, positively the right thing to do". (*Ibid.*, P. 31). According to Fletcher, ethically also one cannot deal with abortion dogmatically or absolutistically or by universalized generalization. (Joseph Fletcher, "Abortion and the True Believer", *The Christian Centuary* vol. xxi . No. 27, (1974), P. 1127). Fletcher is arguing against the role of norm or commandments and only dealing with abortion without considering the arbitrary kind of abortion and its severe consequences. This is found to be one of the main problem with the approach of Fletcher.

Fletcher's perspective on abortion is that the deciding factors are based on reputation, self-respect and also physical and mental health. He stressed the quality of life which is grounded on the argument of deformed fetus or any other genetic defects. He rejects the traditional Christian moral reasoning that advocates for the sanctity of life, the problem of neglecting the normative principle is found in this regard also.

2. The Perception on Euthanasia

In the issue of euthanasia or mercy-killing, Fletcher furnishes the case of a patient who had cerebral hemorrhage over eleven years. The patients voice went off two years ago and she does not hear anything. Her capacity of communication is also ended. For Fletcher the patient is 'dead' since the communication is ended. The communication capacity is one of the indicators of humanhood to Fletcher. Another case is of a sixteen year old youth who received food through the tube and has no sense of pain. Another twenty year old boy is also leading a "living death" and in a coma for four years. An auto crash shattered his cerebral cortex. Since then only the brain stem has sustained life. The fourth case is of a man who suffers from pneumonic suffocation and attempts were made to save him by 'tracheotomy' a hole cut in his throat through which an artificial respirator is used. At last the oxygen is removed and he dies. Another women in her early seventies suffers from bone cancer. Both legs are fractured and she undergoes severe pain. She expressed her willingness to the husband to die!. (Joseph Fletcher, *Moral Responsibility,* P. 141-142).

In all these cases the patients or the relatives feels that their condition is worse and incurable. He condemns those who are not willing to go for the 'loving action' of euthanasia. He states, "Because most people cannot look it in the eye, they cling to irrational, phobic, and sentimental attitudes about voluntary death and the medical control of dying". (I*bid*., P. 143).The pace makers, argued Fletcher, can restart the stopped heart beating and also prolong the suffering. (*Ibid.,* PP. 144-145). He defines euthanasia as a merciful or good death achieved by direct or indirect methods. The direct one is said to be a deliberate action to end life which is murder before the law, and the indirect euthanasia can be done by (1) administering a death-dealing pain killer (2) Ceasing treatment that prolong life or (3) Withholding the treatment altogether. (*Ibid.,* P. 147).

Fletcher calls indirect euthanasia as antidysthanasia. The anti-dysthanasia can be voluntary or involuntary from the patients' part. The popular objections to euthanasia are the following. It is described as murder, suicide or violating Biblical command "Thou shalt not kill". Another objection is that the patients who are pronounced incurable might recover. (Joseph Fletcher, "Our Right to die", *Theology Today* Vol viii (May 1995), PP. 204-210). For him, euthanasia is other-regarding than self-regarding. He says, "to call euthanasia egoistic or self regarding makes no sense, since in the nature of the case the patient is not choosing his own good rather than the good of others". (Joseph Fletcher, *Morals and Medicine,* Boston; Beacon Press, 1965, P. 191. Hereafter Morals and Medicine).

About the criticism on the basis of the Biblical command Fletcher has said that the Bible speaks only of the unlawful killing. He rejected the charge of suicide, and he sees euthanasia as a part of divine plan. He feels that suicide should be considered only the basis of the situation. A Soldier may commit suicide, if he understands that he would be caught by the enemies. So the situations also need to be taken into consideration when one condemns outrightly the persons who committed suicide. He cites in support of it Job 7: 15 where Job contemplated on suicide. (*Ibid.,* P. 198; *Situations Ethics,* PP. 66-67, 74, 97).

Joseph Fletcher approves euthanasia in the extreme cases where a human being becomes a 'vegetable' or the disease is beyond any care. Fletcher comments that the, "incurable pain destroys self-possession and disintegrates personality, as any wide acquaintance with sick beds will teach us". (Joseph Fletcher "Our Right to Die", *Theology Today,* vol. viii, (May, 1951), P. 203). In Fletcher's view euthanasia is other-regarding and love-regarding. It is a loving action. It is an act of loving kindness for Fletcher. He urges to opt for euthanasia in the extreme cases where improvement of health is impossible. In the case of incurability of the disease, Fletcher finds the meaningless suffering, so he advocates for euthanasia as a loving action. Though his approach does not realize the importance of the norm, 'apriori' rules, he considers the context and opt for aposteriori-agapise approach as a solution to the problem.

3. The Idea of Humanhood

The indicators of humanhood are found to be something beside the biological function and are quite important in the understanding of humanness or human being, for Joseph Fletcher (Joseph Fletcher, "Medicine Morals and Religion". *Theology Today* vol. xxxi, (April, 1994), P. 43).In his perspective, in order to become human, human beings have to be something more than biologically classifiable organism of the species of the homo sapiens.(Joseph Fletcher, "The Ethics of Genetic Control:Some Answers", *On Moral Medicine,* P. 356). In order to be human, he says, they should have an individual or separate existence and a functioning of cerebral cortex, that is, some minimal level of intelligence. He infers that "therefore an individual of the species who is not yet human, a fetus, and one who has ceased to be, a "brain dead" patient, is without the status of being human or human being". (*Ibid.*, P. 356). He underlines the fact that the key to humanness is the neocortical functions. Without this trait or capacity the 'fullness of humanness' can't be achieved in Fletcher's view. (Joseph Fletcher "Four indicators of Humanhood the Enquiry Matures", *On Moral Medicine*, P. 275). He states,

> As far as I can yet see, I will stand by my own thesis or hypothesis that neocortical function is the key to humanness, the essential trait the human *sine qua non*. The point is that without the synthesizing function of the cerebral cortex (without thought or mind), whether before it is present or with its end, the person is nonexistent no matter how much the individual's brain stem and mid-brain may continue to provide feelings and regulate autonomic physical functions. (*Ibid*., P. 276).

Joseph Fletcher has discussed in detail the indicators of humanhood. He has framed fifteen positive criteria and five negative criteria. The following are the positive criteria:

(a) Minimal Intelligence

Fletcher argues that an individual of the species homo sapiens who falls below the I.Q. 40- mark in a standard Binet test is a person, below 20-mark and therefore is not a person. (Joseph Fletcher, "Indicators of Humanhood: Tentative profile of Man", *Bioethics,* edited by Thomas A. Shannon, New York: Paulist P ress, 1976, P. 320; Hereafter Thomas A. Shannon, *Bioethics*). 20-mark is regarded as necessary for minimal intelligence and it is essential for decision-making, says Fletcher. (*Ibid*., P. 320).

(b) Self-A wareness

Self-consciousness is absent in lower vertebrates as well as in the non-vertebrates. The irreversible damage to the brain cortex may lead to non-self-awareness or unconsciousness. For Fletcher, this has to do with the judgement on the quality of life. (*Ibid*., P. 320).

(c) Self-control

If an individual is not controllable by others or the individual himself or herself, that would be equal to reaching a low level of life. Furthermore, if the condition cannot be rectified medically the individual ceases to be a person just as the fetus is not a person, explains Fletcher. (*Ibid.*, P. 320).

(d) A Sense of Time

The time consciousness is very important to humanhood. This is meant by Fletcher as 'clock time or chronicles'. (*Ibid.*, P. 320). If a person cannot have the consciousness of the passage of time, he is ceased to be human. (*Ibid.*, P. 321).

(e) A Sense of Futurity

Fletcher argues that nobody can be human if he is unable to realize the futurity or the time that is yet to come. His argument is that subhuman animals do not look forward in time. (*Ibid.*, P. 321). He comments, "subhuman animals do not look forward in time; they live only on what we might call visceral strivings, appetites". (*Ibid.*, P. 321). The sense of futurity is understood by Fletcher as an essential element for humanness.

(f) A Sense of the Past

The memory or the consciousness to recall is a criterion for humanness. (*Ibid.*, P. 321). The uniqueness of man is based on this trait, i.e. the capacity to recall the past.

(g) The Capacity to Relate to Others

Fletcher observes that, "Inter-personal relationships, of the sexual, romantic and friendship kind, are of the greatest importance for the fullness of what we idealize as being truly personal". (*Ibid.*, P. 321). Man is a social being and relating meaningfully in inter-personal dealings is quite important for humanness in Fletcher's version.

(h) Concern for Others

The concern and case for others is part of the criteria for humanhood. (*Ibid.*, P. 321).

(h) Communication

"Utter alienation or disconnection from others, if it is irreparable is dehumanization in Fletcher's view. (*Ibid.*, P. 322).He classifies that his criterion is applicable for patients who cannot hear, speak, feel or see others. (*Ibid.*, P. 322). This can be the result of mental or physical trauma, infection, genetical or congenital disorder or from the psychological causes. (*Ibid.*, P. 322).Completely isolated individuals are subpersonal in Fletcher's perspective.

(j) Control of Existence

Invincible ignorance and complete helplessness is, in Fletcher's words, opposite to humanness. A man who lacks control can't be a responsible person, and an irresponsible one is to be subpersonal. (*Ibid.*, P. 322).

(k) Curiosity

"To be without effect, sunk in anomie, is to be not a person. Indifference in inhuman".(*Ibid.*, P. 322). A human person should have curiosity to know about the developments taking place in the world.

(l) Change and Changeability

According to Fletcher, "To the extent that an individual is unchangeable or opposed to change he denies the creativity or personal beings. It means not only the fact of biological and psychological change, which goes on as a condition of life, but the capacity and disposition for changing one's mind and conduct as well". (*Ibid.*, P. 322). The change and changeability includes the positive attitude to creativity and the capacity to change one's mind and conduct.

(m) Balance of Rationality and feeling

To be 'truly human' is to be a wholesome person, and the wholesome person will have rationality and feeling. (*Ibid.*, PP. 322-323).

(n) Idiosyncrasy

The human being is idiomorphous, a distinctive individual" says Fletcher. (*Ibid.*, P. 323). The identity and to be recognizable and callable by name is the characteristic of a person, for him. (*Ibid.*, P. 323).

(o) Neo-cortical function

The neo-cortical function is the cardinal indicator of humanhood for Fletcher. If the cerebral is not synthesizing properly, that person is not human. The brain death is one of the example for this handicap. In Fletcher's view brain death makes any one non-person, though the body remains alive". (*Ibid.*, P. 323).

Joseph Fletcher also formulated some negative criteria too in this regard. He argues that 1) man is not non- or anti-artificial; the test-tube baby is artificial, but human. His idea is that the humanhood should be ascribed to even the persons who are born by the artificial means. He states, "A baby made artificially, by deliberate and careful contrivance, would be more human than one resulting from sexual roulette - the reproductive mode of the subhuman species". (*Ibid.*, P. 323).2) Man is not essentially, parental. Fletcher states that, people can be fully personal without reproducing, as the religious vows of nuns, monks and celibate priests are also human though they are not married.(*Ibid.*, P. 324).3) Man is not essentially sexual-"Sexuality, a broader and deeper phenomenon than sex, is of the fullness but not of the essence of man". (*Ibid.*, P. 324). Since there is non-sexual reproduction, the sex is not even necessary for the survival of human species. (*Ibid.*, P. 324). 4) Man is not a bundle of rights - The right to live, to die to be healthy are not absolute for him. All rights are imperfect and may be set aside if human need requires it. (*Ibid.*, P. 324).5) Man is not a worshiper - "Faith in supernatural realities and attempts to be in direct association with them are choices some human beings make and others do not". (*Ibid.*, P. 325). The humanhood is not restricted on the aspect of worship.

One cannot easily agree with Fletcher's perspective on humanhood. The brain death and the genetic defects are common, and this does not reduce any one to be subhuman. This criteria will only facilitate objectifying the human beings. The fetus has no consciousness, so it is not a person for him. Fletcher disagrees with the normative understanding of the respect for life and he looked at the issues such as abortion, foeticide and euthanasia with love and mercy in an evaluative manner. The Christian principle is not based on the survival of the fittest, but it teaches to take care of the weak and the handicapped. Not even the comatose can be rejected as a non-person. But at the same, it is important to see the problems that are related to persons whose neo-cortical function is badly affected.

In this case also Fletcher's approach advocate for foeticide and euthanasia, as he suggests that they are more loving than living in misery. So he rejects the norm (apriori rules) and he is very suggestive and applies aposteriori agapeic approach.

4. The Issue of Contraception and Sterilization

Since the contraception and sterilization are the means to control birth, both are taken together for the discussion. The Roman Catholic church rejects the contraception as it is against the nature. Fletcher's fear is that if a Roman catholic husband has found contraception as the only way to control birth, he has no other way but to beget unwanted children beyond a responsible number, since the Roman catholic church is against the contraception. For Fletcher this restricts the love making which is a vital part in marriage. (Joseph Fletcher, *Moral Responsibility*, P. 31). Fletcher rejects the catholic moral claim of "killing" the life in the case of contraception. He argues that though the question of when the life begins is widely debated, the issue of killing in the case of contraception is invalid. (Joseph Fletcher, *Morals and Medicine,* P. 89).

Another means of birth control is sterilization. In the problem of sterilization, Joseph Fletcher has commented that the natural law moralists are trapped into cheating on love or even altogether denying love's demands. (Josepf Fletcher, *Situation Ethics*, P. 80). He feels that "on the ethical side sterilization is plainly a matter of personal freedom and responsibility" (Joseph Fletcher, "The Ethics of Genetic Control: Some Answers", *On Moral Medicine,* P. 360). For Fletcher, sterilization is a means of birth control which is very moral. He also finds the problems with sterilization and he accepted it only with exceptions. He is against irresponsible sterilization which denies the real obligation to propagate. (*Ibid*., P. 360). He also favors the eugenic purpose of sterilization by clarifying that it will enable to curb the misery of having defective children. (Joseph Fletcher, *Morals and Medicine,* P. 160). He also approves the therapeutic function of sterilization which is to enable the mother's life to avoid danger if she gets pregnant. He will also justify the punitive nature of sterilization which is to punish the sex offender or to make it impossible for him to repeat the offense" (*Ibid*., P. 143).Fletcher uses the eugenic reason for sterilization and states that it would seem blasphemous to assert that God will or purposes that defective children should be born. (*Ibid*., P. 164).

Fletcher comments that sterilization is the safer way of contraception. He says, "No method of contraception, however, is as simple and safe as sterilization". (Joseph Fletcher, *The Ethics of Genetic Control*. P. 47). The contraception and sterilization are conception control for him.(*Ibid.*, P. 47).Though Fletcher is against the means of birth control which are irresponsible (especially he rejects these means used to violate the obligation to propagate), he is considering with love the use of contraceptives and sterilization. The sterilization which is therapeutic, eugenic and punitive in nature are accepted by him. He grounded his argument for it is based on love in a way which is situational. It is found that the ethical approach of Joseph Fletcher is critical of the norms which questions the contraception and sterilization. In the issue of birth control, he argues that the means of birth control should not violate the intention to propagate. Though there are exceptions, he dealt with mercy the use of birth control devices. The understanding approach of applying agape in the situation is seen here also. As an inconsistency one can also trace an apriori element in the context. The norm which affirms the right to propagate is given utmost importance by him.

Joseph Fletcher justifies the fertility control by artificial means as he formulates five propositions:

1. Making babies is a good thing but making love is too, and we can and should make love even if no baby is intended. There ought to be no unintended or unwanted babies.

2. The best way to make love without making babies is to prevent their conception; the next best way is prevent fertility itself; and the least desirable way is to end a pregnancy already begun. But any of these methods is good if the good to be gained is great enough to justify the means.

3. Some methods of birth control may be morally better than others, but if so it will be because

they are the most loving and creative means available; it will not be because they are "artificial" or "against nature", because all medicine and art and science are interference with brute nature using it or outwitting it, for the sake of humanly chosen ends. To be artificial or against nature is often the highest good, in terms of moral values. In short, the natural law ethic is self-contradictory, problematic and dead.

4. Only one thing is intrinsically good, that is, inherently and always good and regardless of circumstances; and that one thing is love, namely concern for others. Only love is unconditionally good. Everything is good or bad according to the circumstances, including abortion and sterilization and contraception.

5. Finally: if there are people who believe that any of these things is wrong or sinful let them conduct themselves accordingly. But let them not try to deprive their neighbours who see it differently, of their freedom and responsibility. (Joseph Fletcher, *Moral Responsibility.,* PP. 123-124).

Joseph Fletcher rejects the normative morality which emphasizes the apriori agape, and stress the evaluative dimension of agape as he gives more importance to these cases, that is the posterior realities. The ethical approach of Joseph Fletcher is not quite happy with the norms or apriori principles. It is also to be noted that he is also suggestive and giving some guidelines or principles to look at the use of contraceptives or the sterilization.

5. The Perspective on Artificial Means of Reproduction

The artificial Insemination, Invitrofertilization and the cloning are some of the artificial methods of reproduction.

Fletcher criticizes the English law which validates marriage only by sexual union. According to the English law, though the Artificial Insemination was done from the husband (A.I.H), the court would not pronounce the child as lawful. (Joseph Fletcher, *Situation Ethics*, P. 79). In the view of Fletcher, this child was the seed of their seed and flesh of their flesh. Quoting the levirate system of the Old Testament, he told that artificial insemination by donor (A.I.D) is not adultery. (Josepf Fletcher, "The Ethics of Genetic Control: Some Answers", *On Moral Medicine,* P. 348). Adultery is not included in the act of AID and AIH, for Fletcher. He observes, "No longer can we say that a monogamous marriage agreement means exclusive access to any or all of the wife's or husband's "generative" faculties. It might exclude third party genitalia but not third party sperm and ova, nor graft gonads which can overcome childlessness and barren marriages". (*Ibid*., P. 348).

Artificial Insemination from a donor is often used in order when the husband is a zoospermic or has a low sperm count. Premature ejaculation, malformation and psychological hang ups are also considered as other reasons. (*Ibid*., P. 349). The AID and AIH are used as means to overcome the emotional strain and frustrations in married life. This is a medical possibility and way to overcome the frustrations when the husband or wife suffers from disorders. (Joseph Fletcher, *Morals and Medicine,* P. 101).He says that, "A marriage of barren love puts a heavy emotional strain upon its partners". (*Ibid*., P. 101). There are three objections raised against the artificial insemination. They include adultery, being adulterous the children become bastards and also AID may be pictured as selfish, unproductive and uncreating. According to Fletcher, the artificial insemination would not be forbidden based on these criticisms, since it could not be God's will or man's that a married couple should be condemned to childlessness and to hold on to an unproductive love merely because of psychological or biological accident. (Joseph Fletcher, *Situation Ethics.*, P. 118).

Fletcher goes to the extent of saying that the third-party sperm and ova or graft gonads which can overcome childlessness or sterility should not be understood as adultery. He says, "Adultery cannot apply any longer to the donations of due powers of our "loins" to persons in need just because they are not one's spouse". (Joseph Fletcher, "The Ethics of Genetic Control: Some Answers", *On Moral Medicine,* P. 348). He also sees the problems involved in the artificial methods. He argues, "if the benefits are too meager or the foreseeable consequences too onerous for parents, donors or children, it is wrong in these particular cases". (*Ibid.*, P. 348). He has the opinion that the egg grafts or artificial ovulations from a donor would be perfectly ethical, if the person does not have severe infection of her tubes or if she fears to pass on genetic disease. He also objected the reception of the sperm without the consent and knowledge of the spouse. (*Ibid.*, P. 349). He strongly believes that everyone should help the friends and neighbours, if they need to share our productivity. Fletcher states, "Generosity and human community now have a richer range of depth. Whether or not we ourselves choose to be reproducers - by whatever method - we can and should help our friends and neighbors if they need to share own reproductivity". (*Ibid.*, P. 353). In this matter also, he is not concerned of the Christian norm or apriori principles, but only considered the generosity and love.

The laboratory reproduction such as artificial insemination and invitro fertilization are approved by Fletcher saying, "It seems to me that laboratory reproduction is radically human compared to conception by ordinary heterosexual intercourse. It is willed, chosen, purposed and controlled, and surely these are among the traits that distinguish Homo sapiens from others in the animal genus, from the primates down". (Joseph Fletcher, "Ethical Aspects of Genetic Control", *Bioethics,* edited by Thomas A. Shannon, P. 336).

Fletcher develops his argument on the artificial means of reproduction telling that having babies is not quite necessary in the world. He writes, "In any case women are not baby machines and men are not seed casters. Explaining how we can have babies in many different ways is not beating the drum for making babies. Our bias is for fewer babies and better ones, whether they are made naturally or in the new artificial modes. In the so-called vaginal politics of the women's liberation we have a sound stance morality" (Joseph Fletcher, *The Ethics of Genetic Control;* P. 5).

Fletcher talks about eight modes of parenting. (1) The coital-gestational way (2) Artificial insemination of a wife with her husband's sperm, without any assistance or input from a third party (3) Artificial insemination of a woman with a donor's sperm (4) Egg transfer from a wife, inseminated by her husband and then transferred to another woman's womb for substitute gestation. (5) Egg transfer from a donor to a wife or unmarried woman's womb, before or after insemination - sometimes called prenatal adoption (6) Egg transfer from a female donor, then inseminated by a male donor, and finally transferred to the recipients' womb (7) Artificial gestation or nature of a fetus in a glass womb or similar artifact - which is just a refinement of the incubator and isolate already in use for premature infant plus an artificial placenta; this is often spoken of as ectogenesis (8) Nuclear transplant and cloning, whereby an egg (one's own or another's) is enucleated or denucleated, the original nucleus with its genetic code is removed and placed with the nucleus of either a donated unfertilized egg or the nucleus from a body cell (either a man's or woman's), which is then implanted and brought to term in one's own or another womb - and all this without conception. Only a male or a female seed is used, not both. It is birth from only one parent. (*Ibid.*, PP. 40-41).

Fletcher justifies all artificial means of reproduction except cloning. Cloning is accepted only with reservation by him. He says, "good reasons in general for cloning are that it avoids genetic diseases, bypasses sterility, predeterminates an individual's gender, and preserves family likenesses". (Joseph Fletcher, "The Ethics of Genetic Control: Some Answers", *On Moral Medicine* P. 350). He also agrees with doing in a situation of meeting a family's survival need. (Joseph Fletcher, "Ethical Aspects of Genetic Control", *Bioethics, edited by Thomas A Shannon,* P. 333). He ruled out the lesbian or male homophile extremists who use cloning to reproduce general population of their own sex. The problem he has found in it is the loss of genetic variety due to the a sexual reproduction on a large scale and the undermining effect on the survival of the species. He also questions the use of cloning to create dwarfs, legless people and individuals distorted functionally in various ways. (Joseph Fletcher, "The Ethics of Genetic Control: Some Answers", *On Moral Medicine,* P. 350).

The asexual reproduction (cloning), the surrogate mother, the invitro fertilization and the artificial insemination are the ways in which people overcome the childlessness. According to Fletcher, "sometimes abortion would be right, sometimes wrong; some times egg transfers would be a good thing sometimes not. The same thing holds true with test tube conceptions, sterilizations, artificial gestations, pre-selection of sex, cloning, insemination and involution from storage banks and so on". (*Ibid.*, P. 348). The guidelines he gave on such issues are, compassion, consideration of consequences, proportionate good, the priority of actual needs over the ideal or the potential, a desire to enlarge choice and a courageous acceptance of our responsibility to make decision. (*Ibid.*, P. 348).

The artificial methods of reproduction are understood by him as a great blessing. "Artificial insemination, egg transfers, gonad transplants, substitute gestation and the like, now make it possible to put our generosities very close to home - in one's very own person". (*Ibid.*, P. 348). Fletcher's approach does take seriously into account the importance to the need of overcoming the sterility. In his opinion the love play a crucial role in the situation here. The 'neighbour' comes into the scene to donate the sperm or to furnish the womb. The invitro fertilization is another means, so also cloning. The technological developments are enabling the husbands and wives to overcome the sterility. The use of the technological means is found by Fletcher as a loving and responsible act. The aposteriori- agapeic approach of Fletcher approves the artificial means to overcome the sterility which will create unhappiness and emotional strain on partners. Fletcher stresses the aposteriori-agapeic approach as the normative and rejects the apriori principles of Bible, though the aposteriori-agapeic perspective is only an evaluative principle from Christian perspective. It is important to appreciate this approach of as evaluative approach but not as a normative..

6. The Perspective on Screening

The screening is done to detect the defect of the foetus. According to Fletcher, "screening by one means or other is the obvious way to fulfill our obligation to potential children, as well as to the community which has to suffer when defectives are born". (*Ibid.*, P. 359). The screening is used as a device which enables to prevent hereditary diseases and to cure the genetic and venereal diseases. In Fletcher's thinking, screening is to have a community without physical or genetic diseases or defects. He has opposed the legal restrictions which affirms the privacy and secrecy and claims that the screening is good for all. By rejecting the argument for privacy he has stated that screening is not a violation or privacy, "but to cover a host of terrible distortions of humanity". (*Ibid.*, P. 360).

Fletcher advocates for genetic engineering as he is arguing for quality of life. He states, "Morally, genetic engineering is good when it serves human needs, both health and happiness". (*Ibid.*, P. 355). Supporting the screening process he said, "people who knowingly undertake or who only stumble into the conception of new life are learning that they may be carriers of serious genetic faults. If they have any sense of responsibility for quality in their offspring and of obligation to the community's interest they will want to know as much as they can about their inheritance, their gene pattern". (Joseph F.letcher, *The Ethics of Genetic Control,* P. 59). Joseph Fletcher is uncritically accepting the screening. He is only concerned of the so called 'quality of life' which can be attained through genetic engineering and the technological devices. In the case of screening the aposteriori -agapeic approach of Fletcher is evident. He is concerned of the potentiality and the quality of life rather than the bad effects of screening.

7. The Issue of Organ Transplantation

The organ transplantation and the contribution of organs are understood by Joseph Fletcher as the act of love. The gonad transplants are considered by him as a generosity. (Joseph Fletcher, "The Ethics of Genetic Control: Some Answers", *on Moral Medicine,* P. 353). He calls it as spare parts programme. He says, "we have entered a new era medically, and therefore culturally - ie, morally and ideologically. There are many highly portentous "break throughs" in modern medicine but the one under scrutiny here we can call the spare parts program". (Joseph Fletcher, "Our Shameful Waste of Human Tissue: An Ethical problem for the living and the dead" *Updating Life and Death: Essays in Ethics and Medicine* edited by Donald R. cutler Boston: Beacon Press, 1969, P. 1). This spare parts programme includes the artificial materials such as cardiac pace makers, plastic heart valves or kidney machines.

Fletcher points out the fact that several ones are waiting to get a Kidney either from the living or from the cadaver i.e., the body of another patient who willed his kidneys for extraction and transplant after death. (*Ibid.*, P. 3). The livers are also needed for some patients. He stated that there are situations in which the kidneys are promised by the donor patients, but are refused after the death by the family members. He condemns their sense of hurting or degradation.[247] (*Ibid.*, P. 3). He states that "The body taboo adversely affects not only transplants but medical knowledge and education". (*Ibid.*, P. 5). He warns against the religious ethicists who are trapped by legalism to prevent the organ donation and the transplantation. (*Ibid.*, P. 11).

Fletcher justifies also the adoption of animal organs for human beings. He opines "Man animal combinations are in the same ethical class. If a cow's kidney is "grocon" into a patients thigh to help cleanse his blood, after his own kidney function is gone, that is morally good. If an animal's organ or tissue is used to replace something lost by a human (an interspecific transplant) that is good". (Joseph Fletcher, *The Ethics of Genetic Control,* P. 172). According to Fletcher what counts more is human need and human well-being in such moral decisions.(*Ibid.*, P. 173).The protection of the human beings from danger is very crucial for him in this regard. The role of agape in the particular situation or in each case is crucial in Fletcher's aposteriori-agapeic approach which is concerned of care, love and need of others.

D. The Professional Ethical Issues

Fletcher is also concerned with the ethics which is related to the profession, especially in the field of business and medicine.

1. Ethics and Business Management

Joseph Fletcher points out that there are three characteristic corruptions or distortions of religion and ethics in our culture. They are pietism, moralism and legalism. He states, pietism tends to corrupt religion by separating faith and society; it reduces religion to religiosity by making it a personal and internal or private mystical affair irrelevant to economic or political matters. It encourages the notion that "religion ought not to 'interfere' with politics or business" as if they were divorced dimensions of life. (Joseph Fletcher, *Moral Responsibility*, P. 163).

The moralism, he says, makes the moral life a matter of petty discipline. It fawns upon dancing, card playing and sundry recreation, but never shows much concern over the issues of Justice, comments Fletcher. (*Ibid.*, P. 163). The legalism is the rigid adherence to the letter rather than the spirit of law in Fletcher's version. (*Ibid.*, P. 164). The motive behind law is to minimize obligation to define and to distribute the costs and burdens and restraints of justice and social order, tells Fletcher. (*Ibid.*, P. 167). He says the neighbour concern maximizes obligation.

Fletcher feels that the rigid rules and codes will not work in the area of business enterprise. For him love will go within idea, what, in the situation, is the constructive decision to make, as measured by a primary concern for people, and not for profits alone nor only for the one company's sake". (*Ibid.*, P. 167). The business ethic, for him, is practical (relativistic and situational) as he feels the 'idealist' (legalistic) view of religion (it is always wrong to deceive") is impractical.(*Ibid.*, P. 167, 172). The situation can make it good the merchants lie, according to Fletcher.(*Ibid*., P. 175). In connection with wealth, he said that the greedy or exploitative uses of it should be condemned. (*Ibid*., P. 187).

The business ethics of Joseph Fletcher is also situational in its approach. He is not strictly against the use of lie or misleading in the business. Only the circumstances will decide what tactics should be applied in a particular situation. He wishes to use agape in aposteriori manner. In the case of wealth he is against the exploitation and the aspect of greed.

2. Ethics and the Medical Profession

The most important aspect in this regard is the patients right to know the truth and the medical professionals' responsibility to tell the truth.

Joseph Fletcher holds the view that the "patients are persons, not just bodies". (Joseph Fletcher, "Medicine, Morals and Religion", *Theology Today*. vol. xxxi, (April, 1974), P. 46). He rejects the object-subject relationship in patient-doctor relationship. In his view, the moral status or ethical integrity depends on two things (1) freedom of choice, and (2) Knowledge of the facts and the options among which we may choose. He again explains that as far as medical care is concerned, without patients freedom to choose and the right to know the truth, patients are only puppets. (Joseph Fletcher, *Morals and Medicine*, P. 35). He opposes the idea that the truth should not be told to the patients in certain cases. His view is that the patients have the right to know the truth and everyone is obliged to pay others the rights due to them.

For Fletcher the reservation to the truth telling by the physician will create an 'I-it' relationship. (*Ibid*., P. 38). He affirms that "lying troubles the waters of human relations and take away the one element of mutual trust without which medical practice becomes a manipulation of bodies rather than the care of and for persons". (*Ibid.*, P. 49). In order to assert the validity of patients right to know the truth, he has given some reasons. They are: (1) if the knowledge is denied that is equal to take away the moral quality. (2) denial of facts is a stealing (3) It is a denial of mutual respect and confidence between patient and doctor (4) It is the denial of assuming the responsibilities of the patient, which he only can do. (*Ibid.*, P. 61).

Fletcher warns that this principle of truth-telling does not apply to the questions of telling the truth always. (*Ibid.*, P. 35). This arguments over here are solely related to 'right to know' in doctor-patient relationship. For Fletcher, some situations, if lying will bring good there is nothing wrong in it. In this respect he justifies the lie to murderer when he enquired his enemy who took asylum in a house. He was critical of the imperative that never tell a lie. He was for telling the lie for the sake of love. This description of justifying the lying is applicable only to the question whether the lie is right or wrong in our social relationships. In this case also it is revealed that the Christian evaluative principle of aposteriori-agapeic approach is reduced to be a norm by Fletcher as he doesn't give importance of Biblical norm (apriori principle) 'do not lie'.

Joseph Fletcher is for telling the truth to the patients without any hesitation in all situations. He is for the right to information. He sees the patients as responsible persons. He is unconcerned as to whether it is wise to tell the whole truth to all patients in all situations. It is true that it is not justifiable to hide the facts, if some patients ask about the result of experiments or the present condition of them. The facts should be revealed to the patients of the people concerned when they are demanded. Hiding facts, of course, is an unloving act.

E. The Perspective on Sexuality and Marriage

In Fletcher, the sexuality and marriage take a very dominant place. This issue is taken into account very seriously by him and he had reflected on it elaborately in his writings. There are two aspects we could trace in him about sexuality and marriage. One is the social aspect of it and, secondly the technology and its influence on sexuality and marriage.

1. The Social Aspect of Sexuality and Marriage

The sexuality and marriage in the social relationships is the main discussion over here. Joseph Fletcher has described a case of a woman who was convicted of impairing the morals of her minor daughter. She had tried to teach the child chastity but at thirteen the girl bore the first of three unwanted babies. Her mother asked her to make sure that the boy wears condoms so that the pregnancy can be controlled. On this evidence, she (mother of the girl) was convicted and sentenced. (*Ibid.*, P. 35). Fletcher says that the law and legalistic puritanism had not shown the loving help to the girl, but situation ethics would have praised that woman, it would not have pilloried her. (*Ibid.*, P. 20). A clear instance of Fletcher's aposteriori agapeic approach is evident in this case. But the value of apriori principles or norms are missing in his prospective. Fletcher justifies the girl who had committed the pre-marital sex in this case. He does not find it as a severe crime to be punished, or as a serious ethical problem. Here the ethical approach of Fletcher has to be critically looked upon, his concern over a person when a mistake is estimated is well taken, but his rejection of normative principles is a serious violation of Christian principles.

According to Fletcher, "the triple terrors of infection, conception and detection, which once scared people into "Christian" sex relations (marital monopoly), have pretty well become obsolete through medicine and urbanism".

(*Ibid.*, P. 80). He claims that situationist has no legalistic approach to sex as it does not impose the traditional aspect of chastity. Fletcher does speak of the pre-marital or extra-marital sex only in the situation. The love in the situation has the foremost place in Fletcher's view. He talks about a young unmarried couple who decided to have intercourse (e.g. by getting pregnant to force a selfish parent to relent his overbearing resistance to their marriage), and for Fletcher it is based on the Christian principle of loving concern. He justifies it. He justifies that act as it is not liking, but an act of loving concern. (*Ibid.*, P. 104).Considering psycho-social issues involved in each case and showing mercy or love generously to help a person in a crisis is significant from christian point of view. Fletcher consistently does not show interest in normative rules as he stresses the a posteriori agapeic approach.

Fletcher does not accept the traditional view of the indissolubility of marriage as he understands the divorces as a means to protect the emotional and spiritual welfare of parents and children. In his version, love justifies divorce. In Fletcher's understanding Jesus did not say anything about ethics of sex, except adultery and an absolute condemnation of divorce. (*Ibid.*, P. 133). He says about Jesus that, "He said nothing about birth control, large or small families, childlessness, homosexuality, masturbation, fornication or pre-marital intercourse, sterilization, artificial insemination, abortion, sex play, petting and courtship". (*Ibid.*, P. 139). Fletcher's approach deals with the issues of sex only with love and mercy in an evaluative sense. He argues, "whether any form of sex (hetero, homo or auto) is good or evil depends on whether love is fully served". (*Ibid.*, p. 139; if WIlliam May, *Hello, Lovers:* P. 41).Fletcher also affirms that Paul drops Jesus' absolute prohibition of divorce (based on 1 cor. 7:15). (William E. May, ed., *Hello Lovers; Op.Cit.*. PP. 67-68). But he does not understand the fact that apostle Paul permitted it only on the case of the conversion of any partner to Christian faith. Fletcher does not also want to absolutize Paul's one flesh theory of marriage found in the first epistle to Corinthians (chap. 6). (Joseph Fletcher, *Moral Responsibility,* P. 134). Fletcher understands that Paul's approach was quite agapeic and contextual. While Fletcher was talking about homosexuality also, he argues that the act should be judged right or wrong depending on the situation in which the act was performed. His ethical approach is concerned of the situations or the experience of the people and developed an aposteriori-agapeic perspective.

Joseph Fletcher provides an extra-ordinary example to justify the extra-marital sex. Mrs. Bergmeier was taken off to a prison camp in Ukraine by the Soviet patrol. Her husband and children were unaware of her whereabouts. She was needed there in the family in the situation of hunger, chaos and fear. She wanted to join the family but the law allow it only on two reasons. (1) illness needing medical facilities beyond the camps, in which case she would be sent to a Soviet hospital elsewhere, and (2) pregnancy, in which case she would be returned to Germany as a liability. She found no way to escape and at last she turned to a friendly guard to impregnate her, which he did. Her condition was medically verified and she was sent back to Berlin and to her family. The husband and children welcomed her with open arms. (*Ibid.*, PP. 164-165). Fletcher will justify this act of extra-marital sex as a loving act. For him it is the agape in the situation is important as his approach is concerned of the persons and their ethical need in particular cases.

He defines sexuality as follows: "Dynamic psychology and anthropology, with their idea of the "libidinous component" in emotion and behaviour, have taught us to think of sex as the whole sphere of action and feeling dominated by the relations between men and women: a pervasive force in all aspects of human personality". (Joseph Fletcher, "A Moral philosophy of sex", *Sex and Religion Today,* edited by Simon Doniger, New York? Association press, 1983, P. 186). According to him, "The New Testament is strikingly fragmentary in its treatment of sex problem and ethics. Jesus, for example, had nothing whatever to say about courtship, perversions, masturbation, sex manners, codes of reproduction and parenthood, multiple marriage, incest, birth control, artificial insemination, foeticide and the like". (*Ibid.*, P. 187). Quoting Mathew 5: 28, he said that Jesus' ethical subjectivity is unjust. About John 8:3-11, he has the opinion that it is to do with the evil of self-righteousness and nothing to do with extramarital sexuality. (*Ibid.*, P. 187). Fletcher observes, "Sex in dynamite. Unchannelled by high character it leads to chaos and destruction. It can be the fiercest cement of relationship, but it can also be the lever that breaks people apart. Conceived broadly as "Libido" it is the most "dynamic" of assets as a means to good ends, including love as well as procreation". (Joseph Fletcher. *Moral Responsibility,* P. 91).He understood that sexuality can be a means to enhance the aspects of love and procreation.

Fletcher comments that sexual intercourse may or may not be an act of love. He continues to say that "Love, as understood in the Christian situation ethic, is an attitude of concern and not an emotion of desire". (Joseph Fletcher, "Love is the only Measure", *Commonweal* vol. Lxxxiii, No. 14 (Jan. 14, 1966). P. 429). (He objects the subject-object relationship in sexual act. Fletcher states, "If there is no responsible concern for the other one, for the partner as a subject rather than a mere object, as a person and not a thing, the act is immoral". (*Ibid.*, P. 429). His basic principle is that people are to be loved and things are to be used. According to him, "Immorality occurs when things are loved and people are used". (*Ibid.*, P. 429). The loveless and selfish sexual act is condemned by Fletcher. In this relation, he speaks of sin as the exploitation or use of persons. He calls this exploitation as prostitution. He explains, "Therefore in a familiar phrase, the prostitute is far more sinned against than sinning. She is infinitely closer to righteousness than her customers". (*Ibid.*, P. 430). Fletcher realizes the context in which women are victimized so he is very consciously dealing with issues with a sense of agape in which mercy and care will be rendered to persons as part of Christian responsibility. But as usual Fletcher is unconcerned of the Christian norm.

Fletcher clarifies that the new morality is concerned of the motives along with means and ends. He opines, "In teenage social life if a boy seduces a girl in order to appear in his own eyes or his friends as a Big man, he is using her, he is guilty of sin or "moral evil". If a girl seduces a boy out of curiosity or some such motives, she is committing the same wrong; if she seduces him in order to love him into marriage, she is committing far greater sin than simple fornication ever could possibly be, even if they are married to make it legal". (*Ibid.*, P. 430). Fletcher's argument goes like this: True chastity is a matter of personal integrity, of sincerity and purity of heart. The sexual intercourse is not right or good just because it is legal. (*Ibid.*, P. 431). According to him, "even a transient sex liaison, if it has the elements of caring, of tenderness and selfless concern, of mutual offering, is better than a mechanical, egocentric exercise of conjugal "rights" between two uncaring or possibly antagonistic marriage partners". (*Ibid.*, P. 431).

Fletcher in his discussion on sex ethics asserts that the extra-marital sex and cohabitation cannot be condemned in all situations. He writes, "The personal commitment, not the country clerk, sanctifies sex. A man or wife who hates the partner is living in sin. A couple who cannot marry legally or permanently but live together faithfully and honourably and responsibly, are living in virtue - in Christian love. In this kind of Christian sex ethic the essential ingredients are caring and commitment". (*Ibid.*, P. 431). It is to be noted that Fletcher expresses sympathy, love and concern to the victims of the cohabitation (living together as husband and wife without legal or religious sanction) and even the extra-marital sex. But the problem with his perspective is that the normative perspective has no place in Fletcher's perspectives.

In the context where there is no tenderness and concern the unmarried love is more moral for Fletcher. To Fletcher, "In some situation unmarried love could be infinitely more moral than married unlove, as when the parties to a marriage exercise their legal right of sexual access without the tenderness and concern which alone validate sexual love making". (Joseph Fletcher, "Why New?", *Religion in Life* Vol.xxxv, No. 2 (Spring 1966), P. 188). In the issue of adultery he admits that adultery means an act of sexual intercourse with someone who is not one's spouse, but he argues that judging adultery right or wrong depends only upon the situation. (William E, May, ed. *Hello Lovers!,* P. 37,38). He states, "I am a situationist, and I say that the morality of adultery depends on the situation". (*Ibid.*, P. 39). The concern of applying agape in the cases or what is 'posterior' is crucial in his ethical approach.

About homosexuality, Fletcher stated that it is not unnatural. His argument is that the 'mere fact that a sexual act is homosexual does not establish that it is either good or evil, right or wrong; that will depend upon the situation in which the act is performed - the conditions and consequence. (*Ibid.*, P. 41). As in the issue of adultery, here also he applies the same situational principle that the question of right or wrong is depending on agape in the situation. The feature of aposteriori-agapeic approach comes clear in his exposition over here.

About the question of divorce, Fletcher suspects Jesus absolute prohibition in the gospel of Mathew (5:31-32). (*Ibid.*, P. 67). He says, "Let me simply repeat that the notion of the indissolubility of marriage found in the Gospel accounts of Jesus divorce teaching is so inconsistent with the relativism of his teaching everywhere else that is highly suspect". (*Ibid.*, P. 68). He suspects Jesus' commands on divorce as his ethical approach, consistently, disregard the normative elements found in Christian ethics.

According to Fletcher, Jesus' sex ethic is derived from his insistence on the prohibition of looking at a woman with lustful eye. For Jesus, this is the whole sex code. Fletcher condemns the traditional Christian understanding of sex as inherently evil by telling that it ignores the important ethical issues. He states again that the puritanical Christians (both Catholic and Protestant) have confused morality with sex questions, and virtues with obedience to the sexual taboos. (Joseph Fletcher, *Moral Responsibility,* P. 82-85). The confusion of Fletcher is that the approach takes into account only the evaluative principle, and not the normative rules of the Bible.

Fletcher emphasizes sex as an act of love which serves love. Regarding sex laws, he provides certain guidelines. The offenses should be restricted to (1) acts with the persons under the legal age of consent (2) acts in situations judged to be public nuisance or infringement of public decency, and (3) acts involving assault, violence duress or fraud. (*Ibid.*, P. 111). In this regard Fletcher's concern for sexual offenses has to be appreciated. At least, he admits that some regulations are necessary for any community to uphold the decency and avoid the manipulations. Provision of these guideliness doesn't go against the aposteriori- agapeic approach of Fletcher.

Fletcher agrees with professor Leo Koch's view that sexual intercourse should be condoned among the sufficiently mature to engage in it without consequence and without violating their own codes of morality and ethics, with the due regard for the three qualifying factors -maturity, social concern and integrity. (*Ibid*., P. 129). He sharply condemns the law that "cohabitation" (nonmarital intercourse consistently with the same person) is a criminal offense, since he thinks that it makes the punishment for cohabitation heavier than for promiscuity, thus creating the absurd situation in which a measure of interpersonal commitment between such sexual partners is penalized and promiscuity or casual fornication is preferred. (*Ibid*., P. 130). He also holds that Bible affirms sex as a high order value with the claim that Bible talks about sex solely within marriage is only a inference. (*Ibid*., P. 134). He continued to say that there is nothing explicitly forbidding premarital acts in the Bible, only extra-marital adultery are forbidden. (*Ibid*., P. 134).As the ethical approach does not see the value of apriori rules, he feels that Bible also does not have normative principle.

In Fletcher's understanding the New Testament Teaching on sexuality and marriage is fragmentary and Bible only condemns the extra-marital sex or adultery. Any sort of sex with a valid consent could be understood with concern if it has kept up the love, commitment and integrity. He says that no sexual act between persons competent to give mutual consent should be unlovingly dealt with, except when it involves either the seduction of the minors or an offense against the public order. (*Ibid*., P. 139). Only the sexual act which involves the sadism and the object-subject relationship is condemned by him. The ethical approach of Joseph Fletcher on the issue of sexuality and marriage is certainly agapeic, but he uses agape only in the form of an evaluative perspective. His ethical approach shows interest in what is posterior or the cases.

2. Technological Devices and the Issue of Sexuality and Marriage

The influence of technology has brought tremendous amount of change in the whole perspective on sexuality and marriage. The artificial means of reproduction is the main point of concern in this connection.

Fletcher blames the English law which validate marriage only by sexual union. (Joseph Fletcher, *Morals and Medicine,* P. 118).He favours the Artificial Insemination by Husband (AIH), Artificial Insemination by Donor (AID), Invitro fertilization (IVF), cloning and surrogate mother. According to Fletcher the artificial insemination should not be forbidden since it could not be God's will or man that a married couple should be condemned to childlessness on an unproductive love merely because of psychological or biological accident. (*Ibid.*, P. 118). The A.I.D. and the A.I.H. are the means, for him, to overcome the emotional strain and frustrations in married life. (Joseph Fletcher, *Morals and Medicine,* P. 101). According to Fletcher man has the moral freedom which can be applied also in the area of sexual reproduction that is, the use of artificial means which is children without sexal union. (*Ibid.*, P. 100).

Fletcher explains that Artificial Insemination by Donor is not adultery. Quoting the levitate system of the Old Testament, he said that the artificial insemination by donor is not adultery. (Joseph Fletcher, "The Ethics of Genetic Control: Some Answers" *On Moral Medicine,* P. 348). The sexual intercourse ("one flesh") is the most important aspect in marital life. The procreation, which is the foremost thing in the purpose of marriage is meant to be through the conjugality of the husband and wife. But, the technological devices intervene in this sphere. While explaining the concept of adultery, Fletcher has said that adultery is not a personal and genital act. (*Ibid.*, P. 348). He states, "No longer can we say that a monogamous marriage agreement means exclusive access to any or all of the wife's or husband's "generative" faculties. It might exclude third - party genitalia but not third - party sperm or ova, nor graft gonads, which can overcome childlessness and barren marriages." (*Ibid.*, P. 348). He continued to say that "Adultery cannot apply any longer to the donation of the powers of our "loins" to persons in need just because they are not one's spouse." (*Ibid.*, P. 348). The only criteria he accepts is that the partner's consent should be sought: "To receive an egg or sperm without the spouse's knowledge and consent would be an odd business, hard to justify." (*Ibid.*, P. 349).

The sperm banks is another phenomena. The cryogenic device is used to keep the sperm and it can be used for fertilization later. Fletcher provides an example for it. A married man has oligospermia and his sperm might be collected over a period of time, to aggregate it for fertilization. In another situation he might bank it for a future marriage because he faces a sterilization operation, either for therapeutic reasons or as method of birth control. According to Fletcher, "Stored semen could be used for several inseminations at the ovulation period, thus increasing the chances of a hoped for conception." [310] For Fletcher these devices are a blessing they should be used for man's benefit in marital life. He feels that there is nothing wrong in using the donors' sperm from the sperm banks to have children of quality. (*Ibid.*, P. 353).

Fletcher advocates for the surrogate mother, egg transfers and artificial insemination. He argues for the sharing of the productivity for the sake of friends and neighbours. (*Ibid.*, P. 353). He explains the new development in marriage and family in the following words: Women who have never copulated will have children. Babies without sex, sex without babies. Some children will have only one parent - a parent who may be either a man or a woman. Marriages will be contracted less often than in the past. (*Ibid.*, P. 354). Fletcher describes that, "our traditional morality of baby making is based on heterosexual intercourse or coital conception, and on uterine gestation or fetal nurture in the human womb. This has been superseded or at least become supersedable. Since mores and values always change as conditions and situations change, our morality will and should change too." (Joseph Fletcher, *The Ethics of Genetic Control:* P. 14).

Joseph Fletcher favours cloning. He says, 'good reasons in cloning are that it avoids genetic diseases, by passes sterility, pre-determines an individual's gender, and preserves family likenesses'. (Joseph Fletcher, "The Ethics of Genetic Control: Some Answers", *On Moral Medicine,* p. 348). He justifies cloning in the situation of meeting a family's survival need. (Joseph Fletcher, "Ethical Aspects of Genetic Control, *In Bioethics* edited by Thomas A. Shannon, p. 333). Cloning is reproduction from one parent only (using a body cell instead of combining sperm and ovum), so it is asexual. (Joseph Fletcher, *The Ethics of Genetic Control,* p. 8, 333).The human sexuality has no place over here. Though Fletcher approves cloning, it is with some reservations. It would be wrong, he says, of lesbian or male homophile extremists to want to use cloning to reproduce a general population of their own sex and the production of legless people and dwarfs. (Joseph Fletcher, *The Ethics of Genetic Control,* p. 8, 41).

According to Fletcher, the children born by the artificial means also should be shown the loving concern as those produced in the traditional fashion. (William May, ed., *Hello Lovers!,*p. 133).Fletcher realizes that people use the artificial_means of overcome the infertility . He argued that enabling people to overcome the sterility is a common responsibility of humanity and it is the essential part of loving neighbour . In this respect if some one avail the third party sperms or ova, it has to be considered, with love and generosity but it can not be suggested as a rule to be applied in all contexts.

The ethical approach of Joseph Fletcher concentrates on agape and its role in the particular cases. His ethical approach is not concerned of the apriori principles or norms. Whether it is the pre-marital sex, extra-marital sex, divorce or artificial insemination his approach is aposteriori agapeic as it takes into account the psycho-social factors and also the role of love, mercy, generosity and concern in the particular cases or situation. The ethical approach of Fletcher is reflecting more on the issues which can be termed as posterior, and he was not dwelling on the rules which are apriori. What is to be noted with a critical eye is the suggestion of Fletcher on the certain issues, especially in the use of technological devices, such as idea like no unwanted baby should be born (in the case of contraceptive and sterilization) and the use of third party sperm in the case of artificial reproduction.

F. A Comprehensive Understanding of Fletcher's Ethical Approach and an Appraisal

The section concentrates in a comprehensive look at Fletcher's ethical approach and an evaluation of his approach.

1. A Comprehensive View

The ethical approach of Joseph Fletcher is very agapeic and situational. This is evident from his perspective on the socio-ethical issues, bio-ethical issues and the issue of sexuality and marriage and professional ethics. The foundational aspect of Fletcher's ethical approach also shows clearly that he is influenced by existentialism, utilitarianism, pragmatism, positivism and relativism. As he himself admits his approach is situational and act-utilitarian. He reacted against the natural law ethics, the puritanism, pietism and the moralism. For him these are advocating for a legalistic approach. He questions the universally valid rules and the principles and rules which do not serve love. The deontological ethics is not acceptable to Joseph Fletcher.

The socio-ethical issues expose the fact that the ethical approach of Joseph Fletcher is aposteriori agapeic. He is not interested in the apriori rules and affirms that love (in an aposteriori way) is the only 'norm' He insists more on the evaluative perspective rather than the normative principle. In his view on law and love, he finds no value in loveless rules or principles, but stresses the importance of love in the situations or cases.

The bio-ethical issues also reflect cleanly the situational approach of Fletcher. The dignity of life is for him traditionally rooted on the rigid rules such as 'do not harm' and 'do not kill'. But he questions this traditional understanding as he gives more importance to the 'quality of life'. Abortion of the 'unwanted baby' [baby who is born without real intention (accidental)] or the deformed foetus or any other defects is approved by him. He is for applying euthanasia to the comatose and those are undergoing severe pain and suffering. He even accepts the voluntary and involuntary euthanasia. Even the consent of the relatives is sufficient for him to opt for euthanasia. The euthanasia is love-regarding and other-regarding. Here also his approach is quite aposteriori-agapeic. When we deal with cases, it is important to consider the evaluative approach to show the christian element of love, care and mercy in order to help on person this is very clear in Fletcher's approach.

In the question of humanhood any defects that affect the neo-cortical function is reducing any man to be subhuman. The sense of time, the self-consciousness, the ability to communicate, idiosyncrasy etc. are the criteria he furnishes to affirm humanhood. These are really irresponsible and irrational. This also shows his relativistic approach. In the issue of sterilization and contraception he does not have much hesitation to accept it. They are loving acts for him in order to have a responsible sexual relationship and parenthood. He is very flexible in this issue also. In the case of artificial means of reproduction, Fletcher is advocating for artificial Insemination (by donor or by husband), Invitro fertilization, surrogate mother and cloning. In order to overcome the childlessness he sees these artificial methods as a boon. He is even approving the sharing of the productivity with the neighbour which he meant a loving concern. In the case of sterilization Fletcher rejects only one aspect that is irresponsible sterilization which hinders the responsible act of procreation. In the asexual reproduction (cloning) Fletcher is against creating legless people or dwarfs. Fletcher's is quite approach situational in these issues also. He also advocates for the screening and the organ transplantation which serves good to the humanity in his view.

In professional ethics, the telling lies or 'deception' is not wrong, for Fletcher, in Business Management. For the benefit of the business enterprise, it is necessary to mislead others says Fletcher. In the sphere of medicine, he argues for the telling the truth to the patients about the diagnosis and the related information. For him it is absolutely wrong to hide the fact, and it an unloving act in his understanding. In the social life he says, we have to sometimes lie. This does show that his approach is aposteriori- agapeic

The perspective of sexuality and marriage is the main subject of this research. For him the New Testament is fragmentary and Jesus does not say anything against the homosexuality, pre-marital sex, extra-marital sex, homosexuality and the cohabitation. The divorce is also acceptable to Fletcher only in certain situations where agape and responsibility are denied. The criteria he provides is concern care, and integrity The immorality does include the sex which inflict pain or object-subject relationship in sexual act. In the case of adultery, he said, deciding whether it is wrong or right depending on the situation. In his view, the divorce to overcome the emotional strain and the cohabitation are to be examined in the light of the context. The psycho- social factors are so important to Joseph Fletcher's ethical approach as it considers mainly the cases or the experience of the people in the context.

On the whole, Joseph Fletcher's approach is based on the love. The love is neighbour - regarding and other - regarding. Love, he says, can serve in all situations unlike the principles and fixed rules. Fletcher's approach rejects the apriori norms. Moral decisions should involve the loving concern for Fletcher. The absolute norms and universally valid rules are invalid for him. There is no absolute rules for him as he argues that everything in relative. The good or right is decided depending on the situation or the particular case in Fletcher's ethical approach. It is clear without any doubt that Fletcher's approach is aposteriori; agapeic than normative.

2. An Evaluation of Fletcher's Ethical Approach

Joseph Fletcher is disregarding the principles and rules as he feels that they are rooted on the conventional wisdom and stringent legalism which do not serve love. The words of St. Augustin is very relevant over here as he states, 'love and what you will, do'. Fletcher's ethical approach is, as it is found, *aposteriori agapeic approach.* It is concerned of the experiences and crises of persons in the situation. He depends on the evaluative principle of agape rather than apriori rules or norms. He is also influenced by Paul Tillich's idea that love only can take any form in any situations. (Paul Tillich, *Morality and Beyond,* London: Collin, 1963, P.1ff) Paul Tillich is also influenced by existentialism and the relativism as Fletcher is, According to Basil Mitchell, "Professor Fletcher believes that love and only love, can determine our moral choices. But he does not make it clear how love makes it." (Basil Mitchell, "Ideals, Roles and Rules", *Norm and Context in*

Christian Ethics, edited by Gene Outka and Paul Ramsey, Op.Cit., p. 352). Charles Curran observes that Fletcher is unable to provide the exact meaning and context of agape. (Charles E, Curran, *A New Look at Morality,* London: Sheed and Ward, 1969, pp. 168-169).It is evident that Fletcher's concept of love is away from the Christian normative elements. It can lead to anomie. His rejection of prefabricated rules can lead to relativism and arbitrary subjectivism as Paul Ramsey Claims. (Paul Ramsey, *Deeds and Rules in Christian Ethics,* pp. 218-219). It is true that any misuse of ethics can lead to arbitrary subjectivism.

Fletcher is finding law in contrast to love and he is allergic to law. According to Dietrich and Von Hilderbrand and he confused the divine law with the ecclesiastical and state law. (Dietrich and Alice Van Hiderbrand, *Morality and Situation Ethics,* Chicago: Fransiscan Herald Press, 1966, p. 181). According to Edwin Lutzer, "Love, without rules (or some universal and agreed upon definition) cannot give guidance in making a single moral decisions." (Edwin Lutzer, *The Necessity of Ethical Absolutes*, Michigan: Zonderavan Publishing House, 1981, p. 34). Joseph Fletcher is tremendously influenced by the existentialism, utilitarianism, pragmatism, and personalism. These philosophies are for individual freedom and against the normative principles and rules. Persons and their role in the decision - making at the moment is important than the pre-determined rules. The existential moment and the freedom is affirmed by existentialism. Utilitarianism is grounded on the use or the question of utility. The pragmatism relies on what practically our decision or involvement means; relativism sees everything as varied and denies the absolutes. Positivism depends on what can be verified and observable. Personalism is based on the centrality of the persons. The persons in the context is important so it provides optimum freedom for each individual. The above stated philosophies or phenomenon enable the situation ethicist like Fletcher to bring out an aposteriori-agapeic ethical approach.

Situational approach of Fletcher goes against pietism, puritanism and natural law tradition, as he finds them as legalistic or rule-oriented. He views the case of sex, marriage, abortion, the use of technological devices, the cloning, and his criteria for humanhood from his aposteriori-agapeic approach. The sanctity of sexuality, the dignity of human life and the sacramental aspect of marriage which are based on legalistic rules are given less importance by Fletcher. It is true the Fletcher's approach contributes to democratization process, as Harvey Cox argues. (Harvey Cox, ed. *The Situation Ethics Debate,* Philadelphia: The Westminister press, 1968, PP. 11,13).

The aposteriori-agapeic approach of Joseph Fletcher should be appreciated as an evaluative approach which enables us to show love, concern and mercy to the people who are undergoing crises in the situation (eg. divorce, adultery or prostitution or abortion). But the problem with his ethical approach is that he is not taking into account the normative principles which are apriori rules as his ethical approach is altogether concerned of what can be termed as posterior in nature. It deals about the issues in the situation and the solution to the cases.

The risk factors are not properly dealt by Fletcher. According to Charles Birch and Paul Abrecht, the amniocentesis can lead to hemorrhage, infection, spontaneous abortion and even death. (Charless Birch and Paul Abrecht, *Genetics and the Quality of Life,* Oxford; Pergamon press, 1975, pp. 86-87). J.H. Channer admonishes that abortion can lead to bleeding, tissue damage, kidney failure, pelvic pain, infertility, heavy periods (menorrphagia), miscarriage and depression. (J.H. Channer, Ed. *Abortion and the Sanctity of Human Life,* Exeter: The paternoster press, 1985, PP. 5-20).The manipulation and the physical and psychological problems that these technological devices are to be seriously considered. Fletcher's ethical approach is mainly dealing with what is posterior (the cases), so he does not have to dwell so much on risk factors. What ever might be the risk, in certain cases only an evaluative approach will work.

Fletcher's ethical approach is 'then and there' or aposteriori agapeic this approach can be appreciated as it is an evaluative principle, but the trouble with his approach is that it is not giving importance to what is apriori or the norms. The normative elements are allergic to him. He, in fact, reduces the aposteriori - agape as an absolute norm. As an evaluation, there is strength and weakness found in his ethical approach.

The strength is that as an a posteriori-agapeic approach, his perspective is helping Christians to show love, care and mercy in the situation or cases in order that the understanding and love can be enhanced. The weakness of Joseph Fletchers' ethical approach is that he does not show interest in norms or apriori principles. But this should be understood from the fact that his ethical approach is more concerned of the issues in the context.

Chapter 3

The Biblical Understanding of Sexuality and Marriage

Since the Christian understanding of sexuality and marriage is rooted in the Bible, it is quite significant to find the Biblical understanding of Sexuality and Marriage. This chapter looks into four areas, namely, the Old Testament perspective of sexuality and marriage, sexuality and marriage in the Gospels and the Acts of the apostles, sexuality and marriage in the Pauline writings and sexuality and marriage in the non-Pauline writings and Apocalypse.

A. Old Testament Understanding of Sexuality and Marriage

This section is divided into four: 1) Sexuality and marriage in the pentateuch and historical books, 2) Sexuality and marriage in the poetical literature, 3) Sexuality and marriage in the prophetical books, 4) A comprehensive view of the old testament on sexuality and marriage.

1. Sexuality and Marriage in the Pentateuch and Historical Books

This section concentrates more on the pentateuchal paradigm, since the bulk of the materials on sexuality and marriage are found in the pentateuch.

There are two traditions of creation found in the Genesis account (Gen 1:1-2: 4 and Gen 2:4-24). According to Asher Finkel of Sefon Hall University, "Both man and woman are equally responsible and in the opening story of the Bible the person (Adam) is described as a dual being of two genders. These two complements can enter into a union as equal partners to guarantee procreation." (Asher Finkel, "Women in Biblical Tradition" *Journal of Dharma* vol.XIII, No.1 (March 1998), P.6). Though the polygyny existed in the society, creation story emphasizes monogamous marriage. The sexual bestialities are condemned by the pentateuch. Asher Finkel explains, the second story of creation (Gen 2: 4-24) relates how Adam (Man) should mate only with his own kind and the desired union should be with a partner in a facing position (Kenegdo). This paradigmatic story generates levitical prohibitions against bestiality and homosexuality (Lev 20: 13, 15, 16). Mainly, the story of Adam and Eve offers the ideal model of matrimony. It is a monogamous union, a desired form to be adopted by Moses and Aaron, Isaiah and Ezekiel in a Society that allowed polygyny. (*Ibid.*, P.7).

The marriage is understood as a covenant of sacred agapeic union and it generates care, responsibility and faithfulness. It is also a lasting fellowship of love through life in the pentateuchal tradition, says Asher Finkel. (*Ibid.*, p.7).

According to Asher Finkel, "the second story of creation (Gen .2:23) recalls the nuptial commitment. This one will be called woman ('ishah') for this one was taken of man ('iysh')". 'Taken' is the biblical expression for "married". Thus the story ends in the ideal lesson on marriage. "Therefore a man will leave his father and mother and attach himself to his woman and they shall become one flesh".(*Ibid.*, P.7; Christopher R. seitz observes that "one flesh" bodies the sexual coupling, *Theology Today,* Vol.52, No.2, (July 1995), P.224). According to

Mosaic law the marriage is sacred and it is the 'hardness of heart" that makes a bill of divorce (Dt.24:1) necessary. (*Ibid.*, P.8). It is clear that the Bill of divorce was allowed at least in certain cases because the context has made it necessary. This shows that the context has a role to play in our ethical approach. Though the norm of indissolubility is affirmed by the Bible, the aposteriori approach is applied as an evaluative principle where divorce has taken place. The normative principles (apriori rules) are upheld by the Old Testament.

In the opinion of David F. Hinson, "According to the stories of creation, sexuality is a gift from God, and normal relations between a man and his wife were encouraged and approved. God has said 'be fruitful and multiply' (Gen. 1:2.8; cf. Gen. 2:24). Serious misuses of sex were condemned in the later law codes eg. sexual relations outside marriage (Exod. 22:16), prostitution (Lev. 19:29), homosexual relations (Lev.18:22) and most especially adultery (Lev 20:10)." (David F. Hinson, *Theology of the Old Testament*, New Delhi: ISPCK., 1990, P.114).

In the words of Hinson, the misuse of sex is contrary to the purpose of God. He continued to state that polygamy is not condemned and Divorce is permitted when the marriage relationship is found improper. Divorce was allowed because the woman was not a Virgin at the time of marriage (Deut. 22:13-21), or because a man had married a foreigner (Deut. 7:3; Ezra 10:10,11). (*Ibid.*, P.114). Whatever might be the explanations for divorce, it is to be admitted that the evaluative perspective or the aposteriori approach played a crucial role in the ethical approach found in the Bible.

Joseph Kottackal opines that the family that is constituted by the conjugal covenant of marriage reaches its fullness through fatherhood and motherhood and in marriage man and woman are so firmly united as to become one flesh (Gen 2:24). (Joseph Kottackal, "Family life in the Pentateuchal Traditons", *Bible Bhashyam* (December 1994), P.268). Kottackal observes that in the patriarchal times there was no condemnation of sex and on the contrary sex is viewed as fundamentally good. The sacredness of sex was affirmed (Lev. 18:1-30; 15:16-30; 12:1-8; Dt. 22:13-30). The sex outside marriage was considered to be reproachable by the community. (*Ibid.*, PP.270-271).It exposes the fact that what is apriori has an important place in Biblical perspective on sexuality and marriage.

In the opinion of Joseph Kottackal, sex is lawful and a blessing of God only in matrimonial life (Gen.2:18,24). The pentateuchal tradition condemns the misuse of sexuality. The forbidden categories include adulterous interest on another man's wife (Ex 20: 14, 17; Lev.18:20; 20:10; Dt.22:22-29), the reduction of a Virgin (Ex 22:16), rape (Gen 34; Judg. 19-20), treatment of a female captive taken as war booty (Dt.27: 20,22) incest (Lev. 18:6-18; 20:11-12,14,20; Dt. 27:20,22), causing one's daughter to become a harlot (Gen. 38:24-25; Lev.19:20), and other similar things (Dt. 25:11;23:18; 23:1; Lev. 21:20; Dt. 23:2, 17). (*Ibid.*, P.271).

The pentateuchal tradition and historical books of the Old Testament have listed Abraham, Jacob, Joseph and Solomon as polygamists. Solomon had 700 wives and 300 concubines (1King. 11:1-3). The pre-marital sex (sexual relation with a woman before marriage or betrothal) was considered illegal (Gen. 34:5-7). This is affirmed by the Thamar incident (2 Sam 13:1-14). The punishment for pre-sex is to marry her and not to repudiate her as long as he lives (Dt. 22:28-29). Reuben lost his birth rights because of incest and extra marital sex (1 Chr. 5: 1 ; Gen 49:3-4; Gen 35:22). (*Ibid.*, P. 271-272). The sanctity of sexuality is stressed by the early Biblical traditions. It should be noted that though Reuben and his act was condemned as he was violating the norm or apriori rule, he was not treated without mercy, concern and love. This is true with the case of David also. Though his act of adultery or extra-marital sex was condemned, he was considered with mercy and love. (2 Sam 12) So it is clear from the Biblical perspective that in the issues (which can be termed as posterior) the compassion, care and love play a very dominant role in order to help the people in the critical situation or moral dilemma. An evaluative perspective is found in the Bible.

According to Christopher Wright, the creation narrative clearly implies a monogamous 'one-flesh' relationship between one man and one woman (Gen 2:24). (Christopher J.H.Wright, *Living as the People of God,* Leicester: Inter-varsity press, 1983, P.176). But he observes that "polygamy is certainly present in the Old Testament, but its extent should not be exaggerated. Examples are almost entirely confined to Kings or those in positions of leadership or prestige of some kind. And even in these cases, with a few notable exceptions such as Solomon, it is mostly bigamy rather than polygamy that is evidenced."(*Ibid.*, P.176). The bigamy is also criticized by Deuteronomy (21:15-17). (*Ibid.*, P.176). Marriages were usually arranged by parents. It is clear from the case of Gideon (Judg. 8:20; 6:27). The levirate marriages were also approved by the pentateuchal tradition (Dt 25:5-10). (*Ibid.*, P.155). According to Joseph Kottackal, "Adultery and fornication are considered to be great sins in Israel on the ground that they violate another man's right of possession (Gen. 39:7-10)." (Joseph Kottackal, "Morality of sex in the Old Testament", *Bible Bhashyam* (December 1981), P.153).

The prostitution is considered as a sexual perversion. In ancient Palestine secular and religious prostitutes were common. So also we have allusions about male and female prostitutes in the Old Testament (1 Sam 2:22; 2 king 23:7; 2 chr. 15:10). In Palestine the gods Baal and Asherah were prominent for cultic prostitution (Ex. 3:4; 1 kgs. 14:24;

15:22; 22:47; 2 kgs. 23:7). Kottackal explains that "the radical reform described in II kings 23, is an example of the strong reaction against cult prostitution." (*Ibid*., P.155). The priestly code states that a priest's daughter who acts as a harlot is to be burned to death, and the Israelites prohibited their daughters from Harlotry (Lev. 19:29; Dt 23:18). The girl who is guilty of harlotry is to be stoned to death (Dt. 22:21). (*Ibid*., P.155).

The decalogue (Ex. 20) prohibits the sexual immorality such as adultery. While discussing the commandment "you shall not commit adultery" Brevard S. Childs observes, "the commandment directs its prohibition against any practice that threatens the sanctity of marriage within Israel".(Brevard S. Childs, *Old Testament Theology in a Canonical Context,* London;: SCM press, 1985, P.79). He states that celibacy for religious reasons is not raised in the Old Testament, and homosexuality is universally condemned (Lev. 18:22). (*Ibid*., P.79). The commandment that you shall not covet neighbours wife (Ex 20:7) is also understood as a injunction against adultery. In the opinion of John Shelby Spong, "commandment number seven" you shall not commit adultery", plunges inevitably into a consideration of sexuality, sexual ethics and sexual practices. It arises out of the Judeo-Christian view of the sacredness of human bodies the sacredness of human relationships, and the sacredness of personhood". (John Shelby Spong *The Living Commandments*, New York: The Seabury press, 1977, P.79). The principles which are apriori is found in the case of homosexuality and adultery.

The Israelite marriages were endogamous (Gen. 34) that it excludes the marital relations with communities outside Israel. Exogamy was not the rule for them. Marriages between members of different classes and tribes among Israel was not prohibited. But exogamous or mixed marriages are found in the Old Testament. Esau (Gen.

36:2), Joseph (Gen. 41:45) Moses (Ex. 2:21; married cushite woman) Gideon (Judg.8:31; married non-Israelite women) and sons of Elimelech (Ruth 1:4; married Moabite girls) are the examples. (Joseph Kottackal, "Morality of sex in the Old Testament", *Bible Bhashyam* (September, 1981, PP.150-151). Though there was a strict law against the mixed marriages, it was considered with love and mercy in the situation where the norm is violated.

The Yahwistic and Elohistic traditions do not regard the affinity or blood relationship as a hindrance to marriage. But later, priestly tradition forbids this strictly. (Lev. 18:9). (*Ibid.*, P.152).

Divorce is not usually allowed by the Old Testament. The observations of Raymond Brown are worth mentioned here. Israel's neighbours had the practice of divorcing women on any pretext. The Canaanites have scant regard for sanctity of marriage; divorces and remarriages were common among them. The law (Deut 24:1-4) controls divorce. The woman could not be dismissed from home simply because her husband has no interest in her. The divorce can't be possible unless be found something indecent about her. It can mean some improper conduct. The women have no right to divorce in the Israelite context. The discontented husband has to obtain a legally authenticated letter. This will reduce any hasty action. Marrying again the first husband is not possible even if the second husband is dead. This indicates that marriage union is for life and nobody should break it down. (Raymond Brown, *The Message of Deuteronomy,* The Bible speakes today series, Leicester; Intervasity press, 1993, PP. 228-229).

Joseph Kottackal also observes that divorce was not generally permitted in Israel (Dt 24:1-4), since it was against the original intention of marriage. (Joseph Kottackal, "Morality of Sex in the Old Testament", *Bible Bhashyam* (September 1981), P.152). The sexuality and marriage are quite sacred in the sight of God. The Deuteronomic law even prevents the newly married from involving in war, since it can threaten the stability and happiness of his married life (24.5). It is also to protect the young bride from early widowhood. (Raymond Brown, *Op. Cit* P.229). The procreation and companionship are intended from the marriage. This is clear from the verse "Be fruitful and multiply" (Gen 1:28). This sacred union can't be broken unless there is serious reproach or lewdness (Dt 24:1, serious reproach is indicated by the Hebrew word 'erwa'). (J.Barton Payne, *The Theology of the Older Testament*, Michigan; Zonderavan Publishing House, 1962, P.330).

The pentateuch and historical books provide the picture that marriage is sacramental and sexuality is sacred. So the purity must be kept in all through the life. The marriage is monogamous in its norm, though polygamy has existed in the society. The pre-marital and extra-marital relations were condemned. Divorce is strictly controlled. The covenantal fidelity is stressed. (David Atkinson, *The Message of Genesis 1-11,* Leicester; Inter Varsity press, 1990, p.74). Atkinson emphasizes sexual complimentarity, sexual love, sexual equality, sexual celebration and procreative goal and the covenant-fidelity in marriage and chastity were required from the community on the issue of sexuality and marriage. The unloving sexual acts were not promoted by the Bible. The pentatench and the historical books emphasize the apriori or the normative principles in the issue of sexuality and marriage, but it does not mean that they reject the role of love and mercy in the context where persons already went against norms. Here the aposteriori perspective has found its relevance as an evaluative approach.

2. Sexuality and Marriage in the Poetic Literature

The understanding of sexuality and marriage in the poetic literature is the discussion in their section. The poetic Literature is based on experiential knowledge, and it includes the moral exhortations to regulate the social behaviour. (Gerhard Von Rad, *Wisdom in Israel*, London ; SCM press, 1981, PP.5, 74). Though there is not much material available on the said subject, the resources available will be used to develop the said theme.

The proverbs (3:13-18) hails the preciousness of the wife. The relationship and character are esteemed rather than the marriage gift. The external riches are not given more importance. According to Abraham Pezhumkattil, "she is the possessor of all good things and the immense wealth in the sense that she is the mother of them. The value of marriage rests not in the fact that a man takes a woman as wife, but that he has taken her as one who is capable of begetting all good things for him." (Abraham Pezhumkattil, "Housband-wife Relationship in the wisdom literature", *Bible Bhashyam* (June 1994), P.70). The marital fidelity and marital love are stressed (Prov. 4:5-9,13). (*Ibid.*, P.72). The marriage is understood to be for the life (prov. 2:17; 5:18). The marital bond is so strongly emphasized. The indissolubility of marriage is affirmed. The normative principles are stressed in the context.

The foolish woman is equated to the adulterous one (prov. 9:13-18). The author of proverb mocks the one who entertains other men and involve in sexual immorality, infidelity and sexual abuse. The metaphors 'stolen water' and 'bread eaten in secret' indicate the immoral and illicit sexual relationship.[32] (*Ibid.*, P.76). The good wife's care and concern are primarily about her husband. (*Ibid.*, P.77).The husband is asked to be faithful to his wife (prov. 5;15-20). This instruction is given since, "It seems that the most common error from the part of man is to violate marriage fidelity. He is very easily tempted to have recourse to women other than his own wife" (*Ibid.*, P.79). says Abraham Pezhumkattil. According to him, "The metaphors of drinking water from one's own cistern or well and not scattering one's spring abroad signify primarily the enjoyment of sexual pleasure." (*Ibid.*, P.79).

The wisdom literature admonishes men not to be enticed by woman. The prostitute takes fee as only a loaf of bread, but an adulteress stalks a man's very life (Prov. 6:26). The term 'adulteress' or 'strange woman' (Hebrew- nokrtyyah Zarah) often appears in the wisdom books, denoting a seducing woman who is unfaithful to her husband and the term 'harlot' (Zoneh), denoting either a prostitute or an adulteress." (*Ibid.*, P.80). The adulteress woman forsakes the partner of the youth and neglect the sacred covenant (prov. 2:16-19). Derek Kidner observes that in the book of proverbs the monogamy (one man with one woman) is the norm, and the husband is urged to be faithful and loyal towards his partner (Prov. 5:19; 2:17). (*Derek Kidner, Proverbs: An Introduction and Commentary,* Tydale OT Commentaries series. Leicester ; Inter-varsity press, 1964, p.49). Those who commit sexual sin and keep a low view of marriage flirt with death (Prov. 2:18,19; 6:27-29). (*Ibid.*, p.50).Christopher wright also affirms the fact that wisdom literature advocates for faithful monogamy (Prov. 5:15-20; 18:22; 31:10-31). (Christopher J.H.Wright *Living as the People of God,* Leicester ; Inter-varisty press, 1983, p.176).

The song of songs or song of Solomon elevates the sacredness of love. A love relationship between the lover and lady love. The word 'beloved' denotes sexual partner. (G. Lloyd Carr, *The Song of Solomon,* Tydale old testament commentaries, Illinois ; Inter-varsity press 1984, P. 64). The Hebrew expression 'ra'ya (my love) in the book of songs (1:9,15 ; 2.2,10,13; 4:1,7; 5:2; 6:4) is addressed to the girl which implies friendship or companion. (*Ibid,* P.64). The song of Solomon disclosed the value of love which is intimate and honest. Both lovers respect each other and they show a love which is responsible, caring and undivided. The sanctity of love in the life of would be sexual partners is portrayed in this book.

There is no much references about sexuality and marriage in the books of psalm, book of job or Ecclesiastes. Job (31:1) appears to be overscrupulous in avoiding even the occasion of possible temptation.[42] (Francis I. Anderson, *Job: An Introduction and Commentary,* Leicester; Inter-varsity press, n.d., P.241). The book of Job gives extreme importance to sexual morality. He finds even the lust as the primary cause for sexual promiscuity. The poetic literature is very much concerned of the sacredness of sex and the sanctity of marriage. The importance of responsible attitude to sexuality, and faithfulness in marriage are upheld. The abuse of sex like the pre-marital and extra-marital relationships are ridiculed. The norms or the apriori principles are seriously considered by the poetic literature. It does not mean that the evaluative principles are totally rejected.

3. Sexuality and Marriage in the Prophetical Books

The issue of sexuality and marriage in the prophetical literature is the focus here. It includes the major prophets and minor prophets. In the Old Testament times, the mixed marriages were prevalent, especially among kings. Donald H. Mason describes the situation like this, "Ahab, like his father Omri, and like Solomon before him, made a foreign alliance by marriage." (Donald H. Mason, *Thus Saith the Lord: An Introduction to Prophets of Israel.,* Madras; The Christian Literature Society, 1962, P.32. Hereafter Donald H. Mason Thus said the Lord). Covenant, righteousness and justice were quite important in the thinking of the prophets. Morality and religion were intertwined. (*Ibid.,* P.51). Lust and licentiousness were condemned by prophet Hosea. (*Ibid.,* P.57).

According to Joseph Kottackal, "in contrast to neighbouring Eastern Civilizations, Hebrew belief in a God who is beyond sexuality led to a kind of desacralization of sex. Human sexuality was sacred only in so far as marriage and fertility were part of the plan of the creator God." (Joseph Kottackal, "Morality of Sex in the Old Testament", *Bible Bhashyam*. (September 1981), P.147).Endogamy, exogamy, polygamy and monogamy were prevalent in Israel. (*Ibid.*, P.149).Divorce was also not uncommon in Israel. "A simple form of such divorce certificate may be found in Hosea thus: "she is not my wife, and I am not her husband" (Hos. 2:2)" (*Ibid.*, P.152). says Joseph Kottackal. He states, "The covenant which is meant to unite men with God by a bond of faithful love, is pictured by the prophets as an indissoluble marriage (Hos. 2:2 ff; Is 54:5f). Hence the infidelity of the people is branded as adultery and prostitution (Hos. 2:4)". (*Ibid.*, P.154).

According to Lyle Vander Werff, "marriage is a covenant commitment which protects the mutuality of sex and the meaning of personhood. It acknowledges responsibility for the continued well-being of the other. God is concerned about marriage because He is concerned for persons." (Joseph Kottackal, "Biblical Perspectives on Marriage Divorce and Remarriage", *Bible Bhashyam,* Vol.VIII, No.1 (Jan-June 1975) P.2-3). The fundamental teaching of Malachi is covenant. He found sin as covenant breaking. (Joyce G. Baldwin, *Haggai, Zacheriah Malachi,* Tyndale Old Testament commentaries Leicester: Inter-varsity press, 1972, P.216).Joyce Baldwin states that the broken relationship of Israel with God led on to broken relationships in society, inter marriage (hated inter marriage on religious ground) and divorce being the examples of unfaithfulness quoted by Malachi. (*Ibid.,* P.217). Marriage is described by Malachi as one of companionship (2:14). The life long partnership in marriage is affirmed by Malachi. Wife is portrayed by him as the wife of the covenant and divorce is hateful to God (4:1). The love and fidelity in marriage are emphasized by Malachi.

Divorce is tolerated in the community only because it was sometimes the lesser of two evils. Considering those who violated the apriori norm with mercy and generosity as they are victims of social structure or of psycho-social problems or any other is stressed in the Old Testmant. So the apriori perspective or approach is found in the Bible as an evaluative approach. 'Switching on of mates was considered as a defiling abomination pollute the land and inviting judgement (Jer 3:1; Ezk 16:38) in the understanding of prophets, says Lyle Vander Werff. (Lyle Vander Werff, *Op. Cit,* PP.2-3). He indicates that prophets recount how God's grace works in marriage. In his words, "They find a proto type for marriage for marriage in the divine marriage, in God's persisting love for his people (Isa.5:1 ff ; 54.8; 61:46; Jer 3:8 ff; 5:7; 9:2; 13:27; 23:10; 29:23; Ezk.16). (Lyle Vander Werff, *Op. Cit,* P. 5). Ezekiel's (Chap. 22) ethical teaching includes the condemnation of Judah's immorality such as adultery and incest, says J. Barton Payne. (J. Barton Payne, *The Theology of the Older Testament,* Michign; Zonderavan Publishing House, 1975, P.349).

The covenant relationship is strong in relation to God and man. Jeremiah portrays this strongly through marriage imagery. According to R. K. Harrison, Following the pattern of Hosea, Jeremiah threw deficiencies in the covenant relationship into sharp focus by using the imagery of marriage and contrasting a faithful husband with an adulterous wife (2:1f.; 3:1-13; 31:32 and Hos 1:2-2:50). (R.K. Harison, *Jermiah and Lamentations: An Introduction and Commentary,* Leicester; Inter-varsity press, 1973, P.8). The book of Hosea talks about the need for marital relationship by using the Hebrew word 'Hesed' (covenantal love/steadfast love). Gomer (Hosea's wife) symbolizes Israel's unfaithfulness to God. (Donald H. Mason, *Thus said the Lord,* P. 62).

The prophets were warning the people to shun immorality. The sexual immorality existed in the Israelite society includes prostitution and marital infidelity. Divorce is also found among them. The prophets were protesting against the irresponsible actions and urge them to cling on the covenant and its implications to life.

4. A Comprehensive Old Testament View on Sexuality and Marriage

The understanding of the Old Testament focuses on the covenantal fidelity, the companionship, procreation, mutual love, mutual trust and the Sacramental aspect of marriage. Monogamy was accepted as the norm. The sexuality is considered very sacred and polluting is condemned. The immorality or impurities include incest, rape, prostitution, pre-marital and extra-marital sex and public indecency like nakedness. The normative principle or apriori rules are hailed very much by the Old Testament.

Polygamy was not the accepted norm in the Old Testament, but polygamy was found among the Israelites. It was found, especially among the rich and the royal families. Divorce was not allowed by the law. But as polygamy existed in certain sector as an experience, Bible was considering it with love and mercy to serve good. Though polygamy was not the norm, it was considered within parameters of the evaluative principle of aposteriori agape. The pentateuchal, poetic and prophetic traditions are strongly advocating the chastity and the sane sex order. The Old Testament literature affirm the value of sexuality and its sanity. The poetic literature very vehemently attacked adultery and marital infidelity.

The Old Testament is having a normative dimension on sexuality and marriage which upholds the sacredness of sex and sacramental aspect of marriage. The irresponsible and abusive sexual acts are challenged. Sexuality has to be wisely used in marital relationship. Human sexuality cannot be seen as a means to gain pleasure. Sexuality and sexual union have their high and esteemed purpose in marital relationship. At the same time the role of the evaluative principle is upheld by the old Testament, without denying the normative rules.

B. The New Testament Understanding of Sexuality and Marriage

The understanding on Sexuality and marriage in the Gospels, Acts of the apostles, Pauline corpus, non-Pauline writings and the Book of Revolution are included in this section.

1. Sexuality and Marriage in the Gospels and the Acts of the Apostles

This section deals with the understanding of sexuality and marriage in the gospels and the Acts of the Apostles. The focus of this chapter would be the view of synoptic gospels, the fourth gospel and the Acts of the apostles on the issue of sexuality and marriage. It deals also with the background of the ethical thinking in the Gospels.

(i) Sexuality and Marriage in the Synoptic Gospels

First of all, sexuality and marriage in the synoptic gospels would be dealt with. Then the fourth gospel and thé Book of Acts would be discussed separately. Before entering into the issue of sexuality and marriage in the synoptic gospels, the background and influence of the gospel ethics would be taken up.

(a) The Background of the Gospel Ethics

The legacies of the earlier Hebraic relation, which is very much related to the Old Testament view, and the Judaism at the time of Jesus which is sometimes known as later Judaism and the rules and thinking of the Qumran community are understood as the influences of gospel ethics. The fourth gospel might be even influenced by the Hellenistic thought. According to Ernest Scott, "The two great sources on which Jesus undoubtedly drew were the old testament and the teaching of later Judaism". (Ernest.

F. Scott, *The Ethical Teaching of Jesus,* New York; The Macmillan Co., 1925, PP.14-15). The Johannine background would be discussed when the concept of sexuality and marriage is considered in the sub-section. From the gospel, issues such as sexuality and marriage would be developed. It is evident that the Old Testament and later Judaism have influenced the teaching of Jesus and the formation of he gospels.

(i) The Influence of the Early Hebrew Religion

Judaism is understood as the religion of the Jews. It evolved out of a long history. It also has so many phases. The earlier phase was very much associated to the Torah and the whole Old Testament. According to H.L. Ellison, "Judaism is the religion of the Jews in contrast to the Old Testament". (H.L. Ellison, "Judaism", *The New Bible Dictionary* (revd.) edited by J.D. Douglas, England; Inter-varsity press, P. 670). He regards the beginning of Judaism with the Babylonian exile. (*Ibid.*, P.670). The word 'Hebrew' and Hebraic religion are technically related to pre-exilic phenomenon. The term 'jew' and Judaism are associated with exilic and post-exilic period.

The Decalogue plays a very significant role in the life of the people. According to R.E.O. White, We have the Decalogue in two forms (Exodus 20:1-17; Deuteronomy 34:1-26) both ethical in content; and the third, (Exodus 34:1-26) concerned with ritual. (R.E.O. White, *Biblical Ethics: The Changing Continuity of Christian Ethics* Vol.1, Exeter: The Paternoster press, 1979, P.17). White says, "Exodus 20:22 to 23:19 comprises a social code of ordinances (precedents arising from previous priestly decisions), warnings and exhortations, making together a document described in Exodus 24:7 as the Book of the covenant." (*Ibid.*, PP.21).

White describes the influence of the early Hebraic religion as follows: The principles of the book of the covenant are philanthropy, piety, justice and responsibility which are the whole trend of the Old Testament ethics. The prophetical tradition has also played a dominant role here. Amos rebuked the injustices and licentiousness. Hosea hails the fidelity of God and the covenantal love ('hesed') and protested against the sexual viciousness as an affront to divine love (hosea 2:26). The faithful love is seen as the fount of sympathy, purity and loyalty in all circumstances (Hos. 6:6; 10:12; 2:19,20). The Isaiah of Jerusalem was condemning the sensuality and luxury (3:16, 4:1; 10:1-4; 1:10-17; 29:13-14). Micah insisted the righteousness of God (2:1, 2; 6:8; 3:9-12). (*Ibid.*, PP.22-26).

White states again that the Deuteronomists sought to incorporate the morality of the eighth century prophets which insist on holiness and humanity. In his view, the later prophetic tradition (Jeremiah, Isaiah 40-66; Ezekiel, Jonah, Nahum, Zephaniah, Zacheriah & Malachi) were concerned of the new covenant and emphasized the love and justice. Zephaniah condemned the dishonesty and corruption, Zacheriah called for national repentance (Zeph. 7:1-10), Malachi was aware of the cruelty of divorce (2:13-16; 3:1-3). (*Ibid.*, P.26). Jeremiah has shared the full ethical ideals of the Deuteronomists, but he had no confidence in the code of the moral requirements in the Old Testament and looked for the new covenant (11;1-13; 31:31-34). (*Ibid.*, P.26).

According to R.E.O. White, "Jeremiah Ezekiel and Isaiah 40-66 contributed major insights to the ethical inheritance in to which Jesus came". (*Ibid.*, P.26). The old covenant has given importance to external display rather than inward change. The stress on the new heart and the inner motive of the covenant is very much, fulfilled in and through Jesus. According to Father Antony Edanad, "In the Old Testament it is only Jer. 31:31-34 that speaks about a "new covenant" as such". (Antony Edanad, *Christian Experience and the New Covenant* Bangalore:

Dharmaram Publications, 1987, P.7). The marital infidelity which is the disruption of marriage (Jer. 5:7,8; 7:9; 9:1) is included along with exploitation and injustice in the concept of sin and rebellion by Jeremiah. (*Ibid.*, P.13).

While discussing the new covenant by Ezekiel, Fr. Antony Edanad observes that Ezekiel 36:22-32 (especially verses 24-27) is thematically and even verbally very close to Jeremiah. He states that, "as in the new covenant promises of Jeremiah the forgiveness of sin is the basis of the restoration and internal renewal, in Ezekiel the purification precedes the internal renewal and restoration of the covenant relation and thus serves as their basic condition". (*Ibid.*, P.39).

According to White, holiness code (Lev. 17-26) has a very great significance to Israel since it demands humanity, philanthropy, loyalty to fellow-members, love for God and clear perception of divine holiness. (R.E.O. White, *Op. Cit* P. 29). In the opinion of Fr. Mathew Vellanickal, "Leviticus 17 to 26 attained special importance in later Judaism as the starting point of the moral education of the Jews". (Mathew Vellanickal, "Norm of Morality According to the Scripture", *Bible Bhashyam.* (September 1981) P. 136). The ethical demands of the holiness code includes caring the sojourners and leading a life of holiness. (*Ibid.*, P. 136).

According to Bornkamm, the 'election' `covenant' `law' and promise direct and sustain the people of Israel. (Gunther Bornkamm, *Jesus of Nazareth,* London: Hodder and Stoughton, 1988, P. 36). It is very clear that the old Testament law, covenant idea, and the prophetical teaching have made a very crucial influence in the gospel ethics. The concepts righteousness, justice, holiness, moral purity, and sexual morality have influenced the ethical teaching of the Gospels. The Hebraic religion stressed the significance of the normative principles which are apriori, but it did not reject the evaluative principle based on agape or mercy.

(ii) Judaism of Jesus' Time

For Judaism, the 'Torah' plays a very important place in its theology. 'Torah' means instruction or teaching. According to Lange, "At its narrowest, it is the technical term for the most authoritative of the sacred scriptures, the 'five books of Moses' or pentateuch". (Nicolas De Lange, *Judaism,* Oxford; Oxford Univesity press, 1986, P. 24). He explains again that "central to Rabbinic theology is the concept of the revelation at Sinai". (*Ibid.*, P. 27). Judaism is the way of life of the community. The practices of the Jewish sects such as Sadducees, Zealots, pharisees and Essenes were varied and different in Jesus time.

There were different opinions on law among the Jewish sects. The Sadducees believed in the written law, but the Pharisees respected also the rules of conduct (the tradition of the fathers) which are not recorded in the Mosaic law. On this feature, Lange comments that according to one later explanation, God revealed to Moses the whole Bible, the Talmud, the Midrash and even the answers which would be given at any future time to the questions of a student. (*Ibid.*, P.26). Commenting on this issue, Joachim Jeremias said, "the divine law of the old aeon is laid down in the Torah and the oral Torah. The written Torah comprises the pentateuch." (Joachim Jeremias, *The New Testament Theology* Vol.1, London: SCM press, Ltd., 1971, P.204). He again states that "The Torah has to be interpreted so that it can be applied to the particular instance. Thus the oral Torah arises, named Halakah. It is the work of the scribes. These had a tendency to attach the same authority to it as to the written Torah". (*Ibid.*, P.204). So it is very clear that there was a written Torah and also a 'tradition of the elders' or oral law.

In the words of James Dunn, the interpretation of Torah took two forms - Halakah and Haggadah. In his words, "Halakah was a specific declaration of Gods will in a particular case, a rule of right conduct to guide the inquirer in the way he should go." (James Dunn, *Unity and Diversity in the New Testament,* London; SCM press Ltd.,1981, P. 62). The rulings of the teachers are passed on and preserved and are linked together which is called by evangelist Mathew as 'the tradition of the elders'. According to Dunn, it was first codified and written in Mishnah. The Haggadah is meant for edification and not for regulating conduct which are preserved in Midrashim. (*Ibid.*, P. 63). In the opinion of Dunn, "The Pharisees might see Halakah as part of God's Torah and delight in it - obedience to it was obedience to God." *(Ibid.*, P. 63).

R.E.O. White opines that the Hasidims, Pharisees and scribes saw the supremacy of law and the law dominated the later Judaism. He states that "the standards set by Judaism was high. Against sexual aberrations and infanticide the law was stern; if less on divorce, it was yet more austere than among surrounding peoples". (R.E.O White, *Op. Cit,* P. 42). The importance of the evaluative approach, i.e., the aposteriori-agapeic approach is considered very much in the time of later Judaism so as to input care, love and mercy generously in the cases where people violate the norms because of some reasons, though apriori rule is accepted as the norm.While dealing with the issue of Jewish world of Jesus' time Fr. K. Luke opined that the sadducees emphasized the freedom of will, teaching that man was the author of his own destiny, the Pharisees accepted the traditions of the elders or oral law and the Essenes stressed the observance of continence, purity and sabbath. (K.Luke, "Society Divided by Religion: the Jewish World of Jesus", *Bible Bhashyam* Vol.1, No.3, (September 1975), pp.197-198). The pharisees who appeared in the period of Maccabees under the name "pious" (Chassidim/Hasidim) were rigorous and uncompromising in keeping of the Torah in all spheres and situations of their daily life. (Gunther Bornkamm, *Jesus of Nazareth, Op. Cit* p.39). "According to Bornkamm," the exposition of the scriptures, developed and practiced in this movement, led to the addition to the authoritative letter of the Torah a no less obligatory exposition, which on occasion indulged in the oldest subtleties of casuistry". (*Ibid.*, P.40). The pharisees legalized the law (*Ibid.*, P.40). which was questioned by Jesus. According to Christopher Rowland, the pharisees took seriously the basic cultic Torah and extended to the every day life of the Jews, so that there were strict regulations with regard to purity and tithes (Mt. 15:1ff; Mk. 7:1ff. Lk. 11:42 etc.) (Christopher Rowland, *Christian Orgins,* Fourth impression. London; SPCK, 1991, P.70). F.F. Bruce, has said about the pharisees that "In the course of their study of the law they built up a body of traditional interpretation and application of the law which in the course tended to assume a validity as sacrosanct as that of written law itself." (F.F. Bruce, *New Testament History*, New York; Double day and Co.,1972, P.73). Joachim Jeremias also emphasizes the fact that the pharisees were having strict rules of purity as théir éfforts towards separatedness". (Joachim Jeremias, *Jerusalem in the Time of Jesus,* 3rd edn., London: SCM press, 1969, P.247).

The Sadducees are said to have a very conservative attitude towards the law of Moses. According to Christopher Rowland, "their interpretation tended to be literalistic, and they frowned on the more elaborate exegetical enterprises found among other groups." (Christopher Rowland, *Op. Cit,* P.68).The Sadducees reject the tradition, and exclusively accept the written law. The oral tradition (which is accepted by pharisees) is rejected by Saducees. (F.F.Bruce. *Op. Cit,* P.74). The different value system and perspectives of the movements within Judaism is of great importance, since the Gospel writers and Jesus were confronting those ideologies.

(iii) The Qumran Community

The Qumran community must have originated in the second century B.C. They were a very exclusive community called themselves as 'sons of light' "men of truth" "the members of the covenant" and so on . (William Sanford Lasor, *The Dead Sea Scrolls and the Christian Faith*, Chicago: Moody press, 1977, PP.68-69). The non members of Qumran community are called as 'sons of darkness' 'the treacherous men' the "unclean" and so on. (*Ibid.*, P.69). Lasor states that the Qumran community had repudiated Jerusalem Judaism and the official hierarchy. (*Ibid.*, P.77). So they have formed themselves as a separate community with their own exclusive values and ideology. The influence of Qumran thinking is found in the Gospel of John, especially the 'light' and 'darkness' dualism.

The purity has given extreme importance by the Qumran community. (*Ibid.*, PP.80-87). They concentrate on the study of Torah. Their writings condemn incest, whoredom, murdering orphan, consanguinity and polygamy. (*Ibid.*, PP.120-121). According to F.F.Bruce, the Qumran community addresses themselves as volunteers for holiness and their interpretation of the law was exceedingly strict. (F.F.Bruce, *Second Thoughts on the Dead Sea Scrolls, Exeter*; The parternoster press, 1972, P.113). The essenes were mostly ascetic. In the words of Tenney, "They were usually voluntarily celibate, although some groups allowed marriage, but only for the propagation of children". (Merrill C. Tenney, *New Testament Times,* Michign: William B. Eerdmans Publishing Co., 1965, P.97). The community was sober in temperament and never indulge in pleasure, says Tenney. (*Ibid.*, P.97). According to R.E.O White the Qumran covenantors were for enforced strict rules of discipline as they were for goodness charity, love and monogamy and were against lust. (R.E.O. White, *Op. Cit,* PP.44-45).

The influence of the Old Testament, the later Judaism and the Qumran Community is very much seen in the Gospels, and they have influenced gospel ethics. Jesus was Preaching against the negative elements such as legalism and inhuman attitudes developed by some groups. Joachim Jeremias observes that Jesus has found many references of the pentateuch on the basic norms of the will of God (eg. Mark 7:10ff; 10:19; 12:28-34) (Joachim Jeremias, *New Testament Theology* Vol.1, *op. cit,* P.206). but questioned the wrong perspectives of he the oral traditions in a radical way. Especially, he fought against the Rabbinic Halakah on the Sabbath. The study of the background of the gospel ethics exposes the fact that the apriori rules accepted to be the norm. There is an overemphasis to sanctity, holiness and purity. But it is also found that there is a place for love, mercy and care. So the evaluative approach (aposteriori agape) also has a dominant role to play in ethical thinking.

(b) Sexuality and Marriage in the View of Synoptic Gospels

The law and love have played a prominent place in the teaching of Jesus. The mission of Jesus was for the fulfillments of the law (Mt. 5:17). In the words of George Eldon Ladd, "His messianic mission and the presence of the Kingdom are the fulfillment of the law and the prophets". (George Eldon Ladd, *A Theology of the New Testament,* Michigam; Willian B. Berdmans Publishing Co., 1974, P.123).According to Joachim Jeremias, "In Mark 12: 28-34 par., Jesus describes loving one's neighbour as the greatest commandment after loving God, and in Matt. 7.12 he calls the golden rule the sum of the whole of the New Testament." (Joachim Jeremias, *New Testament Theology* Vol.1, *Op. Cit,* P.212). Jesus was concerned with the fulfillment of the divine will. Bultmann comments, "An interpretation of the will, the demand of God, Jesus message is a great Protest against Jewish legalism - i.e., against a form of piety which regards the will of God as expressed in the written law and in the tradition which interprets it, a piety which endeavours to win God's favour by the toil of minutely fulfilling the law's stipulations." (Rudolf Bultmann, *Theology of the New Testament* Vol.1, London; SCM press Ltd., 1974, p.11).

Jesus was concerned with the intention or the spirit of the law. Forell confirms that, Jesus does not abolish the law, he affirms it. But it is fulfilled in the light of the new situation. This means that it is interpreted not according to its form (letter) but rather its intention (spirit). (George Wolfang Forell, *History of Christian Ethics Vol I: From the New Testament to Augustine, Minneapolis;* Augsturg Publishing House, 1979, P.19).

The sermon on the mount did reflect on the ethical teaching of Jesus and the counter culture that he was advocating for. It is known as the ethics of the Kingdom. It has emphasized the purity of heart. Ladd observes that, "Jesus' ethics embody the standard of righteousness that a holy God must demand of men of any age." (George Eldon Ladd, *Op. Cit* P.128).

The concept of law and love are integral to the ethical teaching of Jesus. It is one of the main thoughts in the gospels, which is related also to the issue of sexuality and marriage. The so called antithesis of the sermon on the Mount (Mt. 5:21-48) also deal with the issue of sex and marriage. Jesus Christ was relating the marriage to the creation story. Ernest Scott says, "But the relation is part of the natural order as God himself designed it; and the sanction involved in it must always remain valid. This idea finds clear expression in the passage (Mt. 19:4-6; Mk 10:5-9) where Jesus bases his conception of marriage on the creation story." (Ernest F. Scott, *Op. Cit* p.99). Earnest

Scott opines that the Gospel of Mathew insist on the saving clause that divorce is allowed only on the ground of adultery (Mt. 5:31,32 cf. Mt. 19:9), but in Marks gospel (10:11,12) divorce is forbidden absolutely. (*Ibid*., PP.99-100). In the question of divorce and remarriage, Scott brings in a crucial issue that whether Jesus condemned divorce or remarriage. In his words, "one point is open to question, - whether it was divorce that Jesus condemned or remarriage while husband or wife was still living".(*Ibid*., P.100). Marriage is understood as indissoluble by Jesus. Houlden also feels that divorce is no longer tolerated according to the Markan Version since God has created man for life- long marriage. (J.L. Houlden, *Ethics and the New Testament,* New York; Oxford University of press, 1977, P.43).Matthean version allows divorce in the case of irresponsibility in the marital life. While affirming the normative principles (apriori rules) on the issue of marriage that divorce is against the commandments, Jesus was also considerate in the cases of divorce and he applied a very evaluative principle. So Jesus was aware of the need of the aposteriori agapeic approach in the ethical thinking. Jesus must have realized the Psycho - social factors (e.g. absence of love and care, the desertion, infidelity, violence over partners etc.) that lead to divorce

Jesus was condemning the attitude which regard women merely as sexual objects. The very look at a girl with lustful eyes was even condemned by Jesus (Mt.5: 28). Benedict Green understands that the Jewish moral teaching in the time of Jesus already extended the scope of the seventh commandment (apart from strictly legal contexts) to cover any sexual activity outside marriage, but Jesus admonishes that there is no distinction between the act and thought. (H. Benedict Green, *The Gospel According to Mathew* (Commentary), Glasgow: Oxford University press, 1975).The sexual purity was of great concern in Jesus' ethical teaching. In the words of John Stott, (commenting on Mathew 5:28) "The teaching of Jesus here refers to unlawful sex outside marriage whether practiced by married or unmarried people". (John R.W. Scott, *The Message of the Sermon on the Mount,* Leicester: Inter-vasrsity press, 1990, P.87). The sexuality is not to be abused, but it should be used in the proper manner. The pre-marital and extra-marital sex are against the norms. Human sexuality should be kept sacred based on the advice that Jesus gives. According to Ladd, "the Law condemned adultery; Jesus condemned lustful appetite". (George Eldon Ladd, *Op. Cit* p.129). The sexual perversions are not permitted by Jesus. The impurity and the insincerity are to be shunned from the sphere of sexuality in the understanding of Jesus. The sexual perversions and sexual unchastity include the extra-marital sex, pre-marital sex, homosexuality and lesbianism.

Commenting on Mathew 5: 27:30, John Stott, the New Testament scholar from England has said, "Once again the Rabbis were attempting to limit the scope of the commandment *you shall not commit adultery*. Although the sin of desiring another man's wife is included in the tenth commandment against covetousness, they evidently found it more comfortable to ignore this". (John R.W. Scott, *Christian Counter-Culture: The Message of the Sermon on the Mount,* (Reprint) England; Inter-varsity press, 1978, P.87).The third antithesis (Mt. 5: 31-32) calls for fidelity in marriage. It is related to Mathew 19:1-9. Stott explains the word 'unchastity' (Mt 5:32; 19:9). The word is 'porneia' in Greek which is translated 'fornication' denoting the immorality of the unmarried, and is often distinguished from 'moicheia' (adultery) which denotes the immorality of the married. Going deep into the word `porneia', Stott comments that it is derived from 'Porne' which means a prostitute without specifying whether she (or her client) is married or unmarried. (*Ibid.*, P.97). This does mean that Jesus asserts the normative and he was against the sexual impurity and the perversions such as pre-marital and extra-marital sex.

John stott argues that the Lord's exposition of the origin of marriage is a divine institution by which God makes permanently one two people who leave their parents in order to form a new unit of society, and he understood from the passage ('become one flesh, should not put to asunder') that marriage is for Jesus permanent and exclusive. The synoptic gospels give the picture on the issue of sex and marriage that sex should not be misused, and it should not be misused even in marriage. The fidelity in marriage recalls the covenant relationship. It is quite crucial to mention the understanding of William L. Lane on the issue of sex based on Mark 7:20-23. He observes that 'fornication' is a broad term referring to all sects of sexual immorality which presupposes the breach of marriage bond and other sexual immorality. (Willaim L. Lane, *The Gospel According to Mark,* Michigm: Wm, B. Eermans and Co., 1975, P.257).

The marital relationship is very sacred. Mark was linking Genesis 2:24 and 1:27 as it is found in Mark 10:6-7. The creation story is considered to explain the Markan version of marital unity thus: "Mark follows the Greek translation of LXX, the two shall become one flesh" (the Hebrew text: "they shall become one flesh"). The addition 'the two' is essential for Mark's argument, for it establishes the connection between the union of husband and wife and the creation of male and female. It is the male and female created by God who are united in marriage as husband and wife". (George Mangatt, "Jesus Teaching on Mariage and Divorce", *Bible Bhashyam*(June 1994), p.95). Mangatt also notes that Mark 10:8a "the two shall become one flesh" is repeated with additional stress in Mark 10:8b "so they are no longer two but one flesh". (*Ibid.*, P.96). The marital oneness is indissoluble. The 'one flesh' concept alludes to the close bodily relationship produced through sexual intercourse, observes Mangatt. (*Ibid.*, P.96).

Discussing Jesus teaching on the unity and indissolubility of marriage, Fr. Paul Savio Pudussery made three important points which are found in Jesus' teaching (Mk. 10:2-12; Mt. 19:3-12 cf Mt. 5:31-32; Lk 16:18) In his words,

He (Jesus) made three important and radical statements: (1) the creation of human kind as man and woman is the foundation for the unity of marriage (Mk. 10:7-9 = Gen 2:24); (2) marriage unites man and woman so deeply and personally that it cannot be dissolved by the law (Mk. 10:7-9 = (Gen 1:27); (3) a man can be answerable to his own wife as an adulterer (Mk. 10:11; cf also Lk. 16:18a); formerly the obligations of a woman to her husband were one-sided, but now they are made mutual; man and a woman in marriage are to be seen as equal partners with equal rights and obligations. (Fr. Paul S. Pudussery, "Jesus Teaching on Family Life", *Bible Bhashyam* Vol. xvii, No.4 (December 1991) p.231; In the bracket `Jesus' is added and this idea has allusion to Paul Hoff mann's "Jesus" saying about divorce and its interpretation in the New Testament tradtion, *Concilium* Vol. 5, No.6 (May 1970), PP.53-55).

The Divorce is also a live issue in the teaching of Jesus. Schnackenburg observes as he reflected upon Mark 10:2-11; Mathew 19:3-9 and the sermon on the Mount, "Jesus brought two earlier scriptural passages (Gen. 1:27; 2:24) into the field against the Mosaic dispensation allowing a bill of divorce to be made out and the Woman sent away (Deut 24:1). From them he argued that the primordial will of God at the beginning of creation intended the indissolubility of marriage". (Rudolf Schnackenburg, *The Moral Teaching of the New Testament,* Kent: Burns Oates, 1982, P.136). He states again that "Moses" commandment was given only because of the "hardness of heart" of the Jews, and now the order established at the creation is once again to prevail, so Jesus announces in

God's name, "What therefore God hath joined together, let not man put asunder". (*Ibid.*, P.137). He is affirming that Jesus is for indissolubility of marriage. Commenting on the "fornication clause" (Mt. 5:32; 19:9 and Luke 16:18), he said that this does not nullify or relax Jesus' fundamental and universal prohibition of divorce. (*Ibid.*, p.36). C.H. Dodd also has made his observation based on Mark 10:2-9 that God intended permanent monogamy and indissolubility of marriage. (C.H. Dodd, *Gospel and the Law,* Cambridge; University press, 1957, P.79). As it is found in the observations of schnackenberg and C.H. Dodd, it is true that monagamy and indissolubility of marriage are the normative principles. But as schnackenberg points out, Jesus had also realized the importance of evaluative principle in the case of divorce, Since the hardness of heart is understood as a reason which is psycho-social where there is irresponsibility in marriage. It is to be noted that the aposteriori -agapeic approach is found very much in Jesus's ethical perspective. But he was not denying the significance of the rules or normative principles.

Joachim Jeremias has made an attempt to disclose the idea of Jesus on sex and marriage. He argues that the right to break up a marriage lies with the husband. It is, according to him, showing a low estimate of marriage. In his opinion, the prohibitions on divorce (Mk 10:116; Mt. 5:32; 19:9; Luke 16:18) are genuine since Jesus ventures to set himself against Torah. And he says, the Old Testament permits the discharge of wife (Deut. 24:1) and Judaism followed this practice. (Joachim Jeremias, *New Testament Theology* Vol.1, *Op.Cit.,* P.224). Gunther Bornkamm feels that Jesus forbids divorce. (Gunther Bornkam, *Op. Cit,* P.99). William Heth and Gordon Wenham have the opinion that God intends marriage to be indissoluble (Mk. 10:2-9 = Mt.19:3-8). And in Jesus' understanding, married couples should not separate or divorce, and divorce followed by remarriage is adultery

(Mt. 5: 32b; Mk. 10:11-12; Lk. 16:18). Divorce, for Jesus, is a kind of adultery and it leads the woman to commit adultery except in the case of unchastity (Mt. 5:32). (William A. Heth and Gordon J. Wenham. *Jesus and Divorce: The problem with Evangelical Consensus*, Nashville; Thomas Nelson Publishers, 1984, P.14).

In the case of irresponsibility, the divorce was permitted by Jesus, since infidelity is found by him as an unloving and irresponsible behaviour. Here Jesus takes into account the norm and context seriously.

There was a dispute among Rabbis on this issue between the Hillel and the Shammai Schools (C.B.C. 20). It was over the phrase *erwat dabar* (Deut. 24:1): "When a man takes a wife and marries her, if she finds no favour in his eyes because he has found some *erwat dabar* in her, and he writes her a bill of divorcement and puts it in her hand and sends her out of his house". The Shammaites translated the words *erwat dabar* as 'something shameful' and interpreted it in terms of a sexual lapse; the Hillelites separated the two words 'shameful (and any other) thing' and understood by 'things', eg. 'if she has let his dinner burn'. (Joachim Jeremias, *New Testament Theology* Vol.1, Op.Cit., p.225). According to Jeremias the explanation of Shammai school is right; this appears to be sound in the context. It would not be reasonable to think that God's command will allow divorce for any selfish reasons.

The ground for divorce is 'hardness of heart' (Mark 10:2-9). Divorce was permitted by the law of Moses and for Jesus it was only a concession to human obtuseness. The Mathean perspective is that 'fornication' is the pre-condition for divorce (5:31-32). The Markan passage has the allusion to Deuteronomy 24:1-4. The sanctity of marriage and chastity are upheld by Jesus' teaching. Jesus was quite strong on the indissolubility of marriage. Commenting on Mark 10:9, George Mangatt observes that "the concluding statement of V.9 (cf. "therefore") summarizes the scriptural argument that it is God who joins the man and the woman He has created into an indissoluble one flesh union according to his creative plan." (George Mangatt, *Op.Cit.,* P.97). He explains again, "the couple is joined together under one *yoke* (that is the meaning of the Greek word used in Mk. 10:9, *sunezeuxen*); and they must work together in a common effort to master the task of wife till the end." (George Mangatt, *Op.Cit.,* P.97).

George Mangatt has made the following observations based on the teaching of Jesus on divorce.

1. Divorce and remarriage constitute adultery (Mk. 10:11-12; Mt.19:9; Lk. 16:18a). What is specially condemned seems to be remarriage which makes the break up of the original marriage final. This is a softening of the absolute prohibition of divorce in Mk. 10:9. Mark alone (10:11) writes "adultery against her" that is against the first wife to whom the man is indissolubly married. This flatly contradicts the Jewish concept of adultery according to which a man cannot commit adultery against his wife. It implies the equality of husband and wife in marriage.

2. The guilt of the husband who by divorcing his wife drives her into an adulterous remarriage is stressed by Mt. 5:32a alone. In the contemporary world a divorced woman would have been forced by socioeconomic reasons to remarry, and thus sin against her former marriage.

3. Marrying divorced woman is declared to be adultery by Mt. 5:32b and Lk 16:18b. The new husband injures the rights of the first husband with whom she is indissolubly bound.

4. Only Mt. 19:9 and 5:32 mention an exception to the prohibition of divorce. In the controversy in

> Mt. 19:3-9, the question of Pharisees is formulated, in comparison with Mk. 10:2, differently: "is it lawful for a man to divorce his wife for any cause?" Corresponding the final answer on 19:9 is changed with the addition of the exceptive clause. It rejects divorce, indeed, for any cause, but allows one exception, the unchastity (unlawful sexual activity of every kind which is the meaning of the Greek word porneia (Mt 19:9) of the wife. The question and answer allude to the rabbinic discussions about the legitimate causes of divorce. In the light of this context, the meaning is clear: it is lawful for a man to divorce his wife and remarry only in the case of the unchastity of the wife. (George Mangatt, *Op.Cit.,*PP.100-101).

The Observation of Raymond F. Collins is also worth to be mentioned: The Essenes prohibited divorce, but the majority of Judaism allowed divorce. Mark is very clear (10:11-12) that whoever, whether man or woman, divorces the spouse and marries another commits adultery. Mark uses the Greek verb 'chorizo' for divorce which means separate. The separation of those who are united in a divinely ordained union contravenes the will of God. Mathean narrative states that whoever divorces his wife commits adultery, except for one single situation, viz, that of unchastity. Lukan version is that the man who divorces his wife and remarries commit adultery (Lk. 16:18). The man who married a divorced woman commits adultery. (Raymond F. Collins, *Divorce in the New Testament,* Minnes sota: The Liturgical press, 1992, PP.81, 99, 113, 179). The Biblical understanding of sexuality and marriage is summarized by Allen D. Verhey as follows: "Divorce was not part of God's creation, but human sexuality was". (Allen D. Verhey, "The Holy Bible and Sanctified sexuality", *Interpretation* Vol.xix, No.1 (Jan 1995) P.38).Verhey views that the sexuality is sacred and it should not be abused. But the divorce is human that it is not permitted by God, as God is for indissolubility of marriage. But it is a fact that the Bible has the record of the practice of divorce as a last resort as in the case of 'Bill of divorce'. This means that Bible takes seriously into account the evaluative principle of agape, though the norm (apriori) ascertains the principle that 'do not commit divorce'

The aspect of celibacy is another very important factor in the teaching of Jesus. According to Werff, "Jesus spoke of marriage as a vocation, stressing the disciples' choice in the matter. Christians may prefer to remain single for legitimate reasons (Matt. 19:10-12)". (Lyle Vander Werff, Biblical Perspective on Marriage, Divorce and Remarriage", *Bangalore Theological Fourm,* Vol.VII, No.1, (Jan-June 1975), P.9.The term "eunuch" (Mt 10:12) refers to those who voluntarily refrain from marriage, comments Benedict Green. (H. Benedict Green, *The Gospel According to Mathew, Op.Cit.,* P.169). The renunciation of marriage to lead a celibate life is a matter of personal calling and gift. (*Ibid.,* P.169). Jesus had a high esteem for celibacy as it is for the sake of the Kingdom of God. The Voluntary celibacy can offer a service out of undivided loyalty to the Kingdom of God.

The synoptic gospels express Jesus' attitude to sexuality and marriage very vividly. Marriage is instituted to be permanent. The norm is apriori and is validated. This is very clear in Jesus' teaching that the marital fidelity is to be given utmost importance, and the unchastity which includes all the illicit form of sexual acts are to be condemned. The synoptic gospels stress the proper use of human sexuality and sacramental and permanent aspect of marriage. The Old Testament, Judaism and the Qumran thinking on sexuality and marriage have influenced or reflected in the synoptic gospels in their view on the issue of sexuality and marriage. But as it is seen in the ethical thinking of Jesus, the aposteriori-agapeic approach plays a critical role as an evaluative principle in which love and mercy are to be shown as the Christian responsibility in the issues.

2. Sexuality and Marriage in the Fourth Gospel

The gospel of John and the synoptic gospels have similarities and at the same time dissimilarities. According to Bultmann, "the Gospel of John exhibits the same literary form as the synoptic gospels". (Rudolf Bultmann, *The Gospel According to John: A Commentary,* trans, G.R.Beasley-mrray; Philadephia; The Westminster press, 1971, P.3). The Johannine perspective is, of course, different. In the opinion of Daniel Harrington, "the synoptic gospels (Mathew, Mark, Luke) provide a "common view" (Synopsis). But John's perspective is different". (Daniel J. Harrington, *John's Thought and Theology: An Introduction,* Goodnews series Vol.33, Willmington; Michael Glazier Inc., 1990, P.9).The background of John's gospel and his view on sexuality and marriage will be considered.

(i) The Background

This is not an exhaustive attempt but only a survey. The hellenistic background also deeply influenced the fourth gospel other than the Old Testament. The later Judaism and the Qumran community also influenced the fourth gospel. The context of sexuality and marriage in the fourth gospel is mainly influenced by the Old Testament and Judaism.

Dualism is one of the features of Johannine thought. One of the influences is Jewish, especially the Qumran sect, and the other is Gnostic. The Judaism is one of the influences of the fourth gospel. According to C.K. Barrett, John was acquainted with Gnosticism and other forms of Hellenism and Jewish elements. (C.K. Barrett, *The Gospel of John and Judaism,* London: SPCK, 1983, P.61). According to Ladd, Johannine dualism is deeply rooted in Greek philosophical and religious thought. Philo of Alexandria and philosopher Plato have their influences at this respect. (George Eldon Ladd, *Op.Cit.,* P.233). Light and darkness, life and death are the examples for dualism.

Philo taught that liberation from early bondage was by knowledge of God. Plato taught that human reason can apprehend the true nature of the world and of man's own being. (C.H. Dodd, *The Interpretation of the Fourth Gospel,* Cambridge; University press, 1953, P.14). The gnostic sources are found in Hermetic writings which reflect a synthesis of Platonism with other philosophies, says Ladd. The hermetists believed that knowledge of God is the only way of salvation. (*Ibid.,* P.15). Dodd states that, to Hermes, the evil of soul is ignorance. (*Ibid.,* P.18).God is light and life for Hermetists. Dodd comments that "this conception of God as life and light clearly belongs to a religious tradition which is also represented in the Johannine writings". (*Ibid.,* P.55).

The Hellenistic Judaism is another influence of John. It is represented by Philo of Alexandria. The real affinity between Philo and John is found in their use of symbolism, says Dodd. (*Ibid.,* P.56). God is light, says Philo, since in the psalms (26:1) it is said 'the Lord is my light and my salvation. It is related to Johannine understanding that Jesus Christ is the light of the world. (C.K. Barret, *The Gospel According to John,* 2nd edn., London; SPCK, 1982, P.32). The non-Jewish elements had influenced the Johannine thought very much. The platonic thinking, the Gnostic philosophy and the Hellenistic Judaism are chief among them.

C.K. Barrett opines that John was dependent on the Old Testament. Judaism is another important influence of John. He feels that John reveals numerous contact with

Rabbinic Judaism. The Rabbinic literature deals with matters of criminal, civil, and religious law. (C.H. Dodd, *op. cit,* P.79). The ethical instruction passes on from law. According to Dodd, John moved within the spheres of the rabbinic conceptions of Torah. He is acquainted with the casuistry of the law. Torah permits circumcision on the day of sabbath, which was a good Rabbinic doctrine. John was aware of this fact. (George Eldon Ladd, *Op.Cit.,* P.234). The Qumran writings also influenced John. The conflict between light and darkness, the spirit of truth and spirit of perversity are the examples of Qumran dualism. (William Sanford Lasor, *Op.Cit.,* P.213).Sanford Lasor noted the similarities between Qumran writings and Johannine literature. They include the ideas of truth and perversity, brotherly love, the foundation of living waters and son of light. (*Ibid.,* P.213).

This is only a survey of the influences of Johannine writings. Though the non-Jewish background is not directly related to the issue of sexuality and marriage which would be the great concern of this sub-section, it is of great importance. The Hellenistic philosophical background has influenced more the Johannine thought rather than the social.

(ii) The View on Sexuality and Marriage

The gospel of John was influenced by the Old Testament, Judaism and Gnosticism. The context of sexuality and marriage in the gospel of John was influenced by the Old Testament and Judaism rather than the Hellenistic background. Both these two contexts are already discussed in this chapter.

We have not much material in the gospel of John on this issue. Whatever material we have on this theme is found in chapters 2, 4 and 8. The context of wedding at Cana (chapter 2) reveals that Jesus had high esteem for marriage. According to Fr. Paul Savio Pudussery, "Jesus held marriage in high esteem and this is evident from the fact that he blessed a marriage at Cana with his presence and support (cf Jn. 2:1-11)". (Paul S. Pudussery, "Jesus' Teaching on Family Life", *Bible Bhashyam* vol. XVII, No.4 (December 1991), P.230). Marriage was considered by Jesus as highly important so he not only did grace the occasion he also filled up what was lacking there.

The next situation one could find is the fourth gospel is the discourse with the Samaritan lady (Chap.4). Jesus discloses her immoral life. William Hendriksen comments on John 4:19 that "the woman does not deny the remarks of Jesus concerning her immoral life. In fact, by calling him a Prophet, (which is to her meant one who can read secrets) she really admits her guilt! It is clear from 4:29 that this stranger's resume of her evil conduct shocked her beyond words". (Willam Hendriksen, *The Gospel of John,* Pennsylynnia; the Banner of Truth Trust, 1976, P.165). Mathew Vellanickal, the well-known scholar in Johannine studies also made a valuable observation in this context. He feels that the Samaritan woman was suddenly aware of her looseness and immorality and was frightened, and she had played a defense mechanism that I have no husband. (Mathew Vellanickal, *Studies in the Gospel of John, Bangalore;* Asian Trading Corporation, 1982, P.91).Though she did not make a public confession, she had realized her sins. This is quite clear from her understanding of Jesus as a Prophet and her commitment to the Messiah.

John 4:18 might indicate that she had five husbands. Some of them have divorced her and others might have died. According to F.F. Bruce, " Jesus words in verse 18 may be taken as a literal summary of her chequered married life". (F.F. Bruce, *The Gospel of John,* Michigm; William B. Eerdmans Publishing Co., 1983, P.107). Interestingly she co-habits with another man to whom she is not legally married. Barrett observes that the rabbis did not approve of more than three marriages though any number was legally admissible. (C.K.Barrett, *The Gospel According to John,* 2nd edn. London; SPCK, 1982, P.235).This might be the reason why she cohabits with a man at present.

Raymond E. Brown also opines that Jesus did uncover the Samaritan woman's evil deeds. (Raymond E. Brown, *The Gospel According to John 1-22*, The Anchor Bible series New York; Double day and Company Inc. 1966, P.177). Jesus was pointing to her that sexuality and marriage were to be kept pure and sacred. Jesus was concerned of the chastity in life. She was leading a very loose life which is against the norms of the Biblical teaching. However Jesus was aware of the social background of the woman, and was willing to accept her as she was responding positively to his message.

Jesus was well aware of the social structure of the time. So he gave serious attention to the socio-economic factor. It was very clear that 'do not commit adultery' is the norm. This apriori rules has to be kept up by everyone. But Jesus was showing love and mercy which included in his concept of forgiveness. So Jesus had accepted the Samaritan woman as he applied the evaluative perspective of agape. The aposteriori-agapeic approach is found in the ethical perspective of Jesus.

John records another important case of a woman (John. 8) who was caught in adultery. Daniel Harrington states that according to Lev. 20:10 and Deuteronomy 22:22-24 the punishment is supposed to be death. Stoning was the mode of capital punishment and the first stone would be thrown by the witnesses (Dt. 17:17). The goal of the pharisees was to test Jesus whether he would be faithful to the letter of the Mosaic law. (Damiel J. Harrington, *John's Thought and Theology: An Introduction,* Goodnews series vol.33, Willington; Michael Glazier Inc., 1990, P.9).

Harrington's comment based on John 8:1-11 is quite useful. Jesus was questioning the integrity of the people who brought them. It reveals the fact that they are also not clear in their moral life. The sexual morality as normative was hailed by Jesus. Jesus neither did condone the illicit sex of the woman nor the immorality of the pharisees. He states about Jesus that, "He forgives the sinner without condoning sin, thus preserving the delicate balance between justice and mercy that is the characteristic of biblical tradition". (*Ibid.,* P.56). The infidelity of the woman is to be punished, but Jesus questioned the integrity of the people who brought the woman to him. He discloses the evil society which entertains the sexual immorality on one side, and that which talks about high morality on another side. The double morality was being challenged. The whole society has the responsibility to maintain morality. Jesus analysed the context and evaluated situation in which she became a prostitute. He found that the unjust structure of the society is responsible for it. Jesus' agapeic approach was considering the context seriously when an ethical judgement had to be made. Jesus understands the victimization of woman as there are psycho-social and economic reasons behind it. It is true that 'adultery' and 'prostituion' are evil, but the divine will also is to help the people in due moral crises and to deal with them with love, care, mercy and generosity. The evaluative perspective of agape-aposteriori or the aposteriori-agapeic approach plays a crucial role in Jesus' ethical prospective in this regard.

3. Sexuality and Marriage in the Acts of the Apostles

The Acts of the Apostles is a history book. It deals with the history of the spreading of the gospel. The author of this book is Luke. According to Marshall, "It begins with the ascension of Jesus, the event which marked the end of the earthly ministry of Jesus (Lk. 24: 50-53) and which also pointed forward to the ongoing work of Jesus through the church." (F. Howard Marshal, *Acts,* Tyndale New Testament Commentaries, Leicester: Inter-varsity press, 1983, P.17). Marshall says to us that the book goes on to tell the exciting story of the beginning of the church in Jerusalem, Judaea, Samaria, Antioch, Asia Minor, Greek and Rome. (*Ibid.,* P.17). Marshall further comments that book of Acts was intended as an account of the Christian beginnings in order to strengthen faith and give assurance that its foundation is firm. (*Ibid.,* P.21). The main message is centred around the theme `you shall be my witnesses' (Acts 1:8). (*Ibid.,* P.25). Though this book does not deal elaborately on sexuality and marriage, it is a very significant book in the new Testament.

The sexual immorality was never tolerated in the Book of Acts (15: 20, 29). The sexual chastity is recognized as an elementary ingredient in Christian holiness, says John Stott. (John R.W. Stott, *The Message of Acts,* Leicester; Inter-varsity press, 1991, P.249). The Christians are asked to abstain from flirting with the world but rather urged to lead a separated life of holiness. The moral purity is expected from a Christian. (Mangford George Gutzke, *Plain Talk on Acts*, Michingan; Zonderavan Publishing House, 1975, P.134). The unchastity is understood (Based on Acts 15: 20) by Marshall as the illicit sexual intercourse. (F. Howard Marshal, *Acts Op.Cit.,* P.253). The book of Acts gives due importance to the normative principles.

The family is of great significance for the author of Acts (Acts 16: 31). He also hails the family of Aquilla and Prisilla (18: 2). Though these references do not say directly anything about married life, these imply the importance of family before God. The family constitute the husband and wife and even the children. The families are within the limit of the saving grace of God. They are also found to be partners in evangelization.

The Acts of the Apostles does give preference to the family or the marital life and the marital fidelity. It also upkeeps the chastity of sexual life. The illicit sex is regarded as means of unholiness. The sexual morality is given foremost importance by Book of Acts.

4. Sexuality and Marriage in the Pauline Eorpus

There are fourteen books traditionally ascribed to Apostle Paul. It includes the epistle to Hebrews. In this study epistle to Hebrews is also included in the Pauline writings. Donald Guthrie discusses the authorship in detail, but there is no conclusive answer given. (Donald Guthrie, *The New Testament Introduction,* Third edn., revised, Leicester; Inter-varsity press, 1970, PP.685-698) .Charles Pfeiffer states, "Neither external nor internal evidence is sufficient to solve the problem of identifying the author of Hebrews. God spoke through him, however, and his message was designed to edify the church of Jesus Christ. (Charles F. Pfeiffer, *The Epistle to the Hebrews,* Chicago; Moody press, 1982, P.7).

Though there are several criticisms against the Pauline authorship of the epistles ascribed to him, the fourteen books are considered for discussion in this study. The Pauline background is considered first, and then his concept of sexuality and marriage would be analyzed.

(i) The Background of Pauline Ethics

Pauline Theology and ethics were influenced by the Old Testament, Judaism and the Hellenistic world and the teaching of Jesus. These sources had a very significant impact in the theological perspectives of Paul.

(a) The old Testament

Paul's heritage is partly Jewish. According to Furnish, "All Pauls' letters attest his indebtedness to the faith of the old Testament and to the traditions of this covenant people." (Victor Paul Furnish, *Theology and Ethics in Paul,* Nashville; Abingdon press, 1978, P.28). He elaborately quoted from the old Testament. The love commandment is quoted (Lev. 19: 18) in Romans 13: 9 and Galatians 5: 14. The Genesis text (2: 24) about man and woman becoming "one flesh" is quoted in Ist Corinthians (6: 16) (*Ibid.*, P.32). In the words of Furnish, "It is not surprising to find that slightly more than forty percent of the scriptural texts Paul employs in ethical contexts are drawn from the Torah. The remainder come, almost equally, from the prophets (virtually always second Isaiah), the psalms, and proverbs. It is not possible to generalize about the subject matter of the contexts in which they appear. Some of them have to do with the responsibility of Christians to give of their "abundance", others with idolatry, personal morality, community relationships, Church disciplines, and one's relationship to the "world." (*Ibid.*, P.32-33).

The figures like Adam and Abraham also play a very key role in the theology of Paul. According to Fr. Pathrapankal, "The most thorough treatment on the meaning of faith given by Paul is an analysis of the historical emergence of the faith of Abraham as the starting point of a faith encounter in the history of salvation." (J. Pathrapankal, *Metanoia, Faith, Covenant: A Study in Pauline Theology,* Bangalore; Dharmaram College, 1971, P.201). It is very clear that the old Testament plays a very dominant role in the theological and ethical development of Apostle Paul.

Fr. Joseph Pathrapankal again states that the background of Paul is Jewish and the Jews criticized the Gentiles for their polytheism, idolatry and immoral practices. This is especially found in the book of Romans (Rom 1: 18-32). (J. Pathrapankal, *Critical and Creative,* Bangalore: Dharmaram Publications, 1986, P.129). The Hebraic religion and later Judaism have exerted their influence on the thoughts of Apostle Paul.

(b) Judaism

Judaism has exerted its influence on Paul. According to John Drane, "Paul himself never mentions Greek or pagan influences, but he makes many statements about his Jewish background and upbringing. He makes a good deal of the fact that he was a good pharisee. (John Drane, *Paul*, A Lion Book, England: Zion Publishing, 1976, P.17). Drane goes on to say that "one of the main rivals of the pharisees was a group called the sadducees. The two groups represented, respectively, the liberal and conservative wings of Judaism. At every point of dispute between the two groups, Paul takes up and often improves the pharisees' view point." (*Ibid.*, P.17).

The centrality of the law was affirmed by Paul as a Jewish Rabbi. He never questions the divine origin of the law, says Ladd. (George Eldon Ladd, *Op.Cit.*, P.363). The unclean food would defile a person in the Jewish teaching. The Idolatry was strongly condemned. In the rabbinic tradition, especially, the pharisees urged for ritual purity. (John D.G. Dunn, *Jesus, Paul and the Law*, London; SPCK, 1990, PP.137-139). Paul was, of course, trying to provide a Christian interpretation as he revised the rabbinic laws on these issues. Paul had to confront the Judaizers in the Church who insisted that circumcision is a pre-requisite to achieve salvation and to become a Christian. (Rudolf Bultmann, *Theology of the New Testament*, Vol.1, London; SCM press Ltd., 1978, PP.108-109).Paul was radically revising the rabbinic thinking as he challenged the standpoint of Judaizers. Furnish states that, "Although there are significant rabbinic elements within Paul's ethical teaching (especially his old Testament exegesis), it is too much to say that the rabbinical tradition finds a Christian representative in him." (Victor Paul Furnish, *Op.Cit.*, P.40).

(c) *The Teaching of Jesus*

The teaching of Jesus had definitely influenced the perspective of Paul. Furnish is stating that Apostle Paul had certainly received the Christian tradition. In order to prove that, he brings some instances: Paul's exhortation to the married that they should not divorce (Cor. 7: 10-11). This reflects Mathew 5: 32; 19: 9; Mark 10: 11-12 and Luke 16: 18. Love your enemies (Rom. 12: 14 = Mt. 5: 44) is found both in Jesus and Paul. Paul was indebted to Jesus in these exhortations. Paul's ethical instructions reflect the influence of Jesus teaching. He upholds the law of Christ which affirms and transcends the old law.

Furnish explains what Paul has meant by Law of Christ (Icor 9: 21): "The general point of the context is clear: although the apostle considers himself free from the legalism of the Jewish law and even emphasizes this freedom in the course of his mission to the Gentiles, he is not therefore to be regarded as a libertinist insensitive to concrete ethical responsibilities." (Victor Paul Furnish, *Op.Cit.,* P.61). Paul was also talking about a life in the spirit. In Furnish's words, for Paul, living and walking in the spirit means living and walking in love. (Victor Paul Furnish, *Op.Cit.,* P.64).

F.F. Bruce also maintain the view that Paul had been influenced by Jesus' teaching. Bruce feels that Paul knows of the apostles of Jesus. He states, "Even where he does not quote actual sayings of Jesus, he shows himself well acquainted with the substance of many of them. We have only to compare the ethical section of the epistle to the Romans (12: 1 - 15: 7), where Paul sets out the practical implications of the gospel in the lives of the believers, with the sermon on the Mount, to see how thoroughly imbued the apostle was with his master's teaching." (F.F. Bruce, *Paul: Apostle of the Free Spirit.* Revised edn., Exeter: The Paternster press, 1988, P.96; *Compare also his book, The Paul and Jesus,* Michingan: Baker Book House, 1982, PP.41-43).It is to be noted that though paul asserted the normative rules which are apriori, he also considers Jesus' evaluative principle of agape (aposteriori-agapeic approach).

It is certain that the Pauline theology and ethics have reflected so much the influence of the teachings of Jesus. The ethical instructions on meekness, renunciation, divorce and the life in the spirit show tremendous amount of Jesus influence on Paul. (F.F. Bruce, *Paul: Apostle of the Free Spirit, Op.Cit.,* P.96, if F.F. Bruce, *Paul and Jesus,* PP.69-80).

(d) The Hellenistic World

The Hellenistic world is one of the main influences in the theology and ethics of Paul. According to Whitely, "It is clear that the thought world of St. Paul and that of contemporary Hellenistic Culture had much in common." (D.E. Whitely, *The Theology of St. Paul*, Oxford; Basil Blackwell, 1972, P.3). John Drane has observed that stoicism was probably the most congenial to Paul. He states, "stoicism was most influential in its ethical teaching about the duty and the unity of mankind. Conscience showed a man what was good, and it was up to him resolutely to set his will to do his duty." (John Drane, *Op.Cit.,* P.21).Drane observes that mystery religions might be another great influence on Paul besides Stoicism. Gnosticism is one of the main influence on Christianity which is an offshoot of mystery religions. The concepts like 'Baptism' and 'salvation' of the mystery religions have something in common with Christian concepts. (John Drane, *Op.Cit.,* P.21).

Gnosticism denotes evil and good in terms of darkness and light. According to Bultmann, "Gnostic thought is so radical that to it the impulse of one's senses, instincts, and desires, by which man is bound to the world, appear alien and hostile-hostile to man's real self, which cannot achieve its own nature in this world at all, and to which this world is a prison in which his real self, related to and derived from the divine world of light, is shackled by the demonic powers of darkness." (Rudolf Bultmann, *Theology of the*

New Testament, Vol.1, London; SCM press Ltd., 1978, P.165). The Gnostic elements were reacted by Paul, as he was admonishing to the unchristian teaching of it. (2 Tim. 2: 23; Tit 3: 9; 1 Tim 1: 4; 4: 7 etc.). (*Ibid.,* P.168).

Bultmann states that the Gnostic language, is very much seen in the Pauline writings. Satan is described by Gnostics as "the god of this world" (2 cor. 4: 4), "the prince of the power of the air" (Eph. 2: 2) are figures of Gnostic mythology. (*Ibid.,* p.173). According to Furnish, "Paul's ethical teaching is, however, indebted to Hellenistic "Sources" in a more general sense." (Victor Paul Furnish, *Op.Cit.,* P.44). He observes that explicit references are not found from secular sources, the Hellenistic terminology is found in panline leffers. It is true that the old Testment, Judaism, Jesus and the Hellenstic world have in flurend the Pauline theological and ethical thought.

(ii) The Understanding of Sexuality and Marriage

Apostle Paul was very much concerned of the sexuality and marriage. He did not tolerate the sexual persuasion, and he had reflected vividly on the issue of marriage, divorc and the celibacy.

(a) The Sexual Perversions

Paul has a list of sexual vices. They include fornication, adultery and homosexuality (1 cor 6: 9- 0). Those who involve in such immorality can't enter into the Kingdom of God. An incident of fornication was pointed out by him from the Corinthian Church (Icor. 5: 1), which was condemned by Paul. Corinthians 5: 9 - 10 also warned against fornication ('porneia'). The list in II cor. 12: 20-21 stressed three vices-impurity, fornication and licentiousness. He also urged the saints to shun fornication (1 cor 6: 18). Prostitution also was viewed by Paul as a sexual immorality (1 cor 6: 15 ff). Prostitution violates the body of Christ and perverts the community of brethren.

(Victor Paul Furnish, *Op.Cit.,* PP.84-85). Fr. Joseph Pathrapankal also comments on the libertinism and sexual promiscuity. He comments, "In 1 Cor. 6: 12 - 20 Paul deals with a bigger problem of Libertinism, sexual promiscuity and prostitution. "The body is not to be used for sexual immorality, but to serve the Lord" (1 Cor 6: 13) Paul wrote. Since Christians formed themselves as part of the body of Christ through baptism and Eucharist, it is not at all proper that these same parts were joined to the body of the prostitute." (J. Pathrapankal, *Critical and Creative, Op.Cit..,* p.132).

Not only fornication but also passion (lust) is mentioned by Apostle Paul in his list of vices (1 Thess. 4: 1 - 8). He urges to have a holy life and to control the body without involving in sexual immortality. Commenting on 1 Thessalonians 4: 3 - 8, John Stott states, "It is not surprising that the apostle begins with sex, not only because it is the most imperious of all our human urges, but also because of the sexual laxity - even promiscuity - of the Graeco - Roman world." (John R.W. Stott, *The Message of Thessalonians*, The Bible speaks today series, Leicester; Inter-varsity press, 1991, P.81). Paul was trying to correct the believers to have a proper vision on sexuality.

The fornication and other sexual immorality are described by Paul in Epistle to Romans (1: 24 - 29). The passionate desire for pleasure, the unnatural sex (it can be homosexuality and lesbianism), and fornication are included among the vices recorded there. The lust (Greek 'epithumia') means the passionate desire for illicit sex here. 'Epithumia' literally means reaching out after pleasure. According to William Barclay, "the stoics defined it as reaching after pleasure which defiles all reason, and 'epithumia' means the passionate desire for forbidden pleasure." (William Barclay, *The Letters to the Romans*, The Daily study Bible series, Revised edn., Bangalore; Theological Publication of India, 1981, P.28).The lust is the motivating force to unchastity. The divine retribution is over the sexual perversions.

The loose living and the unchastity are rebuked by Paul (1 Cor. 5: 1ff). It was an incestual illicit sexual relationship at the Corinthian Church. Paul instructs that do not associate with the fornicators (1 Cor. 5: 9-13), or those who engage in illicit sex. (William Barclay, *The Letters to the Corinthians*, The Daily study Bible series: Revised edn., Bangalore; Theological Publication of India, 1981, PP.43, 46).The event in Corinthian Church (5:1) was that a man was keeping his father's wife, probably his step mother either as wife or as a concubine. It is inferred that either she is divorced or she is seduced by the offender. The Greek Work 'Porneia' is used there for the translation 'immorality' which in the New Testament means pre-marital, extra marital and unnatural sexual intercourse, observed David prior. (David Prior, *The Message of 1 Corinthians,* Leicester; Inter-varsity press, 1985, P.71).

In the case of the man who involved in incest, Paul was advising to grant mercy, if there is repentance. Though he was advocating for the normative principle, aposteriori-agapeic approach is found by him as an evaluative approach.

Ladd also states that the list of vices is dominated by sexual immorality. He comments, "If sexual sins predominate, it is not because such sins were considered worse than others, but because of the notorious immorality of the Graeco Roman world. A famous saying illustrates: 'We have harlots for our pleasure, concubines for daily physical use, wives to bring up legitimate children and to be faithful stewards in household matters' Furthermore, temple prostitution was common. The temple of Aphrodite in Corinth had a thousand prostitutes. (George Eldon Ladd, *A Theology of the New Testament, Op.Cit.,* P.256). Commenting on the list of vices (Rom 1: 29 - 32; 1 Cor. 5:

11; 6: 9; II Cor. 12: 20; Col. 5: 19-21; Eph. 4: 31; 5: 3-4; Col. 3: 5-9), he observes that the sexual sins composed of fornication, uncleanness, lasciviousness, adultery, sodomy and homosexuality, (George Eldon Ladd, *Op.Cit.*, P.526). Paul was strongly condemning the lesbianism and homosexuality (Rom. 1:25-27) as he insists on the normative principle.

Apostle Paul was against the sex outside the marital relationship. He had a high regard for sexuality and moral laxity was disapproved by him. The misuse of sexuality (using sex only as a means for sexual gratification) is formed by him as against the will of God. The homosexuality, sodomy, fornication, lust and adultery are understood by him as sexual perversions which are against the sanctity of the sexuality.

(b) The Institution of Marriage

While discussing the Pauline view on marriage, Herman Ridderbos has stated that marriage is instituted by God and it should be kept sacred. Marriage is not evil (1 Tim 4: 4, 5) and it cannot be forbidden. He questions the ascetic pronouncements which forbids marriage. (Herman Ridderbos, Paul: An Outline of His Theology, trans.John Richard De Witt, Michigan: Wm B. Eerdmans Publishing Co., 1975, P.306).He states that, "The apostle speaks of the institution of marriage by God and the regulation of marriage given with the institution, for example, in I Corinthians 6: 16 and in Ephesians 5: 31, as well as in 1 Timothy 4: 4." (Ibid., P-306). Paul has urged everyone to have his own wife in order to avoid unchastity (fornication) and to lead a sanctified life. (Ibid., P-309). Ridderbos comments, "precisely to prevent fornication every man is to have his own wife, and every woman her own husband (1 cor. 7: 2), and they are not permanently to with hold themselves from marital co-habitation, in order even as married person not to fall into temptation

(vv. 3ff)." (*Ibid.,* P-309). The apriori rules or the normative principle are upheld by apostle paul in the issue of marriage.

Marriage is instituted by God for procreation and to overcome the sexual immorality. Paul had never regarded sexual intercourse within marital relationship as sinful. Ridderbos observes, "Paul values marriage as an institution of God, protected by the express commandment by Christ, to be accepted and experienced in Christian liberty. Even in I Corinthians 7, the chapter to which appeal is made for an opposite opinion, in our view no ascetic - dualistic motive are to be discovered with reference to marriage." (*Ibid.,* P-312). Looking at his higher regard for marriage (which is seen in his admonition concerning the love with which married persons must give themselves to each other, and the expression of marital relationship is related to unity between Christ and Church (Col. 3: 19; Eph. 5: 22ff) in his epistles. We can find out that Paul never understood marriage as a necessary evil, says Ridderbos. (*Ibid.,* P-312)

Lyle Vander Werff also feels that Paul does not oppose the marriage. He states, "Paul counters those forbidding marriage and advocating celibacy. Marriage and its sexual dimensions are to be acknowledged as God's gifts. Marital love involved responsible caring for each other, self control (not prolonged continence), and self giving (1 cor. 7: 1-7; also of Tim, 4: 1-3)." (Lyle Vander Werff, "Biblical Perspective on Marriage, Divorce and Remarriage", *Bangalore Theological Forum,* Vol.VII, No.1, (Jan-June 1995) P.11).

Apostle Paul did argue for the institution of marriage. He realized the original intention of God about marriage and family. He was describing vividly the mutual responsibility of husband and wife, and children and parents (Eph. 5: 21-6: 4) which explicitly upholds the facts that Paul greatly values the marriage and the sacredness of it.

(c) The husband-wife Relationship

Apostle Paul was giving extreme importance to the love, care, the conjugality and fidelity among the partners.

The husband and wife are to love and honour each other (1 Cor 11: 3 - 9; Eph 5: 22; col. 3: 18; 1 cor 14: 34; 1 Tim 2: 11 ff; Tit 2: 5). Ridderbos says that in Pauline perspective, wife and husband are equally important (1 cor 11: 11, 12) and in Christ husband does not have an advantage over the wife (Gal. 3: 28). They should constitute one body (1 cor 12: 13). (Herman Ridderbos, *Op. Cit* P.308-309).

The mutual love is urged by Paul in husband - wife relationship (Eph 5: 33). Joseph Kottackal has stated that the married love bestows sanctifying power on each of the partners (1 Cor 7: 14). He states, "The spouses have a soteriological function to perform for each other. It is in this that the "wonderful mystery concerning Christ and the Church" consists. Hence the couples are instructed in the letter to the Hebrews: "Let marriage be held in honour among all, and let the marriage bed be undefiled; for God will judge the immoral and adulterous" (Hebr. 13: 3)". (Joseph Kottackal, "Pauline Teaching on Marriage", *Bible Bhashyam*, vol.III, No.3 (Sepetember 1977), P.215).

In the marital relationship the partners are asked by Paul to subject to another out of reverence for Christ (Eph. 5: 21). The husband is advised to love his wife as himself (Eph 5: 25, 28, 29). The wife is obliged to respect her husband (Eph. 5: 33). (Mathew Vellanickal, "Family Relationship: A Pauline perspective", *Bible Bhashyam*, vol.XX, No.2,(June 1994), P.108). In the words of Vellanickal, "According to Paul the Christian family is based on a mutual subjection of its members. This is true of all the families which need certain orderliness." (*Ibid.*, P.109). It is in the Lord that the partners subject to each other (Eph. 5: 22; Col. 3: 18).

According to Craig S. Keener, "Mutual Co-operation seems to be the picture of relationships we find in Ephesians 5: 21 - 6: 9. Given the difficulty of loving and serving as radically as this text demands-Paul gives Christ's death as the standard for love, and our allegiance to Christ as the standard for submission. The context in which Paul places this discussion is significant: this is a kind of life that flows from being filled with Christ's spirit (5: 18-21)." (Craig S. Keener, *Paul, Women and Wives*, Massachusetts; Hendriekson Publishers, 1992, P.132). The husband and wife should love and care each other. They have a complementary role in the family.

The husbands and wives are instructed by Paul to upkeep fidelity and sex relations (1 Cor. 7: 2-5; Eph. 5: 31). Commenting on 1 Cor. 7: 2-5. David Prior has said,

The Corinthian rigorists had reacted so strongly against the sexual licence of the city, that they had swung over completely to the other side, forbidding what God has created for us richly to enjoy. Marriage, says Paul, is the gift and plan of God. Sex is the gift and plan of God. To reject both as though they were evil is as much a deviation from the will of God as to indulge in sexual intercourse outside marriage. (David Prior, *The Message of 1 Corinthians*, *op. cit,* P.114).

David Prior discloses that Paul prohibits polygamy ("each man should have his own wife and each woman her own husband") and fornication. (*Ibid.,* P.115).The conjugal right in the marital life is also affirmed by Paul (1 Cor. 7: 3-4). The partners are commanded not to refuse the sexual intercourse (1 Cor. 7: 5). David Prior comments, "Paul's stress on the indispensability of sexual intercourse for the success of Christian marriage is all the more striking." (*Ibid.,* P.117).

The physical aspects are important in the sight of Paul. The husband has the right over wife's body, and wife has the right over husband's body. The "one flesh" aspect is stressed by Paul (1 Cor. 7: 3-4; Eph 4: 31). Paul recalls Gen 2: 24 in Ephesians 5: 31. According to Francis Foulkes, Ephesian 5: 31 warns against polygamy, sexual promiscuity and dissolution of marriage. (Francis Foulkes, *The Epistle of Paul to the Ephesians: An Introduction and Commentary*, Michigan; Wm, B. Eerdmans Publishing Co., 1981, P.161).According to Mathew Vellanickal, "The marriage results in a profound unity between the husband and wife: "the two will become one flesh" (Eph. 5:31). To become one flesh means to share together all the experiences". (Mathew Vellanical, Family Relationship in Pauline Perspective", *Bible Bhashyam* vol.xx, No.2, (June 1994), P.113). This also involves marital fidelity that no sexual perversions are allowed. The extramarital, pre-marital sex and other sexual perversions are against the divine intention of the sex. The Epistle to Hebrews states that marriage is honourable and it should be kept undefiled. The adulterous and immoral would be judged by God (Hebr. 13:4). According to Raymond Brown, "The exhortation and warning found in this verse are strikingly relevant in our own day when such a high percentage of marriage is at risk unless both partners recognize the importance of commitment to Christ and to each other". (Raymond Brown, *The Message of Hebrews,* Bible speaks today series, Leicester Inter-varsity press, 1991, P.253). Apostle Paul stresses the importance of maintaining the norm or apriori rules regarding marriage in marital life which is the will of God.

Ridderbos comments that the partners are not intended to be separated, so fornication is incompatible with belonging to Christ (1 Cor 6:12-20). The believing man cannot at the sametime be one body and one flesh with a prostitute. The unity of Christ and church throws light on the experience of the unity of marriage (Eph 5:22-33). Fornication is strictly forbidden (1 Thes. 4.4). (Herman

Ridderbos, *Op.Cit.*, PP. 309-310). The husband wife relationship is very important in the thinking of Apostle Paul. He advocates for the love, care, conjugality and the fidelity in the marital relationship.

(d) Mixed Marriages

According to Ridderbos, the demand of Paul is that believers should not marry other than a believer (1 Cor. 7:39), but if one partner becomes a believer (another remains unbelieving), the marriage of husband and wife should continue (1 Cor 7:14) and it cannot be broken. (Herman Ridderbos, *Op.Cit.*, PP. 307). The context of 1 Cor 7:12-16 is about the conversion in the new situation. These verses talk about a context in which only one partner has become a Christian. The chief concern here is with the existing situation caused by the conversion of either of the party to Christianity. Joseph Kottackal states that "He forbids the Christian partner to put away the unbelieving one in the case where either party consents to live with the other For the baptized Christian has been consecrated has been made holy (1 Cor. 6: 11). His body is a member of Christ (1 Cor. 6: 15). The unbelieving spouse, therefore, who becomes one flesh with the Christian in the marriage union, shares in this consecration." (Joseph Kottackal, "Pauline teaching on marriage", *Bible Bhashyam*, vol.III, No.3 (September 1977), p.227). The norm is that a Christian should not marry an unbeliever. It is approved by Apostle Paul. But his ethical approach considers the case of a man or woman having a partner who is an unbeliever so he affirms also the evaluative perspective of agape.

The Christian can break the marital bond in the context only if the unbelieving partner disagrees to stay with the other. Joseph Kottackal states, "If the unbelieving partner abandons the marriage the Christian should let him go. For the Christian is not obliged to oppose the separation and involve himself in a life of marital discord, mutual antagonism and continual wrangling." (*Ibid.*, p.227). Paul was concerned of the normative, that is sanctity of marriage. So he allows the partners to continue their marital life if the unbelieving one is willing. Apostle Paul was very conscious of the Christian responsibility of considering the cases or situations with love and mercy in order to help the persons in crises. So he was trying to apply the evaluative principle in order to bring good. The apriori rules or the norm is not betrayed by him, but he applies the agape as an evaluative (aposteriori-agapeic approach) in the case of mixed marriages.

(e) The Divorce and Remarriage

The indissolubility of the marriage is stressed by Paul in 1Cor. 7: 10-11. The husband is admonished not to divorce the wife. The wife is exhorted not to separate from husband. If she separates herself from husband she has to remain single or else be reconciled to her husband.

According to Peter Thomson, Paul prohibits divorce except where an unbelieving partner wishes to separate (1 Cor. 7: 10-16). Paul defines also the conditions for remarriage of widows, repeating the preference for celibacy (1 Cor. 7: 39). (Peter J. Thomson, *Paul and the Jewish Law*, Minnepolis; Fortress press, 1990, p.104). Peter Thomson states that the Hellenistic law allowed divorce at the wife's initiative. He also comments on Rabbinic tradition "while Rabbinic Halakha did a great deal to secure the rights of women, ancient Jewish marriage law was based structurally in biblical patriarchal society. In accepted practice the woman's consent in the marriage was a necessary condition and she could also demand divorce in certain circumstances. Formally the man remained the one who effected marriage and divorce, the woman being 'acquired' or 'sent away'." (*Ibid.*, P.108). Commenting on 1 Cor. 7: 12-14 Peter Thomson opines that "Paul acknowledged legal termination of an informal marriage with a non-believing partner at the latter's initiative. The importance of this acknowledgement should not be overlooked; he generally held the conjugal union in highest esteem and refused to recognise divorce." (*Ibid.,* P.119).

According to Whitely, Apostle Paul forbids divorce and the problem of remarriage is never raised in the case of separation (1 Cor. 7: 10-11). He continues to observe that "It is not clear whether the Christian partner who has been deserted is allowed to remarry or not; Rom. vii. 2-3 would suggest not."[223] (D.E Whitley, *The Theology of St. Paul, Op. Cit,* P.217). The pre-requisite for remarriage is the death of the partner. Commenting on the divorce in the case of unbelieving Christian, Whitely says, "It should be noted that in this section, 1 Cor. 7: 12-16, the problem of remarriage after divorce is never raised: the problem of whether a Christian should insist upon living in marriage with an unwilling non-Christian partner has been raised in so many words." (*Ibid.,* P.217).

Paul was insisting on the norm which goes against the remarriage of the partner after divorce. According to David Prior, "The commitment to marriage by a man and a woman is lifelong, underwritten by God himself and not to be loosened, let alone destroyed, by mere humans." (David Prior, *The Message of 1 Corinthians, Op. Cit,* P.123). Paul avoids the fornication clause that is found in Gospel of Mathew, and also in Pauline perspective adultery does not terminate the marital relationship. (Peter J. Thomson, *Op. Cit,* P.119). J.L. Houlden also made his valuable comments based on 1 Cor. 7: 10-15. Marriage creates a perfect solidarity so divorce is impossible, and if separation takes place, there is no remarriage. In the case of mixed marriage, according to Houlden the divorce is impossible, but remarriage is not permitted. (J.L.Houlden, *Ethics and the New Testament,* New York ; Oxford University press, 1977, PP.73-74). Ladd also holds the same view. He states that 'Paul flatly refuses to countenance divorce on the authority of the Lord himself. If separation occurs, the woman must not marry again, and the husband may not divorce his wife (1 Cor. 7: 10-11). If one partner in a marriage becomes a Christian and the unbeliever does not wish to continue this relationship, the separation is admissible (1 Cor. 7: 12-15). (George Eldon Ladd, *A Theology of the New Testament, Op. Cit,* P.529). Ladd states again that Paul refuses to allow divorce. If the man dies, the wife is allowed to marry again providing the mate is a believer (1 Cor. 7:39). (*Ibid.,* P.529).

Joseph Kottackal states, "Paul proclaims with as much force as the synoptists the indissolubility of Christian marriage. By oral tradition he must have known the Lord's precept. He presents it in a form which resembles the text of Mark, yet with remarkable differences (MK. 10: 9-12)." (Joseph Kottackal, "Pauline Teaching on Marriage", *Bible Bhashyam, Op. Cit,* PP.225-226).

According to Werff, "single persons and widows may remain single (which Paul prefers), marry or remarry. Whatever be the case, love not lust must prevail (1 Cor. 7: 86). Elsewhere he advises young widows to remarry (1 Tim 5: 11 - 14)." (Lyle Vander Werff, "Biblical Perspectives on Marriage, Divorce and Remarriage". *Bible Bhashyam,* vol.vii, No.1, (Jan-June 1975), P.11). Paul warns against the enrolment of widows who remarried after divorce in the Church for Christian Service (1 Tim 5: 9), says Ronald A. Ward. (Ronald A. Ward, *Commentary on 1 and 2 Timothy and Titus*, Texas; Word Books Publisher, 1977, P.83). The widows who are above sixty only are allowed to enroll for Christian services. He promoted the remarriage of the younger widows, since they might loose their concentration, if they join in Christian service, because of emotional strain. (*Ibid.,* P.85).Paul is seemed to be very realistic in his understanding on sexuality and marriage.

Apostle Paul was insisting the normative that marital bond is indissoluble and divorce is not possible. But the ethical approach of Paul was clear that he also dwells on the evaluative principle of agape in which divorce is understood with love, care and mercy. In the case of divorce, the evaluative principle, that is the aposteriori-agape is upheld by paul to help the people in the crises as a Christian response.

(f) The Celibate Life

A voluntary celibacy is approved and advocated by Paul (1 Cor. 7: 25 - 40). In the case of divorce, he advises the partners to remain single (1 cor 7: 11). According to Thomson, "Paul's preference for celibacy reminds one of the attitude which Mathew ascribes to Jesus (Matt. 19: 10-12) and which certain circles associated with John the Baptist. Paul argues for celibacy in view of the things of the Lord." (1 Cor 7: 32). (Peter J. Thomson, *Op. Cit,* P.106).

Paul talks about the preference for single state in 1 Cor. 7: 1-7. He deals again about virgins in 1 Cor 7: 25. Ridderbos comments,

"He lets it be known, moreover, that his urging people to remain unmarried has its basis in "the present distress" (V. 26). What is intended is specifically the distress in which believers find themselves in a world hostile to them, with which Paul himself had and would yet have such an abundant acquaintance (cf. 2 Cor. 6: 4; 12: 10; 1 Thess, 3: 7). What follows relates this with the fact that "the time is short" (V. 29) and "the form of this world is passing away" (V.31). This alludes to the end of things, which is at hand". (Herman Ridderbos, *Op. Cit,* PP.310-311).

Paul feels that the married are more attached to the present life, that they devote themselves to husband or wife and concentrate more in the earthly life than the cause of the Lord. He also fears that more 'tribulation' in the flesh would be for the married. So he advises the unmarried to remain single. At the same time he urges the one who does not have self-control to marry. Paul says especially in the case of virgins that the parents who give her in marriage does well, but he who does not give her in marriage does better (1 Cor 7: 29,31,32,38,39,40). (Herman Ridderbos, *Op. Cit,* PP.310-311).The widows can remain single or remarry (1 Cor. 7:39,40; I Tim 5:9-11).

The ascetic or monastic life was common in the Qumran Community, in the Old Testament times and in Judaism. The celibacy was prevalent. It was told that John the Baptist and Paul were celibates. About Paul, Legrand commented that, "By the time he wrote the first letter to the Corinthians, Paul was agamos, free from conjugal attachment (1 Cor 7:7-8, cf 9:5). This word need not necessarily mean that Paul was a celibate all his life. He might also have been a widower". (L. Legrand,"Virginity in the Bible", *Bible Bhashyam* Vol. III, No.3 (September 1977), P.186). The celibaey is a gift. Legrand states, "In view of this must be said that Christian Virginity is not so much a virtue as a grace, but gift. In fact this was said explicitly by Jesus (Mt. 19:11: "to whom it has been given......." and by Paul (1 Cor 7:7 "each has his own particular gift from God........)". (*Ibid.,* P.190).

Celibacy is understood as a gift from God. It involves the charismatic gift of self-control. According to Kottackal, "God grants many charismatic gifts to his church. But He distributes them "dividing to each one severally as he wills" (1 cor 12:4-11). All these gifts are not intended for all Christians. The entire self-mastery as to the sexual life is a charismatic gift which Paul had from God". (Joseph Kottackal, "Pauline Teaching on Marriage", *Bible Bhashyam, Op. Cit,* P.219). The celibate life is encouraged by Paul in order to have an undivided loyalty to the Lord and to avoid the distress and the tribulation in the flesh.

The Pauline understanding on sexuality and marriage affirms the normative rules such as indissolubility of marriage, sanctity of sex and fidelity in marital life. But he also sensed the context in which these norms are broken and that the persons were undergoing normal crises. So he was also realising the need of the evaluative perspective. He uses agape in the cases or the experience of the people (which are posterior) in order to help them as mercy, love and care are shown in a generous way. He was aware of the need of aposteriori agapeic perspective and applies it as an evaluative approach, even when he advocates the norm.

5. The Sexuality and Marriage In the Non-pauline Writings and Apocalypse

The non-pauline writings do not have much material on sexuality and marriage. so also the Apocalypse. The Apocalypse talks about the bride and the bride groom (Christ and the church) and the celestial marriage banquet. The imagery of marriage in the book of Revelation is of a highly esteemed marriage. This whole section deals generally on the understanding of sexuality and marriage from the non-pauline writings, and the Apocalypse of John.

(i) The Introduction to the Non-pauline Writings and Apocalypse

According to Edmond Hiebert, the non-pauline writings complement the pauline writings.[240] (D.Edmond Hiebert, *An Introduction to the Non-Pauline Epistles,* Chicago; Moody press, 1966, P.20). They constitute comparatively a minor part of the New Testament. Hiebert states, "while each of the New Testament writers gives us his own distinctive emphasis and apprehension of the Gospel message, there is yet perfect harmony between them". (*Ibid.,* P.21). The writers have presented the truth in different perspectives with regard to their context.

These epistles mirror the conditions of the church during the latter part of the apostolic era, except James.

(*Ibid.,* P.21). The developing evil and false doctrines were in prominence in the church context and social context. The context of these epistles and book of Revelation is mostly non-Palestinian. They were written mainly to the scattered Jewish Christians. (Donald Guthrie, *New Testament Introduction,* Leiceser ; Inter-varsity press, 1970: P.791). The Epistle of James tries to correct the understanding of faith. For him faith involves action or good work. The context of I Peter was the persecution of the Church. II Peter, Jude and Johannine epistles were written in the context of moral decay and false doctrines among the members of the Church. (D.Edmond Hiebert, *Op.Cit.,* P.23). The context of the book of Revelation is also the persecution of the Christian Church by Rome. The moral decay was also found from the Churches of Asia Minor, which is portrayed in this book. (Michel Wilcock, *The Message of Revelation,* Leicester ; Inter-varsity press, 1973, P.22).

(ii) The Issue of Sexuality and Marriage

Though the references are scanty, the non-Pauline writings and Apocalypse deal with the sexuality and marriage. The general epistles or the non-Pauline are taken as a group, and the book of Revelation constitute another Section.

(a) Sexuality and Marriage in non-Pauline Writings

The first epistle of Peter (3: 1-7) deals with the husband and wife relationship. Wives are advised to submit to their husbands. They are also depicted as the co-heirs of God's grace. According to Edmond P. Clowney, the Christian wives are urged to submit to their husbands, especially to their non-Christians husbands, since they are God's elect. This is asked to do for Christ's sake. Peter presents this submission as an adornment to women. The role of the wife with an attitude of modesty gives her an opportunity to display Christian love and humility.

(Edmond P. Clowney, *The Message of I Peter,* Leicester ; Inter-varsity press, 1990, PP.128-129).

Apostle Peter brings the example of Sarah who was submissive to Abraham. The husbands are asked to honour their wives (1 per 3: 7). Apostle Paul also writes in Ephesians that the husbands should love their wives. Though the women are supposed to be physically weak, both husband and wife are spiritually equal, being equally destined to inherit eternal life. (C.E.B. Cranfield, *I and II Peter and Jude: Introduction and Commentary*, London ; SCM press Ltd., 1960, P.92).According to Cranfield, "there is the true foundation of the emancipation of the women. Where it is recognized that husband and wife are spiritually equals, there is an end of domestic tyranny." (*Ibid.,* P.92). In the context of Greeks and Romans, the women do not share in the worship. William Barclay commented that even in the Jewish synagogue they had no share in the service. But Christianity has revolutionized the existing attitude that women had equal spiritual rights. (William Barclay, *The Letters of James and Peter,* The Daily Study Bible Series, Bangalore ; Theological Publications of India, 1981, P.223).Though the subordination was urged by Peter from the wives he elevates the women to honour and high esteem as they are co-heirs of God's grace.

The second epistle of Peter talks about the lust (epithumia) and the 'walk after flesh' which might be sodomy (2: 10-14). (Michel Green, *2 Peter and Jude,* Tyndale New Testament Commentaries, Leicester ; Inter-varsity press, 1983, P.103). Commenting on 2 Peter 2:14, Michael Green states, "they lust after every girl they see; they view every female as a potential adulteress." (*Ibid.,* P.111). The heretics rationalized the fornication and prostitution and coloured them as sacred. (*Ibid.,* P.110). The false teachers and false prophets brought in the wrong concept of sexuality which is condemned by Apostle Peter.

The pleasure seekers have distorted the sacredness of sex. The normative element regarding the sexuality and marriage is highly stressed by Petrine writings.

The apostle Jude portrays the immorality that is committed by the fallen angels (6-8). The unnatural sex was their sin. The sin of Sodom and Gomorrah was homosexuality. The unnaturalness of angels can include the going after women. (*Ibid.,* p.167). The immoral acts were punished by God. Jude does not show any favour for immorality whether committed by human beings or angels. The immorality is dealt with seriousness.

The Johannine epistles do not say much about sexuality and marriage. The I John 2: 16 talks about 'lust of the flesh', This indicates the sexual sin. It involves lax in morals. (William Barclay, *The Letters of John and Jude,* Bangalore ; Theological Publications of India, 1981, P.57). The distortion of sex which lacks personal commitment and where love seems to be an empty, mocking illusion, says David Jackman. (David Jackman, *The Message of John's Letters,* Leicester ; Inter-varsity press, 1988, P.63). The sexual immorality which perverts the sacredness of sexuality is challenged by the epistles of John.

It is evident that the non-Pauline epistles provides a sane sex order based on the normative principles which reacted against the sexual immorality like fornication, adultery, homosexuality and very inner attitude of lust.

(b) Seuxality and marriage in Apocalypse of John

The Book of Revelation also does not entertain the sexual immorality. This is quite evident from the messages to the Churches of Asia Minor.

The Church of Pergamum (Rev. 2: 12-17) was warned to get away from the Balam's teaching of Balak. It is none other than fornication. (Leon Morris, *Revelation,* Tyndale New Testament Commentaries, Leicester ; Inter-varsity press, 1983, P.67). In the case of Thyatira (2: 18-29), they were condemned to tolerate the adulteress woman who induces others to practise immorality. The sexual looseness and the immoralities of kind are quite seriously dealt with in the book of Revelation. The unchastity is never tolerated. The immoral are ones to be cast out.

The Book of Revelation also has a high regard for marriage. The heavenly marriage banquet, and the bride and bridegroom concept (Christ and Church) are also used as a powerful imagery which elevates the sanctity of marriage (Rev. 19: 4-9). The celestial marriage is the embodiment of the marriage which takes place here and now. The epistle to Ephesians portrays this fact. The union between husband and wife is described as a sign of the celestial one. (*Ibid.*, P.226-227).

The Book of Revelation gives high importance to the normative principles or apriori rules in the issue of sexuality and marriage. The sexual sins are criticized and the immoral ones are warned vehemently. The marriage also has a very elevated position for the author of the Book of Revelation. It signifies the covenantal relationship of God and mankind. The eschatological marriage reflects the significance of marriage in God's mind.

6. A Comprehensive BIBLICAL View of Sexuality and Marriage

In the Old Testament the sexuality is regarded as sacred and it is found as the gift of God. The original intention of God about marriage is seen in the book of Genesis (Chapter 1 & 2). The male and the female are to unite together in love to form a family for procreation and to live as husband and wife. They are to live as companions which is a life long friendship. Monogamy is the Old Testament pattern of marriage. The covenant fidelity is also very much upheld by the Old Testament. By affirming the normative, the sexual immoralities like pre-marital sex, extra - marital sex and homosexuality are condemned. The evaluative perspective (aposteriori-agapeic approach) is also found applied in the Old Testament in the cases of polygamy, divorce, adultery and prostitution.

The pentateuch, the poetic literature and the prophetical literature give high esteem of the normative principles of sacredness of sexuality and fidelity in marriage. The adultery and the lust for immorality are criticized by the Old Testament. The steadfast love and covenant fidelity are expected from the marriage partners. The cultic prostitution and the illicit sex are questioned by the Old Testament prophets. Amos was very particular about the corrupt practice of cultic prostitution. Malachi talks of about the wife of the covenant that marital fidelity was emphasized by him. The major prophets were also deadly against the sexual immortality. They gave extreme importance for marriage. The poetic literature especially, the Proverbs talks about the undivided loyalty of the partners to one another. It does not encourage polygamy. The Song of Songs emphasizes the purity of love among the lovers. The sexuality and emotional attachment are elevated to an honourable place by Song of Songs. It discloses the fact that the sexuality is not to be suppressed, but it is a subject of high importance to be used responsibly. On the whole, the Old Testament upholds the sacredness of sexuality and marital fidelity. The chastity is expected by the Old Testament.

The gospels are very much concerned of the issue of sexuality and marriage. The covenant and fidelity which is rooted in the Old Testament term 'hesed' which plays a very important role in this regard. Sexuality is sacred and it should not be misused before or after marriage. The pre-marital and extra-marital sex are found to be against the norm. The homosexuality, lesbianism and other sorts of loose sex are considered as sexual immorality. Sex is to be responsibly used in the family (husband - wife) relationship. The fourth gospel and Acts of the Apostles also never condone the sexual impurity. The woman caught in adultery is told to 'sin no more'. Jesus admonished those who look at girl with lustful eyes

The study of gospels and the Book of Acts reveal that marriage is instituted by God and it is indissoluble. The divorce is against the norm or apriori principle.

In the issue of marriage, breaking of marriage bond is allowed by Jesus only in the case of unchastity, that is infidelity. The marriage is a life long relationship. Paul clarifies that remarriage is possible only when one of the partners dies. While the partners are living, no one is permitted to marry another. In the case of divorce, the remarriage is not permitted. This implies that as a norm marriage is not to be dissolved. The marital fidelity should be kept intact till the end of their life by the husband and wife.

The Pauline writings also warned against the misuse of sex and the sexual perversions. The pre-marital sex, homosexuality, and adultery are not tolerated by Paul as they are violations of the norm. The marital fidelity is also urged by him. As the apriori principle the divorce is not permitted, so also the remarriage. Remarriage is allowed only when any one of the partners dies. In the case of unbelieving partner also Paul allows the divorce. The role of the perspective of agape (aposteriori-agapeic approach) has found relevance in his perspective. The 'Pauline' privilage' in the case of the separation of the unbelieving partner (divorce is allowed in this case), Paul makes use of pragmatic, contextual and agapeic approach.

The non-Pauline writings, the Acts of the Apostles and the Book of Revelation also emphasized what is normative in the issue of sexuality and marriage. They challenge sodomy, adultery and lust. The illicit sex was vehemently criticized by them. The marriage is honoured by these writings. The whole New Testament writings highly regard sexuality and marriage. The sexual distortions like lust, fornication, adultery, pre-marital sex, homosexuality and incest are considered as evil. As an apriori rule the polygamy, divorce and remarriage are disallowed.

Jesus was well aware of the social structure of the time. So he gave serious attention to the socio-economic factors. It was very clear that 'do not commit adultery' is the norm. This apriori rules have to be kept up by everyone. But Jesus was showing love and mercy which is integral to his concept of forgiveness. So Jesus had accepted the Samaritan woman and applied the evaluative perspective of agape. The aposteriori-agapeic approach is found in the ethical perspective of Jesus. It is important to note that the aposteriori-agapeic dimension of ethical approach is not rejected by the New Testament. In the New Testament records we see the crucial role of agape in which it is used as an evaluative.

Chapter 4

Attitude Towards Sexuality and Marriage in the Indian Context

This chapter deals with the different perspectives on sexuality and marriage exists in the Indian context. The perspectives of different religious traditions, the tribal communities, the personal laws and the impact of secularization are considered in this study.

A. The Social Changes In India-A Survey

The Indian Society is rapidly changing because of the industrialization, technological development and urbanization. This also has resulted in the secularization of values. The traditional understanding of values are being challenged. The social change also has affected so much the perspectives on sexuality and marriage. This section deals with the social change in India.

The so called modernization is one of the important thing to be discussed over here. According to B. Kuppuswamy, "It involves a transformation of social, political and economic organizations." (B. Kuppuswamy, *Social Changes in India*, Delhi: Vikas Publishing House, 1975, P.54. Hereafter, *Social Changes in India*). Modernization involves the educational facilities. It will also speed up the urbanization and the value system is also affected by it. (*Ibid.*, PP. 55-56.)

According to Kuppuswamy, the western education also has brought a big change in the outlook. Urbanization is usually referred to as the change brought by the British. (*Ibid.*, P. 58). It has influenced our dress, style and education. The western education has promoted rationalism. According to Kuppuswamy, "The humanitarian outlook among the westernized elite led first to social reform movement and later on the Independence movement. They were acutely aware of the existing social evils like child marriage, taboos against widow remarriage, seclusion of women, hostility to women education, untouchability, taboos against inter-caste marriage, inter-caste dining etc. (*Ibid.*, P.58)

The urbanization brings several problems in the society. City comprises of diverse cultures, religious and professions. (Ram Nath Sharma, *Indian Social Problems*. Bombay: Media Promoters & Publishers, 1982, P.17. Hereafter, Ramnath Sharma, Indian Social Problems). According to Ramnath Sharma, the features of the society includes the absence of community feelings (In the villages there is a feeling of oneness, and it might be a homogeneous community), no family unity, moral laxity (The lack of community feeling and family unity and kinship coupled with bad effects of the western civilization have resulted in the fall of moral standards. Due to the high density of population, it is easy to lead a life of anonymity in the city. Therefore, there is considerable increase in the incidence of pre-marital and extramarital sexual relations. The easy availability of vulgar entertainment and sex-oriented literature in the cities contribute to moral laxity), marital problems (In the cities the average age of marriage is quite advanced as compared to rural areas. There is no strict institutional control or restraint on pre-marital and extra-marital sex. Many young men and women prefer to stay single as this affords greater freedom and scope to their aims and activities. In cities the incidence of both love marriage and divorce is more than in the villages. In cities there is commercial sex-oriented entertainment and professional men and women are available to cater to the specialized sex needs of people. This obviously contributes to and complicates marital problems). (*Ibid.*, PP.17-19). According to Sharma, the heterogeneous community also will shake the orthodoxy of any culture. The new and different ideas may come in and this will lead to gradual relaxation of the rigidities of the culture. Particularly it can lead to liberalization of views with regard to sex and marriage.(*Ibid.*, P.21). In Ramnath Sharma's words, "The young people begin to mistrust the old ways and question the reasonableness of traditions and customs of their ethnic groups. Due to meeting and exchange of ideas between different groups which hold permissive and non-permissive sex mores respectively, the family ties are loosened and people dare to flout the orthodoxy of their groups." (*Ibid.*, PP.21-22). According to Sharma, "In villages marriage is considered to be an institution and is regarded a sacrament. But in cities family is more of an association than an institution. It is considered to be like a contract entered into for mutual profit and gain." (*Ibid.*, P.24).

One of the main characteristics of urbanism is that the institutional norms are not effective in controlling or regulating the social behaviour of the urbanites. (D.R.Sachdeva and Vidhyabhushan, *An Introduction to Sociology*, Allahabad: Kitab Mahal, 1979). According to Sachdeva and Vidya Bhushan, "Industrialization and specialization have brought in workshop and factory. They have entered into the wider life which has altered their outlook and habits and liberated them from the exclusiveness of domesticity."(*Ibid.*, P.464).

The technology and communication also affects the society and bring social change. According to Sachdeva and Bhushan "Mechanization has changed not only the economic structure of Society but has also led to a steady devaluation of old forms of social organization and old ideologies." (*Ibid.*, P.464). In their opinion, "Our attitudes, beliefs and traditions have crumbled before technological advance. The spirit of craftsmanship, the divine ordering of social classes, traditions regarding the spheres of the sexes, the prestige of birth all have felt the shock of mechanization. Take a familiar example of the status of women in the industrial age. Industrialism has destroyed the domestic system of production, brought women from the home to their earnings. It has meant a new social life for women." (*Ibid.*, P. 654).

In the words of Kuppuswamy, "It is true that the wheel, the pot, the compass, gunpowder, the printing press, the steam engine, the telephone, the motor car, the radio, the aeroplane and now the atom bomb, have certainly brought about many changes in the society." (B. Kuppuswamy *Social Changes in India,* P.106).The technological factors will bring social and cultural changes. Kuppuswamy states, "still in a broad way we can say that technological developments have brought about many changes in attitudes, beliefs and even in traditions. There is no doubt that the modern factory, the railway carriage, the bus, the restaurant etc., have brought about changes with respect to caste and class behaviour." (*Ibid.*, PP.106-107).

The communication and transportation also have contributed a lot for social change. These elements helped the easy exchange of ideas, enhanced the social relationships, assisted the progress of the sense of universal brotherhood, breaking the barriers to cultural isolation, help to have information and knowledge. (Sachdeva and Vidyabhushan, *Op-Cit* p.646-647). The books and the cinema have influenced the minds of the people. It has brought several changes in the concept of sexuality and marriage also.

The influence of culture is very significant for bringing social change. It has been argued that "there is an intimate connection between our beliefs and our institutions, our valuations and our social relationships. The social and cultural are so closely interwoven that cultural change involves social change." (Sachdeva and Vidyabhushan, *Op-Cit.*, p.658). The transformation of class structures, the breaking up of traditional family system and the disintegration of social nearness are some of the consequences of changes in technology which appear to be the enemy of our culture."(Sachdeva and Vidyabhushan, *Op-Cit.*, p.659).

The tribal communities of India have also undergone social and cultural changes. Among them, "changes have been brought about chiefly by ecological factors, religious changes, education, means of communications, modern technology in respect of agriculture and medicine, industrialization, political changes and changes brought about by government policies and programmes." (M.M.Thomas, R.W. Taylor, eds, *Tribal Awakening,* Bangalore: CISRS, 1988, p.51). Their religion or belief has been largely influenced by Hinduism, Islam and Christianity. Many tribals have turned to Christianity thinking that it may help to fill up the vacuum in the process of change by supplying the tribal with ethical and spiritual guidance. *(Ibid.*, P. 59). The industrialization has brought several changes in the tribal society. "Industrialization also brings other problems involving immorality, drinking and other vices. These constitute a challenge to the tribal people." (*Ibid.*, P. 70). The industrialization in the tribal belt has resulted in the loosening of their traditional social codes and tribal disciplines. (*Ibid.*, P. 72). According to M.E. Prabhakar, "The transition from the traditional to the modern, has deeply affected the tribal people. The modernization processes involving radical politico-economic and technological changes have shaken the foundations of the tribal value systems, social structures, morality and life styles." (M.E. Prabhakar, "Editorial Note", *Religion and Society.* vol . XXXIX, No.4. (December, 1992.)

It is quite true that the transition which is being brought in the Indian sub continent by the industrialization, technological development and the urbanization have positively and negatively affected our society. The traditional values and concept of institutions are challenged. The traditional understanding of sexuality and marriage has also undergone several changes.

B. The Sexuality And Marriage in the Indian Social Setting

This is only an analysis of the forms of sexuality and marriage exist in India today. It also will deal with the use and abuse of sex and marriage. The existing trends in the area of sexuality and marriage are also our concern. It is important to note that the social change has contributed several positive and negative elements in the sphere of sexuality and marriage. The village community is not very much affected by the social change. The social change has reflected more in the urban communities than in the rural communities. The tribal communities are also affected by the social change.

In a study conducted on the transition of family pattern in India, the following reference is made on marriages in the villages. According to the study, "In marriage caste rules are very strictly observed and intercaste marriage are almost unknown. Violating caste rules in marriage means the severe penalty of social ostracism. The usual practice to marry outside one's own village is upheld by the belief that a woman far from her parents' home can be better controlled. It is also required by group exogamy sanctioned by religious and social customs." (P.D.Devanandan and M.M. Thomas, eds, *The Changing Pattern of Family* India, Bangalore: CSIRS,

1966, P.44). Marriages are mostly arranged, and parents try to get their daughters married as soon as they reach puberty. (*Ibid.*, PP. 44-45). "The number of love marriages and divorces is negligible in most villages in India." (Ramnath Sharma, *Indian Social Problems.*, P. 294). But today because of the communication facilities and exposure to the other world, the rural communities are also undergoing several changes. This is evident in the perspective on sex and marriage also.

1. The Traditional Forms of Marriage

The sexuality and marriage can, traditionally, be understood in several ways in India. The endogamy and inter caste marriages, the polygamy and monogamy, the polyandry and polygyny, and the consanguine marriage are some of them.

(i) Endogamy and Inter-caste Marriages

The caste system and its rigidity advocated for endogamous marriages. According to B. Kuppuswamy, "The person of a particular caste has to marry only within that caste. He cannot be married either above (pratiloma) or below (annuloma) except by breaking the caste rules. A man of higher caste could marry a woman of the lower caste according to Manu. But a man of the lower caste could never marry a woman of the higher caste." (B. Kuppuswamy, *Social Changes in India.*, P.173). He states again that "The Mahabharata describes a number of inter-caste marriages. Santanu, the progenitor of the kuru-pandavas first married Ganga and later Satyavati, a fisher-woman, both outside his caste. Manu has classified and named the offspring of annuloma (higher Varna man marrying a lower Varna woman) and pratiloma (Lower Varna man marrying a higher Varna woman) marriages and all that possible combinations of the marriages, indicating that during his time inter-varna marriages were prevalent. He was one of the social thinkers who forbade such marriages." (*Ibid,* P. 183-184). In the caste endogamy, the marriage should take place within the caste, and in the tribal endogamy no one can marry outside ones own tribe.

The endogamy is common in Indian context. According to V.V. Prakasa Rao and V. Nandini Rao, "In the traditional Indian Society, an individual was not allowed to interact socially with certain castes. The members of each caste and sub-castes were to marry within their own endogamous group. Since marriage regulations govern all other regulations, the caste system has made marriage an indispensable and inseparable bond."(V.V. Prakasa Rao & V. Nandini Rao, *Marriage, The Family and Women in India, New Delhi:* Heritage Publishers, 1982, P.107).The inter-caste marriages were rare in the olden days, since they were not even promote by the society. But today we see a gradual change as the love-marriages are coming to the scene. The endogamous nature is enhanced by the arranged marriage system.

(ii) Polyandry and Polygyny

Polyandry is the 'form of marriage where one woman marries more than one man at a given time'. (Sachdeva and Vidyabhushan, *Op.Cit.,* P.291).According to Sachdeva and Vidyabhushan, the Todas of Malabar are supposed to have this institution. There is fraternal polyandry and non-fraternal polyandry. The fraternal polyandry is a 'form of polyandry one wife is regarded the wife of all brothers who have sexual relations with her. The children are treated as the offspring of the eldest brother. Among the Todas polyandry is fraternal." (Sachdeva and Vidyabhushan *Op.Cit.,* P.291). In the non-fraternal polyandry 'one woman has many husbands with whom she cohabits in turn. It is not necessary that these husbands be brothers.' (Sachdeva and Vidyabhushan *Op.Cit.,* P.291). The polyandry is found among the Todas of Nilgiris. In the opinion of Kapadia, the old Nair families had followed the polyandrous marriages, since the conjugal rights were extended to certain others other than the husband also. He observes also that among the Todas of Nilgris the polyandry is prevailed. (K.M.Kapadia, Marriage and Family in India, 3rd edn. Calcutta: Oxford University Press, 1966. PP.79-87).

Though the polyandry is not widely existing among khases today, it is found among them at Jaunsar Bawar pargana of Dehra Dun district in Uttar Pradesh. When the eldest brother marries, his wife is regarded as the wife to his younger brothers also. When the younger brothers marry, their wives are also considered as the wives of all. (*Ibid.*, pp. 63-64).It is true that the wives are common to all, but they are primarily the wives of the one who married them. It is observed that polyandry of the non fraternal type was found among the Nairs of Kerala. (*Ibid.*, P.76). Polyandry is also found among Iravans and Kammala caste in Malabar. (*Ibid.*, P.85). Polyandry is also found among Monpas and Gallongs of Arunachal Pradesh and Sherpas of Nepal. (S.M.Dubey, *Family, Marriage and Social Change on Indian Fringe,* eds S. M. Dubey, P.K. Bordoloi & B.N. Borthakur, New Delhi: Cosmo Publications, 1980 P.17).

The Gonds are found in Madhya Pradesh, Maharastra and Andhra Pradesh. (Christoph Von Furer-Haimendorff., *Tribes of India,* Delhi: Oford University Press, 1980. P.14). The kind of marriage that they follow is endogamous. Polygyny is practiced by the Gond tribes. (*Ibid.*, P.166). The disadvantages of polyandry are also pointed out. It adversely affects the health of women because of the same has to satisfy the sexual desire of several husbands. (*Ibid.*, P.166).In a polyandrous society, divorce is easy to get.(Sachdev and Vidhyabhushan, *Op.Cit.,* P.292).

The system of polygyny is that one husband and many wives at a time. According to Sachdeva and Vidyabhushan,

"Under this system one man has two or more wives at a time. Polygyny is generally called polygamy, but strictly speaking the latter is a general term including both polyandry and polygamy." (Sachdev and Vidhyabhushan, *Op.Cit.,* P.292).Polygyny is found among Hindus and Muslims in India. (Sachdev and Vidhyabhushan, *Op.Cit.,* P.292). It is observed that the polygamy became a practice to obtain more children as numerical superiority is an important factor in the context of war and agriculture. It is also found that in the Himalayan ranges of India, they marry many times in order to protect their property and to obtain help in their agricultural activities. (Ramnath Sharma, Introductory Sociology, Meerut: Rajhans Prakashan Mandir, 1986. P.315).

(iii) The Monogamy

This is one man and one wife system. "Under monogamy one man marries one woman at a time." (Sachdev and Vidhyabhushan, *Op.Cit.,* P.294). Monogamy is the widely accepted marriage. It is very much prevalent among Indians. The Lepchas tribes of Kalimpong are monogamous in their marriage. The Lepchas are living around Kalimpong in Darjeeling district of Bengal and in Sikkim. (S. M. Dubey, P.K. Bordolai, *et al., Family Marriage and Social Change in Indian Fringe, Op.Cit..,* PP. 48-51).The Lalungs (Tiwas) who are found in Due district of Nowgong, Assam also practiced monogamy. The Chorais of Tipra in Tripura are now-a-days strictly following monogamy. (*Ibid.,* p.101).

(iv) Arranged Marriages

Traditionally the marriages are arranged by parents and relatives. "Usually parents (in collaboration with the elderly Kinsmen, friends, or occasionally 'go betweens') start planning their children's marriage well ahead of time. Upon the decision as to when they should get married, the parents initiate, scout around and negotiate with the other potential party for a prolonged period of time."(V. V. Prakasa Rao, V. Nandini Rao, *Marriage the Family and Women in India,* New Delhi: Heritage Publishers, 1982, P. 219). Altekar feels that in the vedic period, probably, the marriages were arranged by parents. There were also references about brides choosing their own husbands he added. (A.S. Altekar, *The Position of Women in Hindu Civilisation*, Delhi: Motilal Banarsides Publishers. 1991. P. 65). P.D. Devanandan and M.M. Thomas also observe that the parents arrange marriages for their daughters, especially in the village set up of India. (P.D. Devanandan & M.M. Thomas, *The Changing Pattern of family in India,* Bangalore: CLSRS 1966. P.44. Hereafter, The Changing Pattern of Family in India).

2. The Traditional Perspective on Sexuality

Gandhiji was fully aware of the conjugal relationship in marriage. He advocated for sexual union only to reproduce and not for the sake of lust. He was never against the sexual instinct, but was totally against the fulfillment of lust. (P.A. Gangadhar, *Mahatma Gandhi's Philosophy of Brahmacharya,* Delhi: ISPCK for CISRS, 1984. P.15). The sexual act is only for reproduction in the context of marriage may be a misconception evident among many men and women in India. Of course, this notion has been changed later. But this view still has a greater impact on people. The homosexuality, pre-marital sex, and extra-marital sex were not traditionally accepted by our society. According to Sachdeva and Vidyabhushan, "As such in Hindu marriage there is no room for romantic love as the basis of marital selection. There is no room for courtship, because the younger people never see each other before marriage." (Sachdeva and Vidhyabhushan, *An Introduction to Sociology,* P. 299). Sex is regarded as sacred, and any abuse of it was condemned by the society. There society followed certain principles or norm in the issue of sexuality.

The women also live with unfulfilled desires. Her sexual fulfilment is not considered by men. The attitude of men to woman is portrayed like this by a women journalist. She goes on to say that when man gets his opportunity he avails of it as hurriedly as he can leaving his wife sexually, roused, unfulfilled and often pregnant. (J.L.Gupta, ed., *Challenges to the Fair Sex,* Delhi: Gian Publishing House. 1988. P. 21). Through the weapon of sex, the male ascendancy is also affirmed, it is argued. (*Ibid.,* P. 21). Sati is also a dehumanizing ritual in which the female sexuality and its rights are neglected. The economic gain that prevent the patriarchal community to leave the widow for remarriage and to have a fair sexual life. The idea that woman was created for the pleasure of man also promotes the view that she is only the property of the husband· (Malladi Subamma, *Women: Tradition and Culture,* New Delhi: Sterling Publishers, 1985. P. 9). Hereafter, Malladi Subamma, Women: Tradition and Culture.

This also will enable to have a negative outlook of men over female sexuality. Malladi Subbamma has depicted the traditional view of men on sex in the following words: "She has to serve her husband sexually with a pleasant face even when, in reality she is in a sorrowful mood." (*Ibid.,* P. 10). Her interest, choice, satisfaction and the mood are not taken seriously. She becomes a sex idol before husbands.

Malladi Subbamma states that "The superstition that intercourse with a girl of immature age will cure several diseases like gonorrhea and syphillis also contributes in no small measures to the offense of rape." (*Ibid.,* P. 22). This illustrates how trivially the men did treat the female sexuality. The personality of women and girls are not considered along with their sexuality. A dualistic understanding on the personality and sexuality of women by men resulted in the abuse of female sexuality. It has been exploited by men for their selfish motives.

According to Malladi Subbamma, the women have several misconceptions about sex. According to her, "Many women are startled when sex is mentioned; some became confused. Yet others shiver in shame. A few get elated. The rest trembled with fear." (*Ibid.,* P. 73). In her words the women are exhibiting an antagonistic feeling towards sex. Malladi Subbamma argues that this antagonistic attitude of women towards sex is developed since men provides no freedom and equal status to women. (*Ibid.,* P. 73).

According to Subbamma, "Avoiding sex and adopting celibacy as a means to attain salvation (Moksha), leading a sex life only for begetting children, treating sex as a step in furtherance of salvation, craving for just sex without any conjunction of love and affection are all stray paths." (*Ibid.,* p. 76).She condemns the practice of one partner using the other partner as a tool. (*Ibid.,* p. 76). She was trying to rectify the misconceptions about sex in our society.

Chidananda Das Gupta analyses the traditional concept of sexuality in India as follows: "In India and a lot of other countries, sex is more moral for men than for women; In a number of Arab and North African countries, the clitoris is cut out in childhood in order to make sure that sex can be enjoyed by men but not by women." (Chidananda Das Gupta, "Indian Daughter- in-law in Chains", *Challenges to the Fair Sex,* edited by J.L. Gupta. Gian publishing house. 1958 P. 25).The sexual morals in the Indian society usually affects badly the women than men. The traditional view projects that the sexual fulfilment of women is given least importance.

3. The Traditional Perspective on Marriage

In ancient times India had the child marriages. But later the child marriages were abolished. According to Ms. Popati R. Hiranandani, "Usually an Indian groom feels it is a favour to marry a woman. Due to this misconception the demands dowry and then the aftermath follows like a logical corollary." (*Ibid.*, P. 76). According to her, marriage restricts the freedom of movement of the girls as she is treated like a slave. (Popati R. Hiranandani, "Lust for Life", *The Illustrated weekly of India* (May 3, 1987), P. 38).

The dowry system has distorted the sacredness of sex and marriage. The material motives reduce the value and significance of sex and marriage. According to V.V. Prakasa Rao and V. Nandini Rao, "Traditionally, it was customary for rich and royal families not only to give the bride as a gift at the time of marriage but also to accompany her with small and formal gifts in cash, land, and for ornaments. These gifts were hardly called dowries in those days as they were presented after the marriage as a symbol of pure affection and love on the part of brides parents. Since the medieval period a number of cases are observed where the amount of dowry demanded has reached alarming proportions in various parts of the country." (V.V.Prakas Rao and Nandini Rao, *Marriage, Family and Women in India,Op.Cit.* P. 224). The original intention of dowry was gone, and it was reduced to become a corrupt practice. Today the sanctity of marriage is challenged by dowry. The money, land and ornaments have taken the place of the sanctity of the marriage. Marriage is reduced to a business which brings profit. To the poor, the marriage has become a burden.

The remarriage was traditionally approved by our society. According to Malladi Subbamma, "Our culture has delineated the ideological structure necessary for binding a woman hand and foot in all sectors of life, including social, economic and moral. It was sanctimoniously stated that a widowed woman cannot be purified by hundred baths. She too should die along with her husband, or she has to end her life otherwise." (Malladi Subhamma, *Women: Tradition and Culture,* P. 76). The oppression over a widowed woman leads her to think that dying is better than living. She is also forced by the relatives of the husband to commit sati because of economic gains.

Subbamma has portrayed the marriage in the Indian situations as follows: "She is compelled to purchase her husband with money. Thus, marriage is not a union of minds, not of affections, and not of individuals; it can be safely affirmed that marriage is between two families, same castes and two layers of status. (*Ibid.,* P. 12). Looking for economic gains and status, the original intention of marriage is sometimes lost.

The divorce cannot be sought by women in the traditional understanding. Subbamma states, "Society looks at a woman who seeks divorce with dismay and disgust. The abhorrent feelings of the society in this respect are beyond description. Even in the case of adultery, the society calls the woman depraved and downfallen. She is compared to a broken pot. But the same attitude is not shown towards a man. He is unblemished. He can marry, beget children and be blessed with happiness. There is the greatest inequality. There is the greatest injustice to women. If the woman is barren efforts will be afoot to get the husband to remarry. But then, a woman who seeks divorce on the ground of impotency of her husband and who longs for motherhood becomes an outcaste in any society." (*Ibid,* P. 32). The sexuality of women and her aspiration for fulfilment is not usually considered by the society. There also we see the double morality where women are not treated humanly by our society.

The traditional marriages are endogamous. The inter-caste marriages were not promoted. The marriages are also, traditionally, arranged by the parents. (P.D. Devanandan and M.M. Thomas, eds., *The Changing Patterns of Family in India,* P. 44). But today, the traditional understanding of marriage is undergoing major changes.

4. Problems in Sexuality and Marriage

The elements of disorganization are playing a dominant role in sexuality and marriage in the Indian context. The rape, the dowry, child marriages, prostitution, devadasi system, divorce, sati and incest are some of the most important aspects of disorganization in the context of sexuality and marriage.

(i) Rape

Rape is a violence over female sex by men. It can also include the child molestation. It is said that the number of rape cases the country as 2,00,000 per annum. (*Malladi Subamma, Women: Tradition and Culture,* P. 21).Usually the poor women become the victim of rape. Rape as an offensive sexual act is very much increasing in our society. According to Malladi Subbamma, "No doubt, grave offenses like rape were committed in the old days. But they are growing in number now." (*Ibid.,* P. 21).While talking about the violence over women Aruna Gnanadasan includes the rape in police lock up and sex forms of torture of women prisoners. (Aruna Gnanadasan, "Women: Violence and non-violence", *Violence / Non-violence,* edited by D.W, Jesudas. Madras: Gurukul Lutheran theological college and Research Institute, 1989.P.4).

It is calculated that a rape is taking place in 54 minutes in India. Many rape incidents are not reported. It is a great threat to Indian womanhood. According to P.N. Premalatha, "Half of the Indian humanity the sisterhood of society has been deprived of self respect and is victim of a number of disabilities such as poverty, destitution, unemployment, unfavourable economic situation ill-treatment and neglect, dowry and woman battering, sexual harassment and eve-teasing, above all the most cruel act of rape." (P.N.Premalatha, *Challenges to the Fair Sex,* edited by J.L. Gupta, Delhi: Gian Publishing House, 1988, P. 17).

Premalatha again explains, "Rape is a crime committed by men upon women. In this act, men are the criminal and women are the victims." (*Ibid.,* P. 17). According to section 375 of Indian Penal Code Rape is that:

1. a man has sexual intercourse with a woman against her will,
2. without her consent,
3. with her consent when her consent has been obtained by putting her in fear of death or hurt.
4. with her consent, when the man knows that he is not her husband and that he is another man to whom she is or believes herself to be lawfully married, and
5. with or without her consent when she is under 16 years of age. (*Ibid.,* P. 18-19).

The rape is classified into two. "There are two types of rapists. The motive of the first group is sex desire only. The other is motivated by an impulse to punish and hurt the victim rather than by sex desire. Gang rapes of deceits, rapes on Harijan women, rapes on women during communal riots and other disputes, and rapes during war all come under this group" says Premalatha. (*Ibid.,* P. 19).

The female sexuality is abused or used by using force by men. This is a very dangerous phenomenon. This is a selfish attitude which even inflicts pain and shame. It brings humiliation to women. Their chastity is taken off by the rape. There are some incidents of rape from different places of India. At Pudukottai, a village in Tamil Nadu, a man around twenty five years old raped a number of women irrespective of age and caste. He entered the house with a knife and raped whoever was there. In another incident a man was murdered by his wife in an attempt to rape his daughter. This kind of incestual rape is also evident in the Indian setting. In the year 1985 at

Wynad (Kerala) a 16 year old dumb tribal girl was raped by the employer."'In Delhi, in January, 1984 three ten years girls were kidnapped and they tried to rape them." (*Ibid.*, P. 20-21). In the case of sex offense like rape, it is understood that there are Psychological factors like emotional disturbance and the exposing to the severe emotional deprivation in childhood also contribute very much. (Stanton Wheeler, "Sex offenses. A Sociological Critique", *The Sociology of crime and Delinquency,* 2nd ed. edited Martin E Wolfang. Leon and Savitz *et al.* New York: John Wiley and Sens, 1970 P.627).

The rape is a common sexual crime in the Indian society. The police, the military men or even parents or relatives cannot be exempted from the issue of rape. In the year 1989, Hasina, a 11 year old girl was lured to Bombay by one of her relatives on the pretext of enhancing the household's income as her father passed away. She was raped and entered into a world of prostitution. (Payal Sing, "The Damned", *The illustrated weekly of India* (June 7, 1987), P.9). The report as follows, "she now faced the tragic reality of stepping into the sordid world of adults. Hasina was raped and thus began her initiation into prostitution. Night after night, the 11 year old child was sexually abused." (*Ibid.,* P. 11). She was sold by her uncle to a brothel owner in Kamathipura in Bombay. The sexual violence, that is, rape is an inhuman act. This is an abuse of human sexuality.

(ii) The Prostitution

Prostitution is having sexual intercourse with a person (not her husband) who offers money for the service which may be coital or extra-coital. The girls may trade their sex for food, entertainment, gifts, money or fulfilling her sexual desire. (Ramnath Sharma, *Indian Social Problems*, Op.Cit., P. 251). The sexual intercourse with a prostitute is transient and impersonal. (*Ibid.,* P. 255). The institution of prostitution is a business today. It has become an exploitative structure where the sexuality of girls and women is abused. The brothel owners are making it a means to get money. Many girls are even deceived and brought to the brothel. They are sold to the brothel owners.

The different types of prostitutes in India are the call girls (independently operating prostitute), the sex workers the street walkers and brothel prostitutes. According to the analysis of Sharma, in India poverty is one of the main factor responsible for prostitution. It becomes the means to earn livelihood. It also can become the means to sexually gratify the employers to get employment. The women who are not remarrying because of the social stigma and the irregular sexuality which unable to satiate the desires also lead to prostitution as a resort. (*Ibid.,* P. 265-67). There are social and economic factors behind the aspect of prostitution. "In a survey of prostitutes in Pune by Vilas Wagh, a Pune based researcher, it was discovered that more than 60% of the women were dalits," (Jean D Cunha, *The Legalization of Postitution,* Bangalore: Word makers for CISRS 1991, P. 2). says Jean D' Cunha. According to Jean D' Cunha, "patriarchy is defined as man's control over woman's sexuality, fertility/reproduction and labour power." (*Ibid.,* P. 14). Women are understood as the sex object and their sexuality is being exploited by the patriarchal structure of Indian Society.

In the words of Jean Cunha, "The double standards of male sexual morality extend to all males as an expression of class and/or male power. Patriarchal society defines male honour in terms of his conduct in public life and permits him the freedom to formulate his own rules in matters of sexuality. It allows him access to sexual pleasure in varied forms and with several women." (*Ibid.,* P. 16). According to her, the society creates the institution of prostitution outside marriage to cater men's diverse sexual needs. (*Ibid.,* P. 16).

The female sexuality is exploited with money by male dominated society. The seamen, businessmen and military men depend on prostitutes to gratify their sexual urge. The tourism industry also makes use of the service of women. This is to attract the tourists to our country. The intention behind is also material gain. The female sexuality becomes an attraction for tourists. The sexuality of women becomes a means to safeguard the national 'interest' that is the material gain. (*Ibid.,* P. 24-25). The female sexuality is sold by women to overcome poverty and to survive, and on other side female sexuality is exploited for the sexual gratification by men. The women also abuse their sexuality to gain money or even as an entertainment.

The inhabitants of Aruvakode in Calicut District is situated three miles away from Nilambur. They are traditionally involved in the craft of pottery. But today they indulge in one trade that is selling themselves. It is the 'flesh trade' or 'meat trade'. The children are also launched into the flesh trade from the age nine. For they say, If we labour in the field we get just Rs. 25. In this job we make Rs. 25 in ten minutes. They earn Rupees 100 to 1000 per day. Their men are lazy and alcoholics, but women involve in prostitution. The men will act as pimps. (*Indian Express* (Indian Express weekend) Kochi edn. (August 3,1991) P.1).Everyone is involved in this business the men and women alike. The men may be using their women's sexuality as a means to gain money. This enables the men to evade from their responsibilities and to involve in carousing, card-play and other entertainments. The deception and selfish motive of the patriarchal society is very much evident here. The men and women devalue the sanctity of both sexuality and marriage by promoting prostitution. The economic benefit is the motive behind the practice of prostitution in this regard

For Jean D' Cunha, prostitution is a thoroughly exploitative practice. She states "prostitution is an institution in which prostitution racketeers, degenerate police officials and vote catching politicians have an economic and political stake and the emotionally impoverished client gratifies his ego and sexuality." (Jean D' Cunha, "Power for the Pimp, Penalty for the Prostitute", *Indian Express,* Kochin edn. (Oct. 5, 1986). P. 8). She continues to say that, "it is an institution fostered by sexist values which sanction and tolerate the abuse of women. Even when voluntarily pursued, prostitution is an exploitative, money spinning market in which the commodities are sex and women's bodies." (*Ibid.*, P. 8). Jean D' Cunha is quite critical of the system that promotes the prostitution. Prostitution will only accelerate a unequal and unjust society.

According to Páyal Sing, almost twenty percent of the prostitutes in Bombay are minors. Kamathipura in Bombay city is the red light street over where around 50,000 prostitutes and, several girls were brought to prostitution who are minors and not yet attained puberty. The minors are forced into prostitution due to rape, abduction, incest or the devadasi system. (Payal sing, "The damned", *The Illustrated weekly of India* (June 7, 1987). P. 10-11). Merlyn Lobo Brito tells the story of a young man who married a girl from Andhra Pradesh without any dowry. The young girl, Basamma was taken to Calcutta after marriage, She was cheated by her 'husband' as she was taken to a brothel and sold her for Rupees ten thousand. (Merlyn Lobo Brito. "Prostitution", *Indian Womanhood Then and Now,* edited by Jessie B. Tellis-Nayak, Indore: Satprakashan Samachar Kendra. 1983, P. 101). The poverty or the economic factors also contributes to prostitution which is to be considered when someone blames the prostitution in the name of morality.

The sexuality is exploited and the concept of marriage is distorted by our society through the institution of prostitution. The consumerism, commercialism and other exploitative trends have promoted the sexual abuse of women. The poverty also contributed to the prostitution which is to be considered when someone blames only the prostitution in the name of morality.

(iii) Devadasi System

The devadasis were the temple dancers. They were dedicated to god or goddesses by their parents. Later, because of the corrupt system, the devadasis become the prostitutes. In Karnataka in the Yellamma temple, the devadasis have to come out in naked in the day of festival. It also has become the practice that the girls were given to god. or goddesses in order to avoid the financial burden involved in marriage. It can be a way to save the money that is given as dowry. The socio-economic factors play a key role in the Devadasi system.

Payal Sing explains that the devadasi system perpetuates the primitive practice of dedicating girls between the approximate ages of five and nine, to Goddess Yellamma. Then the waiting period begins. When the girl attains puberty, a 'bidding' ceremony is arranged and the girl is 'given' to the highest bidder. After which entering prostitution seems to be the next step. Almost 15 per cent of the prostitutes in Bombay are Devadasis. Whereas in the bordering towns of Karnataka and Maharashtra the percentage of Devadasis is as high as 80 to 90 per cent. (Payal Sing, "The damend", *The Illustrated weekely of India*, (June 7. 1987) P. 10.

The devadasi system has degenerated to a sex exploitation and sex service. The abuse of sexuality is evident in it. Chandrika Naik also reports of devadasi prostitution link from the Halvagal Village in the Bellary district of Karnataka. The Harijan women of the village cannot marry as they are termed as devadasis. These women are sexually exploited by the upper caste men. If they give birth to daughters, they also should become devadasi prostitutes. (*Indian Express,* Kochin edn. (January 5, 1994). P.9). This system in that village was followed only for exploiting the sexuality of the Harijan women.

According to Usha Rai, "The young girls dedicated to the Goddesses were among the most attractive in the village for the needs of the Goddesses could only be propitiated by the purest and the best. But, slowly the system was corrupted. As payment for the temple service became erratic, the girls became the mistresses of the priests and the 'important' and wealthy men of the village. (*Indian Express,* Kochin edn. (April 27, 1994). P.9.

The devadasi system became a means to exploit the female sexuality and to promote the institution of prostitution. The devadasi is to clean the temple and to do service in the temple. But she has been abused by the priests and the wealthy. The sacredness of sexuality is neglected by this system. The womanhood become an object of sexual exploitation because of the corrupt social structure. In the devadasi system women are only the victims of the social system

(iv) Sati

The practice of Sati is a means to dismiss the remarriage of the widows. It is an inhuman act imposed on the Indian women by the corrupt and the selfish society. It is a threat to humanity, especially, to the sexuality and marriage. Seeing the injustice involved in it, Raja Ram Mohan Roy and the Serampore Missionary, William Carey had insisted the Government to abolish it. Sati was abolished in 1829. But Sati continued even after the legal decree.

Sati was not affirmed by the Hindu Scriptures. Mahabharta, the vedas or the Dharmasastras are not advocating for sati. The earliest written scriptures of Hindus did allow the widow remarriage by the brother of her dead husband. (M.P. Joseph, "*Suttee: A Critique from an Ethical Perspective*", SATHRI Journal (No. 1/1993). P. 67). Sati was supposed to be encouraged to show the devotion to the husband. But the underlying fact is that by her self immolation, the money she has brought will not go to another man, if she remarries it will go to her new husband. This was the selfish motive behind insisting sati.

The male domination and the selfish motives of the patriarchal structure create the practice of sati. "According to the epic *Ramayana,* Sita agreed for the fire ordeal under coercion by her husband who was afraid that Sita's sexuality had become polluted due to the presence of another male. Her husband's demand represents the general brahiminical view regarding women's sexuality as a cause to the well-being of the society. Apart from the firm containment and stringent control of women's sexuality, the Sita model created a perversive ethics in which the woman's body itself represented a potential danger to the society, a sin," says M.P. Joseph. (*Ibid.,* P.74). Merely eulogizing women's chastity and restricting the women from remarriage is a deception to her sexuality and womanhood.

The Sati Seva Sangh is trying to promote sati. They also organize the Rajputani girls for committing sati. They deify by adding religious colour to those commit sati. According to Indu. B. Nair, "In 1973 an instance of 'sati' shocked the very machinery of the government of Rajasthan. The complaint was that though already informed the police did nothing to prevent it. This 'sati' was performed in the presence of a crowd of 70,000 people, a part of whom had come from the neighbouring villages." (Indu B. Nair, "Unmasking the Faces of Death stories from the lives of Indian women", *Struggle Against Death.*, by the editorial Board, Kottayam: W.C.C. Vancouver Assembly Study Group, 1982 P. 75-76). There are sati temples in Bombay, Calcutta, Manipur, Delhi and Hong - Kong. Indu B. Nair comments that woman is only a property of man, and if the husband dies before the woman she is considered cursed. Indu B. Nair goes on to say that, "the best way for her is to die with him, jumping into his pyre. As a widow is discouraged by her own family as there is no one to give her a new life, death may seen most desirable." (*Ibid.,* P. 76).

In 1987 September 4, one of the shocking incidents of sati was reported from the village of Deorala in Rajastan. The wife of Mann Sing, Roop Kanwar, a 20 year old girl, declared her intention to commit sati with her husband. She got on to the funeral pyre of the husband and put her husbands head on her lap. She was cremated along with her husband. The people cheered 'sati mata ki jai' (Up, up mother sati)· (C.V.V. Raghavan, "Shocking Sati", *Frontline,* (Oct. 3-16, 1987), P. 101).It is interesting to note that this superstitious and inhuman practice has become an entertainment and religious 'rite' for many. The struggle of woman in the particular social structure has to be considered if she is not committing sati. She had to undergo physical and psychological torture.

(v) Child Marriage

In olden days, Child Marriages were common in India. According to V.V. Prakasa Rao and V. Nandini Rao, "Age at marriage has varied in India's history of nearly 60 centuries starting from 4000 B.C. to the present. During this period, the range of age at marriage varied anywhere from six years to nearly 20 years." (V.V. Prakash Rao & V. Nandini Rao, *Marriage: The Family and Women in India,op, cit.,* P. 43). Under the special marriage Act in 1954, the bride and bridegroom should have 18 and 21 years respectively. (*Malladi subbamma, Woman: Tradition and Culture,* P. 83).Talking about the negative aspect of child marriage Prakasa Rao and Nandini Rao says, "with regard to the negative functions, it has been observed that early sexual union is harmful to the development of the females. Little freedom of choice in the marriage is allowed for the young people." (V.V. Prakasa Rao, Nandini Rao, *Op.Cit.*, P. 44).

Though the child marriage is abolished, it has come up in a new form. It is observed that in Hyderabad alone several marriages took place with Arab husbands and girls who have not even reached their puberty. The marriage has been reduced to a game for them. Most of these Arabs try to exploit the sexuality of the girls and see it as a game. The value and significance of marriage is neglected by them. Most of these girls are deserted later on by the Arabs. Farzana of Hyderabad was 13, and married to a 40 year old Arab. His love and romance was short lived. It was only for 18 months and now she is back in Hyderabad with her parents. The minor girls namely Nasreen and Shabeen were also abandoned by their Arab husbands. (*Rasheeda Bhagat, "I Want to Cry Sometimes..", Indian Express*, Kochi edn. (July 14, 1993), P. 9).

Poverty and dowry are the main reasons for this kind of marriages. The Arabs give a few thousand to the parents of the girls, and half of the money would go to the pocket of the middle men. (*Ibid.,* P. 9).This child marriage is an oppressive structure which promotes the exploitation of female sexuality, and it devalues the sanctity of marriage. According to a report in 1985, in Rajasthan, thousands of children were married in keeping with the ancient tradition. An investigation report states that in Rajasthan, in the year 1984, there took place around 25,000 child marriages.(*Indian Express,* (April 28, 1985), P. 7).

Though the child marriages are abolished by the Sarada Act in 1928 (after Mr. Harvilas Sharada, the architect of this legislation), it continues even today. According to a report from Rajasthan in the year 1987, thousands of children were married in Marwar. When these children reach 14 or 15, the marriage has to be consummated. (*Indian Express,* (Express Magazine), (May3, 1987). It is also reported that the child marriages are common in the Malappuram District of Kerala State. It was interesting to note that a pregnant girl aged 10 was brought to the Malappuram District Hospital for delivery. (*Vanitha* (Malayalam Weekly), (Feb., 24, 1994). P. 25)

Child marriages are not uncommon in India. It is practised in several parts of India. Ameena, 11 year old girl from Hyderabad was married to 60 year old Arab Yahya al Sagish, and was deserted, but was rescued. (*Frontline* (Aug., 31-Sept., 13, 199) pp. 24-25, see also *Indian Express* (Feb., 24, 1985) P.5. The aspiration to get their girls married to rich men is one of the reasons for these kind of marriages. It is the socio-economic factors and other selfish motives that promote the child marriages.

Conducting marriage of the children (having no knowledge about sexuality) is to be condemned. The Arab husbands are, of course, marrying the Indian girls for the sake of sexual pleasure. They are the exploiters. The parents give their children to Arabs husbands for economic gains. We cannot reject the socio-economic factors in the issue of child marriages.

(vi) Dowry System

One of the important factors that undermine the value and sacredness of sexuality and marriage is the dowry system. It is one of the worst evils of our society. The marriage is settled depending on the dowry the parents of the girl give. Bargaining over the dowry is common in India. The girls who are from the poor economic background suffer very much since they would be the marginated ones in the marriage market. According to V.V. Prakasa Rao and V. Nandini Rao,

Marriage is such an important personal, religious, and social event that the exchangé of gifts has become an institutionalized custom in India for many centuries. Traditionally, rich and royal families not only gave the bride as a gift at the time of marriage but also accompanied her with small gifts in cash and or ornaments. These gifts were not called dowries in those days as they were presented after the marriage and as a symbol of affection and love. As long as the dowry system was voluntary, it was not a financial obstacle to marriage. Since the medieval period however, dowry demands have increased significantly in parts of the country. (V.V. Prakash Rao & Nandini Rao, Marriage, *The Family and Women in India*. P.61)

Dowry Prohibition Act was passed on 1961 which sees the demand for dowry as offence.

"According to Altekar (1962) there are no references either in Smrithis or Dharmas to the dowry, though Smrithis recommended that the bride should be given in marriage alone (sic) with suitable ornaments, but their number and price are left entirely to the discretion and the ability of the bride's father," (*Ibid.*,P. 80). says V.V. Prakasa Rao and Nandini Rao. In the words of Prakasa Rao and Nandini Rao, "The practice of dowry had become so rigid that parents who owe low on the socio economic scale find it hard to secure partners for their daughters." (*Ibid.,* P.80).

Indu B. Nair narrates the story of a girl named Sashikala who was burnt alive in Delhi on the 26th of June 1981. Sashikala was a graduate of Delhi University and was married to a manager of local business concern. Soon after the marriage the mother-in-law was demanding more dowry. She was later sent home to bring money. She brought only some money which was borrowed by Sashikala's poor parents. Two days after her return, she was burnt alive. The case was registered as 'Suicide'. (Editorial Board for study programme, *Struggling Against Death,Op.Cit.,* P.71). According to a report, in India on an average, two thousand young wives are being murdered by greedy husbands. (*Ibid.,* P. 72).

The dowry deaths are common in India. It is done in the guise of accidents or suicide. The crimes are committed by the husbands and the mothers-in-law. These dehumanizing activities are undermining the dignity of sexuality and marriage. Dowry system devalues the importance of the sexuality of women, and the role of women in marriage. Reflecting on the evils of dowry system Malladi Subbamma says, our idea is that women are created for the pleasure of man, and they should purchase their husbands with money. (Malladi Subhama, Women: *Tradition and Culture,* P.9, 12).

(vii) Divorce

Divorce is one of the main element of disorganization in the family and society. Divorce is common in all communities. The impotence, the drinking or drug addiction and psychological disorders can be the reasons for divorce. The extra-marital love and sex also can lead to divorce. The prosecution like the wife beating also lead to divorce. The marital fidelity and responsibility from both partners are important for a successful marriage.

Shaji P. Jacob brings the history of some of the divorces. Radha discovered her husband who was an engineer, but was sexually impotent. Omana divorced her husband since he had a schizophrenic disorder. (Kala Kaumadi, (Malayalam Weekly), (May 22, 1994), P.15-16).There were also divorces since the husband found dissatisfaction in the beauty of his wife. The economic status also may lead to divorce. Suhra divorced her husband as his family was not economically sound. (*Ibid.,* P. 15-16). (According to Sreedevi, the family court judge, the tendency to divorce is more in the economically self sufficient youngsters. (*Ibid.*, P. 21).

Moncy Joseph reports that in the years 1993 and 1994, around 1500 divorce cases were registered in the Trivandrum (Kerala State) family court alone. This gives the picture of the increasing trend towards divorce. (*Vanitha,* (December 1-14, 1994) P. 4). The partners are not worried about divorce as in the olden days. Divorce even for simple reasons (issues like beauty or economic status, or educational status) is to be condemned. The sacredness of sexuality and marriage are disregarded by the divorces without sufficient and reasonable cause.

S. Pothen, Government New Girls College, Indore (Madhya Pradesh) has made a research on the Hindu Society at Indore about the divorce. Several number of divorces have taken place among Brahmins, Vaishyas and Jains. The reasons for the divorces, according to her analysis, are cruelty of the husbands, the interference by the in-law, lack of tolerance of young Indian women because of modern education and employment and the illicit sex of husband or wife. (S. Pothen, "Divorce in Hindu Society", *Journal of Comparative Family Studies,* vol.XX. No. 3, (Autumn, 1989), PP. 379, 383).

The controversial Shariat and 'Talaq' provide room for the Muslim men to divorce their wives for any reason. The original intention of 'Talaq' might have been distorted by the community. 'Talaq' is a unilateral act, that only men could exercise the 'Talaq'. Several Muslim women were divorced irresponsibly. The marriage of the minor girls from Hyderabad and the consequent divorces by the Arabs and the famous Shah Bano case are the supreme examples for this.

(viii) The Sexual Harassment and Exploitation

The sexual harassment and sexual exploitation are increasing. The unemployment among women and their desire to get job tempt them to fall on the trap of the immoral rackets. They may be led to the brothel or the world of blue film where they have to expose their sex. They may be even ditched by many by promising them to offer job.

M. Madhu reports the story of a girl named Aswati who was enticed by Fatima and led to Madras offering a good job. There was no job given, but Aswati was induced to commit immoral acts (The sexual act with the men for money). There are also rackets which organize women by offering job in gulf. They also undergo sexual exploitation. They are being cheated and sexuality abused. (*Vanitha,* (December 1-14, 1992) P. 15-16).

It is also reported that the working women of this country are undergoing sexual harassment from the male bosses and colleagues. Ranjana Sengupta exposes the stories of several working women who have suffered from the sexual harassment. The sexual harassment involves amusement, condemnations, dirty jokes, touching, leaning over, putting an arm around a woman colleague, telling stories with sexually explicit anecdotes, repeatedly inviting a woman to the cafeteria despite her persistent refusals and demanding that a woman colleague work after office hours whether work pressure exist or not. (Ranjana Senguptha, "Sexual Harassment: The 9 to 5 Menace", *Indian Express* (Sunday Magazine Section I), (October 27. 1991), P. 1) This is, of course, a great threat. Sexual harassment is a sexual exploitation of women.

The tribal female labourers are brought by the agents to the city and are given only low wages. They are economically and physically exploited. They have to live in a hut with very limited facility. Moreover, they are also sexually exploited. According Sushama Sahay Prasad, "It is not uncommon for a tribal female labourer to be locked up and beaten up if she refuses to yield sexually to her employer of local toughs. Apart from being raped by contractors, young tribal girls have to face same fate at the hands of local hoodlooms. Sometimes even the Sardanis (female labour agents) force tribal girls into prostitution." (Sushama Sahay Prasad, "Economic and Physical Exploitation of Tribal Female Labourer", *Challenges to the Fair Sex,* Op.Cit., P. 77).

Sexual harassment of the working women and the sexual exploitation of the children and female labourer are common in the Indian context. The female sexuality is seen as an object to be exploited for pleasure.

5. The New Trends in the Area of Sexuality and Marriage

Despite the traditional forms and perspectives on sexuality and marriage, there are new forms emerged. These forms must have been found in our context in some forms. But today the homosexuality, the lesbianism, pre-marital sex, lover marriages and the gay culture have come in an organized manner, and they even found the approval among at least, some sections of the society.

(i) The Love Marriages

In Indian society, especially in the rural areas the people have a very negative look towards love marriages. The arranged marriages are given more approval by the society. Because of the westernization and the social change in India, the men and women assert their right to choose their partners. According to V.V. Prakasa Rao and V. Nandini Rao, "One of the eight forms of Hindu marriages recognized by the Smritis is Gandharva which involves a love marriage between two consenting parties, even in the early vedic period, instances are observed where young men and women had opportunities to move about freely which resulted in love marriages." (V.V. Prakasa Rao and V. Nandini Rao, *Marriage, the Family and Women in India,* Op.Cit., P. 221-222).

A study among the students reveals that the reasons for an affirmative response to love marriages can be categorized as freedom of choice, intimacy and understanding. (*Ibid.*, P. 222). The love marriage also enhances the inter-caste and inter-religious marriages. According to a research the love marriages disregard allegiance to caste and even to religion and race. (P.D. Devanandan and M.M. Thomas, eds, *The Changing Pattern of Family in India,* P. 83). It states again that "Love marriages are gradually gaining more recognition and respect, at least in certain sectors of the population." (*Ibid.*, P. 85).

(ii) Pre-marital and Extra-marital Sex

Prof. Paul Sachdev had conducted a study among the students who are below 21 in some colleges in Delhi. According to this research, it is revealed that the young men no longer place a premium on the virginity of a bride. Three - fourths of the male students favoured the sexual freedom for women. A third of the male students had experienced pre-marital sex, but only a quarter of the women had lost their virginity. (Usha Rai, "Students see Little in Virginity", *Indian Express.* Kochin edn., (December 1, 1994), P. 17).

'India Today' magazine and MARG had conducted a research among the college students of India, it exposes the trends among the students. 35.5% of the male students and 15% of the girls who come under the survey agreed that they have regular dating. About one-third of the students are in favour of pre-marital sex. The survey was done among 13, 865 selected students. (*India Today,* (Malayalam) (Jan. 21-Feb.5, 1994), PP. 28-30). The tendency towards the premarital sex is on the increase and we see an erosion of the traditional values.

Another study conducted in Madras to know the sexual habits of the people. It is revealed that out of 10,000 subjects interviewed on sexual habits, about 40 per cent had either pre-marital or extra-marital sex. 31.04 per cent admitted that they had their first sexual intercourse between the age of 15 and 20. Around 40.64 per cent said they had sexual intercourse between the age of 15 and 20. The prostitutes, blood relatives, persons of the same sex, and neighbours become the sexual partners to them. The incest was noticed in this sexual promiscuity. Dr. Narayana Reddy, who exposed the study report states that there is one person indulged in sex with his daughter. About 80,000 subjects who had been married, and eight per cent out of them resorted to extra-marital sex. About 71.93 per cent of the subjects also involved in masturbation. *Indian Express*, Kochi edn., (December 2. 1993), P. 11). The studies reveal that the pre-marital sex, the extra-marital sex, incest and the masturbation are very much rooted in our land. It is observed that the children who did not get the parental love and undesirable domestic conditions lead to extra-marital sex or adultery. (Ramnath Sharma, *Introductory Sociology*. Meerut; Rajhans prakashan Mandir 1962. P. 530).About pre-marital sex, it is found that it is opted as a means to express sexual freedom, (Usha Rai, "Students see Little in Virginty", *Indian Express,* (Kochi edn.) December,1, 1994 P. 17).or it is done as a means to please their boy friends by girls, other wise they are afraid that they may loose them. (Elizabeth B. Murlock, *Adolescent Development,* New York: Mc Graw- Hill Book Co., 1973. PP. 288-289). It is clear that the social factors also contributes to the act of pre-marital and extra- marital sex.

(iii) Homosexuality and Lesbianism

The research done at Madras by Narayana Reddy reveals that homosexuality is also not rare among the people. Over two per cent had sex with persons of the same sex, all of them were males." (*Ibid.*, P.11). The urchins and the girls of the ladies hostel are partners of homosexuals and lesbians. This observation is from a study conducted in Ahmedabad. The marriages are solemnized here. The gays are very much in the scene. (*Indian Express,* Kochi edn. (September 14, 1993), P. 9). The homosexuals and the lesbians are asserting their rights, and they are even dared to come out openly. According to Stanley Thomas, "Forced to suppress their sexuality for long, Indian homosexuals are slowly but surely emerging from the claustrophobic cocoon. They had been forced into by a disapproving society." (Stanley Thomas, "In search of an identity", *The Week* (Nov. 28, 1993), P. 37).

The gay culture which goes beyond the normal homosexual relationship also is coming up in India. The gay partnership also is also found in India. The gay partnership crosses beyond the bed room and it may permeate the entire life. (*Ibid.*, P. 38). According to Ashok Row Kavi, a leading gay activist in India, estimates that there are over 40 million homosexuals in India. (*Ibid.*, P. 39).

There are also reports about the gay kingdom from Bangalore. Those who search for jobs are seduced and end up in the bed room of the homosexual for money and job. B. Vijay was forced to become a gay on his rich partner promised that he loves him and live forever with him. But was later cheated, since Vijay found that this richman has other partners too. (M. Gautham Machaiah, "The Gay Kingdom" *Indian Express* (Indian Express Sunday Magazine) (February 20, 1994), P. 9). A Muslim boy from Hyderabad was also initiated into the gay community as he was searching a job.

The Homosexuals and lesbians are organizing themselves and they involve in the sexual activities. The seduction is also used as a means to get people for their sexual pleasure.

The homosexuality, the lesbianism and the gay issue have psycho-social reasons also. According to prof. M.S.

Thimmappa of the Bangalore University, who is a psychologist, "homosexuality can be due to either genetic pre-disposition or because of emotional experiences incurred during childhood." (M. Gautham Machaiah, "The Gay Kingdom" *Indian Express* (Sunday Magazine February 20, 1994), P. 9).

(iv) The Single Woman and Divorce

It is also a new trend that the women in India choose to remain single. They do not want either to marry or to marry legally. Some girls are having their aims and aspirations in life, so they indefinitely postpone the marriage. They even don't care about it. There are also certain men who also have this same excuse. The women do not want to endanger the aspect of freedom through marriage. Some women divorce their husbands and remain single as they are fed up with the married life. There are women who do not see husband as an essential factor for their life. A girl named Pushpa was not even willing to take the risk of cohabitation but to remain single all through her life. (*Vanitha* (August 1-14, 1995), P. 33-35).

According to Suresh Nambath, "The general view among women activists is that women are better off outside of marriage." (Suresh Nambath, "The Invisible Women", *Indian Express* (Sunday Magazine) (Feb.27, 1994), P. 10). The women feel that once married it is a life long struggle for them and to shake off the dependence on male is not easy. The settlement of divorce is always delayed in their view. The conference of women's association at Tirupathi advocated for alternative sexuality. Lesbianism is almost accepted by them as one of the alternatives. (*Ibid.*, P. 10).

Malladi Subamma argues for the motherhood of the unwed girls. She states that the woman has the right to decide whether the father of the child shall be her life partner or not. (Malladi Subamma, Women: *Tradition and Culture,* P.98). Having sexual intercourse with men and beget children through illicit sex by the unmarried and the divorced ones are affirmed by Malladi Subbamma. There are also women who would like to remain single without children. The employment and the economic stability of the girls provide more courage for the girls to divorce their husbands. The aspect of forbearance is not very much seen among the girls today. The reasons like drinking violence (e.g. wife-beating) and quarrel with the mothers-in-law are even causing divorce. (*Vanitha* (December 1-14, 1994). P. 7). Today, poor education, infertility, insufficient income etc. can also be the reasons for divorce. (S. Pothen, "Divorce in Hindu Society", *Journal of Comparative Family Studies,* vol. xx, No. 3 (Autumn, 1989), P. 384).

Traditionally, the remarriage was not accepted. But today remarriages are being approved by the society. Shaji Jacob reports of a girl from Trivandrum divorced her husband and she remarried on the same day when the divorce was allowed by the court. He reports of another girl named Rama who has divorced her husband, and married another without much delay. Another man complained about the beauty of her wife and divorced her. He married another college student. (*Kala Kaumadi,* (Malayalam Weekly) (May 22, 1994), P. 17-18).The divorce and remarriage in the name of impotency, beauty, educational status, financial status or sexual dissatisfaction are common today in India. The hesitation towards divorce or remarriage is not seen very much among the men and women today.

(v) Child abuse or Molestation

The child molestation is a grave issue in the Indian context today. The children are sexually used and abused by the men and women. As already indicated the girl children are the ones widely used in prostitution. A new trend in sexuality is that children (boys and girls) are undergoing molestation. The so called love towards children is usually referred as paedophilia. In a recent report the paedophiles are found in Goa. (Rashmi saksena, "Sex Tourism", (cover story-child prostitutes) *The Week*, August 4, 1996. P. 36). It is noticed that paedophiles from Britain, America, Germany, Australia and the scandinavian countries are coming to third world countries in the garb of tourists to have sex with girls and boys. (*Ibid.*, P. 36).There are two kinds of paedophiles: the preferential and the situational. "Preferential paedophilas are the ones who have clear yearning for sex with children. Situational abusers prefer an adult partner, but find a child less threatening to their self-esteem." (*Ibid.*, P. 37).It can be noted that there are psychological factors also behind the paedophilia.

C. The Secularization of Values and the Sexuality and Marriage

Because of the industrialization, modernization, urbanization and westernization, Indian society had undergone several changes. The rationalism, humanism, and the secularism also have contributed much to the value system. Ethics deals with the values, the ethics of sexuality and marriage also had confronted with there changes.

(i) Defining Secularization

The term secularization was widely used in the wake of French revolution. Napoleon confiscated the vast territories inclusive of the rights and obligations and transferred them to the civil authority. This huge operation is termed as secularization. (Bernard Haring, *Faith and Morality in a Secular age,* Bombay: St. Paul Publications, 1974, P.1). This was termed as secularization since the church's privileges and possessions were all considered to be 'sacred', a transfer to the 'profane' civil society was deemed sacrilegious. (*Ibid.*, P.1). The secular attitudes and views also come from the science and technology, says Haring. (*Ibid .*, P. 6)

According to Harvey Cox, the rise of urban civilization and the collapse of traditional religion are the two hallmarks of this era. He states,

> Urbanization constitutes a massive change in the way men live together, and became possible in its contemporary form only with the scientific and technological advances which sprang from the wreckage of traditional world views. Secularization, an equally epochal movement, marks a change in the way men grasp and understand their life together, and it occurred when the cosmopolitan confrontations of city living exposed the relativity of the myths men once thought were unquestionable. (Harvey Cox, *The Secular City,* Toronto: The Mac Millan Company. 1969, P.1).

Harvey cox feels that secularization undercuts and bypasses religion. It also relativizes the religious world views. (*Ibid.*, P. 2).One of his statement which is noteworthy is that "If secularization designates the context of man's coming of age, urbanization describes the context in which it is occuring." (*Ibid.*, P. 3-4). Urbanization, in Cox's understanding, means a structure of common life in which the diversity and the disintegration of tradition are paramount.

Secularization is a process which is the contribution of science, technology and the urbanization. Secularization is opposed to religionism, says Sachdeva and Vidyabhushan. (Sachdeva and Vidyabhushan, *An Introduction to Sociology,* Op.Cit.., P. 579).The traditional values are also affected by the secularization. The features of secularization are decrease of religionism, differentiation (The differentiation in different aspects of life - the economic, political, legal and ethical questions are separated from each other. Religion does not influence their solution), rationality and scientific attitude (scientific explanations have replaced the religious explanations).

(*Ibid.*, P. 379). According to M.N. Srinivas, "the term secularization implies that what was previously regarded as religious is now ceasing to be such, and it also implies a process of differentiation which results in the various aspects of society, economic, political, legal and moral, becoming increasingly discrete in relation to each other". (M.N. Srinivas, *Social Change in Modern India,* n.p, Orient Longman Ltd., 1977. P. 119). He argues that the tradional concept of sex relations based on caste (traditionally the high caste woman cannot usually have sex relations with an untouchable) system is changed. (*Ibid.*, P. 120).

According to Sachdeva and Vidyabhushan, the causes of secularization are: (1) Modern education - The educated youths tried to find out scientific explanations to the numerous traditional beliefs and practices. The system of co-education demolished several beliefs regarding women's role in society. A secular attitude was adopted towards marriage, occupation and other human activities. (*Ibid.*, P. 580). (2) Development of the means of transport and communication - 'The changes in the modes of transport and communication have increased physical mobility. The inter-mixing of people belonging to different parts of the country led to the removal of much of misunderstanding and growth of liberal ideas. (*Ibid.*, P. 580). (3) Urbanization - The economic problems, fashion, education, urban political and social structure, influence of western culture in urban life and individualism have secularized the urban outlook. (*Ibid.*, P. 580). (4) Social and religious reform movements - The various social and religious reform movements started by Indian leaders like Raja Ram Mohan Roy, Sir Syed Ahmed Khan, Keshub Chandra Sen, Swami Deyanand, Devendranath Tagore and Mahatma Gandhi also encouraged the process of secularization in India. (*Ibid.*, P. 580). (5) Legislation - The Britishers enacted various laws like the widow Remarriage Act, 1856, caste Disabilities Removal Act, 1850, special marriage Act

1872 which attacked the orthodox beliefs of the Indian people. In modern times the Hindu marriage Act, 1955, the Hindu succession Act, 1956, the Hindu Widow Remarriage Act, 1956, the maintenance Act, the Adoption of children Act have led the secularization of the Hindu institution of marriage and family. (*Ibid.*, P. 580). (6) The Indian Constitution - India is declared as a secular republic. Equal rights to all citizens are offered without discrimination of caste, sex or creed. (*Ibid.*, P. 580). (7) Western Culture - The western culture emphasized the materialism, individualism, sensualism, non-religionism and licence. It has influenced the outlook in family relations. The matters regarding sex, marriage and family are not solely determined by religion because of the secularizaion. (*Ibid.*, P. 581).

The secularization also has influenced the values. The traditional values are being challenged. According to B. Kuppuswamy, "One of the chief task of the contemporary Indian society is to bring about a synthesis between the traditional social values and the modern social values." (B. Kuppuswamy, *Social change in India.,* P. 84). According to P.D. Devanandan and M.M. Thomas, the process of secularization in individuals involve giving up of the world view of their traditional culture and taking up another group of ideas. (P.D. Devanandan and M.M. Thomas, *The changing pattern of family in India,* P.104).

2. The Sexuality and Marriage in the Context of the Secularization of Values

According to K.G. Adiyodi, "It is common knowledge that value systems, faiths, beliefs and practices of a society change both spatially and temporally." (K.G. Adiyodi. *"Values in Mad World"*, *Jeevandhara* vol. xxv, No. 149 (September 1995), P. 345) Value system undergoes several changes and it also varies according to the time and space. "Value systems vary not only according to the times but also from religion to religion and even from region to region. Polygamy, for instance, is permitted by Islam under special circumstances, but not by Christianity or Hinduism. In Tamil Nadu, in some Hindu communities, an uncle is permitted to marry his niece. i.e., sister's daughter both of which are unthinkable to a Christian" says Adiyodi. (*Ibid.*, P. 347). There is, of course, the diversity of views and values in the Indian Society. Each community holds their particular norm.

The secularization process challenges the traditional values and ethics. It promotes more room for nationalism, scientific data and individualism. Secularization process even leads to a moral relativity or moral pluralism. The abolitions of sati and the affirmation of widow remarriage are the contribution of the secularization process. The secularization has brought positive and negative effects in the issue of sexuality and marriage. It provided freedom to challenge some of the in human elements, but at the same time it gave room for the sexual promiscuity and the irresponsible dissolution of marriages.

The so called sexual and marriage revolutions are the contribution of modernization and secularization. The traditional concepts of sexuality and marriage have undergone a radical transition. According to A.B. Shah and C.R.M. Rao, the institutions of Hinduism are essentially authoritarian in spirit. They observe that "The modern world view is based on empirical, scientific knowledge and is incompatible with the traditional one on all essential points. It relates ethics to certain basic human urges and looks upon it as a system of norms governing interpersonal relationships." (A.B.Shah and C.R.M. Rao, *Tradition and Modernity in India,* Bombay: Manaktalas, 1965, P.11).It is, indeed quite sure that the traditional authoritarian Hindu institutions are challenged by the secularization.

K.D. Gangrade also analyses the Indian value system and criticizes the anthoritarian structure. He states, "for the traditional Indian value system the authority of the elders and the sanctity of tradition were both supported in opposition to 'rationality' and the right of individual conscience." (K.D. Gangrada, *Crisis of Values,* New Delhi: Chetna publications, 1975. P.5). In North East India also the concept of sexuality and marriage are considerably changed because of the modernization and secularization process. There is sexplosion.

According to a study among the tribals in the North East area, the following aspects have come to the notice. A changed attitude to pre-marital sex, which is not considered to be a taboo. Sexual involvement occurs increasingly in earlier stages of life is another change. The attitude towards sexual morality is guided by subjective or personal morality. Recreational sex mentality is creeping in. People are dared even to have trial or temporary marriages. The consequence of sexplosion includes frequent divorces, teenage marriages and infidelities due to rushed marriages. (Joseph Cilia, "Some Issues of Concern for the Christian churches in the North East", *Religion and Society,* vol. xxxix. No. 4 (December 1992), P. 58-59).

According to Sheela Mohan, counsellor of Trichur family court, the emotional attachment among the husbands and wives is not strong as in the olden days. The women are courageous enough to go for divorce. The life partner concept has changed so much. Even the differences in interests, choice and the behavioural patterns or manners also lead to divorce. This is because the concept of the indissolubility and the sacredness of marriage have come to a fix. (*Vanitha,* (December 1-14, 1994), P. 7). Bigamy is also becoming common. (*Ibid.*, P.8). Vimal Balasubramanyam brings the stories of bigamy. It is observed that the high incidence of bigamy is in Manipur. The bigamists go scot-free since it is difficult for the women to give proof or evidence of a second marriage. (*Indian Express* (Express Magazine) (Jan 6, 1985), P. 2).

The love marriages are being accepted in the society which even transcends the religion or caste. The secularization has given the partners more freedom to decide. There is also a breakdown of joint family where the privacy and the intimacy of the partners are restricted. The sexual activity is only seen as a means to procreate, and not as a means to show their love and belonging together in the traditional family set up. This has been changed considerably. (P.D. Devanandan and M.M. Thomas, The Changing Pattern of Family in India, pp. 83,84,85,87,104).

The secularization has reduced marriage as a social contract. The importance of marriage is being neglected. The girls and boys prefer late marriage. The people also go for love marriage, co-habitation, the inter-caste marriages, the single life, pre-marital sex, extramarital sex, homosexuality and lesbianism. The divorce is common so also the remarriages. (*Vanitha,* (August 1-14, 1995), pp. 33-36; *Kala Kaumudi* (May 22, 1994), pp. 15-24; *India Today* (Malayalam) (January 21-Feb. 5 1994), PP. 28-34). The understanding of sexuality and marriage are so relativized.

The youngsters are involved in dating, and pre-marital sex. The gay culture is also quite alive in our society. (*The Week* (Nov. 28, 1993), PP. 36-42). According to Malladi Subbamma, the modernism condemns, "The idea that woman was created for the pleasure of man, that she is his property, that she should be subordinate to him and that she gets salvation in this world and in after-life only through her husband are being taught to the woman from her childhood." (*Women: Tradition and Culture,* P. 8).

The concept of sexuality is transformed that it is to enhance intimacy, says subbamma. She states,

> Avoiding sex and adopting celibacy as a means to attain salvation (Moksha), leading a sex life only for begetting

> children, treating sex as a step in furtherance of salvation, craving for just sex without any conjunction of love and affection are all stray paths. Appreciating the fact that sex will be useful to bring about or enhance intimacy and for giving the status of a human value at a certain level to the sex act are reflections of a healthy mind. (*Ibid.*, P. 76).

Subbamma is a feminist with very radical ideas on sexuality and marriage. She questions the irresponsibility and the oppressive elements involved in the area of sexuality and marriage.

According S. Pothen, "The tolerance and forbearance of young Indian women for which they are lauded in the past is definitely vanishing due to various factors like modern education, employment and ideas of quality and freedom. Extra-marital relations definitely undermine the very foundation of family and marriage." (S. Pothen, "Divorce in Hindu Society", Journal of Comparative Family Studies (vol.xx, No.3, Autumn 1989.), P. 383). She states that the present studies disclose the fact that there are many cases of extramarital sex by wives and husbands. The negative effect of secularization of values is that it gives more room for irresponsibility and moral laxity in the context of sexuality and marriage.

K.D. Gangrade had studied on the different understanding on sex and marriage by the old generation and the new generation. His study reveals that "the highest percentage of students (36 per cent) were of the view that the boys and girls should be no limitation to the extent of the relationship. With the members of opposite sex it is a personal matter for each individual boy or girl." (*Crisis of Values,* New Delhi: Chetna Publications, 1975, P. 83). About pre-marital sex for the students are having a permissive attitude. Out of 265 students, half of them admitted that marriage is not a must. The reasons are marriage is out of date, marriage is an unnecessary binding with one person and it brings so many responsibilities. In the survey, 46 per cent of the students and 23 per cent parents approved love marriages. The students are found to be more progressive and want to break away from the traditional norms of the society, says Gangrade. (*Ibid.*, PP. 84-87).The study of Gangrade on students reveals that more students from the lower castes than the students of upper castes are favouring the love marriages. It also disclosed that the parents and students are becoming progressive and they favour inter caste, inter religious marriages, inter social strata and inter linguistic community marriages. (*Ibid.,* PP. 88-91). The facts reveal that the students are more progressive in their attitude towards the relationship with the opposite sex. It also reveals that the attitudes and values of the people in India towards sex and marriage have undergone tremendous changes. (*Ibid.*, PP. 88-91).

The research done by V. Narayan Karan Reddy also discloses the fact that the secularization process has influenced so much to the liberal out look to sex and marriage today. (V.Narayana Karan Reddy, *Marriage in India,* Gurgaon: The Academic Press, 1978, P. 39).The marriage can be held even before the legal authority, the room for divorce, the collective marriages provision for re-marriage and love marriages as against the traditional arranged marriages are the contribution of the social change in India, says Narayana Karan Reddy. (*Ibid.*, PP. 40-43).

The secularization of values or ethics have questioned the inhuman practices. Positively, the corrupt, evil and the inhuman practices are challenged by the influence of secularization. In the case of sexuality and marriage also a great change has taken place. Though the attitudes such as the indissolubility of marriage and the monogamy are validated, the bigamy, divorce, pre-marital sex, extra marital sex, homosexuality and lesbianism are being accepted by the society. The sexual ethics has been affected by the secularization process. The positive effects of secularization in the context of sexuality and marriage are that it questions child marriage, and sati.

3. The Influence of Science and Technology on the Sexuality and Marriage

The science and technology have made tremendous changes in our society. With the rise of modern science man has become more and more rational and thereby tried to give a rational explanation of the religious values. (Sajiwan Prasad, "Factors Affecting Religion and Human Development", *Journal of Dharma* (Vol. iii, No.1, Jan-March 1978), P. 20). This has also enabled the religion to come out of its subjectivity and the traditional beliefs which are understood as absolute. According to Sajiwan Prasad, "with the emergence of scientific world-views, man's thinking and feelings have become more and more secularized. (*Ibid.*, p.22). According to him secularization involves changes, great changes, in our attitude to ourselves and to the world. He feels also that the secular man has completely misunderstood religion as he is not realizing the fact that religion also changes with the changing times. (*Ibid.*, p. 24)

In the words of Kuppuswamy, the technological development in India helped for the improvement in the means of communication and transport. It also enabled man to think rationally and objectively about things and events. (B.Kuppuswamy, *Social Change in India*, PP. 110,113). While discussing the challenge of science today, M.G.S. Narayanan opines that "It has been argued that man in modern society is slowly building up new order of life based on a new system of values born of historical experience. A major factor in net-work of natural sciences. (M.G.S Narayanan, "A Historian's Approach", *The Banglore Theological Forum* (vol. xiii, No. 1&2, 1981), P. 23 This whole volume deals with 'the pursuit of truth' and value systems).This has, of course, affected the traditional perspectives on ideas and values. M.G.S. Narayanan writes, "The science oriented modern norm whose mind is liberated from the conventional ideas of God and absolute values will have to confess his limitation, his unenviable predicament where he tries to experiment with the only tool that are available to him, those of natural science and social science." (*Ibid.*, P. 25).

The modern communication medias also has contributed to the social change in India. It also influenced our value system. This is also the effect of the application of science and technology. According to B. Kuppuswamy this communication explosion will bring about changes in attitudes, outlooks and behaviour.. (B. Kuppuswamy, *Social Change in India,* P. 266). A study on the impact of mass media in Kerala reveals that the long term effects of the mass media are that it helped the diffusion of knowledge, new value systems and belief systems on social institutions. (Joseph Velacherry, *Social Impact of Mass Media in Kerala,* Delhi: ISPCK, 1993, P. 245). The positive effect of communication is the availability of information, the correction of the superstitions, and the integration of different cultures and values. The negative effects may include the introduction of the western culture and values. The sexual acts like homosexuality, pre-marital sex and cohabitation are the influence of the mass medias like cinema and television. 'Mast Kalandar' is the first Indian cinema which introduces homosexuality. People like Gore Vidal argues that homosexuals are a minority who suffer discrimination. The 'Bombay Dost' magazine also justifies the gay culture. (Gayathri Sinha, "Bollywood goes gay with abandon", Indian Express Magazine (April 21, 1991), P. 3). These media elements are bringing negative effects in our value system, especially in the issue of sex and marriage.

While talking about the impact of cinema on the society and the value system Manarcad K.M. Mathew states that "Now sex has gone to perversion and violence manifests its most gruesome form. The tragedy is that they have started idealising sex perversions and violence and it moves to an end of no return." (Manarcad K.M. Mathew. "Images of Life and Death in Malayalam Cinema", *Struggle Against Death,* Op.Cit.., P. 56).The influence of video and films also contributes to moral laxity among youths in North-East India. According to Joseph Cilia, the easy accessibility to all forms of films reflects on the youngsters' behaviour: indiscipline and lax behaviour, a gradual loss of respect in boy and girl relationship, interest in pre-marital sex, and disrespect for the sacredness of married life. (Religion and Society, Vol. xxxix No. 4 (December 1992), P. 58).B.K. Ramanujam observes that in the urban areas the advertising media and cinema make an enormous sexual stimulation. (Ramanujam B.K, *"The Indian Family in Transition"*, Social Acttion vol. 22, (Jan-March, 1972), P.23). Girija Rajendran analyses the Indian cinema and states that the male impotency, adultery and extra-marital affairs are openly discussed in cinema. Most Malayalam films do deal with sex as an integral part of the theme. (Girija Rajendran, "Sin Southern Cinema", *The illustrated Weekly of India* (July 17, 1980), P. 31. The sexual excesses and obscene in cinema affects badly the new generation. They are being sexually stimulated and involve in illicit sexual act. These cinema also can form wrong attitudes and perspectives on sexuality and marriage among the youths.

The western science has made a tremendous amount of influence in our society and its values. It also enabled the secularization process in India which abandoned the traditional values and brought in new values. (David L. Gosling, *Science and Religion in India,* Madras: C.L.S. 1976, P. 23). According to Sachdeva and Vidyabhushan, science and technology has made impacts on the social institutions. It has led to the disintegration of joint family system. The employment of women has changed the status of husband-wife relationship and affected the family structure. It has led to liberation of women. Love marriage, inter caste marriage and late marriage are the effects of technology. It has increased the number of divorces. The invention of birth control devices has reduced the size of the family. (Sachdeva and Vidyabhushan, *An Introduction to Sociology,* P. Op.Cit., 649).

The concept of sexuality and marriage has changed very much by the influence of science and technology. According to Joseph Cilia, the facility of birth control devices encourages the pre-marital sex. (*Religion and Society,* vol. xxxix, No. 4 (Dec. 1992), p. 59).The contraceptives and other devices provide room for 'safer sex.' The emergence of Andrology, a new branch of medicine that used surgery to care the sexual dysfunction such as impotency. The impotency affects badly the sexual act and it can even lead to divorce because of the sexual dissatisfaction. Impotency can be Arteriogenic (The arteries supplying blood to the penis do not supply enough cause an erection) Venogenic (The veins develop a leak and hence spill blood, preventing a rigid erection), Neurogenic (Defects in the nervous system), endocrinogenic (Imbalance or insufficiency of sex hormones in the blood stream), or Psychogenic (Problems in the mind). (G. S. Vasu, "Impotence: Shattering Manhood Myths", *Indian Express* Kochi edn. (July 17, 1993), P. 11). The science and technology enable to overcome this dilemma. The modern psychology and the modern medicine have found fruitful means to overcome this serious problem that affects the human sexuality and the sexual act.

The artificial Insemination by husband or donor and the surrogate mother is another technological development that is related to sexuality and marriage. This practice of hiring women to bear child by artificial insemination is on the increase in the west. It is creeping in India also.

(Kusum, "Whose Child is it Anyway", *Indian Express* (February 17, 1985), P. 6). The antagonists of this procedure feels that this might lead to commercialisation and sale of babies. (*Ibid.*, P. 6). Artificial measures are resorted by the childless couples to overcome their sterility. The Invitro fertilization (IVF) is one of the significant ways people resorted to overcome the sterility. The cryo preservation (Cryo Genics) techniques are used for freezing and storing donor sperms. The male may be infertile, and if the wife is healthy and ovulating with no tubal problems, artificial insemination is the best option. (Rasheeda Bhagat, "Cold Facts about Conception", *Indian Express,* Kochi edn. (Sept. 18, 1994), p. 17; Usha Rai", There is no Immaculate Conception", *Indian Express,* Kochi edn., (April 30, 1994), P. 11). There are reports about the test tube babies from Madras and Bangalore. G.G. Hospital (Madras), Apollo Hospital (Madras), Shifa Hospital (Madras) and several centres at Bangalore and Bombay have witnessed to Invitro fertilization. (K. Raghunathan and Jyoti Raghavan, "The Gift and the Grief", *The Hindu* (Hindu Magazine) (Sept. 12, 1993), P.1).

The science and technology have entered into the area of sexuality and marriage. Even the sperm of the donor is received in the artificial insemination. The artificial insemination is through the introduction of the male sperm into the female organism without the normal sexual intercourse. According to George V. Lobo, the renowned catholic moral theologian, the artificial insemination by donor or husband (AID/AIH) will go against the divine plan for the procreation of human life. For him, it completely dissociates procreation from conjugal love. In his understanding, the end of the procreation is to be realized according to human dignity which requires that new life be the fruit of the intimate and exclusive marriage partnership of love. (George V. Lobo, *Current problems in Medical Ethics,* Allahabad: St. Paul Publications, 1980, P. 152). The argument against contraceptives is that it blocks the natural dynamism of the marital act. It also as a barrier to complete intimacy and spontaneity. (*Ibid.*, PP. 131-132).

The science, technology and the area of medical profession should have a human face. Dr. Thomas Kalam is making a crucial comment that "Medicine without clear and conscientious ethical guidelines may be dehumanizing not only to the patients, but also to the medical professionals and scientists themselves." (Thomas P. Kalam, "The Making of an Ethical Doctor", *Jeevadhara,* vol. XXII, No. 132, P. 455). While discussing the issue of artificial insemination, Thomas Srampical has said children are the fruits of the mutual love of husband and wife and every couple longs for them. He states again, "science and technology are supposed to work for the good and happiness of man, and many consider A1 technique to be such a good application of medical technology for the good of the infertile couple." (Thomas Srampical. "Artificial Insemination and Invitro fertilization, *Jeevadhara,* vol. xxii, No. 132 (Nov. 1992), P. 469).

Science sometimes enter into the human life without any control. In the area of sexuality and marriage also it enters and even challenges the importance of sexuality and marriage. But it can help to enhance the love as marriage bond and the science and technology in the form of Artificial Insemination and Invitro fertilization. But at the same time the irresponsible use of science and technology that dominates and manipulates the whole human life may lead to dehumanization.

The issues or the ethical problems such as devadasi system, sati, prostitution, polygamy child abuse, harassment, homosexuality, pre-marital sex, extra-marital sex and divorce are found in the Indian context. The artificial means of reproduction is widely at use. There are also commonly accepted norm or *apriori* rules among each community on those issues of sexuality and marriage. The rules which question the perversions in the context of sexuality and marriage is quite significant to keep up the sexuality responsibility and fidelity in sexuality and marriage.

Though there are clear evidences about the psycho-social and economic reasons behind the issues like polygamy, prostitution, pre-marital sex or homosexuality, there is no proper ethical perspectives based on the principles of mercy, love and concern. From the Christian perspective also what is needed in an ethical approach which would seriously consider the condition of the individuals or communities in the light of the Christian principles of love and mercy.

D. Sexuality and Marriage in the Religious Traditions of India

This section deals with the concept of sexuality and marriage in religious traditions of India. The Indian context is having different religious traditions and they keep up their own idea of sexuality and marriage. Hinduism, Jainism, Budhaism, Sikhism, Parsi religion and Christianity are due dominant religious traditions of India.

1. Sexuality and Marriage in the Religious Traditions

We have in India, mainly the Hindu, Islam, Buddhist and Jainist, Sikh and the Christian religious traditions. These traditions have their own understanding on sexuality and marriage. This survey is only to know the distinctive elements of there religious traditions on sexuality and marriage.

(i) The Perspective of Hinduism

Hinduism cannot be easily defined. It includes several diversified doctrines and beliefs. According to David C. Scott, "Certainly there is no doctrinal and ritual universal to the entire Hindu tradition and what is essential for one group need not be so for another." (David C. Scott, "The Hindu Religious tradition", *Religious Traditions of India,* edited by P.S. Daniel, David C. Scott and G.R. Sing, Calcutta: Indian Theological Library, 1988. P. 75).

In Hinduism there is the goddess concept which is the symbol of life and fertility. They are also the symbols of female principle called 'Shakti'. The fertility symbols, the lingam and Yoni represent the male and female sexual organs. (Raymond Hammer, "Roots: the development of Hindu Religion", *The World Religions* A Lion Handbook, Oxford: Lion Publishing, 1992, P. 173). The sexuality and the related facility have a very significant place in Hindu tradition. Reaching the goal of cosmic consciousness is the goal of Kundalini Yoga. Hatha yoga is one aspect of the Kundalini yoga which helps the body, mind and spirit to come into harmony. (Swami Sivananda Radha, *Kundalini Yoga,* Delhi: Motilal Banarsidass Publishers, 1992, P. 17). According to Swami Sivananda Radha, "Yoga is the oldest known science of physical and mental self development, caring for the body under the intelligent control of the mind. (*Ibid.*, P. 17). For Sivananda Saraswati, Sakti is energy that lies dormant in the Muladhara Cakra in the form of the serpentine coiled power or coiled up power known as the Kundalini Sakti. (*Ibid.*, P. 25). Kundalini Sakti power is symbolized by divine mother, and she is understood as the blissful consciousness. (*Ibid.*, P. 26). Sakti is portrayed in Hinduism as the female principle of cosmic energy.

The yogi has to control the basic instincts. The sex and marriage should go beyond the selfish pleasure, but should be rooted in love. (*Ibid.*, P. 54). Sex is understood as the most powerful life energies and as the beginning of birth. For Swami Sivananda Radha "Sex is, in the basic function, bonding." (*Ibid.*, P. 55). The self-restraint and keeping the purity of sexuality and marriage is important in Hindu philosophy. Sex is not understood as sinful. (*Ibid.*,

P. 195). In the concept of Kundalini yoga, first of all energy is expressed through sex for procreation. (*Ibid.*, P. 195). Swami Sivananda Radha corrects the misunderstanding in the west about kundalini yoga which over emphasizes the aspect of sex and that brought confusion and disaster in human relationships. She clarifies that the sexual union, the marriage and child are to be revered if there exists a complementary role between the male and female. (*Ibid.*, P. 336). The sanctity of sexuality is given utmost importance in Kundalini yoga.

The yoga philosophy also advocates for self control and to keep the chastity of sex. According to Anthony Elenjimattam. "It is the pride of India to have given out the ideal of Brahmacharya of voluntary chastity, sexual continence to the world from the earliest recorded history." (Anthony Elenjimattam, *The Yoga Philosophy of Patanjali*, Allahabad: Better yourself books, 1974, P. 39). The hidden power of continence is discovered by India. Elanjimattam states again, "The rishis in their hermitages and the seekers in the Himalayan jungles realized that abstention from sexual waste, both physical and psychic is the secret key that opened the doors of immortality from the corruptibility of flesh and blood, that opened the doors for higher wisdom in the knowledge and love of God. (*Ibid.*, P. 39).

In order to gain the higher knowledge and wisdom the sexual continence is suggested even the prasna, chandogya and Kata Upanishads. Elanjimattam writes that "From the premises the ideal of Brahmacharya emerges out as the virtue by which a man or a woman voluntarily renounces the pleasures and pains of sex, the orgy of all forms of sexual aberration and sexual madness and concentrates his whole mind and heart to the knowledge of God. (*Ibid.*, P. 40). The self renunciation, overcoming the sexual pleasures and leading a life with self control are the ideals of Hindu philosophy. The ascetic life is very much glorified by Hinduism. The Brahmacharya or the control of carnal desires and passions is a commendable life style in Yoga philosophy of Hinduism. (Satischandra Chatterjee and Dhirendra Mohan Datta, *An Introduction to Indian Philosophy,* Calcutta; University of Calcutta, 1984, P. 302).

The four goals of a man in Hinduism are Dharma (religion/righteousness), Artha (Wealth/Money), Kama (Sex, the duties in the family, especially to wife) and Moksha (liberation). The sex plays an important role in the Hindu ethics and philosophy. The famous 'Kamasutra' of Vatsyayana praises the significance of sexuality in human life. He analyses the different kinds of love making and sex and the types of marriages. Though he is not providing any pattern for sexual act and marriage, his book is a valuable source for human sexuality and marriage. It exposes the intensity and the various dimensions of human sexuality. 'Kamasutra' is a guide to sexual act. The qualification of girls for marriage, he suggests that she could be from good and noble family, three or more years younger than himself and beautiful. (Vatsyayana, *Kamasutra, Delhi: Sahini publications,* 1995, P. 69). The woman is asked to be faithful and loyal to her husband and they are advised not to blame excessively the misconduct of the husbands. (*Ibid*., P. 88-89).A patriarchal structure is very much evident in his perspective.

Vatsyayana admits polygamy as the men could have more than one wife. They can have wives. (*Ibid*., P. 94-95).Kama (sex) for pleasure is not rejected by him. Kama with public women, women belonging to lower castes, women twice married are for pleasure only says Vatsyayana. (*Ibid*., P. 20). He discourages sex with the women who are near relatives or ascetic. (*Ibid*., P. 20). The sexual satisfaction is conceived as an important aspect in human life for Vatsyayana. So he depicts through his book the various techniques of sex. (*Ibid*., P. 170-171).

Rajendra Kumari tries to make some observations in her study on the female sexuality in Hinduism. According to her the religious texts looks for the virginity of women before marriage, and the chastity and fidelity to one's own husband after marriage. She also observes that women by nature is depicted as carnal sensual, and as weak in moral nature. She quotes from Mahabharata: "Milk is possible in cows, devotion is possible in the Brahmanas; unsteadiness is possible among women." (Udyoga parva 5.38.45) There is also suspicion and infidelity created over women, so it is urged to keep them under control. Law of many (ix, 2) says, "Day and night women must be kept in dependence by the males (of) their (families); if they attach themselves to sensual enjoyments, they must be kept under ones control. (Rajendra Kumari, *Female Sexuality in Hinduism,* Delhi: ISPCK., 1988, PP. 12-13). There are references in the Hindu scriptures which dishonour the female sexuality.

Geoffrey Parrinder portrays Shiva as the god of sex and asceticism. He also admires the steadfast love of parvati to Shiva. The linga of Shiva has become the symbol of fertility. The phallic symbol exposes the importance of sexuality. The Hindu gods also have their consort. This also elevates the place of sexuality and marriage. (Geoffrey Parrinder, *Sex in the World Religions,* London: Sheldon 1980, P. 7-8). In the words of Parrinder, sexual intercourse was not only a physical action, it was given the value of a religious ritual. According to Upanishads, he states, sexual intercourse was not unrestricted. Intercourse with the strange women and women belonging to baser caste were forbidden. The Laws of Manu condemns the rape, incest and lesbianism. (*Ibid.*, P. 20-21).

The marriage is Hinduism in another important aspect to be discussed. The sexuality and marriage are inextricably related and they have a very significant place in the Hindu religious tradition. According to B.

Kuppuswamy, the marriages were looked upon as social and religious duty and matrimony was not compulsory for women, and moreover no age limitation was fixed for marriage in the vedic period. In the vedic times there were often love marriages and remarriage of the widow. (B. Kuppuswamy, *Social Change in India,* P. 240). The polygamy was existed. There are references about it in the Brahadaranyaka Upanishad. (*Ibid.*, P. 240). The analysis of Sachdeva and Vidyabhushan reveals that according to traditional Hindu law, marriage in a sacrament and is indissoluble. The second marriages are usually abhorred. The marriage is arranged by parents, and there is not much room for love marriages. (Sachdeva and Vidyabhushan, *An Introduction to Sociology,* P. 299). According to Dr. S. Radhakrishnan, the understanding of marriage in Hinduism is that, "Marriage is not merely of bodies but of minds. It makes us richer, more human, more truly living, and becomes the cause of greater love, deeper tenderness, more perfect understanding. It is an achievement which requires discipline. If it is not the expression of the spirit, it is mere lust." (S. Radhakrishnan, "Hinduism", *The Legacy of India,* edited by G.T. Garratt, Oxford: Clarendon Press 1938, P. 281).

G.T. Manley feels that the Hindu religious tradition upholds the arranged marriages. It allowed men to remarry and not women. The women's duty to her husbands is procreation. The law of Manu says, "Women are created to be mothers" (ix. 26). (G.T. Manley, "Hinduism", *The World's Religions,* edited by J.N.D. Anderson, Michigan: Eerdmans Publishing Co., 1972, P.112). Manusmiriti allows a man of thirty years to marry a maiden of twelve. A man of twenty four could marry a girl of eight years (ix. 94). This sounds like it promotes child marriages; though the reason given is that this is to protect the virginity of the girl under the guardianship of the legally wedded husband until she reaches the age of puberty for marital intercourse. (T.M. Manickam, *Dharma According to Manu and Moses,* Banglore: Dharmaram Publications. 1977). Manu talks about the fidelity among the partners. He urges them to keep fidelity until death (ix. 101). (*Ibid.*, P. 168). "Manu propounds monogamy as the morally ideal form of marriage", says Manickam. (*Ibid.*, P. 170). Manu insists on endogamous marriages (Partners from the same caste) and hypergamy (anuloma marriage) is discouraged. He also tolerated polygamy which was practiced before his time. (*Ibid.*, P. 170). In the anuloma marriage the bride is from lower varna. According to T.M. Manickam, Manu does not encourage divorce as husband is declared to be one with the wife (Manusmriti IX. 45, 47). (*Ibid.*, P. 173).

According to K.M. Kapadia, among the four purusarthas (Dharma, Artha, Kama and Moksha), Kama refers to one instinctive and emotional life of man and provides for the satisfaction of the sex drives and aesthetic urges. He writes again that "Kama as the satisfaction of the instinctive life is recognised as one of the aims of marriage, along with dharma and procreation." (K.M. Kapadia, *Marriage and Family in India,* Calcutta: Oxford University Press, 1966, P. 25). For renunciation sex is the first one to go. In Mahabharata, the traces of polyandry (a woman has more than one husband) is found. (*Ibid.*, P. 53).Draupadi is having five pandavas as husbands "polyandry seems to have been discredited as a cultural trait from the time of the Aitareya Brahman (800 B.C) where it was said that a man could have many wives but a woman could have only one husband. The Mahabharata (1.160, 36) reiterates this tradition" (*Ibid.*, P. 56). says Kapadia. The text of Mahabharata reads like this, `To have many wives is no adharma on the part of men, but to violate the duty owed to the first husband would be a great adharma in the case of a woman'. (*Ibid.*, P. 56). In the vedic literature and epics the devara (Levirate) marriage (the widow is to be married by the brother of her dead husband) are affirmed. (*Ibid.*, P. 58).

The Dharmasastras advocate the fidelity to husband. A husband is not allowed to hand over his wife (Dharmapatni) to another in order to get children, says Kapadia. (*Ibid.*, P. 60). It is reported that among the Nair caste of Kerala polyandry was common. (*Ibid.*, P. 60).Polygyny (a man has more than one wife) was usually socially accepted, though monogamy is the vedic ideal. (*Ibid.*, P. 97). The Hindu religious tradition affirms monogamous marriages, but in the society the polyandry and polygyny were also existed.

In the opinion of A.S. Altekar, "Not only was marriage well established in the Vedic age, but it was also regarded as a social and religious duty and necessity." (A.S. Altekar, *The position Women in Hindu Civilization*, Delhi: Motilal Banarsidass Publishers, 199. P. 31) The vedas gave a foremost place for marriage. The Dharmasastra literature talks about different forms of marriage. 1. The Paisacha form of marriage is the most condemned one. The bride is either duped by making her overdrink or overpowered by bridegroom to make her yield to his passion. 2. The Rakshasa marriage which regards women as price of war. 3. Kshatra marriage is marriage with the bride who is won in battle. 4. Asura Vivaha, under which the husband used to get a bride by paying a reasonable price to her. 5. Gandharva marriage is a love marriage. 6. Brahma, Darva, Prajapatya and Arsha are the four approved forms of marriage. The religious ritual is important for union in these marriages. Arsha marriage is a variety of Asura marriage. When a daughter was offered to an officiating priest, since it was settled while a sacrifice to devas. In the Brahma marriage, the bride, properly bedecked and ornamented is offered to a bridegroom who is speciality invited for that purpose. In prajapatya, the bride is offered according to due rites. (*Ibid.*, P. 45-57). The Hindu literature keeps varied understanding on the approval of the different marriages. Monogamous marriages are the norm, but other forms are also existed with or without the approval of the religious literature.

Altekar opines that "There is no doubt that the later Dharmasastra literature as a whole (200-1200 A.D), while liberally permitting the husband to remarry during life time of the first wife, refuses the remedy of divorce to the wife even when completely forsaken by the husband." (Prabhati Mukherjee, *Hindu Women,* New Delhi: Orient Longman Ltd., 1978, P. 12). Separation from husband by wife is not esteemed by Manusmriti and Mahabharata. It also condemned the women who covet men other than their husbands. (Prabhati Mukherjee, *Hindu Women,* New Delhi: Orient Longman Ltd., 1978, P. 12). In the Hindu religious tradition, the norm is monogamy for marriage and it also gave importance to the Sanctity in sexual life. But the practice of polygamy, bigamy and extramarital sex one are found in the Hindu religious tradition.

(ii) The Islamic Outlook

In India, ninety per cent of the people are Hindus. And Islam holds the second place. But they are a minority in Indian continent. There are around 48,000,000 Muslim in India. (David A. Brown, *A Guide to Religions,* New Delhi: ISPCK, 1973, P. 205). It is usually said that Islam affirms polygamy. But Islam allows only monogamy. It allows polygamy if the husband is economically and physically sound enough to take care of more women, and also in the situation of even when many male members must have died in the fight.

The Islamic Shariah talks about the family laws. Islam does not encourage self-mortification and asceticism, says Sadruddin Islahi. (Sadruddin Islahi. *Islam at a Glance,* traslated by M. ZafarIqbal, Delhi: Markazi Maktaba Islami,1985, P. 98). Islam asks the husbands to be good and kind to wives, and to treat them well. (*Ibid.*, P. 107). Marriage is a permanent companionship. "This permanent companionship of a man and a woman emerges from an open contract which is known in technical terms as "Nikah" (Marriage). It is a sacred relation which is formed with the mutual consent of the two partners and through an open declaration." (*Ibid.*, P. 110). The husband has to provide for his wife and children. This responsibility is understood as legal and obligatory. (*Ibid.*, P. 111).

In Islam, adultery is listed among the worst sins (Quran 25:68). The punishment for adultery is stoning to death or scourging with a hundred stripes. (*Ibid.*, P. 116). According to Sadruddin Islahi, "Islam has also made the institution of marriage simple and convenient. Except for very close relatives marriage in permissible with all others." (*Ibid.*, P. 118). The Islam permitted even four marriages for a man, if he would be just to each of them. "Many of the women, who seem good to you, two or three or four", says Quran (4:3) (*Ibid.*, P. 119).

Islam affirms conditional polygamy, but it treats sexual misconduct like adultery very seriously. Marriage is a sacrament for Muslims. According to Asgar Ali Engineer. "The Quran greatly improved the social status of women and laid down definite norms, as against mere customs and usages. They could no longer be treated as mere chattels to be traded or objects of sexual lust. The married women thus were described by the Quran as Muhsanat, meaning chaste and secured." (Asgar Ali Engineer, "Women Under the Authority of Islam", *Religion and Society,* vol. xxxii, No.2 (June 1985), P. 22). Polygamy is accepted by Quran in a particular social context. The orphans girls or women in order to ensure the justice, polygamy was accepted by Quran.(Mohammad Marmduke Pikthall, *The Meaning of the Glorious Quran*, New Delhi: Universal Book Stall, n.d. P. 91. (Surah IV, 127-129).

According to Kenneth Cragg, Islam prohibits sexual relationship outside marriage except in the case of slavery. (Kennath Cragg. *The House of Islam,* California: Dickenson Publishing Co., 1969, P. 53).

Cragg also agrees with the understanding that a Muslim can have over four wives. Shariah permits four wives (Quran 3:4). The polygamy, says Cragg, should be seen in a different way that 'the whole matter is within the theme of provision for orphans and seems to assume the widowhood ensuing from early warfare.' The Quranic provision is that if one cannot deal the women equally, marry only one. (*Ibid.*, P. 54). The Muslim societies today allow only monogamy as the new exegesis of the test justifies it in the todays context. (*Ibid.*, P. 54). Asgar Ali Engineer also feels that Quran gives general permission to marry up to four wives with certain conditions. He also affirm the fact that polygamy is accepted to ensure justice to slave girls, orphans and in the case of warlike situation where several women may become widows. He also observes that polygamy is accepted on condition of justice on three levels: 'ensuring proper use of properties of the orphans and widows, ensuring justice to all the wives at material level and also dispensing equal love and attachment to all the wives." (Asgar Ali Engineer, "Islam and Polygamy-II", *The Hindu,* (October 17, 1995), P. 12, cf, Asgar Ali Engineer, "Islam and Polygamy-I", *The Hindu,* (October 1995) P. 12).

J.N.D. Anderson opines that marriage is the duty of every Muslim. "Besides Muslim women, he may marry Jewesses or Christians and these may continue to practice their own religion (although, if they do, the spouses will have no mutual rights of inheritance): But a Muslim girl may be given in marriage only to a co-religionist, and there must be no intermarriage of any sort with polytheists. (J.N.D. Anderson. "Islam", *The World's Religions* edited by J.N.D. Anderson, Michigan: Com. B, Eerdmans Publishing Co., 1972, P. 86).

The Sharia of Muslim includes the marriage (Nikah), divorce (Talaq), slavery, concubinage, guardianship, maintenance, wills and inheritance. (*Ibid.*, P. 86). The Shariah has become a contraversial one as the interpretation of the family laws have brought confusion among the Muslims and non-muslims. The Shariah becomes a live issue in the courts in connection with the court verdicts on marriage related problems. The shariah stands for the legal system which means 'way'. The earlier word 'fiqh' stands for 'understanding.' shariah is the sacred law contained both in the Quran and Sunna (practice of the prophet). It is the rule for the right ordinance of the community. (John Alden Williams, ed. *Islam*, New York: 1962, P. 93).Shariah is the all embracing legal system for the Muslims. The official position is decided by 'Ulama' ("the learned"), the 'fuqaha' ("lawyers"), the scholars and custodians of law. (*Ibid.*, P. 94). According to Norman Anderson the shariah has often been classified under five categories: 1. What God has commanded, 2. What had has recommended but not made strictly obligatory, 3. What God has left legally indifferent, 4. What God has deprecated but not actually prohibited, 5. What God has expressly forbidden. (J.N.D. Anderson, "The law of Islam"., The World's Religions, (A Lion Handbook), Oxford: Lion Publishing pic, 1992, P. 322).

According to J.N.D. Anderson, a muslim may divorce his wife at any time and for any reason. When the words of divorce 'talaq' is said once or twice the marriage is revocable at the option of the husband for a short period known as 'idda', during which the husband is responsible for wife's lodging and maintenance. Thereafter a new marriage contract is necessary for the parties to come together. If the words of repudiation (talaq) is said thrice the divorce is irrevocable. The parties cannot remarry unless the wife has first been married to, and divorced by, another man. If wife is pregnant the husband is responsible for the lodging and maintenance until she gives birth to his child in this case. (J.N.D. Anderson, "Islam". *The World's Religions,* edited by J.N.D. Anderson. Michigan: Win B. Eerdmans Publishing Co., 1972, P. 87). The 'idda' (iddah) is usually fixed as three months. (Asgar Ali Engineer, "Women under the Authority of Islam", *Religion and Society,* vol. xxxii, No.2 (June, 1985) P. 31). However, the Islamic law of divorce has become a point of contraversy in the Indian continent.

The analysis of Geoffrey Parrinder also affirms the view that Islam allows polygamy with certain conditions. If one can ensure fairness to all wives and in cases of protection to the widows of war polygamy is permitted. The divorce is permissible in Islam in his understanding marriage in Quran is also meant for procreation. (Geoffrey Parrinder, *Sex in World Religions,* London: Sheldon Press, 1980, PP. 156-159). In Islam marriage is not strictly a sacrament. (*Ibid*., P. 167). According to Malladi Subbamma, "In Islam, marriage is based on contract - may be a holy one - between men and women. Child marriage was not prohibited in Islam." (Malladi Subhamma, *Islam and Woman,* trans. M.V. Ramamurthy, New Delhi: Sterling Publishers, 1988. P. 26). The unbridled sexual intercourse is forbidden by Islam. Mohammed also condemned the sexual exploitation over orphan women and wards (Quran IV, 2 - 6). (*Ibid.,* PP. 28-29). The Mahr (gift) should be paid by the husband to wife, according to Islamic principle (Quran IV, 24). (*Ibid.,* P. 30).

According to Islam divorce are of the following kinds: 1. Talaq - divorce by the husband. 2. Ila - when a person makes a vow to abstain from sexual intercourse for a period of not less than four months and stays away from his wife after informing her, the man is said to make 'Ila' (II. 226, 227) 3. Zihar - If the husband describes his wife as his sister or mother, that if he equates her with a women whom he should not marry, it is divorce pure and simple. 4. Lian - If the husband charges a chaste wife of adultery. 5. Khula - A divorce may be made with the consent and at the instance of the wife if she gives or agrees to give consideration to the husband and for her release from the marriage tie provided that the husband and wife are both of sound mind and past puberty. 6. Mubaraat - A divorce made by the husband and wife mutually agreeing to dissolve the marriage. 7. Faskh - divorce through court. (*Ibid.,* P. 48). The remarriage for the husband and wife is possible if the marriage was unconsummated or after the expiry of the period of 'iddat'. (*Ibid.,* P. 54).

According to Asgar Ali Engineer, Islam gives utmost dignity to women. Divorce the woman is not an easy one (Triple Talaq in one sitting is not permitted by Islam). He states, "The Quran does not mention triple divorce in one sitting. It requires the divorce to be effective over three periods of cleanliness (one cannot divorce ones wife during menstruation) thus giving the couple a chance to reconcile during those three months." (Asgar Ali Engineer, "Islam and Women", Indian Express, Kochi edn. (August 5, 1993), P. 10; (Ranjit Bhushan, "A Separate Identity", *Indian Express* (Sunday Magazine), (July 11, 1993), P. (3). In the midst of disputes on triple Talaq, Seema Alavi describes it as a unilateral act that dehumanizes the women. For Seema Alavi this is an irrelevant and inhuman rule. (Seema Alavi, "Talaq, Talaq, Talaq", *Indian Express,* Kochi edn. (February 27, 1994), P. 10). Furquan Ahmed also questions the wrong attitude behind the triple talaq which is against the spirit of Islam. Dissolution of marriage is the last so he urges the court of law and the religious authorities to be vigilant to help the Muslim women from the tragic pit of triple talaq. He argues that the 'triple talaq' can never be accepted as a weapon against women with all its injustice in the light of Quranic injunctions and teachings of the prophet. ("Understanding Islamic Divorce", *Indian Express* Kochi edn. (August 1, 1993), P. 8).

The normative principle of Islam affirms monogamy indissolubility of marriage and reacted against incest and extra-marital sex. But it is to be noticed that polygamy is permitted in certain situations if equal treatment is provided to all wives. It was allowed because of socio economic and political reasons as it is mentioned earlier. Islam gives due importance to the sexuality and marriage.

(iii) The Vision of Jainism and Buddhism

Jainism and Buddhism have emerged as a protest against Hinduism. While Vardhamana Mahavira is the founder of Jainism, Gauthama Budha is the one who instituted Buddhism. These two religions teach the significance of renunciation and self control in human life. They stood against the desire and lust which are the causes for the suffering and misery in the world. There are around three million Jainist and almost all of them live in India. The Jain followers are asked to conquer their passions and emotions. The Buddhism also holds the same view. First of all this section deal with the Jainist vision on sexuality and marriage, and second, the Buddhist perception.

Mahavira was born around 540 B.C. at Kundagrama near Patna in Bihar and died in 468 B.C. At the age of twenty eight he renounced his family and became an ascetic. (Myrtle Langley, "Respect for all life: Jainism", *The World's Religions* (Lion Handbook) Oxford: Lion Publishing Co., 1992, P. 208). The principle 'do not harm' has a very significant place in Jainism. For the laymen to reach the higher stage the chastity (not involving in adultery) is very important. For reaching the higher stage which is the path of liberation, a Jain layman should even keep away from his own wife and never to scent his body so as to seduce her. (*Ibid.,* P. 214). The ascetic (sadhu) should keep the vow of chastity (to have no dealings with gods, human beings or animals of the opposite sex). (*Ibid.,* P.215). For

Mahavira, women are known to be the causes of all sinful acts. According to him women are the greatest temptation in the world. He urges not to look at women or to claim them as one's own. (Robert Ernest Hume, *The World's Living Religions,* Edinburg: T&T Clark, 1959, P. 54). These references show that Jainism is negative towards marriage and family, and he appeals to keep utmost restraint on sex. Human sexuality has to be controlled.

The Jainists monks are not allowed to indulge in sexual intercourse. (Geoffrey Parrinder, *Sex in World's Religions,* London: Sheldon Press, 1980, P. 61). Hereafter, Geoffry Parrinder, Sex in World Religions. The adultery leads to punishment including amputation of hands and legs. The Laymen should keep chastity that one has to be faithful to his wife at all times, not consummate marriage with a young child, or form a temporary connection with a woman whom it was impossible to marry. The Svetambara sect (white clad) allowed a second marriage during the wife's life time if she bears no children. But the Digambara sect (sky-clad) refuse this view. Both sects forbid the practice of remarriage. It is clear that Jainism encourages monogamous marriages and it promotes rigorous self-control in the issue of sexuality.

Buddha, 'the enlightened one' was born about the year 560 B.C. in Kapilavastu (modern Bhinla, in Nepal) . His name was Siddhartha. He taught Ahimsa and asceticism. (Jaico Publishing House, *Glimpases of World Religions,* Bombay: Jaico Publishing House, 1957, P. 42). Moral purity, self control and self denial are admired by Buddhism. One of the vows is not to do any wrongful sexual acts. (*Ibid.,* PP. 56-59). Buddha taught conquering passion and keep up a life of purity says Satischandra Chatterjee and Dhirendra Mohan Datta. (*Ibid.,* P.71).

The understanding of sexuality in the Buddhist tantrism is useful to be discussed in the section. The sexual intercourse with the partner is also understood as a way of reaching Buddhahood. (Herbert V. Guenther, *The Tantric View of Life,* Berkeley: Shambla Publications, 1972, PP. 59-60). The tantrism preserve the unity of spirituality and sensuousness, and even sex is seen as a means to achieve Budhahood after having the empowerment. Tantrism is looking for the unification which is the consequence of growing awareness which is to merge in the absoluteness of Being. (*Ibid.,* PP.60). According to Guenther, "Throughout Tantrism reference is made to the body as lived by me, perceiving, moving, acting, and so on. Taking this reference as our clue we can say that sexuality in itself a mode of being of the person in question, and is concretely interpreted in the stream of lived experience." (*Ibid.,* PP. 62-63).He states that the 'sexuality of the body manifests itself in a variety of manners so that it is justifiable to say that sexuality expresses a human beings existence in the same way as his existence expressed his sexuality'. (*Ibid.,* P.63).

The embodied bodies have their sex in the tantric philosophy, which does not see sex or sexuality as an object. It is stated, "Although human beings are male and female and although sexuality is coextensive with life, sexuality cannot be reduced to being as such nor can the latter be reduced to sexuality." (*Ibid.,* P.63). Sexuality is apprehended as the dialectic of lived experience. (*Ibid.,* P.63). The sexuality is understood as sacred and meaningful experience in tantric philosophy which is highly philosophical which gives extreme importance to esoteric and erotic elements. The erotic elements also have a significant place in the Buddhist tantrism, so also the way and process to reach Buddhahood also place an importance for sexuality. The Buddhist tantrism, however, does not permit the promiscuity or the misuse of sex. Sex is understood as the means to enjoy the strong affinity and harmonious complimentariness among the partners which leads to the deepest possible experience of being. (*Ibid.,* P.71). It also does not see sex as a mere manipulation of organs, but as that which generates an awareness which may turn into unending love. (*Ibid.*, P.76).

The monks were not allowed to have sexual relationship since it would bring attachment to women which, infact, distract the monk from the vow of chastity and also from the search for liberation, says Geoffrey Parrinder. (Geoffrey Parrinder, *Sex in the World Religions,* P. 45).The masturbation and persuading women for sexual intercourse were considered wrong. (*Ibid.,* P.46).The fidelity from husband and wife is expected in Buddhism among the lay. (*Ibid.,* P.55). Polygamy was found among rich and powerful and was approved by Buddhism. (*Ibid.,* P.55).A Jataka tale goes like this: Brahmin had four daughters, and four suitors came who were respectively handsome, old, noble and virtuous. He was confused as to whom the daughters were to be given. He asked a Buddhist teacher (the story tells it was Buddha himself) about it, he gave the consumer that virtue is the superior quality, so give the daughters to him. (*Ibid.,* P.55). This story affirms the argument in favour of polygamy in Buddhism. The chastity is demanded from both husband and wife. Committing adultery is prohibited in Buddhism, says Robert Earnest Hume. (Robert Earnest Hume, The World's Living Religions, Op.Cit.., P. 73). Ananda K. Coomaraswamy also acknowledges the fact that Buddhism expects faithfulness from the husband and wife. (Ananda K. Coomaraswamy, *Buddha and the Gospel of Buddhism,* Second edn. New Delhi: Manshiram Manoharlal Publishers, 1985, P. 122).

In the opinion of Walpola Rahula, in Buddhism, the love between husband and wife is considered as religious and secred. They are asked to be faithful. (Walpola Rahula, *What the Buddha Taught,* New York: Grove Press inc.1959, P. 59).The chastity, has supreme importance in Buddhism. (Edward J. Thomas, *The History of Buddhist thought,*

London: Routledge and Kegan Paul Ltd., 1951, P. 25). Dharmmapada the Buddhist text advises to keep away from lust and sensual pleasures. (S. Radhakrishnan, *The Dhammapada,* Madras: Oxford University Press, 1977, P. 67).The sexuality and marriage are taken seriously in Buddhism. The classical Buddhism urges to upkeep utmost restraint in sex, and admonishes the husband and wife to be faithful. It also promotes monogamy, but in certain situations polygamy was accepted.

(iv) The Sikhism and its Insights

The Sikh religious tradition had originated during the life time of Guru Nanak (1469-1539). There are about twelve million Sikhs in the world, and eighty percent of them live in India, says Godwin R. Singh. (GodwinR, Singh, "The Sikh Religious Tradition", *Religious Traditions of India,* edited by P.S. Daniel, David C. Scott and G.R. Singh, Serampore: Indian Theological Library, 1988, P. 312). Sikhism is against egoism, lust and greed. According to Godwin R. Sing, "The Sikh Gurus used the word haumai to describe this rebellious attitude. It leads to a scramble for possession of wordly things embroiling human beings into lust (kama), anger (krodh), greed (lobh) and attachment (moha)." (*Ibid.*, P. 324).

The initiated ones are not supposed to indulge in fornication and adultery. (*Ibid.*, P. 327). "Sikhism forbids ostentatious dowry or payments of money at marriage. It allows widow remarriage and recommends monogamy," says Godwin Singh. (*Ibid.,* P.328). The inter religious marriage and child marriages were discouraged, but it promoted widow remarriage and monogamy. According to C.H. Loehlin, 'No account is to be taken of caste, but marriage is to be between Sikhs only. No marriage should be performed between small children; and no payment should be made. Widow re-marriage is allowed. Ordinarily a Sikh should have one wife.' (C.H. Loechlin, *The Sikhs and their Scriptures,* Delhi: ISPCK-LPH, 1974, P. 46).

In 1945 the Sikh Shrine Committee has approved the following guide to the Sikh way of life. The child marriage is to be condemned. Other men's wives should be protected as one's own mother (It means the adultery is not allowed). The husband and the wife should be loyal and faithful to each other. (Geoffrey Parrinder, *Sex in the world's Religions,* p. 69; W. Owen cole and piara Singh Sambhi. (The Sikhs: Religious beliefs and practices, New Delhi: Vikas Publishing House; 1978, P.116. observe that marriage is not a Social contract, but aims at the fusion of two souls. The Sikh religion advocates monogamy and it condemns the adultery and the sexual promiscuity. The sacredness and the sanctity of sexuality and marriage are acclaimed by Sikhism.

(v) The View of Parsi Religion

Parsi (Parsee) religion is the Indian form of Zoroastrianism. Zoroastres proclaimed his teaching in the tenth century before Christ in Persian region. The virtues like honesty and chastity are admired by Zoroastrianism. (Jaico Publishing House, *Glimpses of World Religions,* P. 126). In the wake of Islam persecution, the believers of Zoroastrianism left Persia rather than for sake their religion. (John Hinnels "Courage and Faith: The Parsis", *The World Religions* (A Lion Handbook), Oxford: Lion Publishing Co., 1992, P. 217). They came to India in order to take refuge.

The sanctity and the importance of marriage is affirmed by Parsi tradition. In the words of Geoffrey Parrinder who have reflected on sex in the world religions, "marriage was a good institution, recommended in the scriptures, and it was merit to help others to marry if they were poor." (Gerffrey Parrinder, *Sex in the World's Religions,* p. 71). The aspect of fertility which is an essential element of sexuality is given an important place by Parsi religion. (*Ibid.,* P. 71). The Parsi religion admonishes to keep away from the wives of others and adultery is considered as a great evil. (*Ibid.,* P.71).

The husband or wife could divorce each other if they indulge in adultery. The sexual immortality is not tolerated by Parsi religious tradition. The impotence or sterility also could bring divorce. (*Ibid.,* P.72). Parsis condemned the courtesans (prostitutes), the sexual contact at the time of menstruation and sexual intercourse after the fifth month if the woman is pregnant. (*Ibid.,* P.72).The human sexuality is given utmost care by Parsi tradition. The Parsi religion affirms the indissolubility of marriage and is against divorce and adultery. Divorce is but, allowed in the case of sterility and infidelity (adultery).

(vi) The Perspective of Christianity

This section deals with the understanding of sexuality and marriage by different Christian denominations. The viewpoint of Roman Catholics, the Orthodox Church, the Church of South India (C.S.I) and some of the free Churches are considered over here. The Christians constitute around 3% of the population of India.

(a) The Roman Catholic Church

According to Pope Pius IX (1846-1878), "marriage among Christians cannot be constituted by mere civil contract; the marriage contract among Christians must always be a sacrament; and the contract is null, if the sacrament does not exist." (Lockport Church, *Roman Catholicism,* U.S.A: Lockpart Church, n.d., P. 97). The 'code of the canon law' states, "The marriage covenant, by which a man and a woman establish between themselves a partnership of their whole life, and which of its own very nature is ordered to the well being of the spouses and to the procreation and upbringing of children, has, between the baptised, been raised by Christ the Lord to the dignity of a sacrament." (*The Code of Canon law,* Fourth Reprint,

Bangalore: published by Collins for Theological Publications in India, 1991, P. 189).

The essential properties of marriage are unity and indissolubility according to the Canon law (Can. 1056). The impotence can be a reason to invalidate a marriage. (*Ibid.*, P.193).The marriage can be invalidated if the dissolution of the previous one is not settled with certainty, the women is abducted, if it is consanguine marriage. (*Ibid.*, PP. 193-194).According to Canon law (1141) a marriage that is ratified and consummated cannot be dissolved by any human power or by any cause other than death. (*Ibid.*, P.201).

The spouses have the equal obligation and right to whatever pertains to the partnership and conjugal life. (*Ibid.*,P.201).The responsible use of sexuality has been honoured by the Catholic faith. The analysis of William E. Pinto also states that the obligation of conjugal acts has a foremost place in Catholic marriage. (William E. Pinto, *Law of marriage and Matrimonial beliefs for Christians in India*, Bangalore: Theological Publications in India, 1991, P. 54).

The Oriental code (code of the catholic churches of the east) states that "The matrimonial covenant is instituted by the creator himself. This covenant is the source of the partnership of whole life (consortium totius vitae) established by the free and personal consent of man and woman." (Jose Chiramel, Varghese Palathingal, *Patriarchal and Matrimonial Legislations in the Oriental Code,* Alwaye: St. Thomas Academy for Research, 1992, P. 108). Marriage is indissoluble and conjugal rights should be kept up in married life. (*Ibid.*, PP. 110-111). The capacity to have sexual intercourse is the important criteria to enter into marriage. (*Ibid.*, PP. 121-122).According to Eastern code, "Once a marriage is celebrated and later even if one party commit adultery, the marriage still remains an indissoluble union. It is difficult to prove simulation in the external forum." (*Ibid.,* P.141).

The understanding indissolubility and unity of marriage by the Catholic church does mean that marriage relationship is an exclusive one, i.e., between one man and one wife, and they are not allowed to embrace a second wife or husband. (G. Taylor and E. de Bekker, *Parish Priests and Marriage Cases,* Bangalore: Theological Publications of India, 1986, P. 5). It is a life-long relationship. And the marriage cannot be cancelled by mere human authority. According to the understanding of the Catholic code of the Canon, "a marriage is consummated when the partners have met in the act of sexual intercourse after their marriage contract." (*Ibid.,* P.11). The physical aspects of marriage consummation are: "penetration of the vagina of the woman by the male organ of man; ejaculation in the vagina of the woman even though the male ejaculate is not elaborated in the testicles and so does not contain the male sperms required for fertilization." (*Ibid.,* P.11).

The marriage between a Catholic and a Non-Catholic is allowed by the church. If a marriage case is nullified by the church authorities, the partners are free to marry. (*Ibid.,* P. 14). It means church allows remarriage. The valid marriage should between a woman of fourteen years and man of sixteen years old. The sterility is not a valid cause to invalidate marriage. Impotence can nullify marriage. But impotence means the position in which sexual union is not possible, and it does not include the capacity to fertilize. (*Ibid.,* P. 27). If the male is unable to erect his sex organ, he is impotent. To the women, one can be impotent if she has no vagina, or if the vagina is not penetrable by the male organ. (*Ibid.,* P. 28). There the cases of impotency which is a reason not to marry validly.

According to deliberations of the Second Vatican Council explains clearly the rules for mixed marriages: "It takes the two forms of impediments to marriage: mixed religion and disparity of worship. The first of these forbids marriage between a Catholic and a baptized Non-Catholic, while not taking from the validity of such marriage. The second renders invalid a marriage between a Catholic and a non-baptized person." (Austin Flannery, ed. *Vatican Council II,* Bombay: St. Paul Publications, 1983, P. 431).

The indissolubility of marriage is very much upheld by the Roman Catholic Church. The invalidation of marriage is possible only in the cases of premature marriage in which the married partners have under age or they are impotent. The remarriage is also possible after the legitimate divorce. Mixed marriage is possible with the baptized members of other churches. The Catholic Church gives extreme importance to the sacramental and covenantal aspect of marriage. (George V. Lobo, *Moral and Pastoral Questions,* Anand: Gujarat Sahitya Prakash, 1984, PP. 174-176). So also we say that the Catholic morality gives due respect and importance to sexuality and the responsible use of it.

(b) The Orthodox Church

The sacramental value of marriage and the sacredness of sex are of great importance to the Eastern Church. The celebration of marriage implies that it emphasizes the sacredness of the union between men and women and the connection between the mystery of human love and the love which God has for this creation, says Nicholas Zernov. (Nicholas Zernov, *The Christian East,* Delhi: ISPCK, 1956, P. 69).The Eastern Churches of the Byzantine, however, allow divorce and even remarriage. This, in Zernov's words, does not negate the high esteem for marriage by the Orthodox Church. (*Ibid.*, P. 69).

The Orthodox Church in India also gives tremendous significance to marriage. It does not permit adultery or polygamy, (Kadavil Paul Ramban, *The Orthodox Syrian Church* its Religion and Philosophy, Puthencruz: K.V. Pathrose, 1973, P. 139). Adultery is the only cause for divorce, and the second marriage is not allowed so long as the partner is living. (*Ibid.*, P. 139). The Orthodox Churches are very much concerned of the unity, sanctity and the indissolubility of marriage.

(c) The Church of South India

The constitution of the Church of South India does give utmost importance to the unity and indissolubility of marriage. The minimum age for marriage is fixed by the church. The male should have eighteen years of age, and female should have fifteen years old. (*The Church of South India,* The Constitution of the Church of South India, Madras: C.L.S., 1972, P. 75).

The husband and wife cannot go for the second marriage if one of the partner is living. (*Ibid.*, P. 77). The marriage should be kept sacred and it cannot be dissolved as we like. The divorce is not entertained by the church. Polygamy is not allowed by the Church of South India. The marriage is understood as the holy ordinance of God. (*Ibid.*, P. 81).

(d) The Marthoma Church

According to K.V. Mathew, "Marriage of two young people has a theological significance. They are united in wedlock in which they share love." (K.V. Mathew, *The Faith and Practice of the Marthoma Church,* Kottayam: Mar Thoma Theological Seminary, 1985, P. 58).The marriage involves the love and unity. The husband and wife are bound to remain faithful, and the question of divorce does not occur. (*Ibid.*, P 59).

The Mar Thoma Church perceives marriage as a sacrament, and it considers marriage as permanent. (*Ibid.*, P. 59,60). The responsible sexuality is demanded from the couples. The extra-marital and pre-marital sex are not condoned by the church. (*Ibid.*, P. 60)."When a man and a woman pledge themselves to the life of matrimony they affirm that the married state is for life", (*Ibid.*, P. 63). says K.V. Mathew. The married partners become one in body so they should maintain the unity and love in the married life. The divorce is not visualized in Christian marriage and it is destructive, says K.V. Mathew. (*Ibid.*, P. 64).

The Marthoma Church accepts both partners to be believers in Christ. The proper use of sexuality and the sacredness of marriage is affirmed by the Mar Thoma Church. The partners are to live faithfully and in love together. The members of the church are advised to keep the sanctity of sexuality and the sacramental aspect of holy matrimony.

(e) The Non-Episcopal Churches

This section takes into considerations the idea of sexuality and marriage among the free churches. In India, there are several Baptist, brethren and Pentecostal churches which are advocating holiness and separation. They are very rigid in their view on sex and marriage. These churches argue against polygamy and divorce. Divorce is allowed only in the case of adultery. They usually do not argue for remarriage. The premarital sex, extramarital sex, homosexuality and incest are not accepted by them For them, these are immoral and non-biblical.

The Seventh Day Adventists, one of the Christian sects in India condemns the adultery. (E. J. Chacko, *Keralathile Chila Svatanthra Sabhakal* (Malayalam), Thiruvalla: Theological Literature Committee, 1986, P. 79). They feel that Bible allows divorce and remarriage, but they emphasize the role of forgiveness and reconciliation. They urge that the accused one who committed immorality (illicit sex) should be given an opportunity to repent. If the accused does not do so, it can lead to divorce and remarriage. (*Ibid.*, P. 60). If one partner dies or marries another person, the other partner can go for remarriage, according to their rule. (*Ibid.*, P. 80).

The Late Pastor T.G. Oommen, one of the eminent leaders of the Pentecostal churches has reflected on the issue of Christian marriage and family. He tries to develop a Biblical concept of family. The marriage is appointed for men and women to become companions and to procreate. (T.G. Oommen, *Kudumba Samvidhanam Thiruvachana Velichathil,*(Family Planning in the light of the Bible) (Malayalam), *Kadambanad: Girideepam* Press, n.d., PP. 2-6). The marital impurity is condemned by him. The divorce is not permitted by Bible according to Pastor T.G. Oommen. (*Ibid.*, P. 22-23).He encourages to have utmost restraint in the issue of sex, that he appeals to keep away from adultery and other sexual immoralities. The sanctity of sex is affirmed by him. The indissolubility of marriage is also upheld by him.

The Non-Episcopal churches stress the importance of holiness and moral life. The sexuality cannot be misused or abused. The responsible use of it is looked for. These churches also emphasize the sacramental aspect of marriage.

The Christian churches in India affirm the sacredness of marriage and the sanctity of sex. The divorce is seen as the last resort. It is allowed only in the case of adultery or unfaithfulness. The proper use of sexuality is stressed by them. The sexual misconduct such as pre-marital sex, extra marital sex and homosexuality are not tolerated by them.

The study of the religious traditions and their view on sexuality and marriage reveals that the *apriori* rules or norms one emphasized by them. Most of the traditions make their ethical judgement based on the normative principles. The issues like divorce, prostitution extra-marital sex or pre-marital sex are not seriously dealt with in order to suggest and ethical approach to these issues. The attitude of the Christian churches in this respect also is not promising.

E. The Sexuality and Marriage among the Tribal Communities

The tribal or indigenous communities in India themselves constitute a wide variety of people. There is a unity among them as the tribal communities, but they are diversified because of their values, beliefs and perspectives on different issues. The North Eastern tribal communities are of Mongoloid origin and other tribals are mainly of Dravidian descent. The pluralism of ethical values is the distinctive character of the tribal communities. This section deals with their life is general, and then their understanding sexuality and marriage would be considered.

(i) The Tribal Communities in India

This is only a general survey of the tribal communities. Since it is a vast subject, all the names and the features of the communities may not be referred to. It is also noted that these communities have undergone changes because of the secularization process. The indigenous people practise the religion which is known as primal religions. The tribals are the aboriginals. They have common ethnicity and descent.

One of the consultations in Shillong held in the year 1962 described the tribe as an indigenous, homogeneous unit, speaking a common language, claiming a common ancestry, living in a particular geographical area, backward in technology, pre-literate, loyally observing social, and political customs based on kinship. (M.M. Thomas and Richard W. Taylor, *Tribal Awakening,* Bangalore: CISRS, 1988, P. 2). In India, we have mainly around five hundred tribal groups, beside the sub-tribes. We have around 10 per cent tribal population in India. (*Ibid.*, P. 4). The tribes of India are distributed in three main natural groups:

1. Those living in Northern and North - Eastern India.
2. Those occupying the central belt of the older hills and plateaus along the dividing line between the Indo-Gangetic Plain and Peninsular India.
3). Those scattered over South Western India. (*Ibid.*, P. 56).

The tribals have a solidarity. The have myths, folklores and music. They are honest and sincere. (*Ibid.*, P. 46). The tribals try to find out their own identity and selfhood. Once they were away from the modernization and the related social changes. The religious changes, education, means of communication, industrialization, and modern technology have brought several changes in their outlook. (*Ibid.*, P. 51). The video boon, availability of sex books and the westernization have brought the sexplosion and the erosion of values in North East India. (Joseph Cilia, "Some issues of concern for the Christian churches in the North East", *Religion and Society,* Vol. xxxix, No. 4, (Dec. 1992), PP. 58-59). According to Henry H. Presler, the industrialization and the technological development raised the standard of living, cheapened money and bittled kinship bond among the tribals. (Henry H. Presler. *Primitive Religions of India,* Madras: The Christian Literature Society, 1971, P. 160)

The new civilization that is brought by industrialization and technological development affects the moral order of the tribal society. The old habits and the forms of social control are weakened. It also can lead to individual disorganization. According to Presler,

"Individual disorganization expresses itself in sexual offences, prostitution, drunkenness, purposeless mobility, unemployment, mental derangement, suicide etc." (*Ibid.*, p. 169). The tribal society is an integrated and harmonious society where they have the feeling of oweness and equality. They always entertain a feeling of community. Nari Rustomji writes about the North-east tribals that 'the tribal has preferred to remain independent of any authority outside his own community or village.' (Nari Rustomji, "Emerging from Isolation", The Illustrated Weekly of India (December 14, 1980), P. 12).The tribal life style is undergoing drastic changes today all over India.

(ii) The Sexuality and Marriage among the Tribals

The perspective on the issue of sexuality and marriage among the tribals is not in uniform. They are having different patterns. Leading a life of holiness is very much promoted by the North-East tribals. Adultery and immoral life are not seriously dealt with. (A Wati Longchar, *The Tribal Religious Traditions in North East India: An introduction,* Jorhat: Assam printing Work, 1991, P. 23).Wati Longchar states,

In tribal society, taboo against incest is universal. The strictest from all incest ins sexual relationship between a mother and her son, between father and daughter and between brother and sister. Any sexual intimacy between these sets of relationship is unthinkable in tribal society or even among clan members. The incest taboo is extended even to immediate kin. It is believed that all clansmen are related through blood and have to be avoided in sexual intimacy. (*Ibid.*, P. 34).

According to Longchar, the incest is a severe crime and it will not go unpunished. It was traditionally believed that a warrior should abstain from sexual intercourse at least six days before he goes to war. (*Ibid.*, P. 35). Related to sex, several taboos are found among tribals. The marriages are usually exogamous. "It is taboo to marry a woman from the same clan or phratry. It is also not allowed to marry with aunt and sister-in-law. If his wife does, he can marry his sister-in-law", says Longchar. (*Ibid.*, P. 36).

H. Horam is an expert in tribal studies, especially of North East India. He writes, "Rules governing the sexual life of the tribals are strict and generally observed. Breaches of the rules are sufficiently rare to be talked about and are severely punished. Sexual relationship must be conducted in the proper manner. For instance, it is considered very wrong to force a girl to act against her will and therefore, rape is very rare in tribal society." (H. Horam, *North East India: A Profile,* New Delhi: Cosmo Publications, 1990, p. 93). According to Horam, the bestiality, homosexuality, lesbianism, sodomy, and prostitution are almost unknown to them. But the pre-marital relationship is permitted under certain conditions of discipline and restraint that eventually leads to marriage. (*Ibid.*, P. 93). The sexuality is kept under discipline. It is tabooed to have sexual intercourse before the great festivals, before a hunting expedition and during ceremonial dances and menstruation periods, says Horam. (*Ibid.*, P. 93).

The tribals have no practice of child marriage. But they allow the widow re-marriage. Remarriage is permitted after the death of her husband. (*Ibid.*, P. 98). In Nagaland, the normal pattern is monogamy. (*Ibid.*, P. 176). The Garos are strictly exogamous and marriage is only a civil contract. (Julius L.R. Marak, "Traditional Marriage Customs of the Garos", *Religion and Society,* vol. xxxix, No. 4 (December 1992), P. 22).The love marriages are allowed by the Garo community. The girl goes quietly to sleep with the person of her choice, in the case of love marriages, with a view to get his consent. According to Julius Marak, "If the young man reciprocates her love, he continues sleeping with her without any challenge as their union is thereby legalized and society accepts them as husband wife without further ceremony." (*Ibid.*, P. 24).The Garos also have the custom to have a second wife with the consent of the principal wife. (*Ibid.*, P. 24).The Christian influence have made lot of changes among the tribals. The Christian Garos of North East India do not go for second wife or bigamy, but the non-Christian Garos practise bigamy and polygamy. (*Ibid.*, P. 25-26).

The social change in North East India has made a great impact in the lines of the tribal people. The dropping of youth hostels (Morungs) is one of the contributions. Till their conversion to Christianity, boys and girls after the attainment of puberty, lived in the respective hostels. This practice is not existing very much today. (M. Horam *Op.Cit.*, P. 177). The known ethnic groups in the North East India are Nagas, Mizos, Khasis and Garos. While discussing the issue of family and marriage in North East India S.M. Dubey states, "Among them, polyandry and polygyny, both forms of marriages are practiced." (S.M.Dubey, "Family, Marriage and Social Change", *Family, Marriage, Social change in Indian Fringe* edited by S.M. Dubey: P.K. Bordoloi, B.N. Borthakur, New Delhi: Cosmo Publications, 1980, P. 17). According to Nadeen Hasnain, polygyny (marriage of one man to several women) is found among the Naga tribes. (Nadeem Hasnain, *Tribal India Today,* New Delhi: Harnam Publications, 1983, P. 32).

The observations of Joseph Cilia about the social change and sexplosion among the tribal of North East India is worth mentioning over here. The modernization process has led the young people to moral laxity. The attitude to sexual morality today is guided by subjective/ personal morality. This can lead to relativism. Recreational sex mentality has crept in. There is an increase in teenage pregnancies. This is because of the irresponsible sex. The divorces are also becoming common. The pre-marital sex is encouraged. ("Some issues of Concern for the Christian Churches in the North East India", *Religion and Society,* vol. xxxix, No. 4, (December 1992), PP. 58-59).

The influence of Christianity has encouraged the people to have monogamy and to avoid the pre-marital sex. The tribals of North East are against adultery, rape, incest and homosexuality. Sexuality is considered sacred and they have handled it responsibly. The widow remarriage is permitted. But the polygamy and polyandry are prevalent among the non-Christian tribals of North East India. The secularization process and the consequent relativism which leads to extra marital sex, divorce and early pregnancies.

Other than the tribals of North East India, there are innumerable tribal groups in India. They also have their own views on sexuality and marriage. Those who occupy the central belt and those who scattered over South Western India are included in this group. The contact with non-tribals, the coming of Christianity, the improvement in the means of communication and transportation, the industrialization, and the Western education have brought social change among there tribals. (M.M. Thomas and Richard W. Taylor, eds, *Tribal Awakening,* PP. 66-72). Some scholars note that the industrialization brings the vices like immorality and the tribes were loosing their traditional social codes and discipline. (*Ibid.*, PP. 70,72). The tribal studies of certain scholars point that the tribals are keeping the custom not to marry outside the tribe, and only within a particular clan. They also have no child marriages and are monogamous. (*Ibid.*, PP. 36-37).

In the opinion of Nadeem Hasnain, "Among the Indian tribes, there are many who are following this type of matrimonial alliance. Polygamy has two aspects: (i) polygamy, (ii) polyandry" (Nadeem Hasnain, *Tribal India Today,* Op.Cit., P. 32). He observes that "polygamy is found among the Naga tribes, the Gond, the Baiga, the Toda, the Lushai and most of the other proto Australoid tribes of middle India." (*Ibid.*, P. 32). Polyandry (marriage of one women to several men) is found in the Himalayan tract stretching from Kashmir to Assam and in popular among the Indo-Aryan and Mongoloid tribes. In its classical form it is prevalent among the Tiyan, the Kota, the Khasa (Jounsari) and the Ladakhi Bota. (*Ibid.*, P. 32). The bigamy is resorted by the Holiya and Medara tribes of Mysore. (*Ibid.*, P. 33).

According to Nadeem Hasnain, "Among the tribes of middle India, pre-marital sex relations are overlooked unless of course they lead to pregnancy which is generally regarded as shameful for the girl's parents." (*Ibid.*, P. 37).The extramarital sex is not common or permissible among them, says Hasnain. (*Ibid.*, P. 37). The marriage is only a social contract among the tribes of India, so divorce or dissolution of marriages is widely practised. Remarriage is common among them. According to Nadeem Hasnain, "The ground for divorce, however, varies from tribe to tribe. The Khasis permit divorce for reasons of adultery, barrenness and incompatibility of temperament." (*Ibid.*, P. 38).

The polyandry is found among the Todas of Nilgiri Hills. There are some instances reported of the Nairs of Kerala, the fraternal and non-fraternal types of polyandry. (K.M. Kapadia, *Marriages and family in India,* P. 76). According to Kapadia, "Among the Todas of the Nilgiri Hills, when a boy is married to a girl, all his brothers, including those who are born later, are usually regarded as husbands of the girl." (*Ibid.*, P. 87). Among the Todas, a woman may have one or more recognized lovers, and sex relations are not confined to partners in marriage. Extra marital relations are not recognized as wrong, and there is no ground for divorce. (*Ibid.*, P. 88).The sex laxity is socially approved among Todas. Among the Kotas of Nilgris, the polyandry exists. Man's brothers have sexual access to his wife, and a man has sexual access to all the sisters of his wife. The widow remarriage is also prevalent among them. (*Ibid.*, PP.93-94).

Among the Khasa of Jounsar-Bawar of Uttar Pradesh the eldest brother marries a girl and she will become the common wife of the rest of the brothers. (*Tribal India Today,* Op.Cit., p. 32). They follow the polyandry. Though there is no pre-marital sex relations among them, the extramarital sex relations exist says Nadeem Hasnain. (*Ibid.*, p. 37). G.S. Bhatt also agrees with the fact that the Khasas are polyandrous. (G.S. Bhatt, "Constraints of Being polyandrous Tribal: The case of Jaunsar Bawar". *Family, Marriage and Social Change on the Indian Fringe,* Op.Cit., P. 59).

The monogamy is also very much prevalent among some tribes of India. The Lalungs (Tiwas) of Assam are exogamous and monogamous. The widow remarriage and divorce are rare among them. The illicit sex is also forbidden, observes G.C. Sharma Thakur. (G.C.Sharma Thakur. "Marriage among the Lalungs (Tiwas), *Family Marriage and Social Change on the Indian Fringe,* Op.Cit.., PP. 92-93). The Chorais of Tripura are also strictly following monogamy. The widow-remarriage is restricted. But widowers can remarry. The divorce is impossible for them. According to M.K. Chakravarty, "Divorce is tabooed by the chorais. In the past, there was not a single case of divorce or at present there is not a single case of divorce in the village reported to the investigator." (M.K.Chakravarty. "Marriages and Family Among the Chorias" *Family Marriage Social Change in the Indian Fringe,* Op.Cit., P. 103). The pre-marital sexual relationship is not encouraged by the chorais. (*Ibid.*, P. 104).

The Uralies of Wynad (Kerala) keep monogamy as their rule in marriage. The marriage is arranged by parents. Widow remarriage is allowed. According to Lukose Jacob, "Divorce on the grounds of ill-treatment either by the husband or by wife is allowed among Uralies." (Lukose Jacob, "In and around the Chittalpura: A Study of the Uralies of Wynad", *Religion and Society,* vol xxxviii, No. 3&4 (Sept.-Dec., 1991), P. 70). The pre-marital and extra marital sexual relations are not allowed among the Bhils of Central India. (Bhagwat Bandari, *Tribal Marriages and sex relations,* Udaipur: Himanshu Publications, 1989 PP. 62-69). Adultery in seriously dealt with. Marriages are exogamous and polygynous. (*Ibid.*, P. 68). But today monogamy is accepted as the normal criteria for marriage by the Bhills. (*Ibid.*, P. 75). The right to divorce is also allowed for the husbands and wives among the Bhills.

Generally the marriages are exogamous among the tribal. Pre-marital sex is not permitted. If some one involves in pre-marital sex with a girl, he has to marry her The extra marital sex is normally not allowed. The sexuality is kept sacred in the sense that the bestiality, the homosexuality and lesbianism are not allowed. Polygyny and polyandry are widely common among the tribes of India. Certain tribes are monogamous. The divorce is allowed, but rare among the tribal communities. Though marriage is a social contract, they held utmost restraint and discipline in married life.

F. The Indian Marriage Laws

The Indian constitution affirms the secularism and equality. The different religions and their ideals co-exist in this country. The family laws are important in Indian context, every religious tradition has their own personal laws. The family law includes marriage, sonship, maintenance, devolution of property and even charity endowments. In the religiously and ethically pluralistic country like India, the British recognized the personal laws. (Rajkumar, Agarwala, "Preface", *Conversion and Indian Civil Law, by Julian Saldanha,* Banglore: Theological Publications in India, 1981, P. 5). The Hindus, Muslims, Christians, Parsis and Jews have their own personal laws. The 'Hindu' comprises of Hinduism, Buddhism, Jainism and Sikhism in the personal law. (Paras Diwan and Peeyushi Diwan, *Family law,* 2nd edn., Allahabad: Allahabad Law Agency, 1994, P. 4). The persons who is a convert or re-convert to Jainism, Buddhism, Sikhism or Hinduism is also a Hindu according to law. This section deals with the Hindu, Muslim, Christian and Parsi personal laws which deals with sexuality and marriage.

1. The Hindu Personal Law

The Hindu Marriage Act was enacted by the parliament on 18th may, 1955. (Act No. xxv of 1955) This Act applies to:

(a) any person who is a Hindu by religion in any of its forms or developments, including a Virashaiva, a Lingayat or a follower of the Brahma, Prarthana or Arya Samaj;

(b) any person who is a Buddhist, Jain or Sikhy by religion;

(c) any other person domiciled in the territories to which this act extends, who is not a Muslim, Christian, Parsi or Jew by religion (The following persons are Hindus, Buddhists, Jainists or Sikhs by religion. a. any child, legitimate or illegitimate, both of whose parents are Hindus, Buddhists, Jainists or Sikhs by religion. b. any child, legitimate or illegitimate, one of whose parents is a Hindu, Buddhist, Jaina or Sikh by religion and who is brought up as a member of the tribe, community, group or family to which such parents belong. c. any person who is a convert or re-convert to the Hindu, Buddhist, Jaina or Sikh religion) Central Law Agency, *The Hindu Law* Acts, Allahabad: Central Law Agency, 1995, P. 3, cf., Asutosh Mookerjee, *Marriage Separation*

and Divorce, Calcutta: S.C. Sankar and Sona Ltd., 1986, P. 263).

The conditions for Hindu marriage follow:

(i) neither party has a spouse living at the time of marriage;

(ii) at the time of marriage, neither party -

(a) is incapable of giving valid consent to it in consequence of unsoundness of mind; or

(b) though capable of giving a valid consent, has been suffering from mental disorder of such a kind or such an extent as to be unfit or marriage and the procreation of children; or

(c) has been subject to recurrent attacks of insanity or epilepsy;

(iii) the bridegroom has completed the age of twenty one years and the bride the age of eighteen years at the time of marriage;

(iv) the parties are not within the degrees of prohibited relationship unless the custom or usage governing each of them permits a marriage between the two;

(v) the parties are not sapindars (a relationship with reference to any person extends as far as the third generation in the line of ascent through the mother, and the fifth in the line of ascent through the father. In each cause the person concerned is counted as the first generation) of each other, unless the custom or usage governing each of them permits of a marriage between the two. (Asutosh Mookerjee, *Marriage Separation and Divorce,*Calcutta: S.C. Sarkar and Sons Ltd., 1986, P. 270).

According to the Hindu Marriage Act (1955), no Hindu male can have more than one wife and no Hindu female can have more than one husband. The Hindu widows can remarry. According to this act, no Hindu can marry a non-Hindu. But they can enter into what is known as "civil marriage" through the Special Marriage Act, 1954. The inter-caste marriages are permitted. The marriage between near relations like cousins or uncles and nieces allowed only if their customs allows such marriage. (P.D. Mathew, P.M. Bakshi, *Hindu Marriage and Divorce,* New Delhi: Indian Social Institute, 1994, PP. 2-3).

The impotency, the unsound mind (insanity), the discovery that the wife is pregnant at the time of marriage, the consent of the person is obtained by force, the spouse is not willing to cohabit with the party are the clauses by which annulment of marriage is possible. (*Ibid.,* p. 73, Paras Diwan and Peeyushi Diwan, Family Law, Op.Cit.., P. 90). The grounds for divorce are: - 1. adultery (it means a voluntary sexual intercourse between persons not married), 2. treating with cruelty, 3. desertion for at least two years (Desertion is conduct by way of permanent forsaking of marital obligations), 4. conversion to another religion, 5. incurable insanity of mental order, 6. incurable and virulent leprosy, 7. venereal disease in a communicable form, 8. renouncing the world and becoming a sanyasi, 9. not being heard of for seven years, 10. non-resumption of cohabitation after a decree of judicial separation, for at least one year, 11. non-compliance with a decree of restitution of conjugal rights for at least one year, 12. husband being guilty of rape or unnatural sex after marriage, 13. husband failing to pay the wife maintenance ordered by court; (P.D. Mathew, P.M. Bakshi, *Hindu marriage and Divorce,* New Delhi; Indian Social Instiute, 1994, p. 8; Asutosh Mookerjee, Marriage Separation and Divorce, Op.Cit., PP. 283-291). and 14. by mutual consent. According to Asutosh Mookerjee the bigamy is also a ground for divorce according to the Hindu Marriage Act. (*Asutosh Morkerjee Marriage Separation and Divorce,* Op.Cit., P. 289).

The remarriage is possible after the period of appeal against the decree has expired. (*The Hindu Law Acts,* Op.Cit., P. 12). The Hindu Marriage Law is very much concerned of the sanctity of marriage. The conjugality is given importance that it advises to cohabit with spouse and the impotency and ill-health are taken seriously to become the causes for divorce. The illicit sex and the bestiality are seriously dealt with. The question is whether insanity and ill-health after marriage can be a ground for divorce.

2. The Muslim Personal Law

The Muslim Personal Law is one of the most controversial laws in India. The Muslim Personal Law (Shariat) Act 1937 is applicable to all Mohammadens. A Mohammeden is anyone who acknowledges that there is only one God and Mohammed is the prophet. (*Asutosh Mukerjee,* Marriage Separation and Divorce, Op.Cit., P. 24). The Sunni's and Shias are the major sects in Islam. The Khojas and Cutihi Memons of Bombay are originally Hindus, but are subjected to Shariah Law and they are converted to Islam. A Mohammedan male can marry a Kitabia (a female believer in Christianity or Judaism). This marriage is a valid one. But a Mohammedan women cannot contract a valid marriage with a male believer in Christianity or Judaism. However, the Muslim Woman's marriage with a Non-Muslim is merely irregular and not void. (*Ibid.*, P. 25). Under Shia Law the marriage between a Muslim and Non-Muslim is unlawful and void. But the Muslim male may contract a valid Muta (temporary marriage for enjoyment) marriages with some non-muslims. (*Ibid.*, P. 25). The Muslim belong to different sects can marry each other. So the inter sect marriages are allowed.

The observations and analysis of P.D. Mathew and P.K. Bakshi go like this: The Muslim male can have four wives. But the Muslim female cannot have more than one husband. The Muslim (male or female) who has attained puberty and is of sound mind can marry. (The child marriage is prohibited under the Child Marriage Restraint Act 1929. But it does not nullify the marriage, though it leads to punishment). If a Muslim has not attained puberty, he or she can be married by his or her guardian. (*P.D. Mathew and P.K. Bhakshi, Muslim Marriage and Divorce,* New Delhi: Indian Social Institute, 1989, PP. 6-7).

The prohibited degree of relationship (marriage) are as follows: One cannot marry,

1. one's own mother or grandmother
2. one's daughter or granddaughter
3. one's sister (full or consanguine)
4. one's own niece or grand niece
5. one's own aunt or great aunt (paternal/maternal)
6. the ascendants and descendants of one's wife
7. the wife of one's ascendant or descendant. (*Ibid.*, PP. 8-9).

The divorce is of various categories:

(a) extra judicial divorce, divorce at the instance of the husband unilaterally and without requiring any ground (This is the populous 'Talaq' formula).

(b) extra judicial divorce at the initiative of the husband under constructive category. It is called a 'constructive' category. It is divorce in the form of Ila and Zihar at the initiative of the husband. The husband take a vow of abstinence from sexual intercourse for at least four months and when the vow is fulfilled, it means divorce. This

is the Ila form of divorce which would be settled by the judiciary. In Zihar form the husband compares his wife within the prohibited degrees for marriage. (Such as comparing the wife to the mother) On the husband making such announcement the wife become entitled to seek judicial divorce.

(c) extra judicial divorce by mutual consent as confirmed by statute,

(d) Judicial divorce at the instance of the wife, on specified grounds in statute. (*Ibid.*, PP. 11, 14-15).

The Talaq is a very complex issue today in India. Even in the absence of wife, the Talaq can be pronounced. It is a unilateral divorce by the husbands. According to Shia Law, it must be pronounced orally before two competent witnesses. The Sunni Law prescribes that Talaq may be pronounced orally or in writing. The Talaq may be pronounced as it is said below.

(a) A single pronouncement during the woman's Tuhr (period between two menstruations). This must be followed abstinence during iddat. It becomes effective and irrevocable when Iddat expires (Ahsan).

(b) Three pronouncement made during three successive Tuhrs. There should be abstinence during all the three Tuhrs. Divorce is complete and irrevocable on the third pronouncement (Hasan)

(c) A triple pronouncement made during the Tuhr in one sentence (I divorce thee thrice) or three separate pronouncements during one tuhr such as "I divorce thee. I divorce thee. I divorce thee." (Talak-ul-bidaat).

(d) One pronouncement (single) during Tuhr indicating an intention to divorce irrevocably. It is effective and irrevocable, the moment it is pronounced (Talak-ul-bidaat). A Muslim wife cannot use Talaq in order to divorce her husband. (*Ibid.*, PP. 12-13, cf. Asutosh Mookerjee, *Marriage Separation and Divorce,* Op.Cit., PP. 80-83).

The Muslim wife can sue for divorce under the Act of 1939 on the following reasons:

(a) The whereabouts of the husband is are not known for a period of four years.

(b) husbands failure or neglect to provide maintenance to the wife.

(c) husband being sentenced to imprisonment for a period of seven years or more.

(d) husband's failure without reasonable cause to perform marital obligation for a period of three years or more.

(e) husband being impotent at the time of marriage and continuing to be so till filing of the suit.

(f) husband's insanity for at least two years or husband;s suffering from leprosy or virulent venereal disease.

(g) exercise of right of "repudiation" of marriage by the wife (A wife married by her guardians while she is below the age of 15 years, can repudiate the marriage before attaining age of 18 years provided the marriage has not been consummated).

(h) husband's cruelty (husband's association with women of evil repute, husband's attempt to force the wife to lead an immoral life, husband's obstructing the wife in the observance of her religion practices, husband's unequal treatment of one of his wives, where he has more than one wife.) (*Ibid.*, PP. 17-19).

There was also a question whether a Muslim woman could get maintenance after divorce. In the famous Mohammed Ahmed Khan Vs. Shah Bano (985), the Supreme Court held that the husband must continue to maintain her until her remarriage. But this has undergone change under the law passed by the parliament. The new legislation says that after idaat the wife can get maintenance from the relatives who are her potential heirs. The husband's liability ceases with the idaat (three menstrual courses after the date of divorce - this means three months). Failing maintenance by above relatives, the wife can get maintenance from the Wakf Board. (*Ibid.*, PP.19-20).

The remarriage is allowed to Muslim women with certain conditions. "Under Muslim Law, after dissolution of marriage, by divorce or death a woman is required to wait for certain period, before the expiry of which she cannot remarry." (Parash Diwan, Peeyushi Diwan, *Family Law,* Op.Cit., P. 184). In the case of the dissolution of consummated marriage by divorce, the wife is required to perform Idda of three months. If she is pregnant the Idda will continue till she delivers the child. The Muslim law insists that the husband too cannot remarry during the period wife is undergoing idda. When the marriage is dissolved by death, the wife is to observe the idda of four lunar months and ten days. (*Ibid.,* P. 184).

Most of the conservative Muslim scholars are not willing to modify the Shariat or Muslim personal law in believing that the author of Shariah is God himself. (Muitahid-al-Asr Maulana Syed Ali Naqi, "Can the Shariah- Laws be modified?" *Muslim Law,* edited by F.R. Faridi and M.N. Siddigi, Aligarh: Islamic -Research Circle, 1973, P. 12). Maulana Mohammed Ishaq Sandelvi feels that "Muslim Personal Law, is in fact, another name of the cultural and social freedom of the Indian Muslims." (Moulana Mohammed Ishaq Sahdelvi "Muslim Personal

Law", *Muslim Personal* Law edited by F.R., Faridi and M.N. Siddigi, Op.Cit., P. 16). The Muslims have a close affinity towards their personal law, and they do not favour the modification or reform of it. They also reject the idea of a uniform civil code. For Ishaq Sandelvi, the Shariat is a set of eternal and times rules. Arun Shourie the journalist and social scientist argues for the reform in the Muslim Personal Law in the wake of Shab Bano controversy. But the Muslim fundamentalists are totally for protecting the existing Shariah. (Arun Shourie, "The Shariat", *The Illustrated weekly of India,* (January 5, 1986), P. 7).Shourie argues to reexamine the Muslim personal law in the light of modern secular principles, since he feels that what is known as Shariah today is more the creation of clerics and magistrates than of the Quran and the practice of the prophet.

The Talaq contraversy is also a watershed in the Indian situation. A decree issued by Jamat-e-Ahle Hadis states that the pronouncement of talaq in a row is invalid. According to Sheik Ataur Madani, "A month has to pass before the husband can pronounce a talaq for a second time and another month for it to be pronounced a third time." (Ranjit Bhushan, "A Separate Identity", *Indian Express* (Sunday Magazine), (July 11, 1993) P. 3). Furqan Ahmed also criticises the ignorance of Indian men who used triple talaq in a row which is against the original intention of shariah. The triple talaq is also sometime approved by the Maulavis and judicial court to make divorce irrevocable. These are mistakes. According to Farqun Ahmed, "Under the law of divorce derived from the Quranic injunctions and teachings of the prophet, 'triple talaq' can never be accepted as a weapon against women with all its injustice." ("Understanding Islamic Divorce", *Indian Express* (August 1, 1993), P. 8). In the words of Seema Alavi, the Talaq is a unilateral act. Since the Islam condemns divorce, so the simplistic means of divorce is inhuman and suicidal. ("Talaq,

Talaq, Talaq". *In Indian Express* (February 27, 1994), P. 10). Shenaaz Sheikh was looking for companionship and equality from her husband, but he made her home a prison. When she demanded her rights, triple talaq was the result. (Shenaaz Sheikh, "A Muslim Woman Speaks Out", *Indian Express* (December 9, 1994), P. 8).

The present Muslim Personal Law badly affects the women. The proper perspective is lacking when Shariah is exercised. However, the Orthodox Muslims and scholars are rigid and not for attempting a humane interpretation of it. The Shariah which is found in the enactment of 1937 protects the importance of sexuality as the husbands cannot move as they like. They are insisted to cohabit, and if not after two years it can lead to divorce. The impotence is also given as a reason to divorce, since the conjugal right of women can not be entertained by an impotent man. The marriage is not seriously understood by Muslims as the divorce is quite easy for men even for simple reason. It can lead to irresponsible marriage relationship.

3. The Parsi Personal Law

The Parsi Marriage and Divorce Act was enacted in 1936. (Act III of 1936). The Act applies to Parsi Zoroastrians of India. The consanguinity or affinity can be a cause for making a Parsi marriage unlawful. Bigamy is not allowed. Remarriage is not permitted unless there is a proper dissolution of the first contract. (Asutosh Mookerjee, Marriage Separation and Divorce, Op.Cit., P. 359).

The grounds for divorce are following:

(a) that the marriage has not been consummated within one year after its solemnization owing to the wilful refusal of the spouse

(b) the unsound mind

(c) pre-marital pregnancy

(*d*) that the spouse committed adultery or bigamy or rape

(*e*) that the husband has compelled the wife to submit her to prostitution

(*f*) that the spouse is imprisoned for seven years

(*g*) that the husband or wife deserts the partner for at least three years

(*h*) that the decree or the order for judicial separation has been passed against the defendant, or an order has been passed against the defendant by a Magistrate awarding separate maintenance to the plaintiff and the parties have not had marital intercourse for three years or more since such decree or order.

(*i*) that the defendant has failed to comply with a decree for restitution of conjugal rights for a year or more

(*j*) that the husband or wife ceases to be a Parsi by converting to another religion. (*Ibid.*, P. 366).

The Parsi personal law seriously deals with the irresponsibility in marriage. The conjugal rights are given extreme importance by the law. The married partners are to lead a responsible life. They are not to be involved in adultery or bigamy. The living together is also encouraged by the law.

4. The Christian Personal Law

The Indian Christian Marriage Act (Act XV of 1872) is the main point of discussion in this section. The term 'Indian Christian' includes the Christian descendants of native of India converted to Christianity. The expression Christian means persons professing the Christian religion. The valid marriage should be solemnized if one or both persons is or are a Christian or Christians. (Allahabad Law

Agency, *The Indian Christian Marriage Act,* Allahabad: Allahabad Law Agency, n.d. P. 6).

The law relating to divorce among Christians in India can be found in the Indian Divorce Act, 1869. The Christian husband can seek divorce on the ground that his wife is guilty of adultery. The wife can seek divorce by the following grounds:

(a) husband's conversion to another religion and his having gone through a form of marriage with another woman;

(b) husband's being guilty of incestuous adultery (Adultery is sexual relations by a married person with a person to whom he or she is not married: Incestuous adultery is defined in Section 2(6) of Indian Divorce Act on adultery committed by a husband with a woman with whom, if his wife were dead, he could not lawfully contract marriage by reason of her being within the prohibited degrees of consanguinity or affinity),

(c) husband's bigamy, coupled with adultery,

(d) husband's marriage with another woman coupled with adultery,

(e) husband's being guilty of rape, sodomy or bestiality,

(f) husband's adultery coupled with cruelty,

(g) husband's adultery, coupled with desertion without reasonable excuse, for two years or upwards (desertion implies an abandonment against the wish of the person changing it." (P.D. Mathew and P.M. Bakshi, *Christian Law of Divorce,* 3rd Reprint, New Delhi: Indian Social Instiute, 1993, P. 5).

The marriage can be nullified under the Indian Divorce Act on the following reasons:

(*a*) Respondent (opposite party) was impotent at the time of marriage and at the time of institution of the suit,

(*b*) parties are within prohibited degree of relationship,

(*c*) either party was a lunatic or idiot at the time of marriage; or

(*d*) the former spouse of either party was living at the time of marriage and the marriage was then in force. (*Ibid.*, P. 11; Paras Diwan and Peeyushi Diwan, *Family Law,* Op.Cit., P. 89).

The Christian divorce law is said to be unfair to women. The women cannot seek divorce for mere adultery of her husband. But the husband can divorce his wife just for adultery. The conditional adultery is saving the husband. It is conditional since the adultery should be coupled with incest, cruelty, sexual perversion, bigamy or desertion in the case of husband. According to P.M. Bakshi, the same criteria (adultery as a cause for divorce unconditionally) should be applicable for both husband and wife. He states, "One would have expected that the same remedy would be available to the wife. But unfortunately this is not so." (P.M. Bakshi, "Christian Divorce Law unfair to woman", *Indian Express,* (March 27, 1984), P. 8). There is a move from the progressive men and women to seek a revision of the Indian Christian Marriage Act and law of divorce. Updating the laws are always important. Annie Thayil, the lawyer also pointed out that, the Christian law of divorce is unfair to women. ("Christian Marriage Law", *Religion and Society,* Vol. xxxi, No. 1 (March, 1984), P. 15).

5. The Special Marriage Act

The Special Marriage Act was enacted in 1954. This act is found as an improvement upon the old Act of 1872 which it repeals and contains additions deemed necessary to enable the society to keep pace with the march of civilization in modern times is that it permits inter communal and inter caste marriages. (Central Law Agency, *The Special Marriage Act,* 1954, Allahabad: Central Law Agency, 1955, P. 5). It is enacted as Act No. 43 of 1954.

The conditions for marriage under the special marriage is as follows:

The prohibited relationship includes:

1. relationship by half or uterine blood as well as by full blood ('full blood' and 'half blood' - two persons are said to be related to each other by full blood when they are descended from a common ancestor by the same wife and by half blood when they are descended from a common ancestor but by different wives)
2. illegitimate blood relationship as well as legitimate,
3. relationship by adoption as well as by blood.

The following conditions are to be met by the husband and wife for the solemnization of marriage.

1. neither party has a spouse living
2. neither party is incapable of giving a valid consent in consequence of unsoundness of mind
3. neither party is suffering from epilepsy or insanity or impotency
4. the parties are not within the degree of prohibited relationship
5. the male has completed the age of 21 and the female 18 years. (*Ibid.*, PP. 2-3).

The marriage can be nullified if: - a. the marriage has not been consummated owing to the wilful refusal of the respondent to consummate marriage, or b. the respondent was pregnant at the time of marriage by some other person than the petitioner; or c. the consent of either party to marriage was obtained by fraud. The divorce can be sought by the husband or wife on the following grounds:

(a) the voluntary sexual intercourse with any person other than his or her spouse

(b) desertion of the spouse for a continuous period not less than two years

(c) spouse is undergoing a sentence of imprisonment for seven years for an offence as defined in the Indian Penal Code (Act XLV of 1860)

(d) cruelty

(e) incurable mental disorder

(f) suffering from venereal disease in a communicable form

(g) suffering from leprosy

(h) Not been heard of as being alive for a period of seven years or more by those persons who would naturally have heard of the spouse if the spouse had been alive. (*ibid.*, pp. 8-9; Asutosh Mookerjee, Marriage Separation and Divorce, Op.Cit., PP. 399-404).

The Special Marriage Act does not allow polyandry or polygyny. A person marries under this Act should not have any other spouse. (P.D. Mathew, P.M. Bakshi, Special Marriage Act, New Delhi: Indian Socal Institute, 1991, P. 3).Though the personal laws on marriage and divorce in the Indian law system is giving ample provisions for divorce, the Christian church or other religious communities will allow divorce by those reasons stated in the Marriage Acts. Most of the Christian Churches in India will not usually permit divorce after the consummation of marriage. The law of each communities differ one another. While monogamy is the principle of Christian personal law, polygyny is permitted by Muslim Personal Law. The personal laws are stressing mostly the normative principles.

6. The Personal Laws and Uniform Civil Code

Though there is no unanimity over the issue of the common or Uniform Civil Code among the different religious leaders, this idea is in the air. It is a contraversial topic. While the Hindu religious leaders advocate for uniform civil code, the Muslims are suspicious of it. Since there is different personal laws which conflict each other, the need for a uniform civil code is being discussed today.

Each religious communities were permitted to follow its personal laws in the field of marriage, divorce, inheritance, succession, gifts and adoption of children by the non-interference policy of British rules. (Thomas Kadankavil, "Editorial", *The Journal of Dharma,* Vol. XI, No. 3 (July-Sep. 1986), P. 215).Later most of the personal laws are accepted by the enactment of the Indian Government. The question about the uniform civil code came up in the constituent Assembly of India soon after the independence. According to Fr. Kadankavil, "The main supportive thought behind this thinking was that secularism clearly demands a Uniform Family Law, and that separate family laws for different communities would result in discrimination between the communities which is repugnant to the secular character of the state." (*Ibid.*, P. 215).

The debate over the issue of the uniform civil code came out with the following clause which was adopted as Article 44 (Article 44 appears as 'Directive principles of state policy', part IV, Article 36-50) in the Indian constitution:" The State shall endeavour to secure for the citizens a Uniform Civil Code throughout the territory of

India. (*Ibid.*, P. 215). The 'Directive principles' were not conceived to be mandatory. According to Fr.Thomas Kadankavil, "If the directive concerning the Uniform civil code is made mandatory, it would go against the following fundamental right enunciated in article 25: "subject to public order, morality and health and to other provisions of this part, all persons are equally entitled to freedom of this part, all persons are equally entitled to freedom of conscience and the right to freely profess, practice and propagate religion." *(Ibid.*, P. 216).

One of the contraversial cases with regard to Muslim personal and Uniform civil code is the Mohammed Ahmad Vs Shah Bano (1985), the Judgement that in the case of the divorced woman it is incumbant upon the ex-husband under Section 125 of criminal procedure code, to provide her maintenance if she is unable to maintain herself, till she marries or dies. This verdict was regarded by the Muslim scholars as an interference in the Muslim personal law (shariat) and an indirect attempt to impose the Uniform Civil Code upon them. (*Ibid.*, P. 216).

Tahir Mohmood is suspicious of those who advocate for Uniform Civil Code. He states, "The slogan of a Uniform Civil Code seems to have been adopted by as a camouflage to attempt wiping off the cultural traditions of all the religious minorities in India." (Tahir Mohmood, "Uniform Vs common Civil Code in India" *The Journal of Dharma,* vol. xi, No. 3 (July-September, 1986). P. 228). According to S.N. Balasundaram, "The desire for a Common Civil Code in India is a thrust towards modernity in traditional society which seeks to weld the mutually exclusive communal and religious groups into a united and viable society. It is a laudable but difficult attempt at laying the foundations of secularism which is envisaged by our constitution and, in the context of a religiously pluralistic society means an equal respect to all religions, though thus is not the meaning in which westerners understand the concept." (S.N. Balasundaram, "The Conflict Between Tradition and Modernity, *"The journal of Dharma,* Vol xi, No. 3 (July- Septmber 1986), P. 230).

Balasundaram sees the positive elements of a Uniform Civil Code as the states, By fostering the secular democratic values of liberty, equality and fraternity which form the ideological basis of our constitution,

The children are used or abused by men and women for their sexual gratification. The parents, the relatives and the tuition teachers are reportedly abusing the boy or girl children. There are cases in which the children are sexually abused till the point of death. (Sunil Solomon Ghazan, *Adults Amuzed But child Abused, New Delhi: Navdin prakashan Kendra, 1995.* PP. 22-23). "Today thousands of children keep pouring into the urban cities, either kidnapped, or voluntarily they enter into the cities due to broken homes, step motherly treatment meted out to them by parents, due to the sexual abuse by their own fathers. Pregnant teenagers committing suicide, boy being homosexuly abused, neighbourhood men and women sexually abusing young and innocent children for the pleasure and amusement". (*Ibid.,* P. 10). It is observed that there are social and psychological reasons behind sexual offenses. The unfulfilled sexual desire is one of the reason for it. There are also reasons like emotional instability and impulsiveness of the person. (Stanton Wheeler, "Sex offence: A Sociolgical Critique" *The Sociology of Crime and Deliquency,* edited by Melvin E. Wolfang and et. al Toronto: John Wiley and sons, 1970. P. 628.) we can build an integrated nation. One of the practical means of strengthening the bond of political unity between the different religious communities is to lay the firm base for an integrated Indian Society. It is in this context that the framing of a Common Civil Code assumes great significance. For such a code reflecting the secular spirit of the constitution would strengthen the existing social bonds and foster the political integration of the different religious communities by subjecting them to a common judicial procedure in respect of the personal law. (*Ibid.*, PP. 237-238).

Though the discussion over the Uniform Civil Code is there, it is difficult to come to the agreement on how to do that in religiously and ethical pluralistic society. The Hindus, the Jainists, Buddhists, Islam, Sikhs, Parsees and Christians have their culture, the values and perspectives on the issues like sexuality and marriage. Unless religious leaders come to certain common understanding it is not easy. Though Tahir Mohmood accepts that the Special Marriage Act of 1954 is understood as a step towards Common Civil code, there is noone even presented a concrete picture of the form and contents of the proposed code. (S, Tahir Mohmood, "Uniform Civil code and Islamic Law", *Religion and Society* vol. xxvi, No. 4, (December 1979). PP. 29, 36).

Asgar Ali Engineer talks about the moulding of Hindu customs so also the Muslim. The reform of the Muslim personal law is desirable in his view. In order to do that we should avoid the terms'change' or 'reform' but use the phrase 'creative interpretation in the changed context.' (Asgar Ali Engineer, "Uniform Civil code and Indian Muslims", *Religion and Society* vol. xxiv, No. 4 (December, 1979), P. 84).

Asgar Ali Engineer's observation should be noted that it is important to reform the personal laws of different religious communities. This is applicable to Christian personal law also. The prejudice against the women should be avoided from the Christian personal law. It is necessary to make a 'creative interpretation' of the religious texts in the changed context, in order to make the texts and its principles or teachings relevant to the particular community and the community at large.

Instituting certain common norms and principles based on love justice, equality and humanness is important in any ethically plural context. This can be applied to Indian context also. Asgar Ali Engineer rightly states, "India is a secular nation and as such has to serve all her citizens irrespective of caste or religion on an equal basis and ensuring them all universally accepted human rights. This applies as well to the domain of conjugal relations, inheritance etc. as to any other social or political domain." (*Ibid.*, P. 80).

The ethical pluralism is a reality of the Indian context. The perspective on sexuality and marriage are also diverse in the context of secularization, among the various religious traditions, tribal communities and in the personal laws. The different communities hold their particular norms and practices. There are issues related to the sexuality and marriage which go against what is normative. In the particular cases, it is important to consider the persons in their moral dilemma or crises on to deal them in a loving and merciful way. In this respect, an adequate ethical approach is missing to help the people. The individuals may go among, but it is important to consider them rather than rejecting them.

The issues like prostitution, bigamy, polygamy, child molestation, pre- marital sex, extra-marital sex, and divorce are found in the Indian context, because of secularization, psycho-social, economic or other historial or political reasons. These are to be accepted as the Indian reality. The individuals and communities are undergoing ethical dilemma without getting proper concern, care, love and mercy. The issues related to sexuality and marriage found (in all situations in the religious and secular context). There are several rules found in the different religious traditions in the Marriage Acts or in the personal laws. These norms or *apriori* rules are important. They are good as standing rules for any community of individuals to maintain the order in the society. But what is the role of the Christian principle of love, mercy, care and the concern towards those who are undergoing the crisis, or in a situation which is against the *apriori* norms. There are contributing factors (Psycho-social, economic or political secularization or my other) for this situation. It is important to consider them, rather than criticizing or condemning them on the basis of *apriori* rules. In the cases or issues of the people, it is significant to have an approach to deal them in the spirit of love and mercy. In the question Uniform Civil Code also what is to be considered is the *apriori* norms and also the approach which would look at the issues or the practices of the different communities in the context of sexuality and marriage with love, care and generosity in order to have a loving and harmonious co-existence. An evaluative approach is missing in the Indian context, though there are normative principles.

Chapter 5

The Aposteriori-Agapeic Perspective of Joseph Fletcher as a Basis for an Evaluative Approach for our Times

Having discussed the background of situation ethics, the Aposteriori-agapeic approach to ethical issues with special reference to sexuality and marriage, the Biblical understanding of sexuality and marriage and the attitude towards sexuality and marriage in the Indian context, it is appropriate to discuss the importance and relevance of Joseph Fletcher's agapeic approach for our times. This chapter deals with the following subjects such as

A. Presentation of the Problem

In this section divorce is selected as an issue to be reflected on. It is a very significant issue in the context of sexuality and marriage. It is a live issue which challenges the marital love and covenantal fidelity.

Divorce is a threat to marriage, and it is part of the erosion of values. The negative effect of secularization has contributed to divorce. The marriage is understood in the secularized context as a social contract, and the sacramental aspect of marriage is not given importance. Divorce is a common phenomenon found in most of the communities. The common reasons for divorce are impotence, the drinking, drug addiction, psychological disorders, wife beating, marital infidelity and lack of economic soundness. It is very clear that the secularization and the psycho-social reasons are behind the divorce.

The religious communities have their own particular views on sexuality and marriage. The Hindu religious tradition upholds the fidelity and sanctity of marriage. Separation from wife is not esteemed, but divorces are not uncommon. Islam Shariah permits divorce by mutual consent of partners. The husbands also have the right to divorce their wives by saying 'Talaq'. Parsi religion allows divorce in the case of sterility and infidelity. The Christian churches do not uphold divorce. They emphasize the indissolubility of marriage. Among the tribal communities divorce is practised. Among the Uralies of Wynad, divorce was permitted on the grounds of ill-treatment either by husband or wife (Chap. 4).

The Personal laws also deal with the issue of divorce. According to Hindu marriage Act, adultery, cruelty, incurable insanity and desertion are the reasons for divorce. The extra-judicial and judicial divorce is permitted by Muslim personal law. The Muslim women could divorce if husband is insane, impotent, having venereal disease or deserted his wife. The Parsi personal law permits divorce in the case of adultery, desertion, bigamy, and unsound mind. The Christian personal law allows divorce mainly in the case of adultery. The special marriage Act permits divorce in the case of adultery, desertion, cruelty and insanity.

Marriage is understood as sacrament and indissolubility is hailed, at the same time divorce is becoming a common phenomena. Though marital fidelity and sacramental aspect of marriage is emphasized the divorce is also done because of psycho-social reasons or by some simple reasons (eg. beauty). Among the Muslims, divorce is not a serious matter, and it is an acceptable practice. Among some tribals divorce is common.

It is very clear that diverse views on divorce are held by different religious traditions and personal laws. What is normative is differing to each tradition. While Islam permits divorce even for no serious reasons (privilege of husband in an extra-judicial way - Talaq), Christian churches and Christian personal law do not accept divorce, except in the case of adultery. Divorce brings a moral crisis. It becomes a disorganizing element in the family setting. It affects badly the human relationship. The value of marriage is threatened by divorce. Divorce is an evil, but how should we respond to this issue? Condemning the persons and communities who involved in divorce is a common attitude in the crisis situation, where the persons look for guidance, support or help. It is also important to analyse the issue and deal the persons involved in the case with the Christian principle of love, mercy and generosity. The legalistic attitude has to be examined as it should not badly affect a person or a community.

B. The Values Regarding the Issue

This section deals with the teaching of the church (the teaching of the pentecostals, Catholic church) and the teaching of Jesus.

1. The Pentecostal View

The Pentecostals stand for holiness and they are for the sanctity of marriage and covenant fidelity. The apriori rules or norms are stressed by them. (Steve Dursoff, *Bright wind of the spirit,* New Jersy: Logos International, 1972, P. 78). The homosexuality, pre-marital sex, extra-marital sex and the divorce are not endorsed by pentecostals. They uphold the sanctity of sex and the sacramentality of marriage. According to Pastor T. G. Oommen, one of the early leaders of pentecostals, divorce is against the will of

God and should not be promoted. (T. G. Oommen, *Kudumba Samvidhanam Thiruvachana Velichathil (The title of this Malayalam book means, 'Family planning in the light of the Bible),* Kumbanad: girideepam *Press,* 1971, P. 17). This indicates that pentecostals do not approve the violation of covenant-fidelity.

According to pentecostals divorce is against the Biblical teaching, and divorce was permitted in the Old Testament times because of the 'hardness of the heart' of people. (T. P. Varghese, *ed., Pentecosthu Daiva sasthram (Malayalam, title means 'Pentecostal Theology'),* Thiruvalla: Reader's Publications, *2000, P. 506*). Divorce is understood as an evil by pentecostals. (*Ibid.,* P. 590). The pentecostals are stressing the normative principles, but do not have an evaluative approach in order to help and guide the persons and communities in their crisis.

2. The Teaching of the Catholic Church

The Catholic Church emphasize the sanctity of sex and sacramental aspect of marriage. The Vatican II affirms the love and fidelity between married partners and it rejects the unfaithfulness (adultery) and divorce. Discussing the married love it states, "Endorsed by mutual fidelity and, above all, consecrated by Christ's sacrament, this love abides faithfully in mind and body in prosperity and diversity and hence excludes both adultery and divorce". (Austin Flannery, ed, *Vatican Council II, Bombay:* St Paul Publications, 1975, P. 855).

According to 'The code of the canon law', "A marriage which is ratified and consummated cannot be dissolved by any human power or by any case other than death". (Theological Publications in India, *The Code of Canon Law,* Bangalore: *TPI,* 1991, P. 200). The Catholic teaching advises that the adultery should not necessarily leads to divorce. It states, "It is earnestly recommended that a spouse motivated by Christian charity and solicitous for the good of the family, should not refuse to pardon and adulterous partner and should not sunder the conjugal life". (*Ibid.,* P. 203).

It is clear that the 'Catholic church teaches that marriage is intrinsically indissoluble that is that married people, whether Christian or not can never abandon their own marriage and lawfully contract a new one". (Waldeman Molinski, "Marriage" *Sacramentum Mundi Vols. 3 & 4*, Bangalore: 1989, P. 397). In certain cases the Catholic Church permits 'separation'. Code of the canon law states, "within six months of having spontaneously terminated the common conjugal life, the innocent spouse is to bring a case for separation to the competent ecclesiastical authority. Having examined all the circumstances, this authority is to consider whether the innocent spouse can be brought to condone the fault and not prolong the separation permanently". (*Ibid.,* P. 203). The indissolubility of marriage is upheld by Catholic view but it provides 'separation' in cases where partners cannot get along. (Jose Chiramel and Varghese Palathinkal, *Patriarchal and Matrimonial Legislations in the Oriental Code,* Alwaye: St. Thomas Academy for Research, 1992, P.108).

The oriental code argues that matrimonial covenant is instituted by the creator himself. It affirms the unity and indissolubility of marriage. (*Ibid.,* P. 108). The Catholic Church realizes the importance of normative principles and it also sees the value of an aposteriori-agapeic approach to consider the cases related to marriage so that 'Separation' is allowed. The aposteriori-agapeic approach is very much found in Catholic thinking. It is understood by them as a pastoral approach. But it is found that there is no approach in order to consider the cases in which persons/communities undergo the question of divorce as it is part of moral laxity or traditionally accepted practice, especially in the cases outside the Church. The pastoral approach is confined among the members of the church, and it does not apply to the people outside the church i.e., the community live around us.

3. The Teaching of Jesus Christ

The teaching of Jesus is already discussed (chapter-3). Here the main inferences are stated again.

The Old Testament upheld the importance of sacramentality of marriage and covenantal fidelity. Divorce is not usually allowed by it, as it is against the intention of marriage. The marital bond cannot be broken unless there is some serious approach or lewdness (Dt. 24: 1). The divorce was strictly controlled. Divorce was permitted because of the adamant nature or disobedience of persons.

Jesus stressed the indissolubility of marriage. He permitted divorce only in the case of extreme irresponsibility (e.g. adultery) in married life. Ernest Scott opines that the Gospel of Mathew insists on the saving clause that divorce is allowed only on the ground of adultery (Mt. 5: 31, 32). Divorce was allowed in O.T. because of the hardness of heart of people (Mt. 19). While affirming the normative principles (apriori rules) that divorce is against the commandments, Jesus was aware of the psycho-social factors which may lead to separation or divorce. So an evaluative approach is also found in Jesus. An aposteriori-agapeic perspective is very much found in Jesus' teaching. This was clear in Jesus dealing with the Samaritan women (John. 4) who was in a state of divorce of husbands.

Covenant-fidelity is the norm in which divorce is to be condemned. Here Jesus was hailing the norm as he was against the divorce. At the same time he forgave the sinner without condoning the sin. Jesus' agapeic approach was considering seriously the psycho-social factors when an ethical judgement is made. He deals the cases with love, care mercy and generosity, but he was aware of the deliberate manipulation of the situations by the persons (eg. the pharisees were involved in sexual abuse and exploitation deliberately, and they were so self-righteous and not feeling guilty of their sin). Jesus' evaluative perspective towards the divorce is not legitimizing the immoral act, but evaluate the context and derive at conclusions on the merit of each case. He was affirming the importance of the normative principles which would curb the arbitrariness, and simultaneously granting mercy to those who are in serious crises who look for help, support, guidance and restoration. Value is given extreme importance by the pentecostals, Catholic Church and the teaching of Jesus. What is normative is given serious attention by them. The values are important and no community can exist without the values. The norms are guiding principles of the society. But at the same time an evaluative approach is needed to consider with love and generosity. This is to help those who undergo the crisis situations which can be termed as posterior, but this does not undermine the role of norms or what is normative. Jesus' evaluative approach goes beyond the Jewish community. It was applied to non-jewish persons and communities which confronted the moral crises in their situation.

C. The Attitude of the Church to those who are in the Crisis

The attitude of the pentecostals and the catholic church towards those who are involved in the issue of divorce and are undergoing the crisis is discussed in this section.

1. The Pentecostal View

As it is stated earlier, the pentecostals consider divorce as an evil. It is understood as against marital fidelity. Pentecostals hold that marriage is a sacrament and it should be kept sane. The responsible marital relationship is stressed by them. The act of divorce is criticized by pentecostals. The apriori rules are upheld by them.

In the case of divorce, to those who are in crisis, especially to those who violated the norms and went wrong, there is no perspective developed to guide them. In the cases of break up of partners and planning for divorce, persons are counselled or guided to get away from divorce. But those who are the victims of divorce are not received with mercy and those questions are adequately not addressed. Especially there is no response is developed to those who are in the situation of divorce because of negative effects of secularization and psycho-social and economic changes. The pentecostal churches need to develop an evaluative perspective to deal the issue of divorce from the Christian perspective of love and mercy. They always emphasize what is normative and fail to see the importance of an evaluative perspective.

2. The Catholic View

The catholic church is having more developed view in the issue of sexuality and marriage. They give utmost importance to the covenant-fidelity and sacramentality of marriage. The sanctity of sexuality is upheld by it. The apriori rules are given utmost importance by catholic church.

For catholic church marriage is indissoluble and it asserts the normative rule. It also emphasizes the pastoral approach which accepts 'separation' on the basis of the merit of each case. This is applied to the members of the church. But the approach towards the persons or communities who undergo the moral crises is the question to be taken up here. In this regard, the Catholic Church does not furnish any evaluative approach to consider them with the Christian principle of love and mercy. This does mean that there is no adequate aposteriori-agapeic perspective to consider the victims of divorce, especially to respond to the issues related to the persons who are in the crisis situation.

The Catholic Church stresses what is normative. Their pastoral approach only helps to an extent. An evaluative perspective is needed to deal with the Christian principle of love and mercy. This is important to help the persons who are in the situation of divorce and not accepted by the communities and in crisis.

D. The Role of Sin, Guilt and Conversion

Sin, guilt and conversion play a dominant role in the issue of divorce. Bible understands the divorce as an evil or sin. It is a guilt committed by person. At the same time, those who feel guilty of their sin is having provision to repent and to be restored. If a sinner is conscious of his sin and realize his or her guilt, there is a divine provision of healing. The forgiveness is offered to those who are aware of sin and feeling sorry about their sin. David was a fine example to be discussed here for conversion as he did sin (extra-marital sex), but when the prophet pointed out his sin, he was ready to accept it. He felt a deep sense of guilt about the sin he committed. God granted him mercy as he was repenting of his sin (2 Sam 12; Ps. 51). For the divine act of forgiveness and mercy, one should be convicted of his or her sin and feel a deep sense of guilt.

In the issue of Samaritan woman also (John 4), she was aware of the immorality she was involved in. Jesus pointed out her sins and she was convinced of it. She was in a situation of continuous 'divorce' and 'remarriage'. Jesus was compassionate to those who feel sorry about their sin and seek God's forgiveness. God looks for the repentance or conversion of the people who are undergoing the moral crises. He likes to help them. Jesus was very critical of the self-righteous; this was very clear from his attitude towards the pharisees who do not feel guilty of their sin or seek

God's help for conversion. In the evaluative approach of Jesus also the sin, guilt and repentance are given serious attention by Jesus. 'Sin no more' is the final admonition to the women caught in adultery (John 8). He dealt with sin very seriously as he was aware of the gravity of the moral sin and the bad effects of it in the community. Sin or evil were never legitimized by Jesus, though he forgave the sins of those who repent. The normative elements are held high by Jesus, at the same time he realized the crises of the persons and communities which look for mercy and charity and he applied an evaluative approach in order to help those who are in the crises and are conscious of their plight.

Sin is an offence against God, against self and against neighbour. (Emani Sambayya, *Faith and Conduct,* Madras: C. L. S., 1965, P. 140). Sin is defined as an act against God and as lovelessness. (*Ibid.* P. 142). According to Emani Sambayya, "The corruption of will is the condition of the sinner. Out of this corruption at the centre of his life, proceed evil thoughts, murder, adultery, fornication, theft, false witness and slander. The message of the Gospel is addressed to man in this condition. And the Gospel is that Our Lord Jesus came into the world to rescue penitent sinners from the guilt and power of sin". (*Ibid.,* P. 143). He continued to say that the sinner's need is not only forgiveness from the guilt of sin, but a complete change of his being. (*Ibid.,* P. 144). The Conversion or transformation is the end that those who are in sin and guilt are looking for. One is feeling guilty because of the awareness that there is a commanding law, that one willed to break. (*Ibid.,* P. 144).

Bernard Haering, considers the issue of sin, guilt and the need for conversion. He states, "And the call of grace cannot be rightly understood and followed unless the sinner recognizes his sin, and not merely an injustice and as guilt which only the mercy and power of God can efface! God demands of him also the way of penance and atonement, the perpetual sense of his guilt and of the justice and mercy of God". (Bernard Haering, *The Law of Christ Vol. I,* Bangalore: Theological Publication, 1977, P. 347). According to Haering, conversion means conquest of the old man of sin, held captive of sin, in order to attain a new spiritual form of life created and guided by the Spirit of God. (*Ibid.,* P. 390). He goes on to say that conversion demands total renewal of the heart, and the call to conversion, invitation to pardon, addressed to us by Christ is truly glad tidings, the imperative summons of grace. (*Ibid.,* P. 391) It is very clear that sinner could experience the grace of God by faith if he or she is willing to approach God with a penitent heart.

According to Thomas Aquinas, a sinner is under two burdens, namely, guilt and debt of punishment due. No sin is forgiven without repentance. The forgiveness that pardons the guilt. (*Paul J. Glenn, A Tour of the Summa of St. Thomas Aquinas,* Bangalore: TPI, 1993. P.P. 392-393). According to Thomas Aquinas, sin leads to guilt and it brings crisis in human persons, but God forgives or restores those who return to God with contrition. (*Ibid.,* P. 399).

The Pentecostal view takes seriously the sin, guilt and conversion (repentance). According to Guy P. Duffield and N. M. Van cleave, "Guilt is just desserts of punishment for self-determined violation of law or failure to conform to that law". *(Guy P. Duffiled and N. M. Vancleance Op. cit.* P. 167). They continue to state that, "David's repentance reached its height when he realized that he had not only sinned against Bathsheba and her husband Uriah, but against God". (*Op.. cit.,* P. 167). The repentance or conversion is the remedy for the sin and guilt. God receives gladly the one who repent. The pentecostal churches accepts those who commit sin, but repent their sins and return to God. *(Op cit.,* P. 211). But they have no clear view in the case of divorce, as usually those who involved in divorce cases are not accepted. There is no adequate approach to deal with the issue.

The Catholic Church gives serious attention to sin, guilt and conversion. According to the perspective of Vatican II, sin is a divisive force that leads to evil. It states, "Man therefore is divided in himself. As a result, the whole life of men, both individual and social, shows itself to be a struggle, and a dramatic one, between good and evil, between light and darkness. Man finds that he is unable of himself to overcome the assaults of evil successfully, so every one feels as though bound by chains. But the Lord himself came to free and strengthen man, renewing him inwardly casting out the "prince of this world" (Jn. 12: 31), who held him in the bondage of sin". (Austin Flannery, *ed, Vatican Council II, Op. cit.,* P. 821). Those who feel sorry about their sins can have the remedy of the sacrament of penance. 'The Code of canon law' states, "In order that the faithful may receive the saving remedy of the sacrament of penance, they must be so disposed that, repudiating the sins they have committed and having the purpose of amending their lives, they turn back to God". *(Op. cit.,* P. 178). The Catholic Church also does not consider seriously the people who are in the situation of divorce, especially out side the church, and looking for support and guidance.

Sin, guilt and conversion play a crucial role in the ethical decision making, especially in the case of moral crises of the people. The Christian approach never overlook the importance of inward renewal or repentance. The sinner or the victim of moral evil has to be helped, but he or she has to be conscious of the sin, guilt and the need of conversion.

E. The Significance of Fletcher's Agapeic Approach to the Issue

This section deals with the significance of Joseph Fletcher's agapeic approach to the issue of divorce.

1. The Ethical Need in the Indian Situation

The individuals, groups and communities live with their norms, practices, and issues in Indian context. The norms or the *apriori* rules are prevailing in the communities to guide the life of the people. The Christian churches or communities also hold their norm or apriori rules.

The ethical issues like polygamy, divorce, homosexuality, and extra marital sex are found in the Indian context. It is to be noted that the socio-economic or psychological factors are found behind the issues like divorce. The Christian normative principles are strong that these practices should not be permitted and they should be seriously dealt with. The normative principles are important as standing rules or guide of conduct. The commands and the apriori principles have great value in human life. It is sure that the apriori principles are important, but what would be the Christian approach to the situation or cases or practices (the experience of the persons or what is termed as 'posterior') in which individuals and communities are involved?

In the context of diverse ethical issues, the need is not to condemn the norms and practices of other communities. It is easy to condemn the persons who have violated the apriori principles, but it should be noted that the outright condemnation or judgement will only help to create distrust, hate, and disharmony. The Christian responsibility is to help the people to live in peace and to have harmonious co-existence. It is not difficult to propose or suggest certain rules or principles, but in the context where there are particular norm for each communities, providing an 'apriori' principle or code of conduct is not the ethical need. What is appropriate is to search out how Christians could meaningfully live and relate with other communities in the context of India. The need is to find a solution to the issues in order to deal them with love, mercy and amity.

Though there are different ethical issues related to sexuality and marriage in the Indian context, the religious traditions, the tribal communities or other communities and the personal laws or marriage acts are only keen on the apriori principles or norms, and try to understand the issues on the basis of apriori rules. Apriori rules or norms are important, but what is required in the light of the issues or cases is an approach which can deal the issues with love and mercy.

In the context of the various practices, the experiences or the moral dilemma of the individuals, the groups or the communities, the Christian principles such as love, mercy and generosity play a very crucial role to understand and to deal with them in a spirit of amity and harmony. When the individuals or communities become the objects of mercy, care and love, the Christian responsibility is to understand and to render help to the people in their crises. What is absent in Indian context is an evaluative perspective which can cater to the need. The ethical need is to suggest or propose and evaluative approach which would analyse and understand the situation and to treat the cases with charity and generosity, which would help to maintain and foster love, peace, care, humanness and harmony among communities.

The evaluative approach could analyse the situation to realize the need of the person in the context and to help the persons or communities in their moral dilemmas. It is important to evaluate the situation of a person rather than applying the normative principles disregarding the context. The evaluative perspective is to interpret the situation to know what decision would bring good to the persons. It is a loving and restoring principle to persons and human communities in moral crisis. Evaluative perspective will help to interpret the situations and to assess the would be consequences so that evil effect could be reduced and greater good will be realized in the issues. It enables to avoid what is worse and inhuman.

2. An Ideal or Adequate Solution to the Problem

It is important to suggest or propose an ethical approach as an evaluative in the ethically plural context of India. Since the communities have their normative rules (apriori principles), there is no need to suggest any norms.

What is needed to the moral crises in the Indian context is to propose an ethical approach which can help Christians to relate meaningfully with other communities.It is important to have an approach to help those who are in crisis. The norm of ethics is apriori rules and principles. This is found in all religious traditions. The normative principles are important, but what is required is an evaluative approach in the context of our times. This would help to enhance love, mercy, generosity, peace, and harmony.

The reckless condemnation of any practice or any issue in the context o sexuality and marriage is not the answer to the problem. An ealuative ethical approach which is agapeic and contextual has to b suggested because it can only help the people to deal the issues with care and concern. It is to be noted that socio-economic, psychological and historical factors also have contributed to the crises of the individuals and communities. The individuals and communities are seeking sympathy, compassion, love, and mercy. They look for help and it is the Christian obligation to offer help in the crises of the people, though they have, somehow, moved away from what is normative or the *apriori* principles. It is not to legitimize the evil, but to be more sensitively aware of the issue and try to bring good in the situation as part of Christian responsibility.

Showing generosity or mercy for the good is to be affirmed. In the cases (the experience or what is posterior), the individuals or ommunities are at our mercy. The Christian responsibility is not to condemn those who are the victims of mistakes or crises, but to consider teir welfare and good as part of Christian love or charity. Here one can find the relevance or adequacy of aposteriori-agapeic approach. The norm is certainly the *apriori* rules or principles. The aposteriori- agapeic approach is not suggested as the normative principle, but only as an evaluative one.

The aposteriori - agapeic approach of Joseph Fletcher has to be carefully considered and appreciated in this regard. This does not mean that uncritically one should accept Fletcher's ethical approach. As stated earlier, the ethical approach of Fletcher does not consider the normative principles or apriori rules. For Joseph Fletcher, the aposteriori-agape itself is the 'norm', but from the Christian perspective it is only an evaluative approach. So the ethical approach of Fletcher is to be considered only critically. The Biblical view gives due importance to the norms or the apriori principles even as it sees the significance of the evaluative approach.

The proportionate reason plays a very important role in the evaluative approach. It brings greater good in the situations as it helps to evaluate the situation and to take adequate or appropriate or loving decisions in the context. Miscalculations and faulty evaluations will bring only adverse consequences, so the proportionate reason has to be applied so that the issues can be evaluated on the basis of the Christian principles such as love and mercy. The proportionate reason will enable the people to come out of the rigid rules which are apriori in nature. (Richard Mc Cormick, *Notes on Moral Theology 1967 through 1980, USA;* University press, *1981, pp. 351 ff).*

It is evident that the aposteriori - agapeic approach is not against the Biblical perspective. It is found applied in the Bible, not as normative but as an evaluative perspective. In the context of the different practices and issues of the individuals and communities as they should be looked upon with love and mercy. The Old Testament, Jesus, and Apostle Paul had affirmed the apriori rules as a norm, but the aposteriori agape is found in them as an evaluative approach. So the Bible also gives due importance to the aposteriori-agapeic approach as a solution to the problems of individuals and communities as they seek guidance, help or consideration in the light of the Christian principles of care, love, humanness, understanding and spirit of amity.

3. The Significance of the Agapeic approach of Joseph Fletcher to the Issue and for our Times

About divorce, Joseph Fletcher has his own perspective. He does not accept the traditional view of the indissolubility of marriage. The aposteriori agape plays a significant role in his understanding. He understands the divorce as a means to protect the emotional and spiritual welfare of parents and children (chapter 2). He accepts the fact that Jesus condemned divorce. Fletcher concentrates on the cases in the situation and considered psycho-social factors as his approach is aposteriori - agapeic. Divorce is a loving act for Fletcher, as the psycho-social factors are behind it. Fletcher's approach is to show love and concern to the people in the crisis rather than condemning or rejecting them. For Fletcher, divorce cannot be condemned in all situations. His ethical approach is sympathetic to the victims of divorce. The concern of applying agape in the cases or what is posterior is crucial in his ethical approach.

Joseph Fletcher's aposteriori-agapeic perspective can be understand as an evaluative approach from the Christian point of view only with certain clarification. The normative principles are not his concern. The apriori rules or norms are not regarded by him as he was concerned mostly of the cases or persons in the moral crises. It is important to note that from the Christian perspective, the norms or the apriori rules are very essential for the guidance of the community in order to avoid arbitrariness and antinomianism, so also the evaluative approach in the cases/moral crisis where people look for a generous, merciful and compassionate help from the perspective of Christian charity.

The strength of Joseph Fletcher's agapeic approach is that it considers the persons who are in the moral crises with love and mercy. As an aposteriori-agapeic perspective, his approach, addresses the moral problem without any reservation. It takes care of the situation very seriously and issues are dealt in an evaluative manner.

The problem with the agapeic approach is that he is unconcerned of what is normative, and for him his evaluative perspective is normative. This has to be corrected. From the Christian view one can only understand Fletcher's view of what is normative as an evaluative. Not only that, he does not give importance of sin, guilt and conversion which are very much part of the evaluative approach of Jesus Christ. Jesus did give much emphasis to the values and norms or apriori principles.

Another issue is sin, guilt and conversion, which are not seriously considered by Joseph Fletcher in his agapeic approach. Sin, guilt and repentance are given utmost importance by Jesus in his ethical teaching. Evil is never legitimized by him, though he was aware of the psycho-social factors behind the moral crises. Jesus was evaluative in his approach. Regardless of Jews or non-jews, he was concerned of the persons from all communities in their crises situation.

The evaluative perspective might be understood as pastoral. Of course, it is a pastoral approach which we could also see in Jesus which transcends any particular community. Jesus was very pastoral as he was concerned of the persons who were confronting crises in their life in any community. Jesus was applying a an evaluative approach in order to bring good in the situation. Though Jesus was for the normative principles, he was aware of the need of emancipating the persons from their moral crises. So Jesus was affirming the need of an evaluative approach which is based on care and love. But he was seriously analyzing the attitude of the persons who are in the moral crises. Their plight and attitude of contrition and willingness to repent were the measures by which he evaluated the people and considered their cases.

The Christian churches are affirming the values and they do recognize the importance of normative principles. Divorce is condemned by the Pentecostals and Catholic Church. No adequate response is developed by the churches towards them. The churches fail to have an evaluative approach to the communities where the divorce is a traditionally accepted practice, or where it became bad effect of secularizaion or victims of psycho-social factors.

In the context of moral crises and practices of different communities in our times, Fletcher's aposteriori-agapeic approach can be accepted as an evaluative approach from the Christian view of sexuality and marriage with a critical examination. In the context where persons violate the norms and in moral crises, Fletcher's perspective cannot be recognized as an evaluative approach outrightly as it doesn't give importance to apriori rules and take care the issue of sin, guilt and conversion. In this case Fletcher's agapeic approach can be a fitting Christian response if it can integrate the concept of sin, guilt and conversion. It is also not easy to assume that Fletcher rejects the role of sin as he is concerned of the role of love in the situation. However, one can say that he is not substantial on the issue of sin. It means that the aposteriori-agapeic elements in Fletcher's approach as a Christian evaluative perspective is recognised only with modification or certain clarification. He does understand the aposteriori-agapeic dimension as normative is his ethical approach, but it can be only understood as evaluative from Christian perspective.

Another dimension is about the different communities in which divorce is a traditionally accepted practice. Here the Christian Churches are not considering the issue seriously. The divorce is an accepted norm in some traditional communities, especially among the tribal communities. Here what is significant is not an outright condemnation of the practice of the people, but to help the people to live in love, trust, understanding and harmony. In this respect, Fletcher's agapeic approach will help the Christians to show love and mercy in the situation to bring good. The need of conversion can be presented to them in a loving manner. Though the agapeic approach of Fletcher dosenot show much regard to normative (apriori) principles, it operates as a help in the form of an eye-opener in this respect to be an evaluative approach from Christian perspective. Fletchers' agapeic approach helps to understand the reality and to respond creatively to issues. In this way Fletcher's perspective is understood as a significant Christian response as an evaluative approach in the issue of sexuality and marriage.

Conclusion

On the basis of the study 'The Relevance of the agapeic approach of Joseph Fletcher for the Christan view of sexuality and marriage for our times' it is quite appropriate to make a conclusion including the major observations and inferences.

Analysing the background of situation ethics, it is found that situation ethics is influenced by existentialism, utilitarianism, positivism, personalism and pragmatism and relativism. Existentialism asserts the importance of context and each existential moment. It does not give importance to apriori principles. The personalism contributed to situation ethics to assert that persons are important. So situation ethics would say that persons in the situations are to be considered seriously with their issues. Relativism extends the view that there is historical and cultural relativity. Each situation has its own particularity so there is diversity, though there is unity in certain elements. The historical settings also undergo different changes. These factors also have impact on situation ethics. The experience and context is important for positivism. It is rooted on what is observable. Utilitarianism emphasizes what is useful in the situation. Situation ethics is influenced by these aspects. Situation ethics emerged as a reaction against the legalism of traditional morality. It is observed that situation ethics is allergic to law, especially to natural law and the apriori norms. It is against the legalistic element of the law which goes by the letter of the law than the spirit or the essence of the law. Situation ethics affirms love or agape as norm as it claims that it has the ability to vary in varying circumstances. It challenges the universally valid rules and principles based on conventional wisdom. The agape in the situation is important for situation ethics than anything else. It affirms more freedom and what is practical and loving. It is observed that situationism is an evaluative approach which considers the cases (what is termed as posterior) in terms of love. Situation ethics reacted against the puritanic perspective and the ethical thinking rooted on the natural law theory. Rules are unserviceable tools for situation ethics. The proportionalism also plays a very crucial role in situation ethics. The proportionate good is emphasized by situation ethics.

The aposteriori–agapeic approach of Joseph Fletcher to ethical issues with special reference to sexuality and marriage is discussed in this thesis. The dominant ethical view of Joseph Fletcher is aposteriori–agapeic. He does not give importance to apriori rules. The apriori principles are not loving and human for Joseph Fletcher. In Fletcher's view the apriori rules do not help persons to take responsible decisions in the cases. He reflects on cases like pre-marital sex, extramarital sex, divorce, technological devices like artificial insemination and invitro-fertilization.

He also deals substantially the issues like abortion and euthanasia. The term· agapeic approach and aposteriori-agapeic approach are used in this thesis interchangeably with reference to Joseph Fletcher's ethical approach because his agapeic approach is aposteriori in character. Fletcher's approach considered mostly the cases and the role of love in the particular situation. Fletcher understands agape as the only norm and it helps take fitting decisions in every context. Agape is always considerate and it has a forgiving spirit, so agape plays a very significant role in the ethical decision-making. Agape has the ability to help people to overcome their moral crises.

Joseph Fletcher's ethical approach is understood as aposteriori-agapeic approach. Love is the key category in his ethical perspective and he is dealing the cases with love in the situation. It is considering the victims of certain issues. It is the application of agape in the situation which can be termed as posterior. It is not concerned of what is apriori. The nature of aposteriori-agapeic approach is that it is more contextual. The agape of Joseph Fletcher is not centred on the fixed rules or principles, but it is an act of love in the situation.

Fletcher's ethical approach is agapeic and it is aposteriori agapeic. Love is the only norm in his view. Love is the measure by which every ethical decision has to be determined. He does not deal with what is normative in his approach. He takes cases seriously and applies agape or love in each situation. Each situation is unique in his understanding. The predetermined rule cannot be applied to the cases according to his view. Law is to serve love. He questions the rigidity of law that does not serve love. Though Joseph Fletcher understands his agapeic approach as normative, it cannot be accepted as normative from the Christian understanding. As Fletcher deals with cases, it is an evaluative approach in the light of Christian view.

He considers the cases with love and mercy. Fletcher is aware that there are psycho-social reasons behind the issues.

The agapeic approach or aposteriori-agapeic approach of Joseph Fletcher is understood as an evaluative approach in this thesis. Fletcher's ethical approach is considered by him as normative, but it can be only an evaluative approach as it does not give importance to the apriori rules. His ethical approach does not stand for what is normative from the Christian perspective.

Fletcher's ethical approach is evaluative from the Christian point of view. The evaluative approach helps the persons to take ethical decisions looking at the situation in which one is in. It analyses the situation, especially to know psycho-social factors behind the cases, as to realize the crises a person or persons are undergoing and to help them in order to come out of the crises situation. It does not judge the persons involved in the crises from the Christian normative rules but form the Christian perspective of love and mercy which grant forgiveness to those who violated what is normative. It does not condemn or reject the victims of moral crises outrightly, but seeks to extend help in the situation on the basis of the Christian understanding of love.

The evaluative approach does consider the situation or persons involved in the cases with love, mercy and humanness. It is an approach which undergirds those who are victims of moral crises. The evaluative approach is not to legitimize evil but to bring good in the situation. It is an approach to help those who have violated the normative principles and seeking mercy to be restored. It does not favour the legalism and loveless rules which do not show any concern to the victims of moral crises. It can deal the cases on humanitarian grounds.

Joseph Fletcher develops an evaluative approach for the sexuality and marriage, but he fails to recognize the value of a normative approach. The aposteriori agapeic approach of Joseph Fletcher should be appreciated as an evaluative approach which enables us to show love, concern and mercy to the people who are undergoing crises in the situation (e.g. divorce, adultery or prostitution). But the problem with his ethical approach is that he is not taking into account the normative as his ethical approach is altogether concerned of what can be termed as posterior in nature. Joseph Fletcher's agapeic approach deals only about the issues in the situation and the solution to the cases. Fletcher's agapeic approach is a 'then and there' approach. The danger is that he reduces the aposteriori agape as an absolute norm.

There are certain Christian elements which are missing in the aposteriori agapeic approach of Joseph Fletcher, though there are positive aspects. The situation ethics of Joseph Fletcher provides room for freedom, love, humanness and mercy. It also recognize the importance of persons and their crises in the particular situation. What is missing is the role of sin, guilt and conversion which are very significant from the Christian point of view. Fletcher is found as one sided in his ethical approach as he ignores the aspect of sin and transformation.

It is true that he is not explicitly dealing with sin, guilt and repentance. It is certain that these aspects are very significant from Christian understanding. But one cannot easily blame Joseph Fletcher for this reason. The nature of his ethical approach is also to be considered. The task of Joseph Fletcher's situational approach is not to discuss the aspect of sin and guilt but to help the persons in their issues. The prime task of aposteriori -agapeic approach of Joseph Fletcher is to show love in the situation to help person or persons. It is understood as the act of humanness. His ethical approach is silent on sin, guilt and repentance. One cannot assume that he is against the aspect of sin.

The situation ethics is a corrective to shallow legalism and traditional morality which rejects the context and the role of love and mercy. It is an eye opener to analyse the situation and to make fitting response in the cases. It helps the victims in the crises. In the context of rapid changes, situation ethics helps us to think to form an approach which is more loving in the context. The absolutistic ethics has no much place in Joseph Fletcher's thinking. The puritanic morality and prescriptive rules are not upheld by his ethical perspective. As against the prefabricated rules and principles, Fletcher places the agape as the only norm for making responsible ethical decisions.

The prefabricated rules and principles are not relevant for decision making in Fletcher's understanding. He realizes the importance of the Christian responsibility to deal with the issues with a sense of agape in which mercy and care will be rendered to persons. Even while discussing the sexual ethics, he condemns the sub-object relationship as he rejects any manipulation or exploitation. What he upholds is the agape to help the persons in the situation.

In sexuality and marriage the role of love has very dominant place in Joseph Fletcher's ethical approach. He does not promote any aspect in sexuality and marriage which denies love. The loving concern is very important, for him, in sexuality and marriage. The sex without love or marriage relationship without love is irrelevant in his view. The sexual act without consent and with force are rejected by him. The sexual offences are challenged by Joseph Fletcher as he realizes that they are unloving and inhuman. It is to be noted that he gave extreme care to persons who undergo crises and in need of help.

When we examine Joseph Fletcher's agapeic approach, it is based on love. It is other- regarding. It is against the rigid rules. The good or right is decided depending on the situation or on the merit of each case in Fletcher's approach. He argues that the stringent legalism does not serve love. He tried to view the issues like sex, marriage, abortion and other technological devices from his aposteriori –agapeic perspective. He is not considering the normative elements as he does not give attention to the apriori situations, but to the aposteriori situations. The weakness of Fletcher's agapeic approach is pointed out that it does not show interest in apriori principles, but it should be understood from the approach that his ethical view is more concerned of the issues (what is termed as posterior) in the context.

Joseph Fletcher's ethical approach realizes the fact that ethics is to respond to the issues in the context. Though Christian ethics has to deal with both normative and evaluative elements, he is concentrating only on the evaluative perspective. This is mainly because he found that apriori rules became legalistic which do not give adequate attention to the evaluative dimension of ethics.

This thesis also deals with the Biblical view of sexuality and marriage. The Old Testament perspective is discussed as a background. The synoptic gospels, the fourth gospel and Acts of the Apostles, Pauline corpus and the non-Pauline writings are taken into account in this regard. The Biblical teaching is firm on the normative rules or what is understood as apriori rules. This is clear as Bible affirms the monogamy and indissolubility of marriage. Homosexuality, divorce, extra marital sex and pre-marital sex are understood as against the normative rules. But in the cases which can be understood as what is posterior, the New Testament also recognizes what is evaluative. In fact, the New Testament asserts the importance of both the normative and evaluative aspects.

Though there is the command 'do not commit adultery' (normative or apriori rule) Jesus granting mercy to those who violated it and he considered the cases with love and humanness. This is evident in the case of the woman who was caught in adultery. Apostle Paul also holds the evaluative approach in the case of sexuality and marriage. Though he asserts the normative rules, he also was instructing to forgive those who committed the sexual sins. He instructs the Corinthian community to treat the persons who committed adultery with love and mercy, when they seek forgiveness and restoration. In the case of divorce also he applied an evaluative approach. Divorce was allowed if the partner was not willing to live with him or her because of change of faith. The non- Pauline writings also upheld the sacramentality of marriage and the responsible use of sex.

The New Testament teaching is so strong on the normative aspects in the issue of sexuality and marriage. Sex is to be used responsibly and misuse of sex is condemned by the Old Testament and the New Testament. The sexual immorality is seriously criticized in the Bible. Marriage is an indissoluble bond and divorce was not entertained. The covenantal love and marital fidelity are asserted. In the Old Testament, divorce was, some how, permitted because of the hardness of heart. The normative perspective is highly emphasized in the Bible. But in certain cases, mercy was granted based on the nature of the cases. When persons become victims of certain crises because of psycho-social or economic reasons, an evaluative approach was applied. So both the normative and evaluative perspectives have their own place in the Biblical understanding. Without legitimizing evil, the evaluative dimension is also appropriated. The role of sin, guilt and repentance had an adequate emphasis in Biblical view.

Jesus was very much concerned of the chastity of life in the area of sexuality and marriage. The norms or standards are held high by him. Sexual immorality and marital infidelity are condemned. Divorce is not permitted as marriage is understood as an indissoluble bond in his view. Though Jesus was holding the normative principles, he was also dealing the issues related to sexuality and marriage in the context considering the evaluative perspective. He saw the violation of norm as serious evil, but he was also compassionate to help the persons who were victims of the situation. He was well aware of the psycho-social and economic factors even as he stressed the importance of sin, guilt and conversion. It is to be noted that the New Testament or the Christian perspective always affirms the normative rules even when it sees the significance of what is evaluative in the situation. Comparing to the New Testament, Joseph Fletcher's agapeic approach is not interested in the normative principles.

There is secularized context in India where we see different types and views on sexuality and marriage. The sanctity of sex and sacramental element are questioned in certain context. Cohabitation, lesbianism, homosexuality, pre-marital sex, extra marital sex, divorce and prostitution are legalized by the secularized thinking. Secularization reduced marriage into a social contract. The divorces and the sexual irresponsibility are common in the secularised context, as there is no social binding or authorities to control them. The moral perspectives are deliberatively or ignorantly violated. The misuse of freedom and irresponsibility can be seen in the issue regarding sexuality and marriage.

Different religious traditions and the perspective of tribal communities have also contributed to Indian ethical pluralism. There are norms in the religious communities and the violation of norms are taken seriously by the religious traditions. The ethical pluralism of the Indian context reveals the fact that the individuals and communities live with different issues like pre-marital sex, extra marital sex, polygamy, divorce, and prostitution. Some of these issues are understood by certain groups as legitimate one. Polygamy and polyandry are legitimized by some tribal communities. Polygamy is endorsed by Islam also. What is against the normative is condemned by all traditions though there are diverse practices. Christian churches also take very seriously the normative elements, but they do not give importance to the evaluative approach.

The personal laws are also analysed in this connection. We not only have a common law, but also have enactment of personal laws applicable to persons of different religious communities. The Hindu Marriage Act, the Muslim Personal Law, the Christian Personal Law, the Parsi Personal Law, and the Special Marriage Act are the important ones. The Hindu Marriage Act applies to Jains, Buddhists and Sikhs also. According to Hindu Marriage Act, divorce is possible in the case of adultery, insanity, incurable leprosy or by mutual consent. The Muslim Personal Law allows four wives. The issue of 'Talaq' is also problematic in the Indian context. The Muslim husbands are very irresponsibly using the triple talaq inorder to divorce their wives. There is selfish interest behind it. But it is understood as a practice of a Muslim community. This can be exercised as an extra judicial right by the husbands.

The Parsi Personal Law does not permit bigamy and consanguine marriage. The grounds for divorce include the insanity, premarital pregnancy, imprisonment of the husband for more than seven years of desertion and adultery. The Christian personal law holds on to monogamy. Adultery is considered as one of the important causes of divorce. The special marriage acts accept only monogamy. Insanity, impotency, adultery and cruelty can be the grounds for divorce. The religious traditions have personal laws, the tribal communities and other groups have their norms or apriori principles. What is missing is an evaluative principle which deals with the issues (moral dilemma) in a humane manner in the situation.

In the Indian context there is rapid changes in the understanding of sexuality and marriage. On one side there are conventional practices regarding sexuality and marriage by which the normative elements are upheld and aposteriori aspects are not considered. It is also important to note that even the Christian churches are not so concerned of the need of a aposteriori – agapeic approach. The evaluative approach is very much absent or inadequate in Christianity. The churches regard highly the normative perspective. The existing approach to the victimized one or those who are in crises is very condemnatory and not a helping one. The deontological dimension of ethics is widely used without considering the context. To those who violate the norms or apriori rules, ex-communication is the common type of punishment in the religious and tribal contexts. It is based on the traditional understanding of judgement that those who violate the apriori norms do not deserve for mercy, but for condemnation. This view is to be modified. Here, Fletcher's agapeic approach as an evaluative plays a significant role.

There are factors that one has to consider in the cases of victimized persons. It is observed that there are cases in which the homosexuals and gays are victimized. There are psycho-social and economic factors behind prostitution. For example, poverty and struggle for survival are also pressing women to involve in prostitution. The issues like prostitution, bigamy, polygamy and divorce are to be accepted as the Indian reality. The individuals and communities are undergoing ethical dilemma without getting proper care, guidance, love and mercy. In the cases or issues of the people, it is significant to have an approach to deal with them in the spirit of love and mercy.

Looking at some of the issues that we see in the Indian context, it is observed that Christianity condemns some of the issues like polygamy, polyandry, prostitution and extra marital sex. These practices are against the normative principles for Christianity, so it condemns these practices as evil. But it should be noted that there are psycho social and economic factors behind these cases. Some practices have historically become the essential part of the communities. When we outrightly condemn the practices without having a proper evaluation it will bring disharmony and deny the role of love and mercy in the situation. So it is perceived that what is needed is an evaluative approach which would help Christians and other communities to deal with the issues in a loving and human manner.

An ethical approach is needed to help the people to take responsible decisions in the context. This is very much lacking in the context. The condemnation on the basis of apriori rules or what is normative is not the solution to the problem. The normative elements are to be stressed but there should be a human approach to deal with the victims of several crises. From the analysis of the Indian situation, it is observed that there is no adequate solution to deal with the victims of moral crises in relation to sexuality and marriage. Most of the religious traditions and tribal communities are condemnatory to those who are violating the existing law and do not apply an evaluative approach. From the Christian community also no uniform or adequate response is made to have a solution to the problems.

In the context of secularization, moral diversity and crises, it is very significant to see what should be an adequate Christian approach as a solution to the problem. Divorce is chosen as an example to discuss the problem and to develop an approach. In the context of diverse ethical issues, it is not adequate to condemn the persons or communities which are involved in the issues. The prime responsibility of Christians is not to criticize or condemn them, but to give proper guidance to the victimized. The task of restoration is a Christian responsibility. It is observed that the ethically pluralistic context of India includes the different religious traditions, tribal communities and the secularized context. The dominant ethical view is the normative aspect. The apriori principle or code of conduct is stressed. It is important to explore how Christians could meaningfully relate to the context of the victimized. When the individuals or communities become the objects of mercy, care and love, the Christian responsibility is to provide guidance to come out of the crises.

What is important in the ethically plural context of India is to have an aposteriori approach to deal the cases with love and mercy. This evaluative approach is important as it evaluates the situation of person rather than applying the normative principle disregarding the context. The evaluative approach is to interpret the situation and to bring good to the situation as it does assess the issue. It enables us to avoid what is worse and inhuman. To those who are in crises and look for guidance, it is the Christian obligation to offer help (to the persons and communities in the crisis), though they have, somehow, moved away from what is normative. It is not to legitimize the evil, but to be more sensitive to the issue and to bring good in the situation as part of Christian responsibility. In this regard Joseph Fletcher's agapeic approach (aposteriori–agape) as a Christian response is considered as an evaluative in the context of ethical pluralism of India.

There are diverse views on the issue of divorce. Since the sacramental value of marriage is reduced to a social contract, divorce becomes common in the secularized context. There are certain aspects noticed as reasons for divorce. They are impotence, psychological disorders, wife-beating and marital infidelity. In the Hindu religious tradition, marriage is understood as a sacrament and it is indissoluble. Divorce is not promoted. But the Islamic teaching is not strong on divorce. Even for simple reasons divorce is permitted. Certain tribal communities like Uralies allowed divorce on the ground of ill treatment by anyone of the partners. The personal laws also emphasize different viewpoints. The reasons such as adultery, cruelty, incurable insanity and desertion are endorsed by Hindu marriage Act. The Muslim Personal Law permitted the judicial and extra judicial divorces. In the case of adultery, desertion, bigamy and insanity, Parsi Personal Law allows divorce. The Christian Personal Law allows divorce in the case of adultery.

The covenant fidelity is emphasized by Pentecostals. The normative principles are upheld as they emphasize the sacramentality of marriage and divorce is not permitted. The apriori rules are endorsed by Pentecostals. An evaluative approach is absent to deal with persons who undergo the crisis. The teaching of the Catholic Church also does uphold the covenant fidelity in marriage. It condemns the unfaithfulness and divorce. Marriage is indissoluble for the Pentecostals and Catholics. It is to be noted that there is no adequate approach developed to help those who are victims of the crisis. The Christian churches hold on the apriori rules and principles which is very significant to keep up the normative perspective, but at the same time it is appropriate to give due importance to what is evaluative.

In Jesus' teaching it is observed that the normative principle is given importance. The irresponsibility in marriage bond is never permitted. Divorce is considered as against the intention of marriage. Covenant fidelity is the norm. Though Jesus emphasized the normative perspective in his ethical approach, he was always aware of the psycho social factors. He was sensitive to the issues and helped the persons in their moral crisis. The aposteriori agapeic approach is found in Jesus' teaching.

It is clear in the case of Samaritan woman. He condemns adultery and divorce, but he treated the case with love, mercy, humanness and generosity. Jesus never legitimizes divorce. Divorce is, for him, immoral. He treated with contempt the persons who were involved in deliberate manipulation, so self-righteous and those who did not feel the guilt and the need of conversion. There is possibility for anyone to realize their sin and be transformed. Jesus was also compassionate to those who accept their mistakes and seek God's forgiveness. The element of sin, guilt and conversion are taken seriously by Jesus.

Sin, guilt and conversion are given proper importance by theologians like Thomas Aquinas and Bernard Haering. For Thomas Aquinas sin leads the persons to guilt, but God is willing to restore them if they return to God with contrition. According to him, God demands total transformation of mind. The Pentecostal and Catholic views also take seriously the role of sin, guilt and conversion.

As a Christian ethicist, the aposteriori agapeic approach of Joseph Fletcher provides an evaluative approach which helps Christians to provide guidance to the victimized and to bring good in the context. In the issue of divorce, there are cases where husbands and wives do not act responsibly in marital lives. Husbands and wives desert their partners and even re-marry. In certain cases husbands consider wives as puppets and they are continuously beaten up. In such cases the wives resort to divorce. There are cases in which women are even killed by husbands and relatives. In these cases divorce cannot be outrightly condemned. Taking appropriate and reasonable decisions by evaluating the situations is very crucial.

In relation to the approach to sexuality and marriage, Joseph Fletcher's agapeic perspective does not approve or show interest to normative principles. His agapeic approach does not pay attention to the value of apriori norms. Fletcher's approach also does not give proper attention to the role of sin, guilt and conversion. Even in the case of divorce, he applies the apsoteriori agapeic approach. His approach is sympathetic and loving to the victims of divorce. While the Christians have no adequate approach especially to the cases or what can be termed as posterior, Fletcher's agapeic approach does promote an evaluative perspective.

For the Christian view of sexuality and marriage Joseph Fletcher's agapeic approach is to be accepted only with certain reservations. As in Jesus' ethical approach or the New Testament Teaching, the psycho-social factors are given due importance by Joseph Fletcher's agapeic approach also. Fletcher's approach deals the cases with generosity as it shows love and concern to persons who are victims of moral crises, which is also very much Christian. The Christian task is to help or support the persons who are in moral crises. The Christian churches which do not take seriously the evaluative dimension has to recognize the strength of Joseph Fletcher's aposteriori agapeic approach. As the Christian churches do not have a proper or uniform approach or fitting response to the cases which is posterior in nature, Fletcher's approach can be an eye-opener to develop an evaluative approach. It serves as a great contribution for the Christians to deal with life–relating questions which are crucial in the ethically plural context of India.

There are also weaknesses that one can find in relation to Fletcher's approach. The problem is that what is evaluative from a Christian point of view is normative in his understanding. Fletcher's approach cannot be accepted as a normative Christian principle. While Fletcher stresses the importance of only aposteriori element, Jesus endorsed both the apriori and aposteriori aspects. Another important aspect is the absence of the role of sin, guilt and conversion in Fletcher's agapeic approach. In Jesus' ethical perspective and in the Christian view the role of sin guilt and conversion have tremendous significance. The sin or evil is be condemned, at the same time, the victims of moral crises are to be treated with love and mercy. The sin or evil cannot be legitimized.

Love and humanness have to be shown without legitimizing the evil. It is inferred that Joseph Fletcher's approach is aposteriori agapeic. This approach deals mainly with the cases which can be termed as posterior. Fletcher's ethical approach, though he understands it as normative, is only evaluative from the Christian point of view. It is sure that Fletcher's approach will help bring good in the situation of moral crisis. Fletcher's ethical approach gives motivation to recognize the importance of an evaluative approach as a fitting Christian response to the moral crisis. It helps us to analyse and evaluate the situation and come to decisions in a loving manner.

Joseph Fletcher's ethical approach has the following elements which is very relevant to deal with the issues in the context of ethical pluralism or in the context of our times. It gave foremost importance to particular cases in the particular situation. Another dimension is the role of love or loving concern. The primacy of love is found in his approach as it takes care of the victims of crises with love and mercy which is very essential in the context of our times. The pragmatic emphasis is another significant dimension. The norms and values are important, at the same time, the role of an evaluative perspective is very crucial to have humanness from the Christian point of view.

For our times in the context of moral crisis the agapeic approach of Joseph Fletcher can be a fitting Christian response. It is more appropriate if it takes seriously the concept of sin, guilt and conversion. The

Christian view cannot legitimize the evil. Fletcher's ethical approach cannot be accepted as a normative but only as an evaluative one, as it deals the cases with love and mercy. By giving proper attention to the aspects such as sin, guilt and conversion, Fletcher's ethical approach can be accepted as an evaluative from the Christian point of view.

Joseph Fletcher's ethical perspective is an evaluative approach from the Christian perspective and it has relevance in the Indian context. It is fitting as it can be applied meaningfully to the issues of the persons and communities regarding sexuality and marriage. The normative principles are strong in the context of our times, but what is not strong and adequate is an appropriate evaluative approach to deal with those, who are victims of moral crises with the Christian principle of love and mercy. It is important to show love and mercy, from the Christian perspective, in order to help those who are in the crisis. In the context where people look for guidance in their crises, Fletcher's agapeic approach or aposteriori-agapeic approach can best serve to bring good. Though Fletcher's ethical approach cannot be applied as a normative principle, it can be used as an evaluative approach as his approach is more concerned of the particular situations than what is termed as apriori. Fletcher's ethical approach is relevant because of its special character of dealing with the cases. It is agapeic as it provides sufficient room to take adequate decision in the context. It is more flexible and not rigid. It is sensitive to the issues in the situation. So Fletcher's aposteriori-agapeic approach as an evaluative approach, is a fitting Christian response for our times.

Bibliography

I. PRIMARY SOURCES

A. Books

Fletcher, Joseph. *Situation Ethics: The New Morality*, Phildelphia: The Westminister Press, 1966.

Fletcher, Joseph and Thomas A. Wassmer. *Hello Lovers': An Introduction to Situation Ethics*. New York: Corpus Books and World, 1970.

Fletcher, Joseph. *The Ethics of Genetic Control: Ending Reproductive Roulette*. New York: Doubleday and company, 1974.

Fletcher, Joseph. *Moral Responsibility: Situation Ethics at Work*, (Phildelphia: The Westiminister, press, 1967).

Fletcher, Joseph. *Morals and Medicine* (Boston: Beacon Press, 1865.)

B. Chapters in books

Fletcher, Joseph. F. "A Theological perspective", *Christianity and Property*. edited by Joseph F. Fletcher, Philadelphia: The Westminister Press, 1947. pp. 176-213.

Fletcher, Joseph. "Reflection and Reply", *The situation ethics debate*. edited by Harvey cox, philadelphia: The Westminster press, 1947. pp. 249-264.

Fletcher, Joseph. "Ethical Aspect of Genetic Controls: Designed Genetic changes in man", *Ethics in Medicine: Historical perspectives and contemporary concerns*. London: The M.I.T Press, 1978. pp. 387-393.

Fletcher, Joseph. "Situation ethics", *Encyclopedia of Bioethics Vol. I*. London: Collier Macmillan Publishers, 1978. pp. 421-424.1970).

Fletcher, Joseph, "Situation Ethics", *Encyclopedia of Bio-Ethics Vol.1* edited by Warren T. Reich, London: Collier Macmillan Publishers, 1978.

Fletcher, Joseph. "Medicines scientific developments and resulting ethical problems", *Dial ogue in Medicine and Theology* edited by Dale White, New York: Association Press, 1953.

Fletcher, Joseph. "Technological Devices in Medical Care", *On Moral Medicine* edited by Stephen e. Lammers and Allen Verhey, Grand Rapids: William B. Eerdmans Publishing, 1987.

Fletcher Joseph, "The ethics of genetic control: some answers", *On Moral Medicine* edited by Stephen E. Dammers and Allen Verhey, Grand Rapids: Wm.B. Eerdmans Publishing, 1987.

Fletcher, Joseph, "Situation Ethics", *Encyclopedia of Bio-Ethics Vol.1* edited by Warren T. Reich, London: Collier Macmillan Publishers, 1978.

Fletcher, Joseph. "Medicines scientific developments and resulting ethical problems", *Dial ogue in Medicine and Theology* edited by Dale White, New York: Association Press, 1953.

Fletcher, Joseph. "Technological Devices in Medical Care", *On Moral Medicine* edited by Stephen e. Lammers and Allen Verhey, Grand Rapids: William B. Eerdmans Publishing, 1987.

Fletcher Joseph, "The ethics of genetic control: some answers", *On Moral Medicine* edited by Stephen E. Dammers and Allen Verhey, Grand Rapids: Wm.B. Eerdmans Publishing, 1987.

C. Articles in Periodicals

Fletcher, Joseph. "Love in the only measure", *Commonweal*, Vol. LXXXIII, No.14, (January, 14, 1966), pp. 427-432.

Fletcher, Joseph. "Why New?", *Religion in life*, Vol. XXV, No. 2 (Spring, 1966). pp. 187-190.

Fletcher, Joseph "Love and Utility", *The Christian Century* Vol.XCV, No. 20 (May 31, 1978), pp. 592-594.

Fletcher, Joseph. "Why New", *Religion in Life* Vol. XXXV, No. 2, (Spring, 1966) pp. 187-190.

Fletcher, Joseph. "The end of the era of common sense", *"Religion in Life,* Vol. XXII, No.2 (Spring, 1963) ; pp. 238-246.

Fletcher, Joseph. "Situation Ethics and Watergate", *Theology Today,* Vol. XXI, No. 4 (January, 1995): PP. 343-345.

Fletcher, Joseph. "Critique", *Theology Today* Vol. XXV, No.3 (October, 1968), pp. 366-368.

II. SECONDARY SOURCES

A. Books

Altekar, A.S. *The position of women in Hindu civilization*. Delhi: Motilal Banarsidas publishers, 1991.

Ayer, Alfred Jules. *Language, Truth and Logic* 2nd edn. New York: Dover publication, 1946.

Ayer, Alfred Jules ed. *Logical positivism* Illinois: The free press, 1960.

Anderson, Francis I. *Job: An Introduction & Commentary,* Leicester: Inter-varsity press, n.d.

Anderson, J.N.D. ed. *The World's Religions.* Michigan: Eerdmans Publishing Co., 1972.

Atkinson, David. *The Message of Genesis 1-11.* Leicester: Inter-varsity press, 1990.

Bhadur, K.P. *Caste, Tribes & Cultures of India Vol. VI.* New Delhi: ESS Ess Publication, 1978.

Baldwin, Joyce G. *Haggai, Zachariah Malachi*: Tyndale Old Testament Commentaries, Leicester: Inter-varsity press, 1972.

Barclay, William. *The Letters of James and peter.* The daily study Bible series. Bangalore: TPI., 1981.

Barclay, William. *The Letters of John and Jude.* Bangalore: Theological Publications in India 1981.

Barclay, William. *The Letters of the Romans.* The daily study Bible Series. Revised edn. Bangalore: TPI, 1981.

Barclay, William. *The Letters to the Corinthians.* The daily study Bible Series, Revised edn. Bangalore: TPI; 1981.

Barnett, Paul. *The Message of 2 Corinthians.* England: IVP, 1988.

Barrett, C.K. *The Gospel according to John.* London: S.P.C.K. 1962.

Barrett, C.K. *Essays on John.* London: SPCK, 1982.

Barrett, *The Gospel of John and Judaism.* London: SPCK, 1983.

Beach, Waldo and Richard Neibuhr Ed., *Christian Ethics: Sources of Living tradition*, end edn. (New York: Alfred A. Knopf, 1973)

Bhandari, Bhagwat, *Tribal Marriage and sex Relations*, Udaipur; Himanshu Publication, 1989.

Blackham, H.J. *Six Existentialist thinkers.* London Routledge & Kegam Paul, 1985.

Bornkamm, Gunther. *Jesus of Nazareth*, trans. Irene and Freser Mcluskey with James M. Robinson (Fifth impression), London: Hodder & Stoughton, 1979.

Brocon, David A. *A Guide to religions*. New Delhi. ISPCK, 1973.

Brown, Raymond E. Joseph Fitazmyer *et al The Jerome Bible Commentary*, Bangalore TPI, 1968.

Brown, Raymond E. *The Gospel according to John 1-12*. The Anchor Bible Series. New York: Doubleday & Co; 966.

Brown, Raymond *The Message of Hebrews*. Bible speaks today series. Leicester: Inter-varsity press, 1991.

Brown, Raymond *The Message of Deuteronomy*. The Bible speaks today series. Leicester: Inter-varsity press, 1993.

Bruce, F.F. *Gospel of John* Michigan: William B. Eerdmans Publishing Co., 1983.

Bruce, F.F. *Paul: Apostle of the Free spirit* Revised edn. Exeter: The Paternoster press, 1988.

Bruce, F.F. *Paul and Jesus* Michigan: Baker Book House, 1982.

Bruce, F.F. *Second thoughts on the dead sea scrolls*. Exeter: The Paternoster press, 1972.

Buchler. Justus ed *Philosophical Writings of Pierce*. New York Dover Publications, 1955.

Bultmann, Rudolf *Jesus and the Word*, London: Collins, 1958.

Bultmann, Rudolf *Theology of the New Testament, Vol. I*. London: S.C.M. Press Ltd., 1974.

Bultmann, Rudolf *Theology of the New Testament, Vol. II*, London: S.C.M. Press Ltd., 1978.

Bultmann, Rudolf *The Gospel of John: A Commentary*, trans, G.R. Beasley-Murrey, edited by R.U.N. Hoare amd A.K. Richies, Phildephia: The Westminster Press 1971.

Carr, Lloyd G. *The Song of Solomon*. Tyndale Old Testament Commetaries, Illinois: Inter-varsity press, 1989.

Central Law Agency. *The Special marriage Act, 1954* Allahabad: Cetral law Agency, 1955.

Central law Agency. *The Hindu law Acts*. Allahabad: Central law Agency, 1995.

Chacko, E.J. *Keralathile chila Swantanthra Sabhakal* (Malayalam). Thirivalla: The logical Literature Committee, 1986.

Chatterjee, Satischandra and Datta, Dhirendra Mohn. *An Introduction to Indian Philosophy* Calcutta: University of Calcutta, 1984.

Chatterji, Sharma A. *The Indian Women's search for an Identity*. New Delhi: Vikas publishing House, 1988.

Childs, Brevard.S. *Old Testament Theology in a canonical context*. London L SCM press, 1985.

Chiramel, Jose & Varghese Palathingal. *Patriarchal and Matrimonial Legislations in the Code*. Alwaye: St.Thomas Academy for Research, 1992.

The Church of South India. *The Constitution of the Church of South India* Madras: C.L. S; 1972.

Clowney, Edmond P. *The Message of I peter*. Leicester: Inter-varsity Press, 1990.

Cole, W. Owen and Sambhi, piarasingh. *The Sikhs: Religious beliefs and practices*. New Delhi: Vikas Publishing House, 1978.

Collins, Raymond F. *Divorce in the New Testament*. Minnesota: The Liturgical Press, 1992.

Composta, Doria, *Moral Philosophy and social Ethics* (Bangalore: Theological Publications in India, 1988).

Conzelmann, Hans, *Jesus* (Reprint), Philadelphia: Fortress Press, 1975.

Coomaraswamy, Ananda K. *Buddha and the Gospel of Buddhism* Second edn. New Delhi: Munshiram Manohanlal Publishers, 1985.

Copleston, Frederick. *A History of philosophy vol. VII-IX*. New York: Doubleday, 1977.

Cox, Harvey. *The Situation Ethics Debate*. (Phildelphia: The Westminister Press, 1966).

Cox, Harvey. *Secular city*. Toronto: THe Macmillan company, 1969.

Cragg, Kenneth. *The House of Islam*. California: Dicknson Publishing Co., 1969.

Cranfield C.E.B. *I & II peter and Jude: Introduction and Commentary*. London: SCM Press Ltd., 1960.

Cullmann, Oscar. *The Johannine Circle*. London: SCM Press Ltd, 1976.

Curran, Charles. F. *A New Look at Morality* (London: Sheed & Ward, 1969).

Curran, Charles. E. *Direction in Fundamental Moral Theology*. Dublin: Gill and Macmillam, 1986.

Curtis, C.J. *Contemporary protestant thought*. New York ; The Bruce Publishing Co., 1970.

Daniel, P.S. Scott, David C. *et al Religious Traditions of India* Serampore; I.T.L. 1988.

Das, Somen. *Christian Ethics and Indian Ethios* New Delhi: ISPCK,1989.

Das, Somen. ed. - *Christian faith and multiform Culture in India*, Bangalore: UTC, 1987.

Davis, W.D. *Paul and Rabbinic Judaism* London SPCK, 1962.

D'Cunha, Jean, *The Leqalization of Prostitution*. Bangalore: CISRS, 1991.

Denett, Duncan. M. *A Critique of Modern Hindu Law*. Bombay: Trapathy Pvt. Ltd., 1970.

Devanandan, P.D. Thomas M.M. eds. *The Changing Patterns of Family in India*. Bangalore CISRS, 1966.

Dietrich, Gabriele. *Culture, Religion and Development* Bangalore: CSA Publications, 1978.

Diwan, Paras and Diwan, Peeyushi. *Family law* 2nd edn. Allahabad: Allahabad law agency, 1994.

Dodd, C.H. *Gospel and the Law*, Cambridge: University Press, 1957.

Dodd, C.H. *The Interpretation of the Fourth Gospel*, Cambridge: University Press, 1968.

Drane, John. *Paul*. A lion Book; England: Lion Publishing, 1976.

Dubey, S.M. Bordoloi, P.K. Borthakur, B.N. Eds. *Family, Marriage, Social change in Indian Fringe*. New Delhi. cosmo Publications, 1980.

Dunn, James D.G. *Jesus, Paul and the Law: Studies in Mark and Galatians*. Kentucky: Westminister/John knox Press, 1990.

Edanad, Antony. *Christian Experience and the New Convenant*, Bangalore: Dharmaram Publications, 1987.

Editorial Board. *Struggle against death*. Kottayam: W.C.C. Vancouver Assembly study group, 1982.

Elenjimattam, Anthony. *The Yoga philosophy of patanjali*. Allahabad: Better yourself books, 1979.

Ellis, Earl. F. *The Gospel of Luke*. London: Eerdamans, 1981.

Faridi, F.R. & M.N. Siddiqui. eds. *Muslims Personal Law*. Aligarh: Islamic Research Centre, 1973.

Flannery, Austin. *Vatican Council II*. Bombay: St.Paul Publications, 1983.

Forell, George Wolfang, *History of Christian ethics*, Vol. I *From the New Testament to Augustine*, Minneaplis: Augsburg Publishing House, 1979.

Foulkes, Francis. *The Epistle to the Ephesians: An Introduction and Commentary*. Michigam: Wm.B. Eerdmans Publishing Co., 1981.

Frankena, William.K. *Ethics*. (New Delhi: Prentice-Hall India, 1988).

Fuchs, Joseph. *Natural Law: A Theological Investigation*: Dublin: Gill and Son. 1965.

Fuller, A.G. *A History of philosophy*. Revised edn. New Delhi: Oxford and IBH Publishing Co., 1976.

Furnish, Victor Paul. *Theology and Ethics in Paul*. Nashville: Abingdon Press, 1978.

Gangadhar, D.A. *Mahatma Gandhi's Philosophy of Brahmacharya*. Delhi. ISPCK for CISRS, 1984.

Gangrade, K.D. *Crisis of values*. New Delhi: Chetna Publications, 1975.

Garratt, G.T. ed. *The Legacy of India*. Oxord: Clarendon Press, 1938.

Ghazan, Sunil Solomon. *Adults amuzed but child abused* New Delhi: Navdin Prakashan Kendra, 1995.

Giesler, Norman. *Options in Contemporary Christian Ethics*. Michigan: Baker Book House, 1991.

Gill, Robin; *A text book of Christian Ethics* Edinburgh: T&T Clark, Ltd., 1985.

Glenn, Paul J.A. Tour of the rumma of Thomas Qquinas. Bangalore: TPI, 1993

Gnanadason, Aruna ed. *Towards a Theology of humanhood: Women's perspectives*. New Delhi: ISPCK; 1986.

Green, H. Benedict. *The Gospel according to Mathew*. Glasgow: Oxford University Press, 1975.

Green, Michael. 2 peter and Jude. *Tyndale New Testament commentaries*. Leicester: Inter-varsity Press, 1983.

Gregories, Paulose Mar. *Science for sane societies*. (Madras: C.L.S., 1981).

Guenther, Herbert V. *The Tantric View of life*. Berkeley: Shambla Publications, 1972.

Gupta, J.L. *Challenges to the fair sex* Delhi: Gian Publishing house, 1988.

Gusfafson, James M. *Protestant and Roman Catholic Ethics*. Chicago The University of Chicago Press, 1978.

Guthrie, Donald, *The New Testament Introduction,* Third revised edn. Leicester: Inter-varsity Press, 1970.

Gutzke, Manford George, *Plain talks on acts,* Michigan: Zenderavan Publishing House, 1975.

Haering, Bernard *Free and Faithful Vol.I.* Slough: St. Paul Publications, 1978.

Haering, Bernard. *Free and Faithful Vol.II.* Slough: St. Paul Publications, 1979.

Haering, Bernard. *Free and Faithful Vol.II1.* Slough: St. Paul Publications, 1981.

Haering, Bernard. *The Law of Christ Vol.I.* Trans. Edwin G. Kaiser, Cork: The Mercier Press, 1961.

Haering, Bernard. *The Law of Christ Vol.II* Trans. Edwin G. Kaiser, Cork: The Mercier Press, 1967.

Haering, Bernard. *The Law of Christ Vol.I* Trans. Edwin G. Kaiser, Cork: The Mercier Press, 1967.

Haering, Bernard. *Faith and morality in a secular age*; Bombay: St. Paul Publications, 1974.

Hamilton, Alexander, James Madison *et al. (Compi.) American State Papers*: The Federalist J.S. Mill. Great Books of the Western World series Vol. 43 (24th print) Chicago: Encyclopedia Britannica, Inc. 1982.

Harrington, Daniel. J. *John's thought and theology: An Introduction*, Goodhews series Vol. 33. Wilmington: Michael Glazier Inc., 1990.

Harrison, R.K. *Jeremiah & Lamentations: An Introduction and Commentary*. Leicester: Inter-varsity Press, 1973.

Hasnain, Nadeem, *Tribal India Today*. New Delhi, Hamam Publication 1983.

Heidegger, Martin. *Being and Time* trans. John Macquarrie and Edward Robinson. Southampton: Basil Blackwell, 1983.

Hendrikeen, William, *The Gospel of John*. Pennsylvania: The Banner of Truth Trust, 1976.

Heth, William. A. and Gordon. J. Wenham. *Jesus and Divorce: The Problem with Evangelical Consensus*. Nashville: Thomas Nelson Publishers, 1984.

Hiebert, D. Edmond. *An Introduction to the non-pauline epistles* Chicago: Moody Press, 1960.

Hinson, David F. *Theology of the old Testament*. New Delhi: I.S.P.C.K, 1990.

Horam, H. *North East India: A profile*. New Delhi: Cosmo Publications, 1990.

Houlden, J.L. *Ethics of the New Testament*. New York: Oxford University Press, 1977.

Hume, Robert Ernest. *The World's Living Religions*. Edinburg: T & T. Clark, 1959.

Hunter, David G. *Marriage in the early church* Minnea Police; Fortress Press, 1992.

Islahi, Sadruddin. *Islam at a glance* trans. M. Zafar lqbal. Delhi: Markazi Maktaba Islami, 1985.

Janssens, Louis. Freedom of Conscience and Religion freedom. New York: Alba books, 1965.

Jaico publishing House. *Glimpses of World Religions* Bombay: Jaico Publishing House, 1959.

James, William. *Pragmatism and Four essays from the meaning of truth*. New York: A Meredian Book, 1974.

Jeremias, Joachim, *The New Testament Theology Vol. I*, London: S.C.M. Press Ltd., 1971.

Jeremias, Joachim. *Jerusalem in the time of Jesus*. 3rd edn. London S.C.M. Press, 1969.

Jerudoss, D.W. ed. *Violence/Non-violence*. Madras: Gurukul Lutheran Theological colege and Research Institute, 1989.

Jones, Bevan. L. *The People of the Mosque* Delhi: ISPCK, 1980.

K.M. Kapadia. *Marriage and family in India*. Calcutta: Oxford University Press, 1977.

Kaufmann, Walter ed. *Existentialism from Destoevsky to Sartre*. 24th printing, New York: The world Publishing Co., 1967.

Keener, Craig S. *Paul, Women and Wives*. Massachuetts: Hendrick on Publishers, 1992.

Kidner, Derek. Proverbs: *An Introduction and Commentary* Tyndale Old Testament Commentaries series. Leicester: Inter-varsity Press, 1964.

Kïerkegard. *Fear and Trembling, the sickness unto deàth*, New York: Double day & Co. 1954.

Knitter, Paul F. *No other name?* Philippines: Claretian Publications, 1985.

Kumari, Ranjana. *Female sexuality in Hinduism*. Delhi: ISPCK, 1988.

Kung, Hans and Karl Josef Kuschel *A Global Ethic*. New York: Continuum, 1993.

Kuppuswamy, B. *Social Change in India*. Delhi: Vikas Publishing House, 1975.

Ladd, George Eldon. *A Theology of the New Testament*, Michigan: William E. Eorman's Publishing Company, 1974.

Lammers, Stephen E & Allen Verhey, ed. *On Moral Medicine* Michigan: William B. Erdmans Publishing Co., 1987).

Lane, William L. *The Gospel According to Mark*. Michigan: William B. Eerdman's Publishing Company, 1975.

Lange, Nicholas De. *Judaism*. Oxford: University Press, 1986.

Lasor, William Sanford. *The Dead sea scrolls and the christian faith*. Chicago: Moody Press, 1977.

Lillie, William. *An Introduction to Ethics*. New Delhi Allied Publishers Ltd., 1989.

Lindars, Barnabas. *Behind the Fourth Gospel*. London: SPCK; 1971.

Lion Publishing. *The Worlds Religions* (A Lion handbook), Oxford: Lion Publishing, 1992.

Loades, Ann. ed. *Feminist theology: A Reader*. London: SPCK, 1991.

Lobo, George V. *Christian living According to Vatican II Moral theology today*. Bangalore: TPI, 1991.

Lobo, George V. *Moral and Pastoral Questions*. Anand: Gujarat Sahitya Prakash, 1985.

Lobo, George.V. *Current Problems in Medical Ethics* Allahabad: St. Paul Publications, 1980.

Lochlin, C.H. *The Sikhs and their scriptures*. Delhi: ISPCK-LPH., 1974.

Lockport Church. *Roman Catholicism* U.S.A: Lockport Church n.d.

Longchar, A.Wati. *The Tribal religious traditions in North East India: An Introduction*. Jorhat: Assam Printing Work, 1991.

Lutzer, Edwin. *The necessity of Ethical Absolutes* Michigan: Zonderavan Publishing House, 1981.

Mabry, Hunter. *Christian Ethics: An Introductory Reader*. Serampore: Indian Theological Library, 1987.

Macquarrie, John. *Existentialism* New York: Penguin Books, 1973.

Macquarrie, John. *Twentieth century of Religious thought* Revised edn. London: SCM Press, 1981.

Macquarrie, John ed. *A Dictionary of Christian ethics* London: S.C.M. Press Ltd., 1967.

Meclynn, James V. and Jules J. Toner. *Modern Ethical Theories*. Milwaukee: The Bruce Publishing Co., 1961.

Mckee, James B. *Introduction to Sociology*. New York: Golt, Rinehart and Winston Inc, 1969.

Mc Cormick, Richard, and Paul Ramsey A. *Doing Evil to Achieve Good: Moral choice is conflict situations.* Chicago: Loyola University press, 1978.

Mc Cormick, Richard A. Mow Brane a New World: Dilemmas in Bioethics. London: SCM press Ltd., 1981.

Mamoria, C.B. *Social Problems & Social Disorganisation in India*: Allahabad, Kitab Mahal, 1981.

Manickan, T.M. *Dharma according to Manu and Moses*. Bangalore: Dharmaram Publications, 1977.

Maritain, Jacques. *Moral philosophy*. New York: Charies Scriber's Sons, 1960.

Marshall, I. Howard. *Acts*. Tydndate New Testament commentaries. Leicester: Inter-varsity Press, 1983.

Mason, Donald, H. *Thus Saith the Lord*. Madras: The Christian Literature Service, 1962.

Mathew, K.V. *The Faith and practice of the Marthoma Church*, Kottayam: Marthoma Theological Seminary, 1985.

Mathew, P.D. and P.M. Bhashi: *Special Marriage Act* New Delhi: Indian Social Institute, 1994.

Mathew, P.D. and P.M. Bakshi. *Christian Marriage Law* New Delhi: Indian Social Institute, 1992.

Mathew, P.D. and P.M. Bakshi. *Christian law of Divorce* New Delhi: Indian Social Institute, 1993.

Mathew, P.D. and P.M. Bakshi. *Muslim Marriage and Divorce*. New Delhi: Indian Social Institute, 1993.

Mathew, P.D. and Bakshi. *Law of Wills* New Delhi: I.S.I. 1990.

Mathew, P.D. and P.M. Bakshi. *Hindu Marriage and Divorce* New Delhi: Indian Social Institute, 1994.

Mathew, P.D. & P.M. Bakshi. *Women and the constitution* New Delhi: Indian Social Institute, 1990.

Mathew, P.D. *The Law of Rape*. New Delhi Indian Social Institute, 1994.

May, William E. ed. *Hello Lovers*! Washington: Corpus Books, 1970.

Mookerjee, Asutosh. *Marriage Seporation and Divorce* Calcutta: S.C. Sarkar & Sons Ltd; 1986.

Morris, Leon. *Revolution* Tyndale New Testament Commentaries. Leicester: Inter-varsity Press, 1983.

Mukherjee, Prabhati, *Hindu Women*, New Delhi: Orient Longman, Ltd; 1978.

Murlock, Elizabeth B. *Adolescent Development*. New York: Mc Graw—Hill Book Co, 1973.

Newbigin, Lesslie. *Gospel in a pluralist society* London: SPCK, 1989.

Newman, Jeremiah. *Conscience Versus Law: Reflections on the evolution of natural law* Chicago: Fronsiscan Press, 1971.

Oommen, T.G. *Kudumba Samvidhanam Thiruvachana Velichathil.* (Malayalam), Kumbanad: Girideepam Press, n.d.

Parrinder, Geoffrey. *Sex in the World Religions* London: Sheldon, 1980.

Parisi, Francis. *Pastoral psychology* Manila: East Asian Partoral Institute, n.d.

Pathapankal, Joseph. Christian Life: *New Testament Perspectives*, Bangalore: Dharmaram Publication, 1982.

Pathrapankal, J. *Critical and Creative* Bangalore: Dharmaram Publications, 1986.

Pathrapankal, J. *Metanoia faith Covenant: A Study in pauline theology*. Bangalore: Dharmaram College, 1971.

Payne, J. Barton. *The theology of the older testment*, Michigam. Zonderavan publishing House, 1962.

Peschke, Karl. H *Christian Ethics,* Vol. I. (Bangalore: TPI, 1987).

Peschke, Karl. H. *Christian Ethics*, Vol II. (Bangalore: TPI, 1987)

Pfeiffer, Charles, F. *The Epistle to the Hebrews.* Chicago: Moody Press, 1962.

Pikthall, Mohammed Marmaduke. *The Meaning of the glorious Quran*. New Delhi: Universal Book stall, n.d.

Pinto, Williams. *Law of Marriage & Matrimonial Belief for Christians in India* Bangalore: TPI, 1991.

Podimattam, Felix M. *Current Moral Questions*. Bangalore: A.T.C. Publications, 1984.

Podimattam, Felix.M. *Understanding the Encyclical on Birth Control*. Bangalore: A.T.C. Publications, 1982.

Publication Division India *Society and Literature in Ancient and Medieval periods.* Delhi: Ministry of Information, 1981.

Podimattam, Felix, M. *Relatively of Natural Law.* Bangalore: A.T.C. Publications, 1976.

Popkin, Richard H. and Avrum Stroll. *Philosophy. Made Simple.* London: W.H. Allen, 1969.

Presler, Henry H. *Primitive Religions of India*. Madras: The Christian Literature Society, 1971.

Prior, David. *The Message of I Corinthians.* Leicester: Inter-varsity Press, 1985.

Quinton, Antony, *Utilitarian Ethics*. London: Macmillan Press, 1973.

Radha, Swami Sivananda. *Kundalini Yoga*. Delhi: Motilal Banarsidass Publishers, 1972.

Radhakrishnan, S. *The Dhammapada.* Madras: Oxford University Press, 1977.

Rahula, Warpola. *What the Buddha taught.* New York: Grove press, Inc. 1959.

Ramban, Kadavil Paul. *The Orthodox Syrian Church its religion and philosophy*. Puthencruz: K.V. Pathrose, 1973.

Ramsey, Paul. *Fabricated man: The Ethics of Genetic Control*. New Haven: Yale University Press, 1974.

Ramsey, paul. *The Deeds and Rules in Christian Ethics* (New York: Charles Scribness Sons, 1967).

Rao, Prakasa, V.V. and Nandini Rao. *Mariage the family and women in India*. New Delhi: Hertiage Publishers, 1982.

Reddy, V. Narayan Karan. *Marriage in India* Gurgaon: The Academic Press, 1978.

Ridderbos, Herman. *Paul: An Outline of his theology* Trans. John Richard Dewitt. Michigan: William B. Eerdmans Publishing Co., 1975.

Robinson, John A.T. *Christian Freedom in a Permissive Society* London: S.C.M Press Ltd., 1970.

Robinson, John A.T. *Honest to God*. London: S. C. M. Press Ltd., 1963.

Robinson, John A.T. *Christian morlas today*. Philadelphia: The Westminister Press, 1964.

Robinson, John A.T. *Honest to God*. Philadelphia: The Westminister Press, 1963.

Roubiczek, Paul. *Existentialism: For and Against: Theory of moral life*. New Delhi: Miley Eastern Private Ltd., 1967.

Rowland, Christopher. *Christian Origins*. Fourth impression. London: SPCK; 1991.

Russel, Bertrand. *A History of Western Philosophy*. New York: Simon & Schuster, 1945.

Sachdeva, D.R. & Bushan Vidya. *An Introduction to sociology*. Delhi: KItab Mahal 1979.

Saldanha, Julian. *Conversion and Indian Civil law* Bangalore: Theological Publications in India, 1981.

Samartha, S.J. ed. *Faith in the midst of faiths*. Geneva. W.C.C., 1977.

Samartha, S.J. *One Christ, many Religions*, Bangalore SATHRI, 1992.

Samartha, S.J. *Courage for Dialogue*, N.Y. Orbis Books, 1981.

Sanders, E.P. *Jesus and Judaism*, London: S.C.M. Press Ltd., 1985.

Sandford, Charles. *Studies in Indian Society Culture and Religion*. New Delhi: Caxton Publications, 1988.

Sartre, Jean-paul. *Existentialism and Humanism*. London: Methuen Co., Ltd. 1949.

Schilpp, Paul Arthur. ed., *The Philosophy of John Dewey*. New York: Tudor Publishing Company, 1951.

Schilpp, Paul Arthur. ed. *The Philosophy of C.I.Lewis*. London: Cambridge University Press, 1968.

Schnackenburg, Rudolf. *The Moral Teachings of the New Testament*. Kant: Burns & Dates, 1982.

Scott, Ernest F. *The Ethical Teaching of Jesus*. New York; The Macmillan Co., 1925.

Schweitzer, Eduard. *The Goodnews According to Mathew*. Atlanta; John Knox Press, 1975.

Schweitzer, Edward. *The Gospel According to Mark*. London S.P.C.K. 1978.

Shah, A.B. and Rao C.R.M: *Tradition and modernity in India*. Bombay: Manaktalas, 1965.

Shanti, Margaret & Mary, Corona. eds. *We Dare to speak*.Thiruchirappalli, Woth, 1994.

Sharma, Ramnath. *Indian Social Problems* Bombay: Media Promoters & Publishers, 1982.

Shoeck, Helmut and Wiggins, James W. eds. *Relativism and the Study of man*. Princetom: Vam Norifrand Co., 1961.

Sidgick, Henry, *Outlines of History of Ethics*. Boston: Beacon Press,1960.

Singer, Marcus G. Ed. *Morals and value*. New York: Charles Scribners Sons, 1977.

Spong, John Shelby, *The Living Commandments* New York: The Seabury Press, 1977.

Sreenivas, M.N. Social change in Modern India, N.P: Orient hogman Ltd., 1977

Storkey, Elaine. *What's right with feminism*. London: SPCK, 1985.

Stott, John R.W. *Christian Counter-Culture: The Message of the Sermon on the Mount* (Reprint), England: Inter-Varsity Press, 1978.

Stott, John R.W. *The Message of the Sermon on the Mount*. Leicester: Inter-varsity Press, 1990.

Stott, John R.W. *The Message of Acts*. Leicester: Inter-varsity Press, 1991.

Stott, John R.W. *The Message of Thessalonians*. The Bible speaks today series. Leicester. Inter-varsity Press, 1991.

Subhamma, Malladi. *Islam and Women*. Trans. M.V. Ramamurthy, New Delhi: Sterling Publishers, 1988.

Subbamma, Malladi. *Women: Tradition and Culture*. New Delhi: Sterling Publishers, 1985.

Taylor, G & De Bekker E. *Parish priests and marriage cases*. Bangalore TPI, 1986.

Tellis-Nayak, Jessie B. *Indian Womenhood: Then and now*. Indore: Satprakashan sanchan Kendra, 1983.

Tenney, Merrill C. *New Testament Times*. Michigan: William B. Eerdmans Publishing Co., 1965.

Theological Publications in India. *The code of canon law*. (Fourth reprint) Bangalore: Collins for TPI, 1991.

Thomas, Edward J. *The History of Buddhist thought*. London. Rentledge Kreegam Paul Ltd. p. 1951.

Thomas, M.M, Taylor, R.W. ed. *Tribal Awakening*. Bangalore: CISRS, 1988.

Tillich, Paul. *Morality and Beyond.* (London: Collins, 1963).

Tillich, Paul. *My search for Absolutes*. (New York: Simon & Schuster, 1967).

Tillich, Paul. *Theology of Culture*. New York: Oxford University Press, 1964.

Thomson, Peter J. *Paul and the Jewish law*. Minneapolis: Fortress Press, 1990.

Toffler Alwin, *Future Shock* Londo: Pan Books, 1970.

Vadackumcherry, Joseph. *Natural- Law-Morality Versus Situationism in Morals* (Cochin: Louis Memorial Press, 1969).

Vatsyayana. *Kamasutra*. Delhi: Salim Publications, 1995.

Vaux, Kenneth. *Joseph Fletcher: Memories of an Ex-Radical.* Kentuky : Westminister, 1993.

Velacherry, Joseph. *Social Impact of Mass Media in Kerala*. Delhi: ISPCK, 1993.

Vellanickal, Mathew, *Studies in the Gospel of John*. Bangalore: Asian Trading Corporation, 1982.

Von Hildebrand, Alice and Dietrich. *Morality and Situation Ethics* (Chicago: Fransiscan Herald Press, 1966).

Von Rad, Gerhard. *Wisdom in Israel*. London: SCM Press, 1981.

Von Furer-Haimentorff. *Tribes of India.* Delhi: Oxford University Press, 1980.

Ward, Ronald A. *Commentary on 1&2 Timothy & Titus*. Texas: Ward Books Publishers, 1977.

Warnock, M. *Existentialist Ethics*. London: Macmillan Co., 1969.

Wassmer, Thomas A. *Christian Ethics for Today*. Milwaukee: The Bruce Publishing Co., 1969.

Werkmeister. *Theories of Ethics*. Lincoln: Johnson Publishing Co., 1961.

White, R.E.O. *Biblical Ethics: The Changing Continuity of Christian Ethics Vol. I. Exeter:* The Paternoster Press, 1979.

Whitely, D.E. *The Theology of paul*, Oxford: Basil Blackwell, 1972.

Wilcock, Michael. *The Message of Revelation*. Leicester: Inter-varsity Press, 1973.

Williams, John Alden ed. *Islam*. New York: George Braziller, 1962.

Winn, Ralph B. Ed. *American Philosophy*. New Jersey Adams & Co., 1965.

Wright, Christopher J.H. *Living as the people of God*. Leicester: Intervarsity Press, 1983.

Zernov, Nicolas. *The Christian East*. Delhi: ISPCK, 1956.

B. Chapters in Books

Augustine, Saint "Enchiridion", *Nicene and Post-nicene fathers Vol.III* edited by Schaff Philip, Michigan: WMB. Eerdmans Publishing Co., 1978. pp.237-278.

Cassserly, J.V. Langonead. "Relativism from a theological stand point", *Relativism and the study of man* edited by Helmut shoeck and James W. Wiggins, princetons: D. Van Norstrand Company, 1966. pp. 96-116.

Carmichael, Leonard. "Absolute, Relativism and the scientific psychology of Human nature" *In Relativism and the study of man*. edited by Helmut Shoeck and James W. Wiggins, Princeton: D. Van Nostrond Company, Inc, 1966. pp. 1-21.

Das Gupta, Chidananda "Indian daugher in-law in chains", *challenges to the sex* edited by J.L. Gupta. Delhi: Gian Publishing house, 1958.

Erickson, Millard.J. "Fletcher, Joseph", *baker's Dictionary of Christian Ethics* edited by Carl E. Henry, (U.S.A: Baker's Book House, 1973). p. 247.

Flewelling, R.T. "Personalism", *Encyclopaedia of Religion and ethics Vol. IX* 3rd edition edited by James Hartings, Edinburg: T&T. clonk, 1953. pp. 771-773.

Fletcher, Joseph. F. "A Theological perspective", *Christianity and Property*. edited by Joseph F. Fletcher, Philadelphia: The Westminister Press, 1947. pp. 176-213.

Fletcher, Joseph. "Reflection and Reply", *The situation ethics debate*. edited by Harvey cox, philadelphia: The Westminster press, 1947. pp. 249-264.

Fletcher, Joseph. "Ethical Aspect of Genetic Controls: Designed Genetic changes in man", *Ethics in Medicine: Historical perspectives and contemporary concerns*. London: The M.I.T Press, 1978. pp. 387-393.

Fletcher, Joseph. "Situation ethics", *Encyclopedia of Bioethics Vol. I*. London: Collier Macmillan Publishers, 1978. pp. 421-424.

Fletcher, Joseph. "A moral Philosophy of sex" *In Sex and religion Today* edited by Simon Boniger, (New York: Association Press, 1853).

Fletcher, Joseph, "What's in a rule?: *A Situationist's view", Norm and Context in Christian Ethics* edited by Gene. H. Outka and Paul Ramsey, (London: SCM Press, 1968).

Fletcher, Joseph. "Ethical Apects of Genetic Control", *Bioethics* edited by Thomas A. Shannon, (New York: Paulist Press, 1976).

Fletcher, Joseph. "Indicators of Humanhood: A Tentative Profile of man", *Bio-Ethics* edited by Thomas A. Shannon, (New York: Paulist Press,

Granadasan, Aruna. "Women: Violence and non-violence", *violence / non-violence.* edited by D.W. Jesudas, Madras: Gurukul Lutteraw College, 1989.

Hazetton, Roser. "Humanism and Humanitarianism", *Dictionary of Christian Ethics* edited by John Macquarrie, London: SCM Ltd., 1967).

Heinecker, Martin J. "Pietism", *A Dictionary of Christian Ethics* edited by John Macquarrie, (Nineth impression) London: SCM Press, 1984. pp. 256-257.

H.L. Ellison "Judaism", *The New Bible Dictionary* 2nd edn. reprint) edited by J.D. Druglas, England: Inter-varsity Press, 1982. pp. 631-634.

Janssens, Louis. "International Social Justic", *Christian Responsibility and world ponerty,* edited by Arthur Mc Cormack, London: Burns & Oats, 1963. pp. 273 - 292.

Knox, S.J. "Puritanism", *A Dictionary of Christian Ethics* edited by John Macquarrie, London: SCM Press Ltd, 1984. pp. 284-285.

Kuhn, Harold.B. "Relativism", *Baker's Dictionary of Christian Ethics* edited by Carl F. Henry, (Michigan: Baker Book House, 1981.)

Lavely, John H. "Personalism", *The Encyclopedia of philosophy Vol. 6* edited by paul edwards, New York: The Macmillan Company & Free Press, 1967. pp. 107-109.

Lohff, Wenzel. "Pietism", *Sacramentum Mundi Vol.5*. edited by Karl Rahner and Juan Alfaro *et al.,* Bangalore: TPI, 1975. pp. 24-26.

Lott, Eric J. "Religious faith and the Diversity of cultural life in India" *In Christian faith and multiform culture in India*. edited by Somen Das, Bangalore: United Theological College.

Michalson, Carl "Existentialist Ethics", *Dictionary of Christian Ethics* edited by John Macquarrie, London: SCM Press Ltd., 1967.

Mitchell, Basil, "Ideals, Roles and Rules", *Norm and Context in Christian Ethics*. Gene H. Outka and Paul Ramsey, London: SCM Press, 1968.

Molinski, Waldeman. "Situation ethics", *Sacramentum mundi Vol. 6* edited by Karl Rahner, Juan Alfaro *et al.*, Bangalore: Theological Publications of India, 1975. pp. 9498.

Monden Louis. *Sin, Leberty and law.* New York: Sheed and word, 1965.

Moore, E. Garth. "Proportion", *Dictionary of Medical Ethics* edited by Dunccen A.S., Dunstan, G.R. *et al.*, London: Darton Longmann, Todd, 1977.

Ramsey, Paul. "Justice and Equal Treatment", *On Moral Medicine* edited by Stepehn E, Lammers and Allen Verhey, (Michigan: William B. Eerchmans Publishing Co., 1987.

Mc Cormick, Richard A. "Human Sexuality: Toward a consistant Ethical Method". *One Hundred years of Catholic Thought,* edited by John A. Coleman, New York: Orbis books, 1991, pp. 189-197.

Schlick, Moritz. "What is the aim of ethics?", *Logical positivism* edited by A.J. Ayer, Illinois: The free Press, 1960. pp. 247-263.

Vivas, Eliseo. "Reiferation and second thoughts on cultural relativism", *Relativism and the study of man*. edited by Helmut shoeck and James W. Wiggins, princeton: D Van Norstrand Company Inc., 1966. pp. 45-71.

Wood, H.G. "Puritanism", *Encyclopedia of Religion and Ethics* Vol. 10 edited by James Hastings, Edinburg: T & T Clark, 1980. pp. 507-515.

C. Articles in Periodicals

Badhwar, Inderjit. "Sati: A pagan sacrifice", *India Today,* (October 15, 1987). pp. 98-105.

Cahill, Lisa Sowl. "Sexual ethics", A feminist Biblical perspective", *Interpretation,* vol. XLIX, No. 1 (Jan, 1995). pp. 4-16.

Cilia, Joseph. "Some Issues of concern for the Christian churches in the North-East", *Religion and Society*, Vol. XXXIX, No. 4 (December 1992), pp. 54-60.

Dasgupta, Chidananda. "Lust for Life", *The Illustrated Weekly of India*, (May 3-9, 1989). pp. 38-39.

Dupre, Louis. "Situation ethics and objective morality", *Theological studies* Vol. XXVIII, No. 2 (1967) pp. 245-257.

Fletcher, Joseph. "Medicine Morals and Religion" *Theology Today*, Vol. XXXI, No. 1 (April 1974), pp. 187-190.

Fletcher, Joseph, "Our Right to die", *Theology Today*, Vol. VIII, (May 1951), pp.204-210.

Fletcher, Joseph. "Abortion and the true believer", *The Christian Century*, Vol. LXXXVIII, No. 49 (December, 1979): pp. 1444-1446.

Fletcher, Joseph. "Responsible Decision-Making", *Theology Today*, Vol. XXVIII, No. I (April, 1971), pp. 90-92.

Finkel, Asher "Women in Biblical Tradition". *Journal of Dharma*, Vol. XIII, No. 1 (March 1988). PP. 5-14.

Fuchs, Joseph. "Situation Ethics and Theology", Theology Digest, Vol. II (1954), pp. 25-31.

Gupta, Monobina. "Symbol of Shame in Ameena's Crumbling world", *Frontiline*, (Aug. 31- Sep.13, 1991), pp. 24-25.

India Today (Malayalam), (Jan 21 - Feb. 5, 1994), pp. 28-30

Jacob, Lukose. "In and around the chittalpura: A study of the Uralies of Wynaad", *Religion and Society*, Vol. XXXVIII, No.3&4 (Sept - Dec, 1991) pp. 63-75.

Joseph, M.P. "Suttee: A critique from an Ethical perspective", *SATHRI Journal*, (No. 1/1993) pp. 65-95.

Kadalickad, Mathew; Varghese Saji. "Malappurathu saishava vivahangal", *Vanitha*, (malayalam magazine) (April 15-30, 1994), PP. 25-27.

Kalakaumudi, (Malayalam weekly) 9 May 22, 1994) pp.17-18.

Kalam, Thomas P. "The making of an ethical doctor", *Jeevadhara*, Vol. XXII, No. 132 (November, 1992), pp. 452-467.

Karoth, Pascal. "Hesed - spirituality of the family of Ruth", *Bible Bhashyam*, Vol. XVII, No. 3 (September, 1991) pp. 146-160.

Kidangean, Xavier. "Family in the Indian tradition: Abode of personal and social values", *Jeevadhara*, Vol. XXIV, No. 144, (November, 1994), pp. 425-446.

Kidangean, Xavier. "The biblical perspective on Family", *Bible Bhashyam*, Vol. XX, No.3 (September 1994), pp. 201-216.

Kottackal, Joseph. "Morality of sex in the Old Testament", *Bible Bhashyam*, Vol. VIII, No. 3. (September, 1981), pp. 147-159.

Kottackal, Joseph "Family life in the pentateuchal traditions", *Bible Bhashyam*, Vol. XX, No. 4 (December 1994), pp. 267-279.

Kottackal, Joseph. "Pauline teaching on marriage", *Bible Bhashyam*, Vol. III, No. 3 (September 1977), PP. 213-229.

Kung, Hans. "Towards a world ethic or world religions", *Conclilium*, 1990/2 (1990 April), PP.102-119.

Koya, Mohammed S, M. "Thalakkum Sthreekalude Avakasavum", *Mathrubhumi,* (Malayalam magazine) (Sept. 4-10, 1994), pp. 6-10.

Legrand, L. "Virginity in the Bible", *Bible Bhashyam*. Vol. III, No. 3 (September, 1977), pp. 178-191.

Lucas, Maria. "Origin of marriage in the Bible", *Bible Bhashyam*, Vol. III, No. 3 (September 1977), pp. 161-177.

Luke, K., "Society Divided by Religion: The Jewish World of Jesus Time", *Bible Bhashyam,* Vol. I. No. 3 (September 1975, pp. 195-209.

Madhu, M. "Penkutikalku Pralobhanangalude Kenikal", *Vanitha,* (Malayalam magazine), (December 1-14, 1992), pp. 15-17.

Mangatt, George. "The family of Nazaneth", *Bible Bhashyam* Vol. XVII, No. 3 (September 1991), pp. 181-195.

Mangatt, George. "Jesus teaching on mariage and divorce", *Bible Bhashyam,* (June 1994), P.P. 88-107).

Marak, Julius L.R. "Traditional Marriage Customs of the Garos", *Religion and Society,* Vol. XXXIX, No. 4 (December 1992). pp. 22-26.

Mathias, Gerald.J. "Euthanasia", *Jeevadhara*, Vol. XXII, No. 132 (November 1992), pp. 409-434.

McCormick, Richard A. "Notes on moral theology", *Theological Studies,* Vol. XXXII, No. 1 (March, 1971), pp. 66-76.

Mecabe, Herbert. "The Validity of Absolutes", *Commen Weal* Vol. LXXXIII, No. 14 (Jan, 14, 1966), pp. 432-437.

Milhaven, John. D. and David J. Casey. "Theological Background of the New Morality", *Theology Digest* Vol. XVI, No. 2 (1968), pp. 196-202.

Mollah, Maimoona. "Journey out of childhood", *Frontline*, (Aug.31 - Sept.13, 1991), pp. 22-23.

Noorjihan, K.P. "Thalakkum Quranum", *Mathrubhoomi,* (Malayalam Magazine) (Dec 12-18, 1993), pp. 28-31.

Patil, Vimla. "Sex and the Single girl", *The Illustrated Weekly of India*. (June 8-14, 1986), pp. 24-27.

Pezhumkattil, Abraham. "Husband-Wife relationship in the Wisdom literature", *Bible Bhashyam*, Vol. XX, No.2 (June 1994), pp. 69-87.

Podimattam, Felix. "A Theology of Marital Sexuality and love", *Jeevadhara,* Vol. XXIV, No. 144, (November, 1994). pp. 447-470.

Podimattam, Felix. "A Theology of Marital Sexuality and Love", *Jeevadhara* Vol. XXIV, No. 144 (November, 1994) pp. 447-470.

Pothen, S. "Divorce in Hindu Society", *Journal of comparative family studies*, Vol. XX, No. 3 (Autumn 1989), pp. 376-392.

Prabhu, George M. Soares, "The Dharma of Jesus: An Interpretation of the Sermon on the Mount", *Bible Bhashyam*, Vol. VI, No. 4 (December 1980), pp. 358-381.

Prasad, Sajiwan, "Factors affecting religion and Human Development", *Journal of Dharma,* Vol. III, No. 1 (Jan-March 1978), pp. 17-26.

Pudussery, Paul S., "Jesus Teaching on family life", *Bible Bhashyam*, Vol. XVII, No. 4 (December 1991), pp. 217-241.

Rai, Saritha., Rethanani, Lekha *et al.* "Kalalayangalile Puthiya Thaiamura", *India Today,* (Malayalam) Jan. 21-Feb. 5, 1994), pp. 28-36.

Raghavan, C.V.V. "Shocking Sati", *Frontline,* (Oct. 3-16, 1987), pp. 100-103.

Rajendran, Girija. "Sex in Southern Cinema". *In The Illustrated Weekly of India*. (July 27- August 2, 1980), pp. 28-30.

Ramanujan, B.K. "The Indian Family in Transition", *Social Action* Vol. 22, No. 1 (Jan- March 1972), pp. 16-25.

Ramsey, Paul, "A Christian approach to the question of Sexual relations outside marriage", *Journal of Religion*, Vol. XIV, No. 2 (April, 1968), pp. 202-212.

Sathe, Vasant. "The Love Bug", *The Illustrated Weekly of India,* (June 21-27, 1987). pp. 20-23.

Sebastian, Sunny, "Sati: still seething", *Frontline,* (October 17-30, 1987), pp. 22-23.

Sitz, Christopher R. "Human Sexuality: Viewed from Bibles understanding of the human condition", *Theology Today,* Vol. 52, No. 2 (July, 1995), pp. 236-246.

Sethia, Madhu. "The Social & Courage", *Frontline* (Sep. 14-27, 1991). pp. 83-84.

Shanti, Margaret. "Hinduism and violence against women" *In Voices from the third world,* Vol. XVII, No. 1 (June, 1994), pp. 49-58.

Shourie, Arun. "The Shariat", *The Illustrated Weekly of India,* (January 5, 1986), pp. 6-17.

Singh, Payal. "The Damned", *The Illustrated Weekly of India,* (June 7-13, 1987), pp 9-15.

Singh, Ivy. "Feminism: Various approaches and its values", *Indian Journal of Theology,* Vol. 37/ No. 1, 1995, pp. 58-67.

Srampical Thomas. "Artificial Insemination and Invitrofertilization", *Jeevadhara,* Vol. XXII, No. 132 (Nov. 1992), pp. 468-483.

Thomas, Stanley. "In Search of an identity", *The Week* Vol. II, No. 49 (Nov 28, 1993), pp. 36-42.

Ullrich, Helen E, "Changing Attitudes towards Mariage among Havik Brahmins", *Social Action* Vol. 30, No. 3 (July-Sept 1980), pp. 227-249.

Varghese, Saji. "Vivahathekkurichu Sameepanam marunnu", *Vanitha,* (Malayalam magazine), (August 1-14, 1995). pp. 33-36.

Verhey, Allen D. "The Holy Bible and Sanctified Sexuality: A evangelical approach to seripture and sexual ethics", *Interpretation,* Vol. XLIX, No. 1 (Jan, 1995). pp. 31-45.

Vellanickal, Mathew, "Family relationship in pauline perspective", *Bible Bhashyam,* Vol. XX No. 2 (June, 1994) pp. 108-123.

Vellanickal, Mathew, "Norm morality according to the Scropture", *Bible Bhashyam,* vol. VII, No. 3 (September 1981) pp. 121-146.

Vellanickal, Mathew, "Family life in the Bible", *Bible Bhashyam,* Vol. III, No.3 (September 1977), pp. 192-212.

Vijayan, M. and Murthy A.R. Vasudeva "The approach of natural Science", *Bangalore Theological Forum,* Vol. XIII, No. 442, 1991. pp. 5-14.

War. Juanita. "Family structures, Customary laws and Christianity: The Khasi Context", *Religion and Society,* Vol. XXXIX, No. 4 (December 1992), pp. 14.21.

Webster, John C.B. "Introduction", *Bangalore Theological forum,* Vol. XIII, No. 142, 1991, pp. 1-4.

Werff, Lyle Vander. "Biblical perspective on Marriage, Divorce and Remarriage", *Bangalore Theological forum,* Vol. VII, No. 1 (January - June 1975), pp. 1-16.

Wheeler, Stanton. "Sex offencses: A sociological critique", *The sociology of crime and deliquency,* 2nd edn. edited by Marvin E. Wolfang, Leon and Savitz *et al.* New York John Wiley and Sons.

Zakaria, Rafiq, "In defence of the sjariat", *The Illustrated Weekly of India* (March 9, 1986) pp. 44-47.

D. Articles and Reports in the Newspapers

Ahmed, Furquan, "Understanding Islamic divorce", *Indian Express,* Kochi edn. (August, 1, 1993), p. 8.

Alavi, Seema. "Talaq, Talaq, Talaq", *Indian Express,* Kochi edn. (February 27, 1994), p. 10.

Bakshi, P.M. "Christian divorce law unfair to women", *Indian Express,* (March 27, 1984), p. 8.

Balasubramanyan, Vimal. "A Tale of two wives", *Indian Express,* (Express magazine) (January 6, 1985), p.2.

Bhagat, Rasheeda. "The Ameena speaks out: I want to cry sometimes ....", *Indian Express,* Kochi edn. (July 14, 1993), p. 9.

Bhagat, Rasheela. "Cold facts about conception", *Indian Express,* Kochi edn. (September, 18, 1994), p. 17.

Bhushan, Ranjit. "A Separate Identity", *Indian Express* (Sunday magazine), (July 11, 1993), p. 3.

D'Cunha, Jean. "Power for the pimp, penalty for the prostitute", *Indian Express* Kochi edn. (October 5, 1986), p. 8

Engineer, Asgar Ali. "Shariah courts", *Indian Express,* (November 3, 1993), p. 8.

Engineer, Asgar Ali. "Islam and polygamy -I", *Hindu,* (October 17, 1995), p. 12.

Engineer, Asgar Ali, "Islam and Polygamy - II", *The Hindu,* (October, 16, 1995), p. 12.

Engineer, Asgar Ali. "Islam and women", *Indian Express,* Kochi edn. (August 5, 1993), p. 10.

The Indian Express. "The lesbians and homesexuals of Hyderabad-Part II", *The Indian Express,* Kochi edn. (September 14, 1993), p. 9.

The Indian Express. "Promiscuity creeps into tradition - bound Madras", *Indian Express,* Kochi edn. (December 2, 1993), p. 11.

Jacob, Shaji. "Dowry deaths: The real murderers", *Indian Express,* (Express magazine) (April 9, 1989), pp. 1,6.

Machaiah, M. Gautham. "The Gay Kingdom", *Indian Express,* (Sunday magazine). (February 20, 1994), p. 9.

Menon, Leela "The flesh in willing and the money good", *Indian Express* (Weekend issue) Kochi edn. (August 3, 1991), p. 1.

Naik, Chandrika. "Sisterhood of slaves", *Indian Express,* Kochi edn. (Jan 5, 1994), p. 9.

Nambath, Suresh. "The Invisible women", *Indian Express* (February 27, 1994), p. 10.

Paul, Bulbul. "Where laws divide and women fall", *Indian Express* (Sunday magazine) (October 14, 1984), p. 1.

Paul, Bulbul. "Child marriages in Marwar", *Indian Express* (Express magazine), (May 3, 1987), pp. 1,6.

Pal, Bulbul. "The abandoned brides of Hyderabad", *Indian Express* (Feb 24, 1985), p. 6.

Raghunathan, K.; Raghuram, Jyothi. "The gift and the grief", *The Hindu* (Sunday Magazine), (September 12, 1993), pp. 1-2.

Rahul, N. "Urchins filling prey to footpath perverts", *Indian Express,* Kochi edn. (May 16, 1994), p. 19.

Ramaseshan, Geeta "No way to catch a cradle - Snatcher", *Indian Express,* Kochi edn. (Jan. 16, 1994), p. 10.

Rai, Usha. "Students see little in virginity", *Indian Express* Kochi edn. (December 1, 1994), p. 17.

Rai, usha. "Fiendish marriage", *Indian Express,* Kochi edn. (April 27, 1994), p. 9.

Rai, Usha. "This is no immaculate conception", *Indian Express,* Kochi edn. (April 30, 1994), p. 11.

Sengupta, Ranjana. "Sexual Harassment: The 9 to 5 menace", *Indian Express* (Sunday magazine), (October, 27, 1991), p.1.

Sheikh, Shenaaz. "A Muslim woman speaks out", *Indian Express,* (December 9, 1984), p. 8.

Sing, Payal. "The Damned", *The illustrated weekly of India,* (June 7, 1987) *Vanitha* (Malayalam fortnightly), (Dec 1-14, 1994) pp.7-9. pp. 9-11.

Vasu, G.S. "Impotence: Shattering manhood myths", *Indian Express,* Kochi edn. (July, 17, 1993), p. 11.

